Australian Animal Law

ANIMAL PUBLICS

Fiona Probyn-Rapsey & Yvette Watts, Series Editors

The Animal Publics series publishes original research in animal studies by established and emerging scholars. Animal Publics takes inspiration from varied and changing modalities of the encounter between animal and human – we publish work that engages with and is informed by the field of animal studies across the humanities, social sciences and the creative arts. We encourage monographs that emphasise political, cultural and social transformations in human–animal relations and intersectional approaches encompassing consideration of race, ethnicity, gender, sexuality and disability.

Animal Death
Ed. Jay Johnston and Fiona Probyn-Rapsey

Animal Dreams
David Brooks

Animal Welfare in Australia: Politics and Policy
Peter Chen

Animal Welfare in China: Culture, Politics and Crisis
Peter J. Li

Animals in the Anthropocene: Critical Perspectives on Non-human Futures
Ed. The Human Animal Research Network Editorial Collective

Australian Animal Law
Elizabeth Ellis

Cane Toads: A Tale of Sugar, Politics and Flawed Science
Nigel Turvey

Dingo Bold: The Life and Death of K'gari Dingoes
Rowena Lennox

Engaging with Animals: Interpretations of a Shared Existence
Ed. Georgette Leah Burns and Mandy Paterson

Enter the Animal: Cross-Species Perspectives on Grief and Spirituality
Teya Brooks Pribac

Fighting Nature: Travelling Menageries, Animal Acts and War Shows
Peta Tait

The Flight of Birds: A Novel in Twelve Stories
Joshua Lobb

A Life for Animals
Christine Townend

Meatsplaining: The Animal Agriculture Industry and the Rhetoric of Denial
Ed. Jason Hannan

Obaysch: A Hippopotamus in Victorian London
John Simons

Australian Animal Law

Context and Critique

Elizabeth Ellis

SYDNEY UNIVERSITY PRESS

First published by Sydney University Press

Sydney University Press
Fisher Library F03
University of Sydney NSW 2006
AUSTRALIA
sup.info@sydney.edu.au
sydneyuniversitypress.com.au

A catalogue record for this book is available from the National Library of Australia.

ISBN 9781743328514 paperback
ISBN 9781743328521 epub
ISBN 9781743328552 pdf

Cover design by Miguel Yamin
Front cover image by We Animals Media
Back cover image by iStockphoto

We acknowledge the traditional owners of the lands on which Sydney University Press is located, the Gadigal people of the Eora Nation, and we pay our respects to the knowledge embedded forever within the Aboriginal Custodianship of Country.

For Ben, Libby and Molly Wren

Contents

Preface

As I write, it is more than three years since the Northern Territory passed new animal protection legislation, seven years since the process began to convert the model code of practice for domestic poultry into contemporary animal welfare standards, and a decade or more since the model code of practice for livestock at slaughtering establishments was due to be reviewed. Not one of these processes has been finalised. The Northern Territory Act has still not commenced, the revised draft poultry standards await agreement by the state and territory agriculture ministers, and there appears to be almost no progress in relation to the development of livestock slaughter standards. In the case of the Northern Territory Act and the slaughter standards there is no publicly available information as to the reasons for the delay, while the last official progress report on the poultry standards is dated July 2021.

These inordinate delays are typical of the pace of change in animal protection in Australia. It is all the more remarkable given the very modest nature of the protections that animal reforms routinely contain. It may be that the poultry standards are finalised and the Northern Territory Act commenced by the time this book is published but their contribution to animal protection, while welcome, remains relatively minor. So, too, the various reviews of the legislative frameworks currently underway in a number of jurisdictions. Touted by governments as major reforms, they are largely limited by their terms to fiddling at the margins. Given the groundswell of community concern about animals in recent decades, an increasingly sophisticated scientific understanding of their welfare and the emergence of animal law as a field of significant academic study, it must be asked: why is it so difficult to achieve meaningful and timely animal protection reform in Australia?

This book seeks to address this question by emphasising the systemic nature of the problem. Although animals in some contexts receive greater protection than in others, the legal regulation of *all* animal use shares key characteristics. These include the disproportionate influence of industry in standards development and policy setting, the lack of independent administration of the resulting laws, inadequately resourced and problematic enforcement, fragmented and inconsistent legal and regulatory frameworks, lack of transparency about animal use and its regulation, and interminable delays in effecting even minor reforms. The focus on commonalities not only exposes the yawning gulf between official animal welfare narratives and the facts but also helps to pinpoint key changes required to achieve more meaningful protection for non-human animals.

The first imperative is to transfer responsibility for animal welfare to properly resourced independent statutory bodies, both within the states and territories and at federal level. This critical reform must go hand in hand with much readier public access to information about the actuality of animal treatment and the extent and manner of its regulation. This access should include images of lawful animal use, as well as unlawful conduct where this occurs in the context of government-supported industries. As it stands, we do not see animals – in more than one sense – nor do we see the uses the law permits or how legal powers are exercised. As set out in this book, the law contributes to this non-seeing in myriad ways, through its language, its processes and its substantive provisions. And through its absences. In doing so, the law not only reflects particular power dynamics but also helps to construct ideas about the relationship between human and non-human animals. With these ideas in a state of flux, references to different ways of seeing animals are interspersed throughout this book. They are integrated with the discussion of legal and regulatory failures to help readers appreciate that theories and assumptions about animals have real-world impacts. Uniting the diverse spectrum of views about the nature of the problem is the recognition that animals have interests and value independently of their utility to humans. In this respect, it is abundantly clear that the law has failed both to protect animals and to keep pace with contemporary thinking.

While I hope this book will be a useful resource for animal law students and teachers, it aims to provide a contextual critique that is also accessible to the general public, as well as to animal studies scholars and lawyers without specific expertise in this field. The law is as written at October 2021 but I have updated significant developments where possible during the final stages of the publication process. In writing this book, the purpose has been to expose the highly problematic state of Australian animal law and regulation, not to provide legal advice. The book should be used with that understanding.

Elizabeth Ellis
March 2022

Acknowledgements

I am indebted to many people for assistance in the production of this book, whether reading drafts, providing information or offering support in other ways. Any errors or omissions are my responsibility. My thanks to Margaret Bond, Keely Boom, Ben Bramble, Meg Good, Jed Goodfellow, Scott Grattan, Bidda Jones, Alexandra McEwan, Luke McNamara, Rick Mohr, Dominique Thiriet, Steven White and two anonymous referees. Thanks also to Keely Boom for helping with statutory checks. I am grateful to Sydney University Press for supporting the project and to Jo Lyons and Naomi van Groll for their thoughtful editorial assistance. I owe a special debt to the editors of the Animal Publics series, in particular to former series editor Melissa Boyde for her enthusiastic encouragement and practical advice in bringing this project to fruition. With the hidden nature of much animal use, obtaining appropriate images is difficult and I am grateful to Animals Australia, Teya Brooks Pribac and Diana Simpson for allowing me to include their photographs. Finally, although this book is necessarily critical of regulatory agencies, I acknowledge the hard work of many in this field and express my appreciation to those officials who provided information.

1

What is Animal Law?

On an autumn day in 2016, a pastoral company and its director were each convicted of one count of animal cruelty in the Magistrates Court of Western Australia. This case was unusual as most cruelty investigations don't result in prosecution and those which do are more likely to concern companion animals than cattle. Yet, paradoxically, this case and related litigation reveal a great deal about animal law and its practical operation. By examining these cases, we can begin to explore the complex features and issues that characterise the law and regulatory frameworks governing all Australian animals, not just cattle in Western Australia.[1] The facts of the case are set out in the decision of the Supreme Court of Western Australia which overturned the convictions on appeal.[2] The appellants were also successful in their appeal against the costs order.

1 As humans are also animals, the more accurate descriptor is non-human animals. While the more familiar term 'animals' will be employed for the most part in this book, reference will periodically be made to 'non-human animals' to remind the reader that the division between species is less marked than we tend to think.

2 *SAWA Pty Ltd v Swift* [2016] WASC 331.

An animal law story

SAWA Pty Ltd held a pastoral lease on a cattle station managed by a director of the company. In 2014, SAWA and the director were each charged with animal cruelty offences by Swift, an RSPCA inspector, mostly in relation to the dehorning of 'feral' cattle over the age of 12 months.[3] Some of the original charges were discontinued during trial and some were dismissed but the company and its director were each convicted of one charge of being cruel to an animal contrary to s 19(1) of the *Animal Welfare Act 2002* (WA). This was because the magistrate found that one animal was caused unnecessary harm contrary to s 19(3)(j) when it was dehorned closer to the skull than was necessary. On appeal, Martino J held that the magistrate had failed to identify the law he applied in concluding that the animal had suffered unnecessary harm; the magistrate's reasoning also failed to demonstrate how he decided that the defences under s 23 and s 25 had not been established. These sections provide that it is a defence to a charge under s 19(1) if the defendant proves that the act was done in accordance with a generally accepted animal husbandry practice and in a humane manner (s 23) or in accordance with a relevant code of practice (s 25). At that time, the relevant code of practice was the *Model Code of Practice for the Welfare of Animals – Cattle* (2004), which provided that the dehorning of domesticated cattle without analgesics should be confined to the first muster and preferably when cattle are under six months old [5.8.2]. In relation to feral cattle, the code provided that only under exceptional circumstances, for example range management of older, previously unmustered cattle in extensive operations, should dehorning be implemented without analgesics on animals older than six months [8.3].

Before exploring key features of the above case, there is another, important side to this story as two related cases reveal.[4] The events which led to the prosecution of SAWA and its director took place on private property in a remote part of Western Australia and only came

3 The use of the term 'feral' for some animals living in the wild illustrates the interaction of language and law in the construction of hierarchies of animal protection. See further Chapter 6 this volume.

4 *SAWA Pty Ltd v ABC* [2017] WASC 349; *ABC v SAWA Pty Ltd* [2018] WASCA 29.

to the attention of the RSPCA because they were filmed by a company employee who was concerned about animal welfare.[5] This footage formed a key part of the prosecution case and was tendered in evidence at the trial. The ABC obtained a copy of the video recording pursuant to the *Magistrates Court Act 2004* (WA) with the aim of reporting on the proceedings and related issues, including proposed amendments to the *Animal Welfare Act*. SAWA then sought an injunction restraining publication of the footage while the ABC applied for an order allowing publication pursuant to the *Surveillance Devices Act 1998* (WA). Under s 31 of that Act, the court may make an order that a person may publish a record of a private activity that has come to their knowledge as a result of the use of an optical surveillance device if satisfied that publication should be made to protect or further the public interest. The ABC's application was dismissed by Chaney J on the basis that the broadcaster's purposes could be adequately achieved without using the video recordings and because it would be difficult, if not impossible, to enforce any limitation on their publication. An appeal by the ABC to the WA Court of Appeal was also unsuccessful.

Overview of the legal and regulatory framework

At one level, these cases provide some basic information about animal welfare law and regulation in Australia. First, they illustrate that animal welfare is principally the responsibility of state and territory governments, not the Commonwealth. The majority of jurisdictions include most animal welfare matters within one statute while others have a general animal welfare statute plus additional laws to cover some specific animal uses.[6] In New South Wales (NSW), for example, the *Prevention of Cruelty to Animals Act 1979* is supplemented by the *Animal Research Act 1985* and the *Exhibited Animals Protection Act 1986* but in Queensland only exhibited animals are the subject of separate legislation. Note, however, that some changes to existing legislative frameworks will occur as a result of current reviews in a number of

5 *SAWA v ABC*, [15].

6 Provisions related to animal welfare are also found in legislation governing other regulatory contexts, for example nature conservation legislation.

jurisdictions, as outlined in Chapter 2. The NSW reforms, for example, propose to incorporate the regulation of animal research and exhibited animals into a single animal welfare statute.[7] The Commonwealth's limited legislative responsibility for animal welfare is mainly in relation to live exports and the trade in native wildlife. From time to time, however, the Commonwealth has played a broader role in policy development and national co-ordination, for example in relation to the development of the animal welfare standards referred to below.

Second, these cases demonstrate the key role of codes of practice/standards in the regulation of animal welfare and how they interact with the principal statutes in important ways. Similarly to the *Animal Welfare Act 2002* (WA), most jurisdictions provide that compliance with an industry code of practice is either a defence to a prosecution or exempts the conduct from the operation of cruelty laws.[8] In NSW, compliance with a code of practice does not operate as a complete defence but is admissible in evidence in proceedings under the *Prevention of Cruelty to Animals Act 1979.* The Model Codes of Practice – Animal Welfare are being systematically revised and converted into animal welfare standards and guidelines with the aim of creating enforceable national standards to replace the codes of practice, whose legal status was variable and largely voluntary. For example, the *Model Code of Practice for the Welfare of Animals – Cattle* (2004) referred to in *SAWA v Swift* has been replaced by the *Australian Animal Welfare Standards and Guidelines for Cattle* endorsed in 2016.

Third, these cases make it clear that causing an animal pain or suffering is only a crime if the act or omission is considered *unnecessary.* Words like 'unnecessary', 'unreasonable' and 'unjustifiable' are the standout characteristic of all animal welfare legislation, whatever its form. How these words are interpreted is a crucial element in defining the extent of suffering allowable by law but judicial authority in this regard is limited. This is due to various factors, including the numerous exemptions and defences in animal welfare statutes, the resources and culture of law enforcers, the number and type of prosecutions brought, and the fact that most offences are tried summarily, and result in few appeals.

---

7 Public exposure draft Animal Welfare Bill 2022.

8 Section 4 of the *Animal Welfare Act 1993* (Tas) only exempts compliance with a code of practice in relation to animal research.

This brings us to the final point about the regulatory framework that the cases introduce: namely, that charitable organisations, principally the RSPCA, have an important role in enforcing the criminal law. In some jurisdictions, animal welfare legislation is also enforced by the relevant agriculture department, sometimes pursuant to a memorandum of understanding with the state government which sets out the scope of responsibility in each case. In Queensland, for example, a memorandum of understanding gives responsibility for commercial farming matters to Biosecurity Queensland (Department of Agriculture and Fisheries) while the RSPCA focuses on companion animals and hobby farms. In NSW, the RSPCA has responsibility for enforcing the *Prevention of Cruelty to Animals Act 1979*, along with the Animal Welfare League of NSW. The police also have a role in enforcing animal welfare laws but it tends to be limited to more serious matters, those connected to other criminal activity or where there is no other inspector available.

The above points will be dealt with at length throughout this book but for now they serve as an introduction to key elements of the law relating to animals as a basis for understanding some of its more complex characteristics. It is these less straightforward aspects of animal law, introduced below, that the two *SAWA* cases also illuminate.

Sentience, science and legal 'things'

Sentience may be defined as the capacity 'to consciously perceive by the senses; to consciously feel or experience subjectively'.[9] In *SAWA Pty Ltd v Swift*, Martino J referred at [24] to the magistrate's findings that the feral cattle were 'clearly distressed by the process however the handling of animals, in all such circumstances, will cause such an effect'. From this and other dicta, it is clear that the cattle suffered in the process of dehorning and are rightly considered sentient. While it might seem obvious that cattle are capable of suffering, and that this knowledge ought to guide human behaviour, a long tradition of Western philosophical thought denied moral standing to animals in the belief that they lacked certain

9 Mellor 2019, 440.

Figure 1.1. The law classifies domestic animals as property. (iStockphoto)

qualities considered distinctively human. In the 12th century, St Thomas Aquinas married Aristotelian philosophy with Christian theology to propound a hierarchical order of nature with God at the apex and humans above animals, a superiority that justified an instrumental view of animals whom he believed lacked rationality and an immortal soul.[10] In the 17th century, René Descartes viewed animals as mere automata which could be used for scientific experimentation without regard to analgesia or anaesthetic.[11] Writing in the early 18th century, Immanuel Kant believed that no direct duties were owed to animals because they lacked self-consciousness and the capacity for rational thought. Although he rejected animal cruelty, this was because of its tendency to harden its perpetrators in relation to other humans, not because any moral significance was attached to animals in their own right.[12]

10 Bruce 2018, 13–15.

11 Francione 2004, 110–11.

12 White 2013a, 38.

By the 18th century, however, some philosophers had begun to focus on the capacity of animals to experience affective states and the implications of this for human behaviour. Foremost among these was Jeremy Bentham, a lawyer and social reformer, whose name is synonymous with the development of utilitarian philosophy. In determining right action, utilitarianism considers the consequences of conduct and whether it produces the greatest good for the greatest number but in relation to animals the question remained: how did they fit into this moral calculus? Bentham's answer came in 1789 with the publication of his *Introduction to the Principles of Morals and Legislation*. After noting the neglect of animals' interests by ancient jurists and their consequent degradation into the class of 'things', Bentham argued in a footnote that:

> The day *may* come, when the rest of the animal creation may acquire those rights which never could have been withholden from them but by the hand of tyranny. The French have already discovered that the blackness of the skin is no reason why a human being should be abandoned without redress to the caprice of a tormentor. It may come one day to be recognized, that the number of the legs, the villosity of the skin, or the termination of the *os sacrum*, are reasons equally insufficient for abandoning a sensitive being to the same fate. What else is it that should trace the insuperable line? Is it the faculty of reason, or, perhaps, the faculty of discourse? But a full-grown horse or dog is beyond comparison a more rational, as well as a more conversable animal, than an infant of a day, or a week, or even a month, old. But suppose the case were otherwise, what would it avail? the question is not, Can they *reason*? nor, Can they *talk*? but, Can they *suffer*?[13]

Embodying a shift in focus from rationality to sentience, these oft-quoted words were to have a profound and lasting effect on the place of animals in the moral calculus. Even so, Bentham's position was not without constraint. Notwithstanding his reference to 'rights'[14] and the

13 Bentham 1823, 235–6.

14 Bentham used the word 'rights' not in the popular contemporary sense but as 'a law or rule backed by sanctions': Garrett 2011, 79.

categorisation of animals as 'things', the preceding part of the same footnote makes clear that Bentham was untroubled by the human use of animals:

> If the being eaten were all, there is very good reason why we should be suffered to eat such of them as we like to eat: we are the better for it, and they are never the worse. They have none of those long-protracted anticipations of future misery which we have. The death they suffer in our hands commonly is, and always may be, a speedier, and by that means a less painful one, than that which would await them in the inevitable course of nature. If the being killed were all, there is very good reason why we should be suffered to kill such as molest us: we should be the worse for their living, and they are never the worse for being dead. But is there any reason why we should be suffered to torment them? Not any that I can see. Are there any why we should *not* be suffered to torment them? Yes, several.[15]

For Bentham, the capacity of animals to suffer makes them worthy of moral consideration, but lacking any interest in their own life ('they are never the worse for being dead') their use by humans is uncontested. Indeed, this use is characterised as beneficial for animals on the basis that their death at human hands 'commonly is, and always may be', a speedier and less painful one than awaits them in nature. Bentham's confidence in the potential for humane treatment may have been misplaced but the idea that animals are owed direct duties due to their sentience was a considerable advance. Nevertheless, a crucial question remained: how should the interests of animals in not suffering be balanced against human interests in using them?

The 19th-century response to this question is illustrated by the parliamentary debates during early attempts to legislate against animal cruelty in Britain. With concern about the potential impact of these reforms on human interests, reassurance was found in the ready distinction between animal use and abuse within the prevailing paradigm of the human–animal relationship. On introducing his Cruelty to Animals Bill 1809, Lord Erskine anticipated the following objections:

15 Bentham 1823, 235.

> How, it may be first asked, are magistrates to distinguish between the justifiable labours of the animal, which from man's necessities is often most fatiguing, and apparently excessive, and that real excess which the Bill seeks to punish as wilful and wanton cruelty? How are they to distinguish between the blows which are necessary, when beasts of labour are lazy or refractory, or even blows of sudden passion and temper, from deliberate, cold-blooded, ferocious cruelty, which we see practised every day we live, and which have a tendency, as the preamble recites, to harden the heart against all the impulses of humanity?[16]

In answer to his rhetorical questions, Lord Erskine averred:

> This bill makes no act whatever a misdemeanor that does not plainly indicate to the court or magistrate a malicious and wicked intent; but this generality is so far from generating uncertainty, that I appeal to every member in our great profession, whether, on the contrary, it is not in favour of the accused, and analogous to our most merciful principles of criminal justice? So far from involving the magistrate in doubtful discriminations, he must be himself shocked and disgusted before he begins to exercise his authority over another. He must find malicious cruelty; and what that is can never be a matter of uncertainty or doubt, because nature has erected a standard in the human heart, by which it may be surely ascertained.—This consideration surely removes every difficulty from the last clause, which protects from wilful, malicious, and wanton cruelty, all reclaimed animals. Whatever may be the creatures which, by your own voluntary act, you choose to take from the wilds which nature has allotted to them, you must be supposed to exercise this admitted dominion, for use, or for pleasure, or from curiosity. If for use, enjoy that use in its plenitude; if the animal be fit for food, enjoy it decently for food; if for pleasure, enjoy that pleasure, by taxing all its faculties for your comfort; if for curiosity, indulge it to the full. The more we mix ourselves with all created matter, animate or inanimate,

16 United Kingdom, *House of Lords Debates*, 15 May 1809, 565–6 (Lord Thomas Erskine).

> the more we shall be lifted up to the contemplation of God. But never let it be said, that the law should indulge us in the most atrocious of all propensities, which, when habitually indulged in, on beings beneath us, destroys every security of human life, by hardening the heart for the perpetration of all crimes.[17]

As with earlier attempts to legislate to ban bull-baiting, Lord Erskine's Bill failed and it was not until 1822 that a Bill introduced by social reformer Richard Martin was successfully enacted.[18] Even then, parliamentary support was not unanimous, with one member declaring his opposition:

> … not because he did not concur with the hon. mover, in disapproving of the ill-treatment of animals, but because the offences proposed to be punished by this bill were of too vague and indefinite a nature. Indeed, if the principle were adopted he could not see where the line was to be drawn, or why there should not be a punishment affixed to the boiling of lobsters, or the eating of oysters alive.[19]

Martin's Act was the forerunner of more comprehensive 19th-century reforms which were consolidated in the *Protection of Animals Act 1911* (UK). While the motivation for reform was diverse, 'there seems little doubt that change in the understanding of the moral significance of animals, and of their vulnerability to pain, was important'.[20] These early laws established the framework for modern animal welfare legislation in that nation and served as a broad prototype for Australian legislation, with the first anti-cruelty law introduced in Van Diemen's Land in 1837.[21] As we will see in Chapter 2, the law has evolved considerably since then, extending the level and scope of protection afforded animals and incorporating positive duties to act in relation to their welfare.

---

17 Ibid, 569–70.

18 The *Cruel Treatment of Cattle Act* 3 Geo IV, c 71 extended to horses, sheep and other livestock. For further historical detail of British law, see Radford 2001.

19 United Kingdom, *House of Commons Debates*, 7 June 1822, 873 (Sir James Scarlett).

20 White 2016b, 114.

21 Jamieson 1991, 239.

Yet the underlying ethos of animal welfare legislation in Australia and other western nations remains broadly unchanged and contemporary law continues to reflect the fundamental dilemma that characterised its earliest incarnations. With an implicit acceptance of some animal suffering in the course of their use for human purposes, the animal welfare ethic seeks to regulate the extent and degree of suffering, with conduct only criminalised where the harm is considered unnecessary.

While the concept of necessity is subject to change, ultimately the interests of animals in not suffering must be weighed against human interests in making use of them, a calculus determined by humans. In balancing these interests, science is increasingly called upon to guide our understanding of animals' affective states and the implications of this knowledge for their wellbeing. Yet scientific understanding cannot be divorced from ethical considerations or the broader social and political context, as both historical and contemporary issues demonstrate. In the 19th century, Darwin's ground-breaking work demonstrated that human and non-human animals were part of a continuum rather than fundamentally different, thereby suggesting a non-instrumental basis for valuing animals' lives.[22] At the same time, this approach retained the anthropocentric categorisation of animals according to their similarity to humans,[23] thus reflecting the long tradition of superiority based on human characteristics. More recent times have seen scientific attention to animal welfare increase significantly yet aspects of animal welfare science remain highly contested, as we will see in Chapter 4 in the context of the development of new animal welfare standards for poultry.

In any case, scientific recognition of animal sentience has not altered the fact that, for legal purposes, animals are classed as things. In 1871, Charles Darwin acknowledged 'that the lower animals are excited by the same emotions as ourselves', a fact he considered 'so well established that it will not be necessary to weary the reader by many details'.[24] At common law, however, domestic animals were treated as absolute property and 150 years after Darwin's words, both common law and

22 Chen 2016, 30.
23 Ibid.
24 Darwin 1871 quoted in Dawkins 2006, 4.

statute continue to define animals in terms of goods.[25] The significance of this status is the subject of extensive discussion in the animal law literature. Some lawyers and theorists believe that it is human attitudes and practices that require change rather than animals' property status;[26] others believe that ownership can actually benefit animals by creating a proprietorial interest;[27] others still, argue strongly that meaningful improvement to the lives of animals is impossible without removing their property status.[28] Of those who do favour change, some believe that animals require recognition as legal persons while others support a new category in which humans are the guardians, not owners, of animals.[29] Yet another view is that animals' property classification needs to be replaced 'with a new, transformative legal status or subjectivity' which respects animals 'for what they are – rather than their proximity to idealized versions of humanness'.[30]

As this book unfolds, we will return to the issue of animals' property status and its significance in legal terms. We will also consider some alternative views about the moral significance of animals and their relationship to humans. While comprehensive philosophical inquiry is beyond the scope of this book, it is impossible to evaluate the existing law without some understanding of the assumptions that underpin it. In any case, even acceptance of the current paradigm by no means avoids difficult questions about the moral significance of animals and the adequacy of the law when judged against its own criteria. By returning to *SAWA v Swift* we can start to see these difficulties in the context of contemporary animal welfare issues.

---

25 See, for example, s 2(1) of the *Australian Consumer Law*. For the difference in property status between wild and domestic animals, see Chapter 6 this volume.
26 See, for example, Caulfield 2018, 22–4.
27 See, for example, the chapter by Epstein in Sunstein and Nussbaum 2004.
28 See, for example, the chapter by Francione in Sunstein and Nussbaum 2004.
29 See further Chapter 3 this volume.
30 Deckha 2021, 6.

Unnecessary suffering

You will recall that the relevant law in this case is the *Animal Welfare Act 2002* (WA) (the WA Act). As we have seen, the philosophical justification for animal welfare legislation is the capacity of animals to feel pleasure and pain yet the WA Act makes no reference to animals as sentient. As of 2021, this omission is consistent with all Australian jurisdictions, other than the Australian Capital Territory (ACT), although some changes are pending.[31] Nevertheless, animal sentience is implied in the WA Act's objects as set out in s 3(2) to:

(a) promote and protect the welfare, safety and health of animals; and

(b) ensure the proper and humane care and management of all animals in accordance with generally accepted standards; and

(c) reflect the community's expectation that people who are in charge of animals will ensure that they are properly treated and cared for.

While these objects apply to all animals, as defined in s 5,[32] the effect of the WA Act as a whole, as with other Australian statutes, is that very different levels of protection apply depending upon the setting in which an animal is used. In other words, it is the function of the animal and the context of their use that determine the extent of legal protection. In *SAWA v Swift*, the setting was a cattle station and the context was the dehorning of cattle over 12 months of age, with deficiencies in the magistrate's reasons being determinative of the appeal. The underlying

31 The *Animal Welfare Act 1992* (ACT) was amended in 2019 to recognise that animals are sentient and have intrinsic value. As part of its Animal Welfare Action Plan, December 2017, the Victorian government committed to introducing new principal animal welfare legislation that includes acknowledgement of animal sentience. In Western Australia, the government response to the recommendations of an independent review supports the express recognition of animals as 'living beings, able to perceive, feel, and have positive and negative experiences'. For further information about current reviews of the animal welfare Acts, see Chapters 2 and 8 this volume.

32 For jurisdictional differences in the definition of the term 'animal', see Chapter 2 this volume.

substantive issue, however, was whether the distress caused to the cattle amounted to cruelty in a legal sense, insofar as it was unnecessary and not justified by the available defences. For our purposes, then, let's suppose that the magistrate had set out his reasons more fully: to what legal authorities might he have adverted with respect to the issue of necessity, once the infliction of pain had been established?

The starting point is an old English case, *Ford v Wiley*.[33] This case concerned a successful appeal against a magistrate's decision to acquit the accused of cruelty for, as it happens, dehorning cattle, in that case with a saw. Having found that considerable pain was inflicted, Lord Coleridge CJ held at [209–10] that it is lawful:

> … if it is reasonably necessary; a phrase vague, no doubt, but with which in many branches of the law every lawyer is familiar. This involves the consideration of what "necessary," and "necessity" mean in this regard. It is difficult to define these words from the positive side, but we may perhaps approach a definition from the negative. There is no necessity and it is not necessary to sell beasts for 40s. more than could otherwise be obtained for them; nor to pack away a few more beasts in a farm yard, or a railway truck, than could otherwise be packed; nor to prevent a rare and occasional accident from one unruly or mischievous beast injuring others. These things may be convenient or profitable to the owners of cattle, but they cannot with any show of reason be called necessary. That without which an animal cannot attain its full development or be fitted for its ordinary use may fairly come within the term "necessary," and if it is something to be done to the animal it may fairly and properly be done. What is necessary therefore within these limits, I should be of opinion may be done even though it causes pain; but only such pain as is reasonably necessary to effect the result.

In his judgment, Lord Coleridge CJ emphasised the need for proportionality between the object and the means, as did Hawkins J at [220]:

33 (1889) 23 QBD 203.

> … even where a desirable and legitimate object is sought to be attained, the magnitude of the operation and the pain caused thereby must not so far outbalance the importance of the end as to make it clear to any reasonable person that it is preferable the object should be abandoned rather than that disproportionate suffering should be inflicted.

Notwithstanding the passage of time, *Ford v Wiley* was considered by the magistrate in an Australian decision, *Department of Local Government and Regional Development v Emanuel Exports* (2008) (the *Al Kuwait* case).[34] Coincidentally, this case takes us back to the Magistrates Court of Western Australia and the *Animal Welfare Act 2002* (WA), although the context was not the dehorning of cattle but the live export of sheep, a subject to which we will return in Chapter 4. The magistrate cited from the above passage by Lord Coleridge CJ and emphasised the need for proportion between object and means. Applying this reasoning to the facts, she found that a particular class of sheep had been transported in a way that causes, or is likely to cause, unnecessary harm in breach of s 19(1). The defendants were acquitted, however, because the magistrate found an 'operational inconsistency' between the Act and the Commonwealth law regulating live exports, with the relevant provisions of the Act rendered invalid by the operation of s 109 of the *Constitution*.[35]

With a lack of Australian authority on the meaning of unnecessary suffering, this case illustrates the continuing relevance of the principle in *Ford v Wiley*: harming animals is only lawful if it occurs in pursuit of a legitimate end and is proportionate to that purpose. The implications of this approach and the judicial scope it affords attract different

34 Unreported, Magistrates Court of Western Australia (Criminal Jurisdiction), Crawford M, 8 February 2008.

35 The magistrate's finding on the s 109 issue has been questioned: Morfuni 2011; McEwen 2008. Note also that in a preliminary hearing in another prosecution of the same company in 2021, a different magistrate ruled that s 19(1) and s 19(3) of the *Animal Welfare Act 2002* (WA) are not inconsistent with Commonwealth laws governing live exports: *Department of Primary Industries and Regional Development v Emanuel Exports*, unreported, Magistrates Court of Western Australia (Criminal Jurisdiction), Shackleton M, 3 June 2021. See further Chapter 4 this volume.

views among animal law scholars. Citing extensively from a Canadian case,[36] Sankoff argues strongly that there is virtually no end to those purposes considered legitimate within a paradigm that privileges human interests.[37] While the means adopted must be proportionate to the legitimate end, suffering is only unnecessary if it may reasonably be avoided after taking into account human interests, including economic efficiency, social costs and even mere convenience.[38] By contrast, some scholars take a less pessimistic view. For Radford, the flexibility of the concept of unnecessary suffering allows its application to a wide variety of factual circumstances and its reinterpretation by the courts in the light of changing attitudes to animals.[39] In the context of animal welfare politics, Garner argues that the imprecision at the heart of the concept is also its strength because what is considered unnecessary 'can be altered by subjective political debate'.[40]

It is true that the decision in *Ford v Wiley* expressly rejected 'the notion that economic expediency of itself can justify a harm-causing practice and protect it from scrutiny'.[41] Moreover, the potential for a broader application of his reasoning was recognised by Lord Coleridge CJ at [215] when deciding the case:

> I am not afraid of the possible application of the principle to other practices which have not yet been attacked, but which may hereafter turn out to be prohibited by law.

In fact, as we have seen, this potential was realised in the magistrate's reasoning in the *Al Kuwait* case, notwithstanding the outcome on the s 109 issue. Accordingly, *Ford v Wiley* arguably 'provides a robust analytical framework for enabling stringent review of painful animal husbandry practices'[42] but its utility is subject to qualification. As identified by Lord Coleridge CJ at [210], the practice under consideration was no longer in general use when *Ford v Wiley* was decided:

---

36 *R v Menard* (1978) 43 CCC (2d) 458.
37 Sankoff 2013, 18.
38 Ibid, 20.
39 Radford 2001, 258.
40 Garner 2006, 166.
41 Goodfellow 2015, 110.
42 Ibid, 111.

> ... as to necessity, it is found in the case that for twenty years the practice of dishorning has been entirely disused throughout England and Wales. It has not been thought necessary in all that time to perform it on any of the millions of cattle which during that time the farmers of England of all sorts have reared, and sold, and eaten. We learn further ... that except in three counties, Fife, Forfar, and Kincardine, it is unknown in Scotland ... It is incredible to me, at least, that an operation for many years discontinued in England and Wales, and, with the above exception, in Scotland also, should suddenly have become "necessary" so as to except it, if it be cruel, from the mischiefs against which the statute is directed. It was not unknown, but it has been discontinued.

In other words, the disuse of the practice in most of Britain at that time appears to have been an influential factor in determining the issue of necessity and the application of the proportionality test may well be different where husbandry practices enjoy widespread industry support. In White's view, 'it is perhaps doubtful that a court would regard a *usual* animal husbandry practice as being unnecessary, if the legitimacy of the practice was otherwise accepted'.[43] Dehorning in Australia today is just one example of a common farming practice whose legitimacy is widely accepted, with 'an estimated 122,294 calves dehorned every year without the use of pain relief'.[44] According to the NSW Department of Primary Industries (DPI), dehorning has 'been an accepted part of cattle management for generations'. While noting that 'past methods can no longer be accepted without question', the DPI states that the 'temporary discomfort caused by the operation is completely outweighed by the

43 White 2016a, 195. In relation to the application of the proportionality test in the Al Kuwait case, several factors should be noted. First, a separate charge, that the sheep were confined in a manner likely to cause unnecessary harm, was dismissed by the magistrate. Second, the prosecution case was confined to a class of fat adult sheep constituting 13,163 sheep out of a total of 103,232 sheep loaded. The confinement of the argument in this way allowed the case to be framed as a problem with a specific aspect of the voyage rather than with the live export trade more generally: see Caulfield 2008, 203–4.

44 Animal Health Australia 2013, 28.

long-term benefits'.[45] These benefits, as listed by the DPI,[46] are that horned cattle:

- can cause more severe injury to other cattle, especially in yards, feedlots and transport;
- can damage hides and cause bruising which reduces the value of carcases;
- are harder to handle in yards and crushes;
- can be potentially more dangerous to handlers;
- require more space at a feed trough and on cattle trucks;
- are not as tractable and quiet to handle;
- may suffer discounts at sale especially if they are destined for feedlots.

Notably, only one of the listed benefits relates to animal welfare, while the impact of dehorning is described as 'temporary discomfort'. Yet, according to the European Scientific Committee on Animal Health and Animal Welfare, painful husbandry procedures, including dehorning, present one of the main risks to cattle welfare.[47] Similarly, a discussion paper prepared for the Australian cattle standards and guidelines development process, notes that dehorning appears to be 'one of the most aversive procedures used on cattle, based on the magnitude of acute stress responses'.[48] The same discussion paper concludes, however, that 'the procedure is necessary for cattle husbandry'.[49] In other words, within specified age limits, dehorning cattle without pain relief is considered an acceptable practice, carried out for a legitimate purpose, notwithstanding the suffering involved.

---

45 NSW Department of Primary Industries, n.d. The DPI notes that '[d]ehorning by veterinarians using sedation and local anaesthesia is accepted practice in Europe and should be encouraged in this country where practical, such as in small intensively managed situations'.

46 Ibid.

47 Scientific Committee on Animal Health and Welfare 2001 cited in Animal Health Australia 2013, 23.

48 Cattle Standards and Guidelines Writing Group 2013, 7.

49 Ibid, 2.

Exemptions and defences

In any case, the question of whether a common farming practice might fall foul of the concept of necessity is largely moot given the exemptions and defences included in animal welfare statutes. These provisions have a long history. In response to rural agitation and concern about the fining of Victorian farmers, dehorning was exempted from cruelty legislation in 1908 in South Australia when 'performed with a minimum of suffering to the animal'.[50] This exemption was adopted by other Australian jurisdictions over the next 20 years, with further farming exemptions to follow.[51] While there are jurisdictional differences, *SAWA v Swift* provides a contemporary example of the effect of these kinds of provisions, as well as illustrating the ambiguity of animal welfare legislation. Remember, s 23 of the WA Act provides a defence to a cruelty charge if the relevant act was done in accordance with a generally accepted husbandry practice, other than a prescribed practice, *and* in a humane manner. Dictionaries define 'humane' in terms of showing kindness, sympathy and compassion and its opposite as 'inhumane' and synonymous with cruel. Accordingly, if a generally accepted husbandry practice *is* humane within the ordinary meaning of the word it would be unlikely to fall within the definition of cruelty in s 19 and therefore would not be subject to prosecution. However, with regard to the purpose of the WA Act and the whole of its provisions, a cruel husbandry practice might be construed as 'humane' for the purposes of s 23 provided that reasonable care is taken to avoid suffering. As Radford notes in relation to Britain, a practice expressly or impliedly permitted by legislation will be considered legitimate by the courts, 'provided it is carried out in a reasonable manner … even though there may be an alternative means of achieving the same end which causes less suffering'.[52]

But there was another relevant defence in *SAWA v Swift*, and one not qualified by reference to humane practice. Section 25 of the WA Act provides a defence to a charge under s 19(1) where the defendant can prove that the impugned act was in accordance with a code of practice, as prescribed by the regulations in accordance with s 5(1). To put this

50 Jamieson 1989 quoted in White 2016b, 120.
51 Ibid.
52 Radford 2001, 249.

into context, the prosecution case on the dehorning charges involved four feral animals, three of whom were dehorned at the base of the skull and returned to the paddock to put on weight prior to their sale. By contrast with tipping the horns, this practice causes considerable suffering, but was undertaken to avoid repeating the process before the animals were ready to be sold. The fourth animal was being shipped. While this journey required cutting the animal's horn to within 12 cm of its skull, it was cut to within about 7 cm instead. During the trial, the magistrate accepted that the relevant code of practice permitted dehorning of previously unmustered older cattle when being returned to the paddock but concluded that the act of aggressively cutting the horn of the animal being shipped caused unnecessary harm.[53] On appeal, however, Martino J held that the magistrate's reasons failed to demonstrate how he had concluded that the defences under both s 23 and s 25 had not been established, leaving open the possibility of establishing these defences in relation to the matter on appeal.[54] Either way, the company and its director had already been able to rely on the code of practice to justify the dehorning of the other animals. As Goodfellow maintains, the risk that many farming practices might be challenged under the general legislative standard 'is precisely why State governments have sought to exempt the practices prescribed in the codes of practice from the application of animal welfare law'.[55] In relation to Western Australia, the independent panel commissioned to review the operation and effectiveness of the *Animal Welfare Act 2002* concluded that:

> Many of the codes adopted under the AW Act have not been updated for many years, and the recommendations in many codes do not reflect advances in animal welfare science or community expectations. The use of outdated provisions as a defence against a charge of cruelty may provide a defence for the use of practices

53 *Western Australia Police v Nicolaas Francois Botha*, unreported, Magistrates Court of Western Australia (Criminal Jurisdiction), Tavener M, 30 March 2016, [102], [104].

54 As noted in *Sawa v Swift* [35] the prosecution decided not to seek a retrial.

55 Goodfellow 2016, 204.

> that are less humane than practically available options, which is inconsistent with the objectives of the AW Act.[56]

The independent panel also found that '[g]iven the move towards national endorsed animal welfare standards, the need to retain a broad, undefined defence for "normal animal husbandry" is questionable and not supportive of contemporaneous and progressive animal welfare legislation'.[57]

Conflicting interests

Chapters 2 and 4 will consider codes of practice and their conversion into national standards and guidelines in detail. They will also examine the different ways in which states and territories incorporate exemptions and defences into the principal statute. For now, some background material serves further to illustrate how codes of practice and animal welfare standards interact with other characteristics of the regulatory framework to exempt the majority of animals affected by human activities from the operation of cruelty laws in substantial ways.

Codes of practice originated in the context of increasing community concern about animal welfare in the second half of the 20th century. In Britain, technological and scientific advances, combined with the reduction of government farming subsidies in the 1950s, fuelled the expansion of intensive farming to contain costs and increase productive efficiency.[58] Similar developments occurred in Australia from the 1960s.[59] In 1964, Ruth Harrison's account of intensive farming in Britain[60] alerted the public to practices such as housing chickens, calves and pigs in tiny cages, crates and stalls, thus exploding 'the pervasive myth that farm animals were well-treated and enjoyed a bucolic, pastoral life'.[61] In response to community concern,

---

56 Western Australia, Department of Primary Industries and Regional Development 2020, 86.

57 Ibid, 84.

58 Woods 2012, 16. See also Goodfellow 2015, 31–2.

59 Senate Select Committee on Animal Welfare, Parliament of Australia 1990, 21.

60 Harrison 1964.

61 Rollin 2019, 155.

the Brambell Committee was established by the British government to inquire into intensive livestock systems,[62] following which the first comprehensive standards for regulating farmed animals were written. In 1975, the publication of Peter Singer's seminal work, *Animal Liberation*, drew further attention to the treatment of animals in large commercial systems and laboratories. In this environment, the impetus to develop codes of practice in Australia came from industries fearful of challenges to methods of livestock management and animal experimentation.[63] By documenting minimum accepted standards of animal treatment, the codes aimed to facilitate national consistency and provide guidance to industry on acceptable practices, while reassuring the public that animal welfare was being managed.[64] In this way, they acted as a shield against criticism of animal industries even though the codes' provisions generally reflected existing husbandry and management practices.[65] Further, while compliance with the codes was voluntary in most jurisdictions, legal protection for industry was obtained through the effective exemption of otherwise cruel practices from the operation of animal welfare legislation, as *SAWA v Swift* illustrates.

Between 1983 and 2006, 22 model codes of practice were endorsed by the (then) Primary Industries Ministerial Council (PIMC).[66] The early 2000s, however, saw two developments in animal welfare regulation. First, a review of the model codes was commissioned amidst concern that Australia's position as a major livestock producer and exporter was facing 'international scrutiny and rising community expectations'.[67] The Neumann Review identified major shortcomings with the code process, including inconsistent application and enforcement of codes, lack of transparency and public consultation, and inconsistent use of animal welfare science.[68] Second, the Commonwealth took a leadership role in the creation of the Australian Animal Welfare Strategy (AAWS).

---

62 Brambell 1965.
63 Geoff Neumann & Associates Pty Ltd 2005, ii, 3, 10.
64 Ibid, 5.
65 Ibid, ii, 10.
66 Australian Animal Welfare Strategy 2009, 3.
67 Geoff Neumann & Associates Pty Ltd 2005, 10.
68 Ibid, 11.

Endorsed by the PIMC in 2004, the AAWS aimed 'to provide the national and international communities with an appreciation of animal welfare arrangements in Australia and to outline directions for future improvements in the welfare of animals'.[69] The National Implementation Plan developed by the AAWS included converting the existing codes of practice to mandatory national standards and guidelines, with Animal Health Australia (AHA) commissioned to facilitate the standards development process. Following the election of the Abbott government in 2013, however, the Commonwealth withdrew from any leadership role in national animal welfare initiatives, with the result that 'the AAWS is now simply a document with no governance or administrative structure, or sustained funding source to ensure its implementation'.[70]

With the termination of the AAWS, an Animal Welfare Task Group (AWTG) comprised of deputy secretaries of state and territory departments with responsibility for agriculture/primary industries was formed to oversee the standards development process under the auspices of the Agriculture Ministers' Forum. AHA was retained as the overall project manager, with the contract management of developing individual standards the responsibility of a nominated state. It had originally been envisaged that all existing model codes of practice would be reviewed by 31 December 2010[71] but as of March 2022 only four sets of standards for farmed animals have been finalised: the land transport of livestock in 2013, sheep standards in 2016, cattle standards in 2016, and standards for livestock at saleyards and depots in 2018.[72] As we discuss in Chapter 4, development of standards to replace the 2002 poultry code of practice commenced in June 2015 but nearly seven years later the development process remains unfinished.

Lengthy delays are not the only problem with the standard-setting process. Although badged as animal welfare standards and guidelines, the dominant players in the process are government agriculture/primary industries departments and industry stakeholders. This can be illustrated by reference to the cattle standards and guidelines, endorsed

69 Australia, Department of Agriculture, Fisheries and Forestry 2005, 5.
70 Goodfellow 2015, 101.
71 Australian Animal Welfare Strategy 2009, 8.
72 Standards for exhibited animals were endorsed in 2019. See further Chapter 5 this volume.

in 2016 and referred to in *SAWA v Swift*. The writing group responsible for drafting the cattle standards and guidelines was comprised of representatives from the Animal Welfare Committee (AWC), Cattle Council of Australia, Australian Lot Feeders' Association Inc, Dairy Australia, CSIRO, the Department of Agriculture and an independent chair, and was supported by AHA.[73] At that time, the AWC comprised representatives from each of the state and territory departments with responsibility for animal welfare (typically primary industries/agriculture departments), the CSIRO, and the Commonwealth Department of Agriculture, Fisheries and Forestry.[74] AHA is a not-for-profit public company whose vision is a 'national biosecurity system that provides every opportunity for Australian agriculture to succeed at home and overseas'.[75] Support and comment was provided by a standards reference group (now the stakeholder advisory group) which comprised representatives from the same federal, state and territory departments, 12 industry stakeholders, two animal welfare organisations and the Australian Veterinary Association.[76] It is unsurprising then that animal welfare organisations are much more critical of the standards that result from this process than the industry bodies directly affected by them.[77]

The extent of industry influence in the standards-setting process has been the subject of considerable criticism by academics and lawyers, as well as animal welfare groups. So too the fact that the government departments responsible for animal welfare are principally concerned with the promotion of efficient and profitable agricultural industries.[78] In NSW, for example, the *Prevention of Cruelty to Animals Act* is administered by the Department of Primary Industries, whose ultimate goal is 'increasing the economic contribution of primary industries to the state'.[79] The interplay of competing interests can be illustrated by the NSW DPI's views on the practice of dehorning, referred to earlier

73 Australian Animal Welfare Standards and Guidelines 2020c.
74 Tim Harding & Associates in association with Rivers Economic Consulting 2013, 13.
75 Animal Health Australia 2020.
76 Tim Harding & Associates in association with Rivers Economic Consulting 2013, 14–16.
77 See, for example, Oogjes 2011.
78 See Chapter 4 this volume for further discussion and references.
79 NSW Department of Primary Industries 2017, 5.

in this chapter, and in the Western Australian context, by the minister's instruction to withdraw the appeal already commenced by the State Solicitor's office in the *Al Kuwait* case.[80] That government agencies might favour productivity gains over animal welfare is unsurprising. As the Productivity Commission notes, the welfare of animals 'is likely to be of secondary importance when the primary objective of the agency responsible for livestock welfare is to promote a productive and profitable agricultural sector'.[81] The extent to which these interests conflict turns, in part, on how animal welfare is conceptualised. Industry bodies tend to equate welfare with productivity, a very narrow view rejected by animal welfare organisations and by contemporary science.[82] In a comprehensive study of farmed animal regulation in Australia, Goodfellow found that while many government regulators reject the notion that productivity and animal welfare are synonymous, 'their perspective of the overall role of animal welfare within the agricultural sector is not inconsistent with that of the livestock industries'.[83]

Apart from problems with delay and conflicting interests, the key aims of creating national consistency and mandatory regulation have not been achieved. In NSW, the sheep and cattle standards have not been regulated but only prescribed as guidelines under s 34A of the *Prevention of Cruelty to Animals Act*. This means that compliance or noncompliance with the standards is admissible in evidence in cruelty proceedings but industry compliance with the standards is not mandatory. This approach gives effect to a 2015 memorandum of understanding between the NSW Liberals and Nationals and the NSW Farmers Association which incorporated a commitment to non-mandatory animal welfare standards in order to drive agricultural growth within the NSW economy.[84] Even where standards are being regulated into law, there are different legislative routes to enforceability

80 Western Australia, *Parliamentary Debates*, Legislative Council, 19 March 2008, 1147b (Ljiljanna Ravlich).
81 Productivity Commission 2016, 224.
82 Goodfellow 2016, 214.
83 Goodfellow 2015, 200.
84 The MOU, *NSW Farming: Investing Locally, Connecting Globally*, was signed on 25 March 2015 by Troy Grant on behalf of the NSW Liberals and Nationals and the President of the NSW Farmers Association, Fiona Simson.

and the process of implementation is very slow.[85] As a result, jurisdictional differences continue even though the ongoing support of some industries for the standards is contingent upon the 'successful harmonisation of state and territory welfare legislation'.[86] Any failure to regulate new standards through legislation also means that some animals are denied even the relatively weak welfare protections they contain. Further, where the standards are mandatory, enforcement remains a major issue. First, in many cases, the same government agencies involved in setting the standards are responsible for their enforcement, with the attendant problem of conflicting interests this entails. Second, resourcing of animal welfare within government agencies is limited.[87] Where the RSPCA is responsible for livestock welfare, resources are simply inadequate to the task of monitoring and enforcing the law across a wide range of industries, over large distances and involving millions of animals.

These and other concerns about the national standards process were recognised by the Productivity Commission in its 2016 report, *Regulation of Australian Agriculture*. The report identified three areas where the regulation of farm animal welfare could be improved, including greater independence and transparency in the standards development process and the application of rigorous scientific principles.[88] To this end, the Productivity Commission recommended the establishment of an independent body, the Australian Commission for Animal Welfare, to assume responsibility for developing national standards and guidelines.[89]

Inconsistent laws, fragmented administration

It is instructive to contrast the legal protection of farmed animals with the laws regulating companion animal welfare. The latter topic will

85 See, for example, the progress report on the cattle standards endorsed in 2016: Australian Animal Welfare Standards and Guidelines, 2020a.
86 Animal Health Australia 2014, 15.
87 Productivity Commission 2016, 242.
88 Ibid, 228.
89 Ibid, 236.

be examined in detail in Chapter 3 but a few examples here serve to highlight the distinction. With a qualified definition of cruelty and various exemptions and defences, animal welfare legislation typically allows castration of young farmed animals without pain relief although performance of the same procedure in the same way on a dog or cat would incur criminal liability. Similarly, to confine a companion animal to a small cage without any opportunity for exercise is a criminal offence but to confine millions of hens in a similar way is perfectly legal. In NSW, this is achieved by exempting stock animals (other than horses) from the requirement in s 9(1) of the *Prevention of Cruelty to Animals Act* to exercise confined animals, in conjunction with the *Prevention of Cruelty to Animals Regulation 2012* which adopts the stocking densities for laying fowl set out in the poultry code of practice. With limited exceptions, other jurisdictions use a variety of legislative approaches to achieve the same result.[90]

Even the same species of animal attracts a different level of legal protection depending upon the setting. A rabbit, for example, kept as a pet receives a higher level of protection than one considered feral or one used in laboratory research. Again, these differences may be illustrated by reference to NSW. Section 15 of the *Prevention of Cruelty to Animals Act* confines the prohibition on the administration of poison to domestic animals, while s 24(1)(b) provides a defence to a cruelty charge if the act or omission occurred, *inter alia*, in the course of, and for the purpose of, hunting an animal, subject to the ambiguous proviso of no unnecessary pain. Another defence is provided by s 24(1)(e)(i) where the animal is harmed in the course of, and for the purpose of, carrying out animal research in accordance with the provisions of the *Animal Research Act 1985* (NSW). While a rabbit kept for laboratory research is accorded some protections under the *Australian Code for the Care and Use of Animals for Scientific Purposes*, the s 24 defence is acknowledgement that a rabbit

90 Battery cages were banned in the ACT by legislation passed in 2014. Under the *Animal Welfare (Domestic Poultry) Regulations 2013* (Tas), keeping layer hens in cages is not permitted in Tasmania unless a person is an existing cage producer or the purchaser of all or part of an existing egg operation: Tasmania, Department Primary Industries, Parks, Water and Environment, Biosecurity Tasmania 2021.

or other animal can legally be subjected to great cruelty in certain circumstances.

To sanction the differential treatment of non-human animals for reasons other than their sentience is to sever animal welfare legislation from its philosophical base. In turn, this begs the questions: what determines the level of protection an animal receives and what justifies the difference? Significantly, Goodfellow's study of farmed animal regulation in Australia found that 'none of the regulators associated the role of animal welfare regulation with any kind of ethical foundation', with animal welfare framed not by reference to sentience but solely in terms of instrumental benefits.[91] This inconsistent protection of animals depending upon their context and use is in marked contrast to much government rhetoric about animal welfare and raises issues of regulatory legitimacy which will be considered throughout this book. In addition, because there is no overarching philosophical and policy framework within which animal welfare laws are developed, their administration and enforcement are spread across diverse agencies, both within and between jurisdictions. The result is fragmented regulatory responsibility, including in contexts inherently risky to animal welfare, such as slaughter, which is largely regulated through food safety laws. As we will see when we consider enforcement in detail, this kind of fragmented responsibility can lead to communication problems, divided resourcing, and a lack of accountability and transparency. With no overarching framework, animals are also very vulnerable in regulatory contexts less obviously associated with their welfare. For example, land clearing and the consequent habitat loss are a major cause of injury, starvation and death for wildlife, including threatened native species.[92]

Hidden animals, opaque law

Animal welfare is a unique regulatory field because it governs the use of sentient beings who are also recognised by the law as a human resource. In these circumstances, it might be expected that animal use

91 Goodfellow 2015, 198.
92 Taylor et al. 2017.

and its regulation by law would be highly transparent. In fact, animal use is largely hidden, particularly in commercial contexts, and detailed information about its regulation is not readily available. Again, the *SAWA* litigation is instructive. The events in question took place on a remote private property where cameras were prohibited and thus would have escaped public attention without the footage obtained by the employee. The restriction on cameras was said to be due to occupational and health considerations but also because 'standard practices conducted in the cattle industry are confronting to the general public' and are capable of bringing the company 'into disrepute if publicly broadcast'.[93]

In conjunction with the failure of the ABC's application to broadcast the footage, this statement illustrates the invisibility of much animal use, as well as the problematic nature of the surrounding secrecy. That standard industry practices are too confronting to reveal might suggest problems with the practices or, at the very least, a need to subject them to closer scrutiny. Further, the reasoning that denies access to this knowledge is circular: the public must be protected from practices they don't understand but they don't understand the need for the practices because they lack industry knowledge. This reasoning also reflects a view that only those with industry experience are sufficiently informed to speak with authority about animal welfare. This belief was clearly evident in a Senate inquiry into a private senator's Bill to establish an independent office of animal welfare.[94] It is also hinted at in a report to the NSW DPI as part of the poultry standards consultation process which notes that 'many community and animal welfare representatives had little understanding of the poultry industry and practices'.[95] This bifurcation of the public response to animal welfare reinforces another divide which itself has a long history – that between urban and rural Australians. In relation to early Australian animal welfare laws, Jamieson notes that the 'historical concentration of animal protection legislation

93 Nicolaas Botha's affidavit evidence cited in *SAWA v ABC*, [26].

94 The Voice for Animals (Independent Office of Animal Welfare) Bill 2015 was introduced by Senator Lee Rhiannon for the Greens. The proceedings of the Senate Rural and Regional Affairs and Transport Legislation Committee, 14 September 2015, may be viewed at http://parlview.aph.gov.au/mediaPlayer.php?videoID=275719.

95 Roth 2018, 10.

on domesticated animals had early fostered its perception by the rural community as mere urban meddling'.[96] The framing of concern about animal welfare as uninformed, urban meddling is commonly found in contemporary debates, as the 2015 Senate inquiry also illustrates.

The hidden nature of much animal use is reinforced by a lack of transparency about regulatory activities.[97] With respect to the enforcement activities of charitable bodies, information is generally available but lacks detail. For example, basic data about cruelty complaints, prosecutions and routine inspections are included in RSPCA Australia's national statistics but more comprehensive data, such as the number of penalty notices issued, is not and the information in state and territory RSPCA annual reports is typically limited.[98] In relation to government activities, not all agencies publish animal welfare compliance and enforcement data and, where it is available, detail is usually lacking. This applies generally, not just to farmed animal welfare. The NSW DPI, for example, is responsible for enforcing the *Exhibited Animals Protection Act 1986* (NSW) but provides no information in departmental annual reports or on its website about compliance and enforcement, other than a general guide to licensees in relation to the audit process. Available data about animals used in research varies by jurisdiction, and key information, such as details of site inspections, is strictly limited.[99]

Even when the exposure of major animal welfare issues compels greater disclosure, significant knowledge gaps remain, as recent events in relation to live exports illustrate. As part of its response to the footage of the suffering of live sheep, broadcast in 2018[100] and generally regarded as shocking, the federal government placed 'independent observers' on live export voyages. The Department of Agriculture, Water and the Environment, however, only publishes brief summaries of its reports,

96 Jamieson 1989 quoted in White 2016b, 120.
97 White 2007, 359.
98 The RSPCA is a federated organisation whose state and territory member societies are independently responsible for investigating and prosecuting cruelty complaints.
99 See further Chapter 7 this volume.
100 Bartlett 2018.

often after substantial delay.[101] Even after lodging an FOI application at considerable cost, RSPCA Australia only gained access to heavily redacted observer reports and photographs six months later, with the department still refusing to release the video footage.[102] In July 2019, the Senate passed a motion noting that less than half the independent observer summary reports from 2018 had been finalised and no 2019 reports had been released.[103] More generally, all of the above problems in accessing information are exacerbated by the fragmentation of responsibility for animal welfare. Without a national agency, or even state and territory agencies, which bring together data on all animal welfare matters, locating the required information is difficult and time-consuming even where it is available.

The use of animals in private contexts, the conflicting interests of regulatory agencies, the lack of transparency, and the cultural and resource problems associated with enforcement mean that serious animal cruelty often comes to light only when exposed by whistle-blowers or activists, with the help of the media. Cruelty in the live export industry is the prime example but others include the non-livestock sector, such as the 'horrific practice'[104] of live baiting in the greyhound racing industry exposed in 2015.[105] In the subsequent NSW inquiry into the industry, it was discovered that Greyhound Racing NSW had deliberately misreported the extent of racetrack injuries and failed to make publicly available information about deaths of greyhounds both during and after racing.[106] While these kinds of exposés have led to some beneficial regulatory change, governments have also responded by seeking to introduce harsher penalties for those who engage in undercover activities.

---

101 See, for example, *Independent Observer Summary Report on MV Al Shuwaikh Sheep and Cattle Exported to Kuwait, Qatar and United Arab Emirates in June 2018*, Report 7, May 2019.

102 RSPCA Australia 2019c.

103 Commonwealth, *Parliamentary Debates*, Senate, 24 July 2019, 63–4 (Mehreen Faruqi).

104 McHugh 2016, vii.

105 Meldrum-Hanna 2015b.

106 McHugh 2016, 9.

The story so far

By using the cases arising from one incident, in one jurisdiction, this chapter has sought to chronicle the law governing all animals in all parts of the nation. This account reveals not only the mechanics of the law but also a more complex story about the law's role in reflecting and constructing the human and non-human animal relationship. A careful reading of the statutes regulating this relationship reveals that the protection they afford animals is considerably more limited than their titles and objects suggest. In turn, the restrictive nature of these legislative provisions is reinforced by other regulatory features which further limit the law's protective reach.

Animal law then is defined by the following key characteristics:

- law regulates the extent and degree of animal suffering in connection with human conduct but harming animals is only criminalised where it is considered unnecessary;
- the level of legal protection is based on the animal's setting and function not on the animal's sentience;
- the result is inconsistent laws governing different species and even the same species in different settings;
- inconsistent laws go hand in hand with fragmented administration and enforcement;
- inconsistencies within jurisdictions are amplified by inconsistencies between jurisdictions;
- there is a heavy reliance on codes of practice and animal welfare standards developed through non-parliamentary processes, with disproportionate input from industry;
- the law is typically administered by government departments whose principal purpose is the promotion of productive and profitable agricultural and other industries;
- the law is enforced by these same departments and/or by charitable organisations;
- animals have the legal status of property, with their use in commercial contexts hidden from public scrutiny; and
- comprehensive information about the operation of laws that regulate animal use is not readily available to the public.

While this chapter has focused on farmed animals for illustrative purposes, these characteristics apply to all animal settings, to varying degrees, including those that attract the greatest legal protection. The breeding and sale of companion animals, for example, are also regulated by codes of practice typically developed under the auspices of primary industries departments with significant input from the pet industry. Similarly, regulation related to their welfare is fragmented and inconsistent, both within and between jurisdictions, while government action to address the problem of companion animal overpopulation has been piecemeal and inadequate.

In the following chapters, we will explore in detail the characteristics listed above in relation to major animal settings: companion animals, farmed animals, animals used for entertainment, sport and recreation, animals in the wild, and animals used in research and teaching. We will map the pervasiveness of these characteristics across the different regulatory settings and the way they contribute to an animal law narrative which is widely promoted but factually inaccurate. First, however, we need to examine the overall legal and regulatory framework and the breadth of the boundaries it sets for lawful animal use in Australia.

2
Legal and Regulatory Framework

> *[T]he* Animal Welfare Act *no longer meets the needs of Territory animals or lives up to community expectations when it comes to the health, safety and welfare of animals.*[1]

> *[I]t is always nice to add to the debate on legislation, particularly one that is so long overdue in providing reforms that will have a direct, positive impact on our community.*[2]

These words were spoken in the Northern Territory Legislative Assembly in 2018. More than three years later, the outdated *Animal Welfare Act 1999* remains on the statute books and the 'long overdue' legislative reforms are still not operative. Although the Animal Protection Bill was passed in 2018, the new Act's commencement was made contingent upon the finalisation of the necessary regulations.[3] As of January 2022, this had not occurred, despite advice from the Northern Territory Department of Primary Industry and Resources in April 2018 that the

1 Northern Territory, *Parliamentary Debates*, Legislative Assembly, 30 October 2018, 4721 (Lauren Moss).
2 Northern Territory, *Parliamentary Debates*, Legislative Assembly, 30 October 2018, 4719 (Kate Worden).
3 Legislative Assembly Social Policy Scrutiny Committee, Parliament of the Northern Territory 2018, 55.

drafting process was anticipated to take approximately six months.[4] The Northern Territory experience exemplifies the lengthy delay in securing even modest animal welfare reforms in Australia. It also suggests the hotly contested nature of this area of law and policy. While the reasons for the extensive delay in the Northern Territory are unknown, the critical role of the regulations in prescribing codes of practice might be a relevant factor given that compliance with these codes will provide a defence to a prosecution under the 2018 Act.

As well as the Northern Territory changes and recent amendments to the law in the ACT, major revision of other animal protection frameworks is underway in most of the states. As part of its *Animal Welfare Action Plan* published in December 2017,[5] the Victorian government committed to introducing new principal animal welfare legislation. In October 2020, public consultation was opened to inform the development of a draft Bill in relation to proposed changes contained in a Directions Paper, with an Engagement Summary Report released in 2021.[6] In May 2019, the Western Australian government commissioned a public review of the operation and effectiveness of that state's *Animal Welfare Act 2002* by an independent panel whose report was published in December 2020.[7] A legislative review is also underway in NSW, with publication by the DPI of an Animal Welfare Reform Issues Paper in February 2020, a Discussion Paper in July 2021 and a public exposure draft Animal Welfare Bill in January 2022.[8] In December 2020, the Queensland government announced that it would conduct a 'full review' of Queensland's animal welfare legislation,[9] with a Discussion

4 Ibid.
5 Victoria, Department of Economic Development, Jobs, Transport and Resources 2017.
6 These documents and other information about the Victorian reform process are available at https://engage.vic.gov.au/new-animal-welfare-act-victoria.
7 The report, the government's response and other information about the Western Australian review are available at https://www.agric.wa.gov.au/animalwelfare/review-animal-welfare-act-2002.
8 It appears that the Issues Paper is no longer available online. The Discussion Paper and other information about the NSW reform process are available at https://www.dpi.nsw.gov.au/animals-and-livestock/animal-welfare/animal-welfare-reform.
9 Furner 2020.

Paper released in 2021 and the Animal Care and Protection Amendment Bill introduced into parliament in May 2022.[10] In September 2021, the Minister for Primary Industries and Water announced that the Tasmanian government would introduce a Bill to amend the state's *Animal Welfare Act* 'to further strengthen enforcement and support the prosecution of animal welfare breaches'.[11] The information in this book reflects the law as at October 2021 unless otherwise stated but it is important to be mindful that legislative changes will occur as a result of the above reviews.

Because of the Commonwealth's limited role in animal protection, the state and territory laws are the most useful starting point for understanding the legal and regulatory frameworks governing animal welfare in Australia. Each jurisdiction has a principal animal protection statute as set out below. While the following discussion refers to provisions in the *Animal Protection Act 2018* (NT) (the 2018 NT Act), remember that the *Animal Welfare Act 1999* (NT) will continue to apply until the 2018 Act commences operation.

- *Animal Welfare Act 1992* (ACT)
- *Prevention of Cruelty to Animals Act 1979* (NSW)
- *Animal Welfare Act 1999*; *Animal Protection Act 2018* (NT)
- *Animal Care and Protection Act 2001* (Qld)
- *Animal Welfare Act 1985* (SA)
- *Animal Welfare Act 1993* (Tas)
- *Prevention of Cruelty to Animals Act 1986* (Vic)
- *Animal Welfare Act 2002* (WA).

Legislative objects

The objects clauses of the above animal welfare Acts suggest a wide-ranging concern to prevent cruelty to animals and to promote their welfare.[12] For example, s 3 of the *Prevention of Cruelty to Animals Act 1979* (NSW) provides that its objects are:

10 The Discussion Paper is available at https://bit.ly/3FAKCUf.
11 Barnett 2021.
12 There is no objects clause in the SA and Tasmanian statutes.

(a) to prevent cruelty to animals, and

(b) to promote the welfare of animals by requiring a person in charge of an animal –

(i) to provide care for the animal, and

(ii) to treat the animal in a humane manner, and

(iii) to ensure the welfare of the animal, and

(c) to promote the welfare of dogs and cats by requiring information about them to be provided when they are advertised for sale.

The 2018 NT Act and the Victorian Act include an educational object. For example, the purposes of the Victorian Act set out in s 1 are to:

(a) prevent cruelty to animals; and

(b) to encourage the considerate treatment of animals; and

(c) to improve the level of community awareness about the prevention of cruelty to animals.

The objects of the Queensland and WA Acts include reference to community expectations, while the objects of the ACT Act recognise animal sentience, the first Australian jurisdiction to do so:

4A Objects of Act

(1) The main objects of this Act are to recognise that –

(a) animals are sentient beings that are able to subjectively feel and perceive the world around them; and

(b) animals have intrinsic value and deserve to be treated with compassion and have a quality of life that reflects their intrinsic value; and

(c) people have a duty to care for the physical and mental welfare of animals.

Only in Queensland do the objects explicitly reflect the balancing exercise between human and animal interests discussed in Chapter 1. Section 3 of the *Animal Care and Protection Act 2001* (Qld) provides that the purposes of the Act are to:

> (a) promote the responsible care and use of animals;
>
> (b) provide standards for the care and use of animals that—
>
> > (i) achieve a reasonable balance between the welfare of animals and the interests of persons whose livelihood is dependent on animals; and
> >
> > (ii) allow for the effect of advancements in scientific knowledge about animal biology and changes in community expectations about practices involving animals;
>
> (c) protect animals from unjustifiable, unnecessary or unreasonable pain;
>
> (d) ensure the use of animals for scientific purposes is accountable, open and responsible.

Through consideration of key provisions in the principal animal welfare statutes of each state and territory, this chapter will help you to evaluate the extent to which each Act is consistent with the purposes identified in its objects clause. It will also illustrate the pervasiveness of the characteristics identified in Chapter 1. While the focus is on commonalities, it is important to stress that there are jurisdictional differences, not all of which can be covered here.

Definition of an animal

The dictionary in the ACT Act, s 4 of the NSW Act, s 11 of the Queensland Act and s 3(3) of the Victorian Act define an animal in broadly similar terms as:

- a live member of a vertebrate species, including any amphibian, bird, fish, mammal (other than a human being) or reptile; or
- a live crustacean (but in the ACT only when intended for human consumption and in NSW only when at a building or place where food is prepared or offered for consumption by retail sale).

There are some other variations, however, in these provisions, for example the inclusion in the ACT and Queensland Acts of cephalopods, such as octopus or squid. The other animal welfare Acts also define animals by reference to vertebrate species but with some differences. Section 3 of the Tasmanian Act restricts the definition to any live vertebrate animal but includes any other prescribed creature. Clause 4 of the *Animal Welfare (General) Regulations 2013* prescribes a creature of the class of Cephalopoda for the purposes of Part 4 of the Act (animal research). Section 5 of the 2018 NT Act defines an animal as a member of a vertebrate species but only includes bony or cartilaginous fish, as well as cephalopods or crustaceans, in the possession of or under the control of a person. A fish, cephalopod or crustacean is not in the possession or under the control of a person only by reason that it has been caught with fishing gear permitted under the *Fisheries Act* but is still in its usual aquatic habitat. Section 3 of the SA Act and s 5 of the WA Act exclude fish and crustaceans but include any prescribed animal (SA) and a live invertebrate of a prescribed kind (WA). The definitions broadly reflect current thinking about animal sentience but the jurisdictional variation indicates that non-scientific factors are also relevant. In the UK, for example, a review drew on over 300 scientific studies to evaluate the evidence of sentience in cephalopod molluscs, including octopods, squid and cuttlefish, and decapod crustaceans, including crabs, lobsters and crayfish. The review recommended that all cephalopod molluscs and decapod crustaceans 'be counted as "animals" for the purposes of the *Animal Welfare Act 2006* and included in the scope of any future legislation relating to animal sentience'.[13] In NSW, the draft Animal Welfare Bill 2022 includes decapod crustaceans and cephalopods in the definition of 'animal'.

13 Birch et al. 2021, 7–8.

General cruelty provisions

While the statutory objects apply to animals as defined above, not all legislative provisions apply to all animals, as we saw in Chapter 1. We will consider the various exemptions and defences in more detail after we examine the nature of the offences that the statutes contain.

All the principal animal welfare Acts include a generally expressed prohibition against cruelty which applies to any person:

- *Animal Welfare Act 1992* (ACT) s 7;
- *Prevention of Cruelty to Animals Act 1979* (NSW) s 5(1);
- *Animal Protection Act 2018* (NT) s 24;
- *Animal Care and Protection Act 2001* (Qld) s 18(1);
- *Animal Welfare Act 1985* (SA) s 13(2);
- *Animal Welfare Act 1993* (Tas) s 8(1);
- *Prevention of Cruelty to Animals Act 1986* (Vic) s 9(1);
- *Animal Welfare Act 2002* (WA) s 19(1).

These Acts incorporate the cruelty prohibition in various ways and use some different terminology, for example the SA Act refers to 'ill treatment' rather than cruelty. In Queensland, s 18(2) provides a non-exhaustive list of conduct taken to fall within the general cruelty prohibition in s 18(1) while the NSW Act includes a definition of an 'act of cruelty' in the general interpretation section. All jurisdictions, however, have a common characteristic: the offence of cruelty is qualified by words such as 'unnecessary', 'unreasonable' or 'unjustifiable'. This is illustrated by s 4(2) of the NSW Act set out below:

4 Definitions

(1) …

pain includes suffering and distress

…

(2) For the purposes of this Act, a reference to an act of cruelty committed upon an animal includes a reference to any act or omission as a consequence of which the animal is unreasonably, unnecessarily or unjustifiably –

(a) beaten, kicked, killed, wounded, pinioned, mutilated, maimed, abused, tormented, tortured, terrified or infuriated,

(b) over-loaded, over-worked, over-driven, over-ridden or over-used,

(c) exposed to excessive heat or excessive cold, or

(d) inflicted with pain.

5 Cruelty to animals

(1) A person shall not commit an act of cruelty upon an animal.

(2) A person in charge of an animal shall not authorise the commission of an act of cruelty upon the animal.

(3) A person in charge of an animal shall not fail at any time:

(a) to exercise reasonable care, control or supervision of an animal to prevent the commission of an act of cruelty upon the animal,

(b) where pain is being inflicted upon the animal, to take such reasonable steps as are necessary to alleviate the pain, or

(c) where it is necessary for the animal to be provided with veterinary treatment, whether or not over a period of time, to provide it with that treatment.

The above definition of 'pain' includes suffering and distress but does not make specific reference to mental suffering as some jurisdictions do, for example Queensland. Yet animals' capacity to experience mental suffering is a function of their sentience and its recognition in law is consistent with animal welfare science which acknowledges the importance of animals' affective states. This understanding of animal welfare supports an interpretation of 'suffering and distress' as inclusive of mental suffering, as do related terms in the NSW Act, such as 'tormented', 'terrified' and 'infuriated'. To avoid any ambiguity, however, the definition of 'cruelty' in the draft Animal Welfare Bill 2022 uses the language of 'harm' instead of 'pain' and includes specific acknowledgement that harm includes psychological suffering.[14]

Each of the following animal welfare Acts also creates an offence of aggravated cruelty where the animal dies or suffers serious harm as a result of the act or omission:

- *Animal Welfare Act 1992* (ACT) s 7A;
- *Prevention of Cruelty to Animals Act 1979* (NSW) s 6(1);
- *Animal Protection Act 2018* (NT) s 25;
- *Animal Welfare Act 1985* (SA) s 13(1);
- *Animal Welfare Act 1993* (Tas) s 9(1);
- *Prevention of Cruelty to Animals Act 1986* (Vic) s 10(1).

In Queensland, an indictable offence of serious animal cruelty was inserted as s 242 of the *Criminal Code* (Sch 1 of the *Criminal Code Act 1899*) in 2014. Acts or omissions authorised by the *Animal Care and Protection Act 2001* or another law are exempt from liability under this section. In NSW, s 530 was inserted into the *Crimes Act 1900* in 2005,[15] with exemption from liability created by s 530(2):

530 Serious animal cruelty

(1) A person who, with the intention of inflicting severe pain:

(a) tortures, beats or commits any other serious act of cruelty on an animal, and

(b) kills or seriously injures or causes prolonged suffering to the animal, is guilty of an offence.

Maximum penalty: Imprisonment for 5 years.

(1A) A person who, being reckless as to whether severe pain is inflicted:

14 NSW Department of Primary Industries 2021, 12.

15 Section 530 was amended in 2017 to include s 530(1A).

(a) tortures, beats or commits any other serious act of cruelty on an animal, and

(b) kills or seriously injures or causes prolonged suffering to the animal, is guilty of an offence.

Maximum penalty: Imprisonment for 3 years.

(2) A person is not criminally responsible for an offence against this section if:

(a) the conduct occurred in accordance with an authority conferred by or under the Animal Research Act 1985 or any other Act or law, or

(b) the conduct occurred in the course of or for the purposes of routine agricultural or animal husbandry activities, recognised religious practices, the extermination of pest animals or veterinary practice.

...

The inclusion of s 530(2) in the NSW Act is a clear indication that the law permits the infliction of severe pain or prolonged suffering if the conduct is considered necessary or justifiable. The use of the words 'routine' and 'recognised' also illustrates the way that existing practices dictate the scope and content of animal cruelty laws. In considering the proper construction of s 530, Bell P in the NSW Court of Appeal observed that:

> It might be thought to be somewhat extraordinary and indeed shocking that such abhorrent conduct including the torture of animals and acts of serious cruelty to them could occur either:
>
> (a) in accordance with an authority conferred by or under the *Animal Research Act 1985* or any other Act or law, or
>
> (b) in the course of or for the purposes of *routine* agricultural or animal husbandry activities, *recognised* religious practices, the extermination of pest animals or veterinary practice ...

> This is, however, what s 530(2) seems to contemplate in absolving a person who engages in such conduct from criminal responsibility under s 530(1).[16]

Specific offences, positive duties

In addition to the general prohibitions against cruelty, the principal animal welfare Acts include a wide variety of specific offences, either in the form of an omission or the commission of a prohibited act. Typical offences include failure to provide appropriate food, water, vet treatment, accommodation and exercise, as well as the abandonment of animals. In some jurisdictions, these offences are included in the same section as the general cruelty provision while other jurisdictions list them as separate offences. Failure to provide food, water and shelter, for example, falls within the general cruelty provision in s 9(1) of the *Prevention of Cruelty to Animals Act 1986* (Vic) and within the definition of ill treatment of animals in s 13(3) of the *Animal Welfare Act 1985* (SA). By contrast, they are listed as separate offences in s 6B and s 6C of the *Animal Welfare Act 1992* (ACT) and in s 8(1) of the *Prevention of Cruelty to Animals Act 1979* (NSW). There are numerous other specific offences contained in the animal welfare Acts but the jurisdictional variation is considerable. These offences relate to a wide range of activities, including transportation, surgical procedures, use of traps and electrical devices, baiting and poisoning, and prohibited events. Specific offences are also found in the regulations. For example, the tail docking of dogs except by a vet on therapeutic grounds is prohibited by statute in the ACT, NSW, NT, Queensland and Victoria but in SA, Tasmania and WA it is prohibited by the regulations.

Increasingly, specific offences are being framed in terms of breach of a duty of care as, for example, in s 17 of the Queensland Act:

---

16 *Will v Brighton* (2020) 104 NSWLR 170, 184, [60]. With respect to the mental element of s 530(1), however, the court considered the words 'with the intention of inflicting severe pain' and held that they mean 'an actual subjective intention to bring about this result as opposed to an intention to do acts which have the consequence of causing severe pain' at 184, [62] (Bell P). See further Chapter 6 this volume.

17 Breach of duty of care prohibited

(1) A person in charge of an animal owes a duty of care to it.

(2) The person must not breach the duty of care.

...

(3) For subsection (2), a person breaches the duty only if the person does not take reasonable steps to –

(a) provide the animal's needs for the following in a way that is appropriate –

(i) food and water;

(ii) accommodation or living conditions for the animal;

(iii) to display normal patterns of behaviour;

(iv) the treatment of disease or injury; or

(b) ensure any handling of the animal, including any confinement or transportation of the animal, by the person, or caused by the person, is appropriate.

...

Meaning of animal welfare

A duty to care for the physical and mental welfare of animals is recognised in the objects clause of the ACT Act. In the 2018 NT Act, ss 22–23 impose a duty of care on a person in control of an animal which is breached if the person fails to provide the minimum level of care, as defined in s 6, with the requisite state of mind. Section 6 of the Tasmanian Act imposes a general duty on a person who has the care or charge of an animal to take all reasonable measures to ensure the welfare of the animal. Animal welfare, however, is only defined in some jurisdictions and, even then, only in very general terms. In the Queensland Act, for example, 'welfare' is defined in the dictionary to mean 'issues about the health, safety or wellbeing of the animal'.

Nevertheless, inclusion of duties that go beyond meeting an animal's basic physical needs reflects an evolution in scientific thinking about the meaning of animal welfare[17] and the need for the relevant legislation to take 'a proactive approach'.[18] In the 1980s and 1990s, science focused on animals' biological functioning but animal welfare is now widely recognised as a complex phenomenon which includes animals' mental states, or feelings, as well as 'their ability to function according to how they have been shaped by evolution'.[19] With contemporary ideas about good welfare extending beyond meeting animals' basic needs and avoiding negative physical outcomes, the emphasis is increasingly on the achievement of positive welfare states and the concept of a 'life worth living'.[20] This evolution of the concept of animal welfare has ramifications for all animal uses but it assumes a particular significance in those regulatory settings where the interests of human and non-human animals are most likely to diverge. For this reason, we will return to the meaning of animal welfare in greater depth in Chapter 4, in the highly contested context of commercial animal uses.

Criminal liability

By contrast with the general cruelty provisions, specific offences are typically expressed to apply to the person in charge of an animal, a term which extends beyond an animal's owner. In NSW, for example, *person in charge* is defined in s 4(1) to include:

> (a) the owner of the animal,
>
> (b) a person who has the animal in the person's possession or custody, or under the person's care, control or supervision,

---

17 Goodfellow 2015, 116, 118.

18 Western Australia, Department of Primary Industries and Regional Development 2020, 16.

19 Veit and Browning 2021, 13.

20 Western Australia, Department of Primary Industries and Regional Development 2020, 19.

(c) where a person referred to in paragraph (b) is bound to comply with the directions, in respect of the animal, of any servant or agent of the owner of the animal, that servant or agent, as the case may be, and

(d) where the animal, being a stock animal, is confined in a sale-yard:

(i) the owner of the sale-yard, or

(ii) where the sale-yard is the subject of a lease, the lessee of the sale-yard.

Similarly, s 12 of the Queensland Act provides that:

(1) A person is *a person in charge* of an animal if the person—

(a) owns or has a lease, licence or other proprietary interest in the animal; or

(b) has the custody of the animal; or

(c) is employing or has engaged someone else who has the custody of the animal and the custody is within the scope of the employment or engagement.

(2) Despite subsection (1)(a), a person who holds a mortgage or other security interest in an animal only becomes a person in charge of the animal if the person takes a step to enforce the mortgage or other security.

The ACT Act also uses the phrase *person in charge*, as does the Victorian Act. In the Northern Territory, the relevant terminology is a *person in control* of an animal, the South Australian Act refers to the *owner*, and the Tasmanian Act refers to a person who has the *care or charge* of the animal or has *possession or custody* of it. While the terminology differs, all these provisions, as defined in their respective Acts, extend responsibility for an animal's welfare beyond that of the owner.

The meaning of a *person in charge* has been the subject of legal challenge, including in the *Al Kuwait* case about live sheep exported from Western Australia, discussed in Chapter 1. Section 5 of the WA Act defines a person in charge as:

> (a) the owner of the animal; or
>
> (b) a person who has actual physical custody or control of the animal; or
>
> (c) if the person referred to in paragraph (b) is a member of staff of another person, that other person; or
>
> (d) the owner or occupier of the place or vehicle where the animal is or was at the relevant time.

Once the sheep were on board the ship, Emanuel Exports no longer owned the animals or had physical control of them but the company had engaged a stockman to care for the sheep during the voyage. Although the defence argued that the stockman was not paid by the company and was not its employee, the definition of staff in the WA Act includes all the people working for, or engaged by, a person whether as officers, employees, agents, contractors, volunteers or in any other capacity. The magistrate found that the stockman on the voyage was responsible for caring for the sheep and that he had been engaged by the company, at least 'in any other capacity'.[21] Accordingly, Emanuel Exports was a person in charge for the purposes of the Act.

In deciding this issue, the magistrate in the *Al Kuwait* case had regard to the purposes of the WA Act and to the test in *Song v Coddington*. In that case, Greg James J considered the term *person in charge* as defined in s 4(1)(b) of the *Prevention of Cruelty to Animals Act 1979* (NSW) and held that to meet the definition it is necessary for the person:

> … to have some responsibility or authority of an immediate kind for the physical control of an animal rather than merely having some legal responsibility to undertake a limited function in connection with the animal even if that function involves a visual

21 *Department of Local Government and Regional Development v Emanuel Exports*, unreported, Magistrates Court of Western Australia (Criminal Jurisdiction), Crawford M, 8 February 2008, [35].

> looking over of the animal. The concept of person in charge, in my view, in the *Prevention of Cruelty to Animals (General) Regulation* 1996 particularly refers to a person's ability and authority (to) take positive steps to effect the immediate physical circumstances of the animal so that person's authority might be employed to ensure care, treatment in a humane manner and the welfare of the animal.[22]

While the reasoning in *Song v Coddington* resulted in a positive finding in the *Al Kuwait* case, the test as set out by Greg James J is arguably a narrow one. The case involved an appeal by a veterinary officer employed by the Australian Quarantine Inspection Service, Dr Song, from his convictions under cl 5(1)(b) of the *Prevention of Cruelty to Animals (General) Regulation 1996* (NSW). The proceedings arose out of Dr Song's authorisation of the export by plane of a consignment of 1,137 live goats, contained in eight three-tier wooden pallets. A subsequent inspection by the RSPCA found that some of the goats were unable to stand upright without coming into contact with the ceiling of the tier in which they were loaded. In allowing the appeal, Greg James J rejected the magistrate's finding that the goats were under Dr Song's supervision and held that in order:

> ... to be a person in charge of the goats, it is not enough that the person perform some ancillary legal function in relation to the goats but it is necessary that the person, whether on their own or in combination with others, have that degree of authority and responsibility as would enable the person to engage in the physical disposition of the goats.[23]

Song v Coddington was considered by the Supreme Court of New South Wales in *RSPCA (NSW) v Elliott*.[24] The case involved an appeal by the RSPCA against a magistrate's decision to acquit Ms Elliott of 23 offences under the *Prevention of Cruelty to Animals Act 1979* (NSW) of failing to provide veterinary treatment and proper and sufficient food for a number of greyhounds. Ms Elliott did not own the greyhounds

---

22 (2003) 59 NSWLR 180, 194, [66].

23 Ibid, 195, [66].

24 [2012] NSWSC 585.

but had volunteered to help with cleaning the kennels and feeding the dogs. At first instance, the magistrate made reference to Greg James J's 'restrictive interpretation' in *Song v Coddington* to conclude that Ms Elliott was not a person in charge. On appeal, however, Schmidt J held that the magistrate erred in his understanding of what was decided in *Song* and remitted the matter to the Local Court to be determined according to law.[25]

Another of the elements of criminal liability which has been tested in the courts is whether animal cruelty offences require proof of *mens rea*; that is, a positive state of mind such as intent, recklessness or knowledge. The common law presumption that *mens rea* is an essential element of every offence may be displaced by statute, having regard to the words and subject matter of the legislation.[26] In Victoria, for example, most of the offences in the *Prevention of Cruelty to Animals Act 1986* have no *mens rea* element.[27] In *Will v Brighton*, Bell P stated that s 5 of the *Prevention of Cruelty to Animals Act 1979* (NSW) 'creates a general offence where a person commits or authorises, by act or omission, an act of cruelty upon an animal. Section 5(3) makes it clear that a subjective intention to commit an act of cruelty is not required for this offence to be made out'.[28] In *Pearson v Janlin Circuses Pty Ltd*,[29] Windeyer J referred to the decision in *Bell v Gunter*[30] and that of the NSW Court of Appeal in *Fleet v District Court of NSW*[31] and held that s 5(2) of the *Prevention of Cruelty to Animals Act 1979* (NSW) does not require proof of *mens rea*. This was also the view of the Supreme Court of Tasmania in *Mitchell v Marshall*[32] in relation to ss 7, 8(1) and 9 of the *Animal Welfare Act 1993* (Tas). Note, however, that s 9 of the Tasmanian Act was repealed in 2015 and the following section substituted:

25 Ibid, [29].
26 *He Kaw Teh v R* (1985) 157 CLR 523.
27 Sentencing Advisory Council, Victoria 2019, 14.
28 (2020) 104 NSWLR 170, 175, [16]. For the court's interpretation of the mental element of s 530(1) of the *Crimes Act 1900* (NSW) see note 16 above.
29 [2002] NSWSC 1118.
30 Unreported, Supreme Court of NSW, Dowd J, 24 October 1997.
31 [1999] NSWCA 362.
32 [2014] TASSC 43.

9 Aggravated cruelty

(1) A person must not do any act, or omit to do any duty, referred to in section 8, if the person knows that, or is reckless as to whether, the act or omission will, or is reasonably likely to, result in –

(a) the death, deformity or serious disablement of an animal; or

(b) harm to an animal that endangers the life of the animal; or

(c) an injury to an animal that, either alone or in combination with the health of the animal at the time of the injury, results in a significant and longstanding injury to the animal.

...

This amendment illustrates the use of statutory language to make clear that a particular state of mind is an essential element of an offence. Where *mens rea* is not an element of an animal cruelty offence, a number of Australian cases establish that the defence of honest and reasonable mistake of fact is available to an accused person.[33] In criminal law terms, this is referred to as strict liability; where proof of *mens rea* is not required and the defence of honest and reasonable mistake of fact is not available, liability is said to be absolute. In the case of some offences, statutory provisions specify whether liability is absolute or strict, for example s 15A(3) of the *Animal Welfare Act 1992* (ACT).

Defences and exemptions

While the lack of a *mens rea* element for some offences makes the prosecution's task easier, the qualified definition of cruelty means that much pain and suffering falls outside the ambit of the animal welfare Acts. This is just one of several means by which a great many

33 Sentencing Advisory Council, Victoria 2019, 14.

animals are effectively excluded from the law's protective reach. Other mechanisms are the exemption of certain classes of animal, or animal uses, from the application of key parts of the legislation, as well as the inclusion of defences to a cruelty charge. These defences and exemptions are commonly, though not exclusively, applicable to conduct which accords with an adopted or prescribed code of practice, or an accepted husbandry practice, as illustrated by the *SAWA* case in Chapter 1.

Summarised below are key defences and exemptions in each of the principal animal welfare Acts. The list is not intended to be exhaustive but to convey the scope of activities effectively excluded from the application of animal welfare laws.

Australian Capital Territory

Animal welfare offences are contained in Part 2 of the ACT Act. Section 20 provides that, other than the provisions it specifies, Part 2 does not apply to conduct in accordance with an approved or mandatory code of practice. The prohibition in s 19 on carrying out medical or surgical procedures by non-veterinary practitioners does not apply in some circumstances. These include procedures carried out in accordance with accepted animal husbandry practice in relation to farming and grazing activities, zoo management or the management of native animals, or in accordance with a licence or authorisation, subject to any written direction of an animals ethics committee.

New South Wales

A wide range of defences to a cruelty charge are listed in s 24 of the NSW Act, many of which relate to husbandry practices. For example, s 24(1)(a) includes defences related to the ear-tagging and branding of stock animals, the castration of pigs and stock animals under a certain age, the dehorning of cattle under 12 months of age and the mulesing of sheep less than 12 months old. Section 24(1)(b) covers conduct related to hunting, shooting, snaring, trapping, catching or capturing an animal or destroying the animal, or preparing the animal for destruction, for the purpose of producing food for human consumption. All these defences are subject to the proviso that the conduct inflicts no unnecessary pain. Other defences in s 24 include conduct in accordance with the provisions of the *Animal*

Research Act 1985 and destroying an animal, or preparing an animal for destruction, in accordance with the precepts of the Jewish religion or any other religion prescribed for the purposes of the provision. In the case of these defences, there is no qualifying requirement that the conduct be carried out in a manner that inflicts no unnecessary pain. The NSW Act also excludes stock animals (other than horses) and animals usually kept in a cage from the requirement in s 9 to exercise confined animals, while s 34A(3) provides that compliance or failure to comply with guidelines or codes of practice prescribed or adopted by the regulations for the purposes of s 34A(1) is admissible in evidence in cruelty proceedings.

Northern Territory

Section 21(2) of the 2018 NT Act provides a defence to a prosecution for conduct in accordance with a code of practice adopted or prescribed by regulation. Sections 27 and 28 which govern the administration and laying of poison do not apply, *inter alia*, to conduct or circumstances exempted by regulation. Section 110(2) provides a defence to a cruelty prosecution, other than for an offence against s 24(3), if the person is an Aboriginal person and the conduct complied with Aboriginal traditional law or custom.

Queensland

Section 7 of the Qld Act provides that a person who lawfully does an act or makes an omission authorised under the *Fisheries Act 1994*, the *Racing Act 2002* or the *Racing Integrity Act 2016* which would otherwise constitute an offence under the Qld Act is taken not to commit the offence by reason only of doing the act or making the omission, unless the act is the use of an animal for a scientific purpose. Section 40 of the Qld Act provides an offence exemption for acts or omissions compliant with the requirements of a code of practice or the scientific use code. Section 41A exempts the killing of an animal under Aboriginal tradition, Island custom or native title provided the act is done in a way that causes the animal as little pain as is reasonable. Section 42 exempts acts done to control feral or pest animals which do not involve the use of a prohibited trap or spur and is done in a way that causes the animal as little pain as is reasonable and complies with any prescribed conditions. Other exemptions include s 45 which governs slaughter under religious faith.

South Australia

Section 13(5) of the SA Act provides a defence to a charge of ill-treating an animal if the defendant proves that the offence did not result from any failure on the part of the defendant to take reasonable care to avoid the commission of the offence. Section 43 of the SA Act provides that nothing in the Act renders unlawful anything done in accordance with a prescribed code of practice relating to animals.

Tasmania

Section 4(1) and (2) of the Tasmanian Act provide that the cruelty offences and the baiting and shooting offences do not apply to the hunting of animals or to practices used in fishing or angling provided these are done in a usual and reasonable manner and without causing excess suffering. Section 4(3) exempts animal research carried out with approval and in accordance with a code of practice from the general cruelty offences and s 4(4) exempts the feeding of an animal from baiting and shooting offences if carried out in a reasonable manner, having regard to the natural behaviour of the animal. Unlike other jurisdictions, the Tasmanian Act does not contain defences or offence exemptions for compliance with codes of practice, other than in relation to scientific research. Usual husbandry practices are nevertheless unlikely to fall foul of the law due to the qualified nature of cruelty offences which incorporate the terminology of unreasonable and unjustifiable pain or suffering.[34]

Victoria

Section 6(1) of the Victorian Act exempts a wide range of activities carried out in accordance with a code of practice from the application of the Act. These include any act or practice with respect to the farming, transport, sale or killing of any farm animal and the handling, transportation, killing, hunting, trapping, husbandry or management

34 Cao 2015, 219.

of any other animal. Other exemptions in s 6(1) include the slaughter of animals in accordance with the *Meat Industry Act 1993* or any Commonwealth Act, anything done in accordance with the *Catchment and Land Protection Act 1994*, and fishing activities authorised by and conducted in accordance with the *Fisheries Act 1995*. Section 6(1B) exempts anything done in accordance with the *Wildlife Act 1975*. The Act also contains various defences, for example s 11 relating to reasonable self-defence against an attack, or threat of attack, by an animal.

Western Australia

Sections 20–30 of the WA Act set out a wide range of defences to a cruelty charge under s 19, for example s 22 in relation to acts authorised by law and s 24 in relation to killing pests. As illustrated in Chapter 1, the defences include acts done in accordance with generally accepted animal husbandry practice (s 23) or done in accordance with a relevant code of practice (s 25). The husbandry practices in s 23 are not limited to farming or grazing activities but extend to the management of zoos, wildlife parks or similar establishments, animal breeding establishments and the training of animals. Other included defences relate to killing pest animals, stock fending for itself, the prescribed use of devices and prescribed surgical operations. Other offence provisions in the Act also contain defences, for example s 32 in relation to shooting, hunting or fighting captive animals.

In addition to the principal animal welfare Acts, relevant exemptions or defences may be included in other statutes. Section 4(3) of the *Livestock Management Act 2010* (Vic), for example, provides that it is a defence to an offence under the *Prevention of Cruelty to Animals Act 1986* if the person was carrying out a regulated livestock management activity and acting in compliance with a prescribed livestock management standard. Note also that the animal welfare Acts typically confer broad regulation-making power, for example s 35(2) of the NSW Act:

35 Regulations

(1) …

(2) A provision of a regulation may –

(a) apply generally or be limited in its application by reference to specified exceptions or factors,

(b) apply differently according to different factors of a specified kind,

(c) authorise any matter or thing to be from time to time determined, applied or regulated by any specified person or body, or

(d) exempt any person, or any specified class of persons, either absolutely or subject to conditions, from the operation of any specified provision of this Act,

or may do any combination of those things.

(3) …

Similarly, the ACT Act provides:

111 Exemptions by regulations

A regulation may –

(a) exempt a person from the requirements of all or any of the provisions of this Act; or

(b) provide for all or any of the provisions of this Act to apply, or not to apply, in relation to an animal.

In addition, specific provisions in animal welfare Acts authorise the regulations to prescribe permitted uses in relation to an otherwise prohibited act. A typical example is s 16(3)(a) of the *Prevention of Cruelty to Animals Act 1979* (NSW) which authorises the use of an electrical device on an animal of a prescribed species. Remember also that most animal welfare Acts provide that conduct in accordance with a code of practice adopted or prescribed by regulation is exempt from cruelty offences or constitutes a defence. In some jurisdictions, the animal welfare Acts specifically require the tabling of these codes of practice or classify them as disallowable instruments.[35] Where this is not the case and codes of practice are adopted by regulations simply as a list, they are effectively incorporated into law without any parliamentary scrutiny.[36]

Legal status of codes and standards

Clearly, codes of practice play an important role in the regulation of animal welfare. As we saw in Chapter 1, compliance with codes of practice for farmed animals has largely been voluntary but has advantages for animal use industries through access to the defences or exemptions which compliance brings. We also noted that the Model Codes of Practice are being converted into national Animal Welfare Standards and Guidelines, a topic we examine further in Chapter 4. In addition, national Animal Welfare Standards and Guidelines for exhibited animals were endorsed in 2019 and the *Australian Code for the Care and Use of Animals for Scientific Purposes* developed by the National Health and Medical Research Council is in its eighth edition. As with the Model Codes of Practice, the status of national Animal Welfare Standards and Guidelines depends on how they are incorporated into state and territory laws, a process which to date has been both slow and variable. The position is further complicated by the development of different codes of practice by state and territory governments and their inclusion in some cases in animal welfare legislation. Consideration of the NSW and WA Acts illustrates both the complexity and the jurisdictional variation.

As described in Chapter 1, s 34A(3) of the NSW Act provides that compliance or failure to comply with codes of practice prescribed or adopted by the regulations for the purposes of s 34A(1) is admissible in evidence in cruelty proceedings. Clause 33(1) of the *Prevention of*

35 *Animal Welfare Act 1992* (ACT) ss 22 and 23; *Animal Care and Protection Act 2001* (Qld) s 14; *Prevention of Cruelty to Animals Act 1986* (Vic) s 7.

36 Legislative Assembly Social Policy Scrutiny Committee, Parliament of the Northern Territory 2018, 29–31.

Cruelty to Animals Regulation 2012 originally prescribed eight codes of practice or guidelines for this purpose, all in relation to farmed animals and related commercial activities. In 2017, the codes of practice for sheep and cattle were omitted from cl 33(1) following the development of the national standards designed to replace them. At the same time, the *Australian Animal Welfare Standards and Guidelines for Cattle* and the *Australian Animal Welfare Standards and Guidelines for Sheep*, both endorsed in 2016, were adopted as guidelines by cl 33(3) for the purposes of s 34A(1). By contrast, the *Prevention of Cruelty to Animals (Land Transport of Livestock) Standards* were regulated in 2013 by their inclusion in Sch 1 of the *Prevention of Cruelty to Animals Regulation 2012* which, in conjunction with Part 4 of the Regulation, governs animal trades. Among other requirements, Part 4 makes it an offence for proprietors and employees of a prescribed animal trade to fail to comply with each relevant code or standard listed in Sch 1. Various codes of practice developed at state level under the auspices of the NSW DPI are also regulated under the animal trades provisions and mandate compliance. Examples are the *Animal Welfare Code of Practice – Animals in Pet Shops* and the *Animal Welfare Code of Practice – Breeding Dogs and Cats*. Like all the states and territories, NSW has also adopted the *Australian Code for the Care and Use of Animals for Scientific Purposes* but, unlike other jurisdictions, it is incorporated through separate animal research legislation, not through the principal animal welfare Act.

In Western Australia, the *Australian Animal Welfare Standards and Guidelines – Land Transport of Livestock* 2012, as amended from time to time, are adopted by cl 6(1) of the *Animal Welfare (General) Regulations 2003* under s 94(2)(d) of the *Animal Welfare Act 2002*. The *Australian Animal Welfare Standards and Guidelines for Cattle* 2016 and the *Australian Animal Welfare Standards and Guidelines – Livestock at Saleyards and Depots* 2018 are also adopted by this clause. This means that compliance with these standards and guidelines can be used as a s 25 defence to a charge under s 19(1) of the Act. Clause 6(1) also includes a number of codes of practice developed by the WA Department of Local Government and Regional Development, for example circuses and rodeos. In addition – or separately – standards can be directly regulated to mandate compliance, as for example the

Animal Welfare (Transport, Saleyards and Depots) (Cattle and Sheep) Regulations 2020 which currently implement the *Standards for Land Transport of Livestock* and *Livestock at Saleyards and Depots* in relation to cattle and sheep.[37] Regardless of whether standards are regulated in this way, their status as a s 25 defence is dependent upon their adoption by regulation under s 94(2)(d). The same applies to codes of practice developed by the state. The operation of some codes of practice as a s 25 defence is modified by reference to national standards, as itemised in the table in cl 6(2) of the *Animal Welfare (General) Regulations 2003*. This table includes codes developed at state level, for example the *Code of Practice for Sheep in Western Australia* first published by the Department of Local Government and Regional Development in 2003. This code, adopted by cl 6(2) under s 94(2)(d) of the Act, is modified as follows:

> To the extent that the Code applies to the transport process for sheep in Western Australia, the transport process is to be undertaken in accordance with the *Australian Animal Welfare Standards and Guidelines – Land Transport of Livestock* (Edition 1, Version 1.1, 21 September 2012), published by Animal Health Australia (AHA), Canberra, as it is amended from time to time.

Administration and enforcement

The current arrangements for administration of the animal welfare Acts are set out in Table 2.1. While these departments are subject to reorganisation or change of name from time to time, the general point remains that animal welfare is typically administered by departments of primary industries or agriculture.

The animal welfare Acts typically authorise the responsible minister or departmental head to appoint inspectors to enforce the legislation. These are usually drawn from the ranks of the various state/territory RSPCAs and relevant government departments, but other appropriately

---

37 For a progress report on the implementation of these standards across Australia, see http://www.animalwelfarestandards.net.au/saleyards-and-depots/.

Table 2.1. Animal welfare administrative agencies

Animal Welfare Act	Administrative agency
ACT	Transport Canberra and City Services
NSW	Department of Primary Industries
NT	Department of Primary Industry and Resources
QLD	Department of Agriculture and Fisheries, Biosecurity Queensland
SA	Department for Environment and Water
TAS	Department of Primary Industries, Parks, Water and Environment, Biosecurity Tasmania
VIC	Department of Jobs, Precincts and Regions, Agriculture Victoria
WA	Department of Primary Industries and Regional Development

qualified persons may also be appointed in some cases. In jurisdictions which incorporate the use of animals for scientific research within their animal welfare Act, there may be different criteria for appointment of these inspectors, as well as differences in their functions and powers. The highly unusual involvement of a charitable organisation in criminal law enforcement reflects the RSPCA's historical origins and functions in 19th-century Britain.[38] In Australia, the first Society for the Prevention of Cruelty to Animals was established in Victoria in 1871, followed by New South Wales in 1873, South Australia in 1875, Tasmania in 1878, Queensland in 1883 and Western Australia in 1892. The societies received the Royal warrant in 1923, and in 1955 and 1965, societies were

38 See further Radford 2001.

established in the ACT and the NT respectively.[39] Today, the RSPCA is comprised of eight autonomous state and territory societies and a federal body, RSPCA Australia, which sets national animal welfare policies and works with government and industry to address animal welfare issues.[40]

Officers of the state and territory RSPCAs are currently authorised to enforce the principal animal welfare Act in all jurisdictions except the Northern Territory. In most jurisdictions, the RSPCA has responsibility for enforcement, backed up by departmental officers and the police. Where compliance and enforcement responsibilities are divided between government agencies and the RSPCA, departmental officers typically have responsibility for commercial livestock and the RSPCA for other animals. In Queensland and Victoria, this division of responsibility is formalised in a memorandum of understanding. Police officers in Queensland are not appointed as inspectors under the *Animal Care and Protection Act* but have some relevant powers under the *Police Powers and Responsibilities Act 2000*. In NSW, enforcement of the *Prevention of Cruelty to Animals Act 1979* (POCTAA) is the responsibility of approved charitable organisations, currently RSPCA NSW and the Animal Welfare League, and the police.[41] An inspector within the meaning of the *Greyhound Racing Act 2017* is also included in the definition of inspector in s 24D(1) of the NSW Act. Inspectors may also be appointed from other classes of persons for specific purposes in some jurisdictions. In Western Australia, for example, s 33(2) and s 35(1) of the *Animal Welfare Act 2002* provide for the appointment of local government officers as general inspectors but restrict the exercise of their powers to their local government district except in specified circumstances. Importantly, whether or not the relevant government departments have any enforcement function, they are influential in policy terms and have a key role in advising ministers, developing codes of practice and standards, and promoting animal welfare generally.

---

39 RSPCA Australia n.d. Our History.

40 RSPCA Australia n.d. About Us.

41 Section 4(1) definition of 'officer'; s 24D(1). Although employees of the DPI may be authorised by the minister to enforce the NSW Act, this has not occurred. The DPI plays an important role, however, in relation to stock welfare panels established under s 24T.

Note also that, in most jurisdictions, RSPCA inspectors are subject to various forms of oversight and control by these departments through such means as conditions of appointment, training requirements and reporting obligations.[42]

Enforcement options

A hierarchy of formal enforcement options is contained in the animal welfare Acts. Although most include written directions, penalty or infringement notices for prescribed offences and prosecution, there is the usual jurisdictional variation. In Queensland, for example, penalty infringement notices are only being considered as part of the current review of the *Animal Care and Protection Act 2001*.[43] In practice, educational activities and informal action appear to make up a significant part of the work of all enforcement agencies. According to RSPCA Victoria, for example, the promotion of animal welfare 'is often best achieved through providing assistance and education, rather than employing a criminal justice response'.[44] Similarly, the Queensland government maintains that '[e]ducation and/or the use of animal welfare directions usually see improved outcomes for animal welfare'.[45] In Western Australia, both the RSPCA and the relevant department have 'supported the value of education as the most appropriate method of achieving compliance' with the legislation.[46] In 2020, the independent panel's review of the WA Act noted that it 'is likely that all inspectors, whether employed by the RSPCA or [Department of Primary Industries and Regional Development], deal with minor incidents and "first time offenders" by education rather than enforcement action'.[47]

The Queensland government has also expressed the view that '[f]ailing to meet an animal's needs has many causes and is rarely

42 Goodfellow 2015, 280–1.
43 Queensland Government 2021, 19.
44 Sentencing Advisory Council, Victoria 2019, xiii.
45 Queensland Government 2021, 19.
46 Easton et al. 2015, 28.
47 Western Australia, Department of Primary Industries and Regional Development 2020, 59.

intentional or malicious' and that prosecution is 'appropriate for deliberate acts of cruelty and more serious incidents of neglect'.[48] Remarks of this kind suggest that regulatory agencies may be importing a de facto *mens rea* element into enforcement decisions and only prosecuting if they think moral fault is present in some way, even if it is not a requirement of the offence. In any event, only a very small percentage of complaints received by all enforcement agencies, whether charitable organisations or government bodies, result in prosecution, as figures in relation to NSW, Victoria and Queensland illustrate. In NSW, in the financial year 2018–19, the RSPCA investigated 15,673 complaints, issued 248 written directions, 7 official cautions, 37 penalty infringement notices and commenced 77 prosecutions, involving 353 offences and 4,397 animals.[49] In Victoria, 79,006 complaints of animal cruelty were received by the key enforcement agencies between 2011 and 2017, of which 6,135 were substantiated and 2,775 charges sentenced.[50] In the financial year 2018–19, RSPCA Queensland investigated 17,810 complaints, charged 340 people and conducted 154 successful prosecutions, with 238 cases pending.[51] In the same period, Biosecurity Queensland received 2,818 animal welfare complaints, all but 390 of which were closed with only one complaint resulting in prosecution. No other information is available from Biosecurity Queensland about its regulatory action in response to these complaints.[52]

Law enforcement is a complex activity, as the following chapters will illustrate. A low prosecution rate is not necessarily an indication of failure but the efficacy of current approaches by all enforcement agencies needs to be tested rather than assumed. It appears that these approaches focus heavily on education and other informal action, with recourse to even the less punitive formal options, such as written directions or penalty notices, relatively rare. It may be that informal responses are effective tools in the achievement of the statutory objects but it is unclear what, if any, evidence is relied upon by agencies in making this claim. As the culture of enforcement agencies and the values and assumptions

48 Queensland Government 2021, 19.
49 RSPCA NSW 2019, 34.
50 Sentencing Advisory Council, Victoria 2019, 17.
51 RSPCA Queensland 2019, 26.
52 Martin and Reid 2020, 76–7.

of individuals inevitably influence the exercise of discretionary powers, routinely available data about the choice of regulatory tools is needed to evaluate the efficacy of current approaches. Qualitative research would also help to shed light on the exercise of discretionary powers in relation to animal welfare. Apart from the direct consequences for animals, the way these powers are exercised plays an important part in constructing notions of cruelty in the context of the human–animal relationship.

Penalties

Nearly all animal cruelty offences are summary offences dealt with by Magistrates Courts. Section 178 of the *Animal Care and Protection Act 2001* (Qld), for example, provides that offences under the Act are summary offences, while the offence of serious animal cruelty under s 242 of the *Criminal Code* (Qld) is dealt with by the District Court. Research suggests that a moderate fine is the most frequently imposed penalty for offences prosecuted under animal welfare legislation.[53] In Victoria, for example, 60% of animal cruelty charges received a fine in the ten years from 2008 to 2017 inclusive, compared with 55% for all offences sentenced in the Magistrates Court. Where it was not part of an aggregate sentence covering more than one charge, the average fine was $1,355.[54] The second most common outcome in Victoria was an adjourned undertaking, with 4% receiving a term of imprisonment, including partially suspended sentences.[55] Of the prison sentences imposed, 88 were part of an aggregate sentence; of the remaining 38 non-aggregate prison sentences, 31 were for a period of less than six months.[56] In Queensland, a fine was imposed in 68.2% of cases for offences against animals from 2005–06 to 2017–18, with an average fine

53 Sentencing Advisory Council, Victoria 2019, 3.

54 Ibid, 31–2. The Victorian report analysed 35 animal cruelty offences operational during the reference period in relation to the *Prevention of Cruelty to Animals Act 1986*, the *Prevention of Cruelty to Animals Regulations 2008*, the *Prevention of Cruelty to Animals (Domestic Fowl) Regulations 2016*, the *Domestic Animals Act 1994* and the *Racing Act 1958*.

55 Ibid.

56 Ibid, 34.

of $1,460.[57] The second most common penalty was probation, followed by community service, with a custodial penalty imposed in 9.2% of cases. The latter included wholly suspended sentences and intensive correction orders, with a term of imprisonment imposed in less than half of the cases (33 of 76) where a custodial penalty was ordered. The average length of imprisonment in these cases was five months.[58]

The maximum penalties for offences under the principal animal welfare Acts vary between jurisdictions, as Table 2.2 illustrates. This table sets out the maximum penalties for the general cruelty and aggravated cruelty offences in the states and territories as compiled by the NSW DPI in 2018. For ease of comparison, the monetary penalties are expressed as amounts, not as a number of penalty units, as in most jurisdictions.[59]

The purpose of including this table is to illustrate jurisdictional variability only and current amounts in some jurisdictions will be greater than listed here. In NSW, for example, the *Prevention of Cruelty to Animals Act 1979* was amended in June 2021 to increase substantially the penalties for various offences. These include an increase in the maximum penalty for a s 5 cruelty offence from 50 penalty units (currently $5,500) and/or six months' imprisonment to 400 penalty units (currently $44,000) and/or imprisonment for one year for an individual and from 250 penalty units (currently $27,500) to 2,000 penalty units currently ($220,000) for a corporation. The maximum penalty for a s 6 aggravated cruelty offence has been increased to 1,000 penalty units and/or imprisonment for two years for an individual and 5,000 penalty units for a corporation. Some jurisdictions also include penalties for continuing offences; for example, s 79 of the WA Act which provides for a penalty of $1,000 for every day on which the offence is taken to continue. There are also higher penalties for the indictable offences of serious animal cruelty which are decided in the intermediate or District Courts. In Queensland, the maximum penalty for serious animal

57 Queensland Sentencing Advisory Council 2019, 12–13. The Queensland report considered offences under the *Animal Care and Protection Act 2001* and s 242 of the *Criminal Code.*

58 Ibid.

59 The value of a penalty unit is not uniform throughout Australia and is subject to regular increase.

Table 2.2. Maximum penalties: principal animal welfare Acts 2018*

State or territory	Cruelty to animals offence	Aggravated cruelty to animals offence
ACT	Individual – $15,000 and/or one year's imprisonment Corporation – $75,000	Individual – $30,000 and/or two years' imprisonment Corporation – $150,000
NSW	Individual – $5,500 and/or six months' imprisonment Corporation – $27,500	Individual – $22,000 and/or two years' imprisonment Corporation – $110,000
NT	$23,100 or 18 months' imprisonment	$30,800 or two years' imprisonment
QLD	Individual and corporation – $252,300 or three years' imprisonment	N/A but note the *Criminal Code* offence
SA	$20,000 or two years' imprisonment	$50,000 or four years' imprisonment
TAS	Individual – $15,900 and/or 12 months' imprisonment Corporation – $79,500	Individual – $31,800 and/or five years' imprisonment Corporation – $159,000
VIC	Individual – $39,642.50 or 12 months' imprisonment Corporation – $95,142	Individual – $79,285 or two years' imprisonment Corporation – $190,284
WA	Individual – $50,000 and five years' imprisonment Corporation – $250,000 Mandatory minimum penalty: Individual – $2,000 Corporation – $10,000	N/A

* NSW Department of Primary Industries 2018, 4–5.

cruelty under s 242 of the *Criminal Code* is seven years' imprisonment; in NSW, s 530 of the *Crimes Act 1900* provides a maximum penalty of five years' imprisonment for serious animal cruelty where the infliction of severe pain is intentional and three years where it is reckless.

In addition to imposing penalties for offences, courts have power under the principal animal welfare Acts to make various orders, including a prohibition or control order prohibiting a convicted person from acquiring or possessing any animal for a specified period or applying conditions that must be complied with by a person in charge of an animal. Some of the Acts also provide for the recognition of interstate prohibition or control orders, for example s 31AA of the NSW Act and s 12A of the Victorian Act. According to the Victorian sentencing study, prosecutors emphasised the importance of control orders in maximising animal welfare outcomes but some stakeholders expressed concern that magistrates lack knowledge of them as a sentencing option.[60] The Queensland Sentencing Advisory Council study found a considerable increase in the proportion of cases that resulted in a prohibition order, from 25.7% of cases in 2011–12 to 50.7% in 2017–18.[61]

Enforcement problems

Enforcement will be considered further in Chapters 3–7 in the context of specific animal uses. Broadly, however, current problems with enforcement are associated with one or more of the following issues: ambiguous legislation, insufficient resources, lack of transparency, inadequate powers, agency culture, conflicts of interest and fragmentation of regulatory responsibility. The interrelated nature of these issues compounds their effect.

Ambiguous legislation

As we have seen, general cruelty offences are characterised by qualifying words, such as 'unnecessary', 'unjustifiable' and 'unreasonable'. The balancing act required by this terminology means that it may be

60 Sentencing Advisory Council, Victoria 2019, 39, 42.
61 Queensland Sentencing Advisory Council 2019, 12.

easier to establish a breach of a specific offence provision than the general cruelty prohibition. For example, between 2009 and 2017 the most common charge laid by RSPCA Victoria was failing to provide veterinary treatment, followed by failing to provide food, drink or shelter.[62] Specific offences, however, are also commonly drafted in general terms; for example, s 10(1) of the NSW Act which prohibits the tethering of animals for an unreasonable length of time. Even where provisions specify a time limit or other restriction on an activity, for example the maximum period in which a sow may be confined to a stall, it is very difficult to establish a breach in the absence of constant monitoring. While it is mandatory to keep relevant records in some cases, this raises a further issue as to when and how this requirement is monitored and enforced.

With cruelty offences routinely heard in Magistrates Courts, published information about animal welfare proceedings is typically limited and higher authority lacking.[63] Enforcement agencies may be reluctant to prosecute if the meaning of unnecessary suffering, or other provisions, is unclear but the absence of judicial authority might reinforce a view that cruelty offences lack application in particular contexts. The ultimately unsuccessful *SAWA* prosecution considered in Chapter 1 is an example of these difficulties. Notwithstanding the outcome in that case, the independent panel's review of the WA Act noted the very high success rate of prosecutions conducted by the RSPCA in Western Australia. According to the review, this 'might be attributed to high quality investigations and the prosecution's sound

---

62 Sentencing Advisory Council, Victoria 2019, 19. Note that the RSPCA in Victoria is not responsible for investigating cruelty complaints about commercial livestock. See also White 2016, 483. Heikkila argues that prosecutions for breach of duty of care under s 17 of the *Animal Care and Protection Act 2001* (Qld) have largely replaced prosecutions for cruelty offences, particularly omissions, under s 18: 2018, 281.

63 In some cases, an offence may be dealt with by a higher court exercising summary jurisdiction: see, for example, s 34(1) of the *Prevention of Cruelty to Animals Act 1979* (NSW). The serious animal cruelty offences included in general crimes legislation are indictable offences, for example s 530(1) of the *Crimes Act 1900* (NSW).

advocacy. It could also suggest that only the most clear-cut cases are commenced'.[64] The panel observed that:

> Commencing only the clearest of cases may prevent a worthy prosecution from occurring and hinder the continuing evolution of our understanding of the AW Act. Prosecutions which test the boundaries of the AW Act (whilst still having a reasonable prospect of success) are critical to clarify the law and improve the prospects of future convictions.[65]

In NSW, the RSPCA advised a parliamentary inquiry in 2019 that no accused person had been acquitted and no conviction in proceedings undertaken by RSPCA NSW had been overturned on appeal to the District Court in the last two years.[66] According to RSPCA NSW, however, it does not avoid testing the limits of the NSW Act, although whether a matter can be 'characterised as a "test case"' is not 'an appropriate consideration' in deciding whether to prosecute.[67]

Insufficient financial and human resources

As the Productivity Commission has noted, funding for animal welfare enforcement is limited.[68] With respect to the RSPCA, government grants for the various inspectorates constitute only a fraction of the cost of this work, with the remainder subsidised by public donations, bequests and other fundraising activities. In NSW, for example, the annual state government grant specifically for the RSPCA's inspectorate has remained at $424,000 since 2005–06; by contrast, the inspectorate's direct expenses in 2018–19 were $6,233,041.[69] Government agencies responsible for compliance and enforcement activities also fare badly, with services related to animal welfare attracting only 'a fraction of one

---

64 Western Australia, Department of Primary Industries and Regional Development 2020, 58.

65 Ibid, 59.

66 RSPCA NSW 2019, 41.

67 Ibid, 39–40.

68 Productivity Commission 2016, 242.

69 RSPCA NSW 2019, 18.

per cent of most department of agriculture funding arrangements'.[70] In Queensland, for example, White found 'a high degree of government complacency in animal protection policy and regulatory activity, marked by minimal staffing, resourcing and expertise'.[71] These findings are borne out by an independent Queensland inquiry into animal cruelty in the management of retired racehorses, whose 2020 report we examine in detail in Chapter 5.[72] Among other problems, a lack of resources may make it less likely that the scope of cruelty provisions will be tested in the courts, regardless of which agency is tasked with enforcing the law.[73] Exacerbating this situation is the restriction in some animal welfare statutes of the traditional right of any person to initiate a private prosecution. In NSW, for example, s 34AA was inserted in the POCTAA in 2007 to limit the authority to prosecute to official agencies, except with the written consent of the minister or departmental secretary.

Lack of transparency

Reactionary rather than proactive law enforcement is the likely result where financial and human resources are limited. Complaint-driven enforcement is particularly problematic in a regulatory context where animals have no voice and their use is largely hidden. In commercial contexts, especially in intensive production systems or remote locations, the treatment of animals is usually witnessed only by those with a vested interest, whether as owner, manager, contractor, service provider or employee. In these circumstances, the number of complaints about animal welfare will not reflect the actuality of animal treatment. Given the lack of public scrutiny, ready access to information about regulatory activities is especially important yet animal welfare regulation is similarly opaque. In 2009, the Gemmell review of the AAWS noted the lack of national statistics and recommended that consideration be given

70 Goodfellow 2015, 191.
71 White 2016a, 323.
72 Martin and Reid 2020.
73 In the case of RSPCA NSW, this is disputed: RSPCA NSW 2019, 40.

to producing a periodic public report to compel the development of data and indicators to measure animal welfare.[74] This has not occurred.

As noted, RSPCA Australia provides regular statistics about the work of the various inspectorates but comprehensive detail about their compliance activities and enforcement outcomes is lacking. Even less information is available in the case of government agencies. In addition to the examples cited in Chapter 1, the following instances are revealing. In Queensland, there is no detailed public disclosure of information about the Department of Agriculture and Fisheries' animal protection activities or of the resources available to the department to engage in them.[75] The department's Annual Report for 2019–20, for example, simply states (under the heading 'Keep Queenslanders healthy') that 1,395 animal welfare investigations were undertaken, and that some additional funds were made available in response to Covid and the inquiry into retired racehorses noted above.[76] The 2020–21 Annual Report includes more references to animal welfare but in relation to compliance activities only records that 1,684 investigations were undertaken.[77] In NSW, s 34B(3) of POCTAA and cl 34 of the *Prevention of Cruelty to Animals Regulation 2012* require the RSPCA and the Animal Welfare League to report annually to the minister in detail about their enforcement functions but these reports are not published by the government,[78] even though RSPCA NSW has indicated it has no objection to the reports being made public.[79] In some cases, government data may be available but it is generally limited and more comprehensive information from government agencies is usually very difficult to obtain. In relation to the critical issue of slaughter, there is

74 Gemmell 2009, 18.

75 White 2016a, 298. See also Martin and Reid 2020, 76.

76 Queensland Department of Agriculture and Fisheries 2020, 4, 12–13.

77 Queensland Department of Agriculture and Fisheries 2021, 24.

78 Access to information in these reports currently requires an application under the *Government Information (Public Access) Act 2009*. The review of animal welfare legislation in NSW proposes a new requirement for the tabling of these reports by the minister: NSW Department of Primary Industries 2021, 27.

79 Evidence to the Legislative Council Select Committee Inquiry into Animal Cruelty Laws, Parliament of NSW, Sydney, 13 February 2020, 63 (Steve Coleman, CEO of RSPCA NSW).

a lack of public information about complaints received by regulatory agencies and the outcome of investigations.[80] Even information about the number of abattoirs, poultry processors and knackeries in each jurisdiction is not readily available to the public, nor information about the number of establishments approved to conduct slaughter without prior stunning.[81] More generally, statistical information about animal cruelty offences when matters are dealt with by the courts is not always easy to find, with the Australian and New Zealand Standard Offence Classification including animal cruelty under 'Offensive Conduct', a subdivision of 'Public Order Offences'.[82]

Inadequate powers

In broad terms, general inspectors under the state and territory animal welfare Acts have power to enter and search dwellings and other places, to require the provision of certain information, to gather evidence, to examine and care for animals, and to seize animals and other property. The power to enter dwellings usually requires the occupier's consent or the authority of a search warrant but in some jurisdictions an inspector can enter if he or she reasonably believes or suspects that an animal is in imminent danger or there are other urgent circumstances.[83] The absence of this power in some jurisdictions is problematic and illustrates the lack of uniformity in animal protection laws across Australia. Issues also arise in relation to powers of seizure. In Western Australia, for example, in the absence of an offence or likely offence, there is no power

---

80 RSPCA Australia 2021a, 34.

81 Ibid, 8, 13–14. According to RSPCA Australia, as of October 2020 there were nine abattoirs and poultry processors with approval to conduct slaughter without prior stunning for religious purposes to produce halal meat (under Islam) or kosher meat (under Judaism). The RSPCA Australia report further notes 'that all export and the vast majority of domestic slaughtering establishments conducting halal slaughter in Australia ... comply with standard practice where animals are stunned prior to slaughter, on the condition that reversible stunning methods are used': 2021a, 14.

82 ABS, Australian and New Zealand Standard Offence Classification (Catalogue No 1234.0, 2011, 3rd edition).

83 Western Australia, Department of Primary Industries and Regional Development 2020, 27. See, for example, *Prevention of Cruelty to Animals Act 1979* (NSW) s 24E(2).

to seize an animal where it is being held in contravention of a prohibition order or where a person has failed to comply with an animal welfare direction.[84] With reference to the different approach under the Qld Act, the independent panel which reviewed the WA Act recommended that an inspector 'be authorised to seize an animal under a warrant in circumstances where either the animal's welfare, safety and health is at risk, or there has been repeated non-compliance with a direction'.[85]

More generally, as part of the Victorian reform process, the Directions Paper noted in the context of monitoring compliance that:

> The current POCTA Act is typically enforced by an animal welfare inspector or officer authorised under the Act to respond to "reasonable" suspicion that cruelty has occurred. A shift to requiring people to meet a minimum standard of care for animals may require enhanced proactive monitoring tools, such as routine or unscheduled audits and inspections.[86]

Monitoring compliance with legislative requirements is particularly important in relation to commercial operations that are not open to the public. With the hidden nature of much animal use, it is critical that enforcement agencies have the power to inspect commercial premises routinely and without notice. In most jurisdictions, however, a search warrant is required to enter these premises without the occupier's consent or a reasonable suspicion of an animal welfare breach. In 2019, the WA Attorney-General pledged to toughen that state's enforcement powers after an exposé on ABC TV called 'The Final Race' about the fate of retired racehorses, which included footage of gross cruelty to horses at a Queensland abattoir.[87] Referring to the need for a reasonable suspicion that cruelty is happening before inspectors can enter commercial premises in Western Australia, the Attorney-General stated:

> … how can they have that if they haven't been inside. It's a catch 22. That silly circle has got to be broken by statutory force to allow

84 Ibid, 34.
85 Ibid.
86 Victoria, Department of Jobs, Precincts and Regions 2020, 44.
87 Meldrum-Hanna and Donaldson 2019.

> inspectors to go in and that will obviate the need for trespassers to go in and take secret footage.[88]

In their review of the *Animal Welfare Act 2002*, the independent panel found that the 'lack of power to enter non-residential places and vehicles to monitor compliance with the AW Act does not align with other similar WA legislation, or with contemporary community expectations of a proactive compliance regime'.[89] The panel recommended that inspectors be appropriately trained and able to enter any non-residential place for the purpose of monitoring compliance with the WA Act and Regulations. It also recommended, however, that this entry be subject to a requirement to provide reasonable notice, unless the inspector reasonably suspects that to do so will jeopardise its purpose or the effectiveness of any search.[90] The Animal Welfare and Trespass Legislation Amendment Bill 2021 (WA) authorises entry at any time to an intensive production place, abattoir and knackery for the purpose of monitoring compliance with specified provisions of the *Animal Welfare Act*. This power is limited to designated inspectors employed by the Department of Primary Industries and Regional Development. The same Bill creates a new offence of aggravated trespass in relation to land used for 'animal source food production'. With a maximum penalty of two years' imprisonment and a fine of $24,000, the proposed offence doubles the usual maximum penalty for trespass in Western Australia.[91]

In relation to Queensland, the inquiry which followed the ABC program noted that there are no powers under the *Animal Care and Protection Act* that allow Biosecurity Queensland inspectors 'to enter without consent and have a presence at slaughtering establishments to routinely monitor and enforce animal welfare standards'.[92] In Victoria,

88 Mochan 2019.
89 Western Australia, Department of Primary Industries and Regional Development 2020, 29.
90 Ibid, 31.
91 Western Australia, *Parliamentary Debates*, Legislative Assembly, 23 June 2021, 1912–13 (John Quigley).
92 Martin and Reid 2020, 62. The Qld Act provides for the creation of monitoring programs but s 108(1)(c) requires that the occupier be given at least 48 hours' notice of proposed entry, in the absence of specified circumstances.

s 24L of the *Prevention of Cruelty to Animals Act 1986* provides additional entry powers for specialist inspectors but requires the written authority of the minister. In South Australia, s 31 of the *Animal Welfare Act* allows routine inspections of premises but reasonable notice of the proposed inspection must be given to the occupier in most cases. Section 24G of the NSW Act allows routine inspections without notice of certain commercial premises but financial and resourcing constraints limit the RSPCA's capacity to utilise this. In 2018–19, RSPCA NSW conducted 94 routine inspections of animal trades, mostly breeding kennels, pet shops/markets and saleyards, although it is unclear whether these inspections were unannounced.[93] In 2019–20, 139 routine inspections were conducted.[94] In a submission to the NSW parliamentary inquiry into animal cruelty laws, the RSPCA noted that more funding would, among other things, 'increase proactive auditing and inspection for compliance across all s 24G animal trade establishments, including assessing compliance with DPI Standards and Guidelines'.[95]

In addition, a lack of surveillance powers in some jurisdictions may impede the ability of some law enforcement agencies to gather the kind of evidence needed to prove animal cruelty where it occurs on private property and away from public scrutiny.[96] Instead, this kind of cruelty often comes to light only through the work of activists. While typically expressing shock and disgust at the revelations of cruelty, state and federal governments have moved to introduce new laws and tougher penalties for farm trespass in an attempt to deter animal activists from procuring or publishing covert footage, including footage of the conditions in which animals are lawfully kept.[97] In June 2021, the Farm Transparency Project announced a High Court constitutional challenge to provisions of the *Surveillance Devices Act 2007* (NSW), arguing that they breach the implied freedom of political communication by inhibiting public exposure of systemic animal

93 RSPCA NSW 2019, 36.
94 RSPCA Australia 2020d, Table 5.
95 RSPCA NSW 2019, 20.
96 Animal Defenders Office 2019, 6.
97 For example, the *Criminal Code Amendment (Agricultural Protection) Act 2019* (Cth). For further information about 'ag-gag' laws, see Gelber and O'Sullivan 2020.

cruelty.[98] The matter was heard on 10–11 February 2022, with the High Court reserving its judgment.[99]

Agency culture and conflicts of interest

Strengthening inspectorial powers is one thing; the extent and manner of their exercise is quite another. Apart from the level of resourcing, the exercise of these powers depends upon an agency's culture, including its conceptualisation of animal welfare within a framework of competing interests. Animal welfare is not a high priority for government agencies whose central goals are economic growth, industry sustainability and biosecurity.[100] Even more concerning is the inherent conflict of interests in this administrative arrangement. This conflict crosses all commercial contexts but is particularly acute in the case of farmed animals. The belief that agriculture departments have a 'vested interest not a conflict of interest'[101] is only tenable if animal welfare is equated with productive efficiency. The expression of this belief by regulators tends to support Goodfellow's argument that agriculture departments 'have adopted the same instrumental approach to animal welfare as that advanced by the livestock industries'.[102] He further argues that the 'various regulatory failures and process deficiencies' of these departments present 'a strong case for the existence of regulatory capture'.[103] Significantly, the impact of this conflict of interests is felt not only in decisions about enforcement, where government agencies have this function, but also in the provision of ministerial advice, standard-setting and other key administrative responsibilities.

---

98 Farm Transparency Project 2021.

99 For further information about this case, see *Farm Transparency International Ltd v NSW*, S83/2021 at https://www.hcourt.gov.au/cases/case_s83-2021.

100 Martin and Reid 2020, 75–7.

101 Evidence to Legislative Council Select Committee on the Use of Battery Cages for Hens in the Egg Production Industry, NSW Parliament, Sydney, 13 August 2019, 4 (Scott Hansen).

102 Goodfellow 2016, 195.

103 Ibid.

Fragmentation of regulatory responsibility

All of the above issues are compounded by the fragmentation of responsibility that pervades the regulation of animal welfare. This fragmentation occurs most obviously across different animal use sectors, as for example where enforcement is split between a government department and the RSPCA in the case of farmed animals and companion animals. Even within the same animal use sector, however, it is not uncommon for more than one agency to be involved. An example is the regulation of slaughter, where food safety authorities have a major role in addition to other government authorities or the RSPCA. Further examples of divided responsibility are set out below. In the following chapters, we will return to this issue in greater detail to illustrate how fragmented regulatory responsibility can exacerbate problems with accountability and transparency in a wide range of animal settings.

Other state and territory animal welfare legislation

Not all state and territory animal welfare provisions are found in the principal animal welfare Acts. While most jurisdictions also regulate the use of animals for research and testing in this legislation, NSW has a separate *Animal Research Act 1985*. Regulation of exhibited animals is even more fragmented. Two jurisdictions, NSW and Queensland, have specific legislation governing exhibited animals, while the sector is regulated in the ACT through its principal animal welfare Act and Regulations. The remaining jurisdictions employ a mix of regulations and codes of practice as regulatory tools, although their scope and coverage are patchy. In addition, a limited number of animal welfare protections are contained in other statutes, with different ministerial portfolio responsibility and different enforcement agencies. In NSW, for example, the *Biodiversity Conservation Act 2016* makes it an offence to harm, or threaten to harm, a protected animal or an animal that is of a threatened species or part of a threatened ecological community. This legislation is administered and enforced by the NSW Department of Planning and Environment. In relation to companion animals, statutes designed primarily for their control and management also contain regulatory measures relevant to their welfare, such as microchipping.

These statutes are typically administered by local government, not primary industries or agriculture departments. In NSW, for example, the *Companion Animals Act 1998* is administered by the Office of Local Government and enforced by local council officers. This mosaic of protections is further complicated by the regulatory frameworks for horse and greyhound racing, as well as hunting and 'pest' animal control, all of which include provisions relevant to animal welfare.

Role of the Commonwealth

Australia has a federal system of government with legislative power divided between the Commonwealth and the states. Under the *Australian Constitution*, the Commonwealth has specific legislative powers, with general legislative power retained by the states. Note, however, that a valid Commonwealth law has paramountcy over state law by virtue of s 109 of the *Constitution*. This section provides that where a state law is inconsistent with a Commonwealth law, the former is invalid to the extent of the inconsistency. An example is the finding of the magistrate in the *Al Kuwait* case about live sheep export discussed in Chapter 1. The territories also have power to legislate generally but this power is subject to Commonwealth control as the territories lack sovereign status.[104]

The limited role played by the Commonwealth in animal protection reflects a mix of constitutional and political factors. With no specific head of Commonwealth power with respect to animal welfare or animals generally, the states and territories have borne responsibility for legislating in this field. The Commonwealth, however, relies on some of its other heads of power to play a limited legislative role in animal welfare. A notable example is Commonwealth regulation of the live export trade supported by the trade and commerce power, s 51(i) of the *Constitution*.[105] This power also enables the Commonwealth to regulate

104 The *Euthanasia Laws Act 1997* (Cth) is an example of the exercise of Commonwealth power to restrict territory legislatures, in that case by removing their power to make laws for voluntary euthanasia.

105 This head of power is restricted to interstate and overseas transactions and does not include intrastate trade except where the latter is incidental to the former.

slaughter establishments that supply animal products to overseas markets. The external affairs power, s 51(xxix), is another important source of Commonwealth power. In reliance on this power, the Commonwealth regulates trade in native or endangered animals through provisions in the *Environment Protection and Biodiversity Conservation Act 1999* (EPBC Act) which give effect to Australia's obligations as a signatory to the *Convention on International Trade in Endangered Species of Wild Fauna and Flora.*[106] In the event of an international treaty on animal welfare to which Australia was party, the external affairs power would allow the Commonwealth to legislate to implement its terms.[107] Other relevant heads of power in s 51 are the postal and telegraphic power, quarantine, fisheries and the corporations power. Various heads of power may be relied on in combination, as for example in the case of the *Industrial Chemicals Act 2019* (Cth) which, in conjunction with other measures, implements a ban on cosmetic testing on animals from July 2020, as discussed in Chapter 7.

Notwithstanding some constitutional limits, there is scope for a more expansive Commonwealth legislative role in animal welfare. According to Victorian barrister Graeme McEwen, adequate constitutional power exists to support the establishment of a national statutory authority responsible for all animals, with the Commonwealth able to rely on its powers in respect of Commonwealth instrumentalities, the public service and the territories, in addition to the s 51 powers referred to above.[108] Indeed, in reliance on a number of these powers, the Australian Democrats introduced the National Animal Welfare Bill in the Senate in 2005. It was referred to the Rural and Regional Affairs and Transport Legislation Committee which recommended that the Bill not proceed, though not for any want of constitutional power. Instead, subject to a dissenting report by the Democrats and Greens Senators, the committee accepted

106 White 2007, 368.

107 See further Chapter 8 this volume.

108 McEwen 2011, 232. As White notes, in the case of any doubt about the Commonwealth's constitutional reach, 'an alternative avenue would be the preparation of a model bill, with adoption by each state and territory': 2016a, 320.

- most sentenced offending involved failure to provide food, water, shelter or vet treatment;
- three months was the average length of imprisonment imposed where the offender was sentenced exclusively for animal cruelty offences;
- appeals against a sentence of imprisonment were successful in 17% of cases, with either the duration of the imprisonment reduced or the sentence converted into a non-custodial one;
- a control order was imposed in 20% of cases;
- there was a context of family violence in at least 15% of animal cruelty offending.[28]

The heavy reliance on fines and a low rate of imprisonment as sentencing options noted in the Victorian review are broadly consistent with earlier research into animal cruelty sentencing in Australasia,[29] and with recent data compiled by the Queensland Sentencing Advisory Council also discussed in Chapter 2.[30] According to the Victorian Sentencing Advisory Council, the high rate of fines is one of three key issues warranting further consideration, along with the importance of control orders and the need to develop guidance on animal cruelty sentencing, including judicial education.[31] The lack of consistency between the objects clauses of animal welfare statutes and their substantive provisions is relevant in this context. As Markham argues, sentencing outcomes have failed to give effect to legislative intent and '[t]here is also a sense in which existing sentencing practice treats animal cruelty as a purely regulatory offence, rather than locating it in its proper context on a continuum of other forms of violent and anti-social behaviour'.[32] Animal welfare Acts which are confused and inconsistent in content and scope contribute to the construction of animal cruelty as a regulatory offence and make it difficult for judicial

28 Ibid, xiv, 34, 36, 61.

29 See, for example, Markham 2013; Boom and Ellis 2009.

30 Queensland Sentencing Advisory Council 2019.

31 Sentencing Advisory Council, Victoria 2019, 61. With respect to fines as a sentencing option more generally, previous research by the Sentencing Council has found that over a nine-year period, only 53% of all fines imposed on individuals for all offences were completely paid, 7% were partly paid and 40% were not paid at all: 2019, 62.

32 Markham 2013, 224.

> the arguments put forward by many that all levels of government in Australia, industry groups and research bodies are working together through the current mechanism provided by the Australian Animal Welfare Strategy to improve the welfare of all animals in Australia. In the committee's view, the strategy provides the best approach to achieve improvements in this field. Accordingly, the committee urges all those concerned for animal welfare to work towards improving compliance with the strategy and with the various codes of practice now in existence.[109]

In 2015, a Bill to establish a national independent office of animal welfare was introduced in the Senate by the Greens but was again rejected by the majority in the Rural and Regional Affairs and Transport Legislation Committee to which it was referred. Instead, the committee's brief report appeared to express confidence in the existing regulatory arrangements involving co-operation between the Commonwealth and state agriculture departments, with input from industry.[110]

The apparent reluctance of the Commonwealth to assume a more prominent legislative role in relation to animal welfare is in marked contrast to some other regulatory fields. As White notes, 'the Commonwealth has been much more respectful of "States' rights" in the area of animal welfare' than in other fields formerly regulated by the states, such as industrial relations, where it has intervened extensively.[111] Nevertheless, the Commonwealth did take on an important, indirect role in animal welfare for a limited period. As noted in Chapter 1, the Commonwealth assumed the lead in developing a national animal welfare framework, in the form of the AAWS, endorsed by the Primary Industries Ministerial Council in 2004. In the context of adverse publicity about the live export trade and the mulesing of sheep, a key concern of the AAWS was to signal Australia's animal welfare credentials to the international community, particularly our trading partners.[112] Funded and coordinated by the then federal Department of Agriculture, Fisheries

109 Senate Rural and Regional Affairs and Transport Legislation Committee, Parliament of Australia 2006, 13.

110 Senate Rural and Regional Affairs and Transport Legislation Committee, Parliament of Australia 2015.

111 White 2007, 348.

112 Dandie 2005, 2.

and Forestry, the AAWS developed a National Implementation Plan overseen by a national Advisory Committee. Animal sector working groups were also established for each of six areas: animals in research and teaching; native and introduced wildlife; animals used for work, recreation, entertainment or display; aquatic animals; livestock and production animals; and pets and companion animals. A key policy objective of the AAWS was to move from voluntary codes of practice for livestock welfare to national standards and guidelines, with agreement to extend the latter to non-production animals.[113] In 2013, however, the Commonwealth ceased funding the AAWS and disbanded its Advisory Committee,[114] with the work of developing standards and guidelines handed over to the states and territories. This development is difficult to reconcile with the finding of the Senate Rural and Regional Affairs and Transport Legislation Committee in 2006 that the AAWS provided the best approach for improving animal welfare in Australia.

Promise and practice

At first glance, the principal animal welfare Acts appear to offer substantial protection to animals, an appearance reinforced by administrators and politicians alike. This confidence is not borne out by a close examination of the law's operation. With a qualified definition of cruelty, extensive defences and exemptions, conflicting interests of administrative agencies, and major issues with enforcement, the protection afforded animals is at best patchy and at worst almost entirely lacking. As noted, however, some changes have resulted from legislative reviews finalised recently, for example the 2019 acknowledgement of animal sentience in the *Animal Welfare Act 1992* (ACT). Changes will also occur in New South Wales, Queensland, Tasmania, Victoria and Western Australia as a result of the reviews underway in those jurisdictions. These reviews appear to acknowledge growing public concern about animal welfare and questions about the adequacy of existing legislation. For example, 98% of people surveyed as part of the

113 Australia, Department of Agriculture, Water and the Environment 2011.
114 Vidot 2013.

consultation process for Victoria's Animal Welfare Action Plan said that protecting animals was important and 75% said that animals need better protection.[115] Industry stakeholders are generally more supportive of existing arrangements and express concern about a stricter regulatory framework.[116]

The extent to which the current reviews will increase animal protection as opposed to tinkering at the margins is a matter for debate. To enhance existing levels of protection it is necessary to address the more difficult legal and regulatory failings, as opposed to focusing on less contentious, and largely symbolic, reforms, such as tougher penalties. A major problem in this regard is that reviews are usually overseen, and reforms implemented, by the very departments currently tasked with animal welfare regulation whose conflicting interests have been widely noted. In NSW, for example, the Department of Primary Industries published its Animal Welfare Reform Issues Paper in February 2020 as part of the government's plan to 'modernise the policy and legislative framework for animal welfare in NSW'.[117] Although described by the Director-General as an 'almost once-in-a-generation opportunity to reform' animal welfare legislation,[118] the issues paper, the discussion paper and the draft Animal Welfare Bill 2022 are narrow in scope and fail to address key matters such as regulatory conflicts of interest and the inadequate protection of animals in commercial and industry contexts. It may be instructive to compare the outcome of the New South Wales reform process with that in Western Australia where an independent panel was responsible for reviewing that state's *Animal Welfare Act 2002*, although overall control of the reform process remains with the Minister for Agriculture.[119] Whatever the outcome of these reviews, information will need to be much more freely available if any changes to animal welfare regulation are to be properly evaluated.

---

115 Victoria, Department of Economic Development, Jobs, Transport and Resources 2017, 12.

116 Western Australia Agriculture Authority 2020, 2.

117 NSW Department of Primary Industries 2020c, 4.

118 Evidence to the Legislative Council Select Committee Inquiry into Animal Cruelty Laws, Parliament of NSW, Sydney, 12 February 2020, 11 (Scott Hansen).

119 Note, for example, the different scope of the independent panel's report published in 2020 and the NSW Discussion Paper published the following year.

But underlying these important concerns is an even larger issue. Existing legal frameworks are based on the animal welfare paradigm which accords limited moral significance to animals. Although their use as human resources is subject to the humane treatment principle, this book illustrates how animal protection is readily traded away when it collides with human interests. This failure suggests the need to examine other ways of thinking about the moral significance of non-human animals. One influential strand of theorising comes from Peter Singer – like Bentham, a utilitarian philosopher, but whose development of the concepts of speciesism and equal consideration of interests would radically expand the protections afforded animals.[120] By contrast, animal rights' advocates generally eschew the use of animals for human purposes, emphasising their autonomy and inherent value.[121] Other approaches still, for example some feminist perspectives, criticise both utilitarian and rights theories as too abstract and look instead to redefine our relationship with animals, incorporating qualities such as kinship and empathy.[122] With substantial 'arguments in favour of significant change in the way we conceptualise animals, and especially how we protect their interests in law',[123] we will return to these philosophical issues after more detailed consideration of existing regulatory failures.

---

120 Singer 2011.
121 See, for example, Regan 1983.
122 See, for example, Donovan and Adams 2007; Gruen 2014.
123 White 2013a, 59.

3
Companion Animals

Under the Australian Consumer Law, buying a pet from a pet shop or professional breeder is the same as buying any other product.[1]

So says the WA Department of Mines, Industry Regulation and Safety in its guide to consumer rights when buying a pet. The advice is correct. Animals are defined as 'goods' under the Australian Consumer Law which means that the same consumer protections apply to their purchase as the purchase of any other 'product'. This definition reflects the legal classification of animals as property. Its anachronistic nature is highlighted in this context, however, because many Australians regard their companion animal as part of the family, as the WA guide acknowledges. According to a 2019 Australian survey, 63% of dog owners and 60% of cat owners regard the animal as a member of the family,[2] a finding difficult to reconcile with animals' property status. But this is not the only inconsistency. In 2019–20, 45,364 cats and 28,072 dogs were received by the RSPCA across Australia;[3] many others were taken in by council pounds, other animal charities, or disposed of elsewhere. Despite considerable efforts to rehome animals, a significant

---

1 Western Australia, Department of Mines, Industry Regulation and Safety n.d., 1.
2 Animals Medicine Australia 2019, 6, 20.
3 RSPCA Australia 2020d, Table 2.

proportion continue to be killed.[4] These facts are easier to reconcile with the notion of companion animals as products than as family members. So too is the law governing animal welfare which does not criminalise the killing of animals *per se* but only killing considered unnecessary or accompanied by gratuitous pain or suffering. Under the *Animal Welfare Act 2002* (WA), for example, s 85 provides that the death of an animal must be taken into consideration by the court in cruelty proceedings but is not sufficient, on its own, to prove that the person committed the offence.[5] Further, while it is an offence to abandon an animal, it is not an offence to surrender an animal to a pound or shelter, sell it or give it away. In combination with a traditional reluctance to curb excessive breeding, or to restrict opportunities for sale, these laws contribute to the commodification of companion animals, notwithstanding a measure of progress in some jurisdictions.

Even so, companion animals are comparatively well protected by existing laws. Arguably, three reasons account for this. First, companion animals are more visible to the general public than, for example, farmed animals or animals used in research.[6] Second, the extra protection they receive is a recognition by legislators of the special bond and 'familial' relationship between humans and companion animals.[7] Third, our interest in animals as companions coincides much more closely with their interests than our use of animals for other purposes, such as fibre and food, so that little is sacrificed by according them greater

---

4 Killing in this context is commonly referred to as euthanasia. As Broom argues, however, the use of this term should be confined to circumstances where the killing occurs for the benefit of the animal and is done humanely; if the benefit is for someone else, the appropriate term is 'killing' or 'humane killing': 2017, 16. Accordingly, the latter terms are used in this work except where quoting or paraphrasing regulatory authorities, reports or legislation which use the term euthanasia.

5 In 2019, doubt was expressed as to whether a Perth man could be prosecuted under the Act after killing a kookaburra by tearing off its head. He was subsequently fined under the *Biodiversity Conservation Regulations 2018* (WA) for the offence of taking fauna without lawful authority: Australian Associated Press 2020.

6 O'Sullivan 2011 argues that the extent of legal protection different animals receive is a function of their level of visibility, as well as their species membership.

7 White 2009a, 862.

protections. Nevertheless, the law regulating companion animal welfare is not immune from the inconsistencies and irrationality that characterise animal protection generally. Nor from the influence of the market. By identifying the enhanced legal protections companion animals receive, in conjunction with key constraints, this chapter will suggest ways in which companion animal regulation reflects the broader themes identified in Chapter 1, notwithstanding the different regulatory setting. Finally, the chapter will interrogate the property status of companion animals by reference to alternative conceptualisations of their legal classification and the moral significance of animals.

Regulatory framework

As with animal welfare generally, the Commonwealth plays a very limited role in relation to companion animals. Apart from Commonwealth legislation prohibiting the import of certain dog breeds and international trade in domestic cat and dog fur,[8] companion animal regulation is the province of state and territory governments. Within these jurisdictions, local government also has a significant role. This is due to the way companion animal regulation is conceptualised: as an animal welfare issue on the one hand and a problem of animal management or control on the other. While the former is dealt with under the state and territory animal welfare Acts, companion animal management is typically relegated to local government authorities and governed by separate legislation. The objective of animal management is apparent in the confinement of this legislation almost exclusively to cats and dogs, although many other animals are kept as companions in Australia. Nevertheless, animal management legislation is relevant to companion animal welfare in important ways, as we will see later in this chapter.

---

8 Cao 2015, 175.

Animal welfare legislation

Companion animals fall within the general definition of animals in the animal welfare Acts and are therefore protected by the prohibitions against cruelty, as well as by the specific offence provisions and duty of care requirements considered in Chapter 2. A few offences apply specifically to animals commonly kept as companions, such as provisions in relation to declawing cats and debarking dogs, but there is no separate category of companion animal in the animal welfare Acts, or sub-set of laws that applies exclusively to them. In that sense, companion animal is not a legal term but a convenient classification of animal function.[9] This is illustrated by s 13(2)(b)(i) of the Queensland Act which provides that a code of practice may be made about the use of animals as companions. This function is critical to the level of protection companion animals receive because animals kept in a domestic context for non-commercial purposes are much less likely than other categories of animal use to be excluded from key welfare provisions. As we have seen, many industry practices are exempt from a cruelty charge if carried out in accordance with a prescribed or approved code of practice. By contrast, companion animals are generally not excluded from key provisions and thus derive the benefit of animal welfare legislation in a way often denied to animals in other settings.[10]

In Chapter 1, we saw how exemptions and defences make it legal to perform various procedures on farmed animals without pain relief and to accommodate them in cramped spaces even though it would incur criminal liability to treat a domestic cat or dog in the same way. Companion animals also benefit from enhanced statutory protections in relation to basic welfare needs, such as food, water and shelter. These contrast with the minimum requirements for farmed animals set out in codes of practice and animal welfare standards which typically incorporate a lesser standard of care. An example is the *Australian Animal Welfare Standards and Guidelines – Land Transport of Livestock*

---

9 The term 'companion animal' is preferable to 'pet' as it emphasises the mutuality of the relationship rather than the entitlement of property ownership.

10 For a detailed discussion of companion animal regulation, see White 2009a and White 2016a.

whose specifications include requirements in relation to food and water for different species while being transported by land. The maximum time off water, for example, is 48 hours for sheep over four months old and for cattle and goats over six months old, and 28 hours for lambs under four months and goats under six months old. These standards are adopted in NSW by Part 4 and Sch 1 of the *Prevention of Cruelty to Animals Regulation 2012*. By contrast, the *Prevention of Cruelty to Animals Act 1979* (NSW) indicates what is considered appropriate for animals generally. Section 8(1) of the NSW Act requires a person in charge of an animal to provide the animal with food, drink and shelter which is proper and sufficient and which it is reasonably practicable in the circumstances for the person to provide. Section 8(2) provides that a failure to provide clean water during a period of 24 hours is evidence of failure to provide the animal with proper and sufficient drink. In relation to livestock, however, cl 37A of the *Prevention of Cruelty to Animals Regulation 2012* (NSW) provides an exemption from s 8(1) in respect of providing animals with drink during transport for a person who complies with the relevant livestock transport standards. The different standards for transporting livestock appear to reflect convenience and cost rather than scientific evidence, despite the acknowledged stress of transportation.[11]

Where codes of practice about companion animals are incorporated in animal welfare legislation, they are mostly concerned with commercial settings, such as pet shops, boarding facilities or breeding establishments, although shelters and pounds are also typically regulated. These codes generally reflect the stronger standards considered appropriate for companion animals. For example, the NSW codes of practice for animals in pet shops and for cat and dog breeders state that clean water must be available at all times. There is, however, considerable jurisdictional variation in the type and content of these codes and whether and how they are incorporated in law. There are also differences within jurisdictions as to how codes of practice for different animals are referenced in the principal animal welfare legislation. In NSW, for example, codes of practice relevant to companion animals are included in the Animal Trades provisions of the *Prevention of Cruelty*

11 Animal Health Australia 2008, v.

to Animals Regulation 2012, not listed in cl 33 as a code of practice to which s 34A of the Act applies. In some jurisdictions, companion animal codes of practice are incorporated in animal management legislation, not the principal animal welfare Act. In Victoria, for example, codes of practice regulating pet shops and breeding businesses are made under the *Domestic Animals Act 1994*, not that state's animal welfare legislation. With minimum welfare standards for animals in commercial establishments, these kinds of codes illustrate the overlap between animal welfare and animal management legislation. In some cases, their provisions may have relevance to the broader issue of companion animal overpopulation. For example, in Victoria, the *Code of Practice for the Operation of Breeding and Rearing Businesses* made under s 59 of the *Domestic Animals Act 1994* now limits the number of litters for both female cats and female dogs.

Enforcement of animal welfare legislation

Legal protections for companion animals are only as effective as their enforcement. Issues relevant to a successful enforcement regime include the adequacy of resources, the way in which discretions are exercised by enforcement agencies, and the decisions of judicial officers when sentencing offenders. As discussed in Chapter 2, the resourcing of animal welfare enforcement is inadequate, either because the task falls to underfunded charitable organisations or because resourcing the animal welfare activities of government agencies is a low priority. Inadequate resourcing promotes reactive rather than proactive investigative activity and may be a factor in determining the response of enforcement agencies when breaches of the law are found.[12] In Victoria, for example, an independent review of the RSPCA noted that prosecutions completed in 2014–15 made up less than 1% of cruelty reports received, with the workload of inspectors a factor in this relatively low number.[13] In the review of the WA Act, the Independent Panel observed that 'RSPCA Inspectors might be reluctant

12 Note White's argument, however, that a decline in the number of prosecutions annually in Queensland 'reflects a strategic decision rather than a simple lack of resources': 2016a, 296.

13 Comrie 2016, 54.

Table 3.1. RSPCA Australia National Statistics: Complaints and Prosecutions 2014–15 to 2019–20*

	2014–15	2015–16	2016–17	2017–18	2018–19	2019–20
Complaints	60,809	62,563	55,405	57,092	57,982	73,997
Prosecutions finalised	274	264	340	370	376	359

* RSPCA Australia 2020d, Table 6.

to commence prosecutions that are not highly likely to succeed' because of 'the burdensome costs of conducting a prosecution and the risk of an adverse costs order if a prosecution is unsuccessful'.[14]

The RSPCA is the agency primarily responsible for cruelty complaints about companion animals in all jurisdictions, except the Northern Territory. Where the RSPCA is also responsible for other animals, as in NSW, the bulk of enforcement activity is nevertheless in response to complaints about companion animal cruelty.[15] Although RSPCA member societies are responsible for enforcing the law in their respective jurisdictions, national prosecution statistics are compiled on an annual basis by RSPCA Australia. The most recent available prosecution data at the time of writing is set out in Table 3.1.

As discussed in Chapter 2, enforcement of animal welfare legislation is a complex task but these kinds of prosecution rates have nevertheless been described as 'astonishingly low'.[16] According to RSPCA member societies, however, prosecution decisions accord with general state policies and guidelines in relation to the criminal law. In NSW, for example, '[p]rosecutorial decision-making in the context of animal cruelty is the same as prosecutorial decision-making in the general criminal context and the prosecutorial guidelines applied by RSPCA NSW adopt the

14 Western Australia, Department of Primary Industries and Regional Development 2020, 58.
15 RSPCA NSW 2018b, 9, Table A.
16 Markham 2013, 211.

guidelines of the NSW Office of the Director of Public Prosecutions to the extent they are applicable'.[17] In Western Australia, the 'decision of whether to prosecute is made in accordance with the RSPCA Compliance Enforcement and Prosecution Policy, which is designed to be consistent with the DPP Statement of Prosecution Policy and Guidelines'.[18] With formal policies and guidelines framed in very general terms, however, the critical factor is their interpretation and application in the field, something which requires detailed empirical investigation.

There are no national statistics with respect to the exercise of other regulatory mechanisms, nor is this data routinely included in the annual reports of the state and territory RSPCAs available to the public, although it may be accessible elsewhere. For example, the submission by RSPCA NSW to the Legislative Council inquiry into animal cruelty laws provides some insight into the use of the formal enforcement mechanisms. In the financial year 2018–19, RSPCA NSW received 16,696 complaints, carried out 15,673 investigations, issued 248 written directions, 7 official cautions, 37 penalty infringement notices and commenced 77 prosecutions.[19] The lack of formal action following most investigations is arguably consistent with the high number of complaints about neglect-related offending rather than deliberate cruelty and accords with the RSPCA's emphasis on community education and support. RSPCA NSW, for example, 'considers the levels of "formal" action taken in matters investigated by the Inspectorate to be appropriate in circumstances where POCTAA regards community engagement and educational efforts by the Inspectorate to be representative of success in achieving its objects'.[20] In addition, public misunderstanding of what constitutes an offence under animal welfare laws is likely to contribute to the substantial gap between complaints and prosecutions,[21] although

17 RSPCA NSW Response to Supplementary Questions and Questions on Notice, Legislative Council Select Committee on Animal Cruelty Laws in NSW, 12 March 2020, 18.

18 Western Australia, Department of Primary Industries and Regional Development 2020, 57.

19 RSPCA NSW 2019, 34. Information about the use of the range of regulatory options by RSPCA NSW is also available in the Annual Report of the Board.

20 RSPCA NSW 2020a, 13.

21 Morton et al. 2020, 492.

there is also evidence of under-reporting of cruelty.[22] As the Sentencing Advisory Council in Victoria observes, 'the reported number of complaints is, in a way, both an underestimation and an overestimation of the rate at which animal cruelty occurs'.[23] Meanwhile, evidence to the NSW parliamentary inquiry into animal cruelty laws suggests that opinions about current standards and approaches reflect very different concerns. For example, Animal Care Australia, a national lobbyist for those who keep and breed animals, advocated 'a stronger focus on education and welfare over prosecution';[24] by contrast, the NSW Cat Protection Society, a registered charity, expressed the view that existing standards for cats and dogs 'are too low' and their breach 'too difficult to prosecute'.[25]

Where cases are prosecuted, the resulting sentences are not noted for their severity even though the low rate of prosecutions suggests that it is only the most serious offending that ends up in court. According to Markham, the 'true prevalence of animal cruelty offending' is masked by the low prosecution rate; in turn, this impacts on sentencing outcomes as the prevalence of offending is a factor affecting the level of sentence in most jurisdictions.[26] Notably, however, there is 'surprisingly little information' on sentencing for animal cruelty in Australia, in part because most matters are decided in Magistrates Courts.[27] This lack of data, in combination with recognition of community concern about animal welfare, prompted the Victorian Sentencing Council to produce the comprehensive review of Victorian animal cruelty sentencing referred to in Chapter 2. Although the review is not confined to companion animals, it provides a useful insight into sentencing matters given that they comprise the largest cohort of animals in cruelty cases. In addition to the matters noted previously, key findings include:

---

22 Ibid, 488.
23 Sentencing Advisory Council 2019, 18.
24 Evidence to the Legislative Council Select Committee Inquiry into Animal Cruelty Laws, Parliament of NSW, Sydney, 13 February 2020, 25 (Michael Donnelly).
25 Evidence to the Legislative Council Select Committee Inquiry into Animal Cruelty Laws, Parliament of NSW, Sydney, 13 February 2020, 23 (Kristina Vesk).
26 Markham 2013, 211.
27 Sentencing Advisory Council, Victoria 2019, 3.

officers to discern legislative intent in a coherent fashion. Similarly, while there is evidence that the public support tougher penalties for animal cruelty, attitudes about appropriate punishment may depend upon the species and context.[33] In other words, the ambiguity and inconsistency of animal welfare regulation extend to the sentencing process, a problem not susceptible of remedy by increasing maximum penalties. Moreover, while there are 'legitimate criticisms' of sentencing practices,[34] penalty escalation is of 'limited effectiveness' as a policy tool for addressing the causes of animal cruelty[35] and may be a distraction from more pressing regulatory reforms.

Animal management legislation

The principal companion animal management legislation in each jurisdiction is set out in Table 3.2. As the titles of these Acts suggest, they are chiefly concerned with the management of cats and dogs. While the *Companion Animals Act 1998* (NSW) defines a companion animal as a cat, a dog or any other animal that is prescribed by the regulations, no other animals have been prescribed for this purpose to date. In Australia in 2019, there were an estimated 5.1 million dogs and 3.8 million cats but also an estimated 11.3 million fish, 5.6 million birds, 614,000 small mammals (including guinea pigs, rabbits, mice and ferrets), 364,000 reptiles (including turtles, tortoises and frogs) and 1.8 million other companion animals (including horses).[36] For the first time in 2020, the annual Household, Income and Labour Dynamics in Australia Survey (HILDA) included questions about 'pet ownership'. The statistical report showed that almost 62% of people own at least one pet and, of this group, almost 72% have a dog, 37% have a cat, 16% have a bird, 18% have a fish, 3.6% have a horse and 17% have some other type of animal. Of 'pet-owning' individuals, approximately 59% have only

33 See, for example, Geysen, Weick and White 2010; Taylor and Signal 2009a, 2009b.

34 Markham 2013, 224.

35 White 2016a, 312.

36 Animals Medicine Australia 2019, 6, 10.

Table 3.2. Principal companion animal management legislation

Jurisdiction	Act
ACT	*Domestic Animals Act 2000* *Domestic Animals Regulation 2001*
NSW	*Companion Animals Act 1998* *Companion Animals Regulation 2018*
NT	*Local Government Act 2019**
Qld	*Animal Management (Cats and Dogs) Act 2008* *Animal Management (Cats and Dogs) Regulation 2019*
SA	*Dog and Cat Management Act 1995* *Dog and Cat Management Regulations 2017*
TAS	*Cat Management Act 2009* *Cat Management Regulations 2012* *Dog Control Act 2000* *Dog Control Regulations 2021*
VIC	*Domestic Animals Act 1994* *Domestic Animals Regulations 2015*
WA	*Cat Act 2011* *Cat Regulations 2012* *Dog Act 1976* *Dog Regulations 2013*

* The Northern Territory has no specific companion animal management legislation and relies largely on local council by-laws made under the *Local Government Act 2019* for this function. See, for example, Part 3, Darwin City Council By-Laws 1994.

one type of animal, 24% have two types and 17% have three or more types of animal.[37]

Where an objects clause is included in these Acts, it typically makes reference to the management of the animals as well as to their responsible care. In South Australia, for example, s 3 of the *Dog and Cat Management Act 1995* states the objects as:

> (a) to encourage responsible dog and cat ownership;
> (b) to reduce public and environmental nuisance caused by dogs and cats;
> (c) to promote the effective management of dogs and cats.

There is considerable jurisdictional variation in the content and scope of companion animal management legislation but the following matters are typically included:

- the identification and registration of animals;
- responsibilities for control of dogs;
- responsibilities for control of cats;
- powers and responsibilities in relation to dangerous dogs;
- procedures for dealing with seized or surrendered animals; and
- functions of local government authorities.

While this legislative framework is primarily concerned with the management and control of domestic cats and dogs, it includes provisions that contribute to their welfare. In some cases, however, the control function can also impact the welfare of animals, for example the provisions governing dangerous dogs.

Dangerous dogs

Overall, governments have tended to regulate the problem of dangerous dogs more readily than issues associated with companion animal welfare. Subject to considerable jurisdictional variation, the regulatory response typically includes provisions in relation to dangerous and, in

37 Wilkins et al. 2020, 151–2.

most jurisdictions, menacing dogs, plus separate provisions governing specific or restricted breeds that are presumed to be dangerous.[38] These breed-specific provisions are controversial, with both the Australian Veterinary Association (AVA)[39] and the RSPCA[40] describing them as an ineffective regulatory response to a more complex problem. The definition of 'dangerous' typically applies where a dog has attacked or killed a person or animal without provocation or has repeatedly threatened to do so. A classification of 'menacing' typically applies where a dog harasses or displays unreasonable aggression towards a person or animal or has attacked them but with less serious consequences.[41]

A declaration by a local government authority, or a court in some cases, that a dog is a dangerous, menacing or restricted dog, has consequences for the animal and their owner. The latter is typically required to comply with a range of conditions relating to the animal, for example mandatory desexing; the premises in which the dog is kept, such as warning signs and enclosure requirements; and control of the dog in public, such as muzzling and mandatory leashing. A lack of compliance with these obligations attracts a penalty and may result in the dog's seizure.[42] The death of the dog may be authorised in certain circumstances by a local government authority or by court order.[43]

Clearly, the behaviour of some dogs poses a risk to humans and other animals but legislative change tends to be a reaction to the publicity generated by dog attacks in public places, even though most dog bites occur in the dog's own home.[44] According to the AVA, the key to preventing dog aggression lies in early identification of potentially dangerous dogs and a well-resourced regulatory framework that incorporates factors such as a nationally consistent reporting system,

---

38 See, for example, s 55 of the *Companion Animals Act 1998* (NSW).

39 Australian Veterinary Association 2012, 4.

40 RSPCA Australia 2019d.

41 See, for example, ss 33–33A of the *Companion Animals Act 1998* (NSW).

42 See, for example, ss 51–52 of the *Companion Animals Act 1998* (NSW).

43 See, for example, s 48 and s 58G of the *Companion Animals Act 1998* (NSW). See *Isbester v Knox City Council* [2015] HCA 20 for a rare superior court decision about a dog destruction order. The dog's owner was successful in having the order quashed because of a reasonable apprehension of bias in relation to a member of the council panel convened to hear the matter.

44 Australian Veterinary Association 2012, 2.

temperament testing and education.[45] While human behaviour is a significant contributor to the problem of canine aggression, the dog bears the legal consequences in terms of a more restricted environment and, in some cases, loss of life. More emphasis on responsible dog ownership, community education and tighter regulation of breeding and sale would arguably benefit both the public and dog welfare.

Overpopulation

Identification requirements are conducive to animal welfare as they facilitate the rehoming of lost animals but, as the NSW parliament has acknowledged, ascertaining the rate of microchipping in the community is difficult.[46] While data provided by the NSW Office of Local Government (OLG) shows that at 30 June 2017 there were at least 2.5 million dogs and 803,000 cats microchipped in NSW,[47] the total owned cat and dog population is unknown, as is the proportion of contact details on microchips whose currency is accurate. Certainly with respect to cats who end up in pounds and shelters in Australia, there is evidence of a very low rate of both microchipping and registration. In South Australia, for example, only 1% of cats received at the RSPCA and AWL's shelters in 2019 were microchipped[48] and in NSW only about 3% of cats and kittens coming to RSPCA shelters are microchipped and registered.[49] A report prepared for the NSW OLG advised that, as at 30 June 2017, 59% of microchipped dogs and 45% of microchipped cats in NSW were also registered,[50] despite cl 14 of the *Companion Animal Regulation* requiring registration by 12 weeks of age or when the animal is first sold, even if younger.[51] Although this suggests a significant lack

45 Ibid, 20–4.

46 Joint Select Committee on Companion Animal Breeding Practices in NSW. Parliament of NSW 2015, 50.

47 Acil Allen Consulting 2018, Section 2.1.

48 RSPCA South Australia and AWL 2019, 10.

49 Evidence to the Legislative Council Select Committee Inquiry into Animal Cruelty Laws, Parliament of NSW, Sydney, 13 February 2020, 67 (Steve Coleman).

50 Acil Allen Consulting 2018, Section 2.1.

51 Prior to 4 July 2016, the relevant age for registration was six months.

of compliance with the *Companion Animals Act*, the OLG only collects information on the number of penalty notices issued in relation to dog attack investigations.[52]

Animal management legislation also has a role to play in relation to companion animal overpopulation. With more animals born than homes available, thousands are humanely killed every year in Australia, although the only national statistics are those compiled by the RSPCA in relation to its shelters.[53] The number of cats and dogs euthanased in Australia by the RSPCA for the period 2015–16 to 2019–20 is set out in Table 3.3. The problem remains acute, particularly in relation to cats, despite some decrease in the number received and the proportion euthanased. The RSPCA national statistics give the reasons for the euthanasia of dogs and cats as infectious, medical, behavioural, legal and other. In 2019–20, the most common reason given for euthanasing dogs was behavioural (2,392 of 3,466 dogs) while 4,205 of the 9,714 cats were euthanased for unspecified 'other' reasons.[54]

No national figures are available with respect to companion animals humanely killed by other animal charities and council pounds but the scope of the problem may be illustrated by NSW data. The NSW Companion Animals Taskforce found that in 2010–11 approximately 64% of cats and 33% of dogs impounded by council pounds, the RSPCA, the AWL and the Cat Protection Society were euthanased.[55] Notwithstanding some encouraging downward movement, more recent data indicates an ongoing problem, particularly for cats, with the euthanasia of over 40% of cats received by NSW council pounds in 2017–18,[56] over 40% of cats received in 2018–19[57] and over 38% of

52 Email from Darren Sear, Manager, Program Delivery, NSW Office of Local Government, to author, 17 July 2020.

53 The RSPCA National Statistics 2019–20 include council animals in the RSPCA NSW data for 2019–20: Table 3, n 2.

54 RSPCA Australia 2020d, Table 3.

55 NSW Companion Animals Taskforce 2012b, 4.

56 Based on 8,404 cats euthanased out of a total of 20,630 received by NSW council pounds for the period 1 July 2017 to 30 June 2018: NSW Office of Local Government, n.d. Pound and Dog Attack Statistics.

57 Based on 9,419 cats euthanased out of a total of 23,368 received by NSW council pounds for the period 1 July 2018 to 30 June 2019: NSW Office of Local Government, n.d. Pound and Dog Attack Statistics.

Table 3.3. RSPCA National Statistics Cats and Dogs*

	2015–16	2016–17	2017–18	2018–19	2019–20
Cats received	55,570	53,912	53,011	51,170	45,364
Cats euthanased	16,205	14,563	12,610	11,740	9,714
Dogs received	45,256	44,770	40,286	33,863	28,072
Dogs euthanased	5,872	5,763	5,577	4,308	3,466

* RSPCA Australia 2020d, Table 2.

cats received in 2019–20.[58] It may be that more recent statistics, when available, will show a decrease in the number of companion animals killed as enforced lifestyle changes accompanying the coronavirus pandemic have led to a surge in adoption rates.[59] It remains to be seen, however, whether there will be a post-pandemic increase in surrenders and/or a decrease in adoption applications if most available homes have already acquired a companion animal.

As noted by the Companion Animals Taskforce, factors commonly associated with the abandonment and surrender of companion animals 'include unwanted litters due to lack of desexing and impulse buying'[60] but attempts to regulate these matters have been mixed. In NSW, the Companion Animal Register shows that at 30 June 2017, 44% of microchipped dogs and 45% of cats were desexed[61] but more

58 Based on 7,906 cats euthanased out of a total of 20,432 received by NSW council pounds for the period 1 July 2019 to 30 June 2020: NSW Office of Local Government, n.d. Pound and Dog Attack Statistics.

59 Roy 2020.

60 NSW Companion Animals Taskforce 2012b, 54.

61 Acil Allen Consulting 2018, Section 2.1.

recent reforms may lead to some improvement in the rate of desexing. In addition to the discounted registration fee for desexed animals, amendment of the *Companion Animals Act* in 2018 means that from 1 July 2020, an annual permit of $80 is payable by owners of cats not desexed by four months of age, subject to some exemptions, in addition to the one-off fee for pet registration. According to the NSW OLG website, the need for an annual permit will create a stronger incentive to desex cats, improve their health and wellbeing, lower demand on pounds, reduce euthanasia rates, and help to address concerns about feral, stray and roaming cats.[62] It is unclear how the annual permit requirement will be enforced, however, or whether any additional resources will be dedicated to monitoring compliance.

Some jurisdictions have gone further than NSW by mandating the desexing of companion animals, subject to various exemptions, typically for approved breeders. In South Australia, s 42E of the *Dog and Cat Management Act 1995* mandates the desexing of dogs and cats in accordance with the regulations, which currently require desexing before six months of age or within 28 days after the owner takes possession of the dog or cat. Section 18 of the *Cat Act 2011* (WA) requires the desexing of cats that have reached six months of age and the *Dog Amendment (Stop Puppy Farming) Act 2021* (WA) inserts a prospective requirement into the *Dog Act 1976* for the mandatory sterilisation of dogs that have reached the prescribed age (proposed to be two years).[63] In Tasmania, the requirement in s 14 of the *Cat Management Act 2009* to desex cats more than six months of age will be reduced to four months when s 10 of the *Cat Management Amendment Act 2020* commences in March 2022. By contrast, the Animal Welfare League Queensland[64] and RSPCA Australia recommend mandatory desexing *before* four months of age and *prior to* sale or transfer.[65] These measures need to be accompanied by public awareness programs and actively enforced. At present, even in those jurisdictions that mandate desexing, regulatory effectiveness is impacted by a lack of compliance and other factors. In the ACT, for example, desexing of cats and dogs has been a legal

62 NSW Office of Local Government, n.d. Annual Permits.
63 This provision commences on a day to be fixed by proclamation.
64 Animal Welfare League Queensland 2018.
65 RSPCA Australia 2018b.

requirement since 2001 yet research reveals a lack of compliance by pet owners, with minimal enforcement of the legislation, and a significant proportion of vets unaware of the relevant law.[66]

Other measures relevant to cat and dog welfare in animal management legislation relate to commercial breeding and sale, the upgrading of companion animal registers and improved traceability mechanisms. Some of the more recent reforms have been a response to media publicity about major animal welfare problems in puppy farms, defined by the RSPCA as 'essentially commercial operations with an emphasis on production and profit with little or no consideration given to the welfare of the animals'.[67] In Victoria, for example, the *Domestic Animals Act 1994* was amended to address issues around puppy farms and backyard breeders.[68] As originally drafted, the Domestic Animals Amendment (Puppy Farms and Pet Shops) Bill 2016 limited to ten the number of fertile female dogs allowed to be kept by a domestic animal business. The Bill was subsequently revised to allow the minister, on the advice of the chief veterinary officer, to approve commercial establishments with 50 fertile female dogs.[69] Other changes introduced by the Bill include a restriction on pet shop sales to cats and dogs sourced from shelters, pounds and registered foster carers, and the creation of new offences in relation to the publication of advertisements for dogs or cats for sale without the inclusion of specified identifying information.[70] The latter provision extends to animals given away. Note, however, that the considerable jurisdictional inconsistency in companion animal regulation in Australia has implications for animal welfare. The tougher regulations in relation to breeding practices in Victoria, for example, have raised concerns that some breeders will simply relocate to NSW;[71] meanwhile, Victorians can still purchase animals from interstate.

66 Orr and Jones 2019, 5–6.
67 RSPCA Australia 2010, 1.
68 Victoria, *Parliamentary Debates*, Legislative Council, 30 November 2017, 6616 (Jaala Pulford).
69 Ibid, 6617; *Domestic Animals Act 1994* (Vic) ss 58AA–58AL.
70 *Domestic Animals Act 1994* (Vic) ss 12B–12C, s 63AAB.
71 Peck 2021.

Case study: regulation of breeding and sale in NSW

With a plethora of inquiries but relatively little action, the recent history of regulating cats and dogs in NSW highlights the difficulties of effecting meaningful change even for those animals favoured by animal welfare laws. In 2009, the NSW Parliament debated a Bill introduced by the Independent MP Clover Moore to regulate the advertising and sale of cats and dogs, including a ban on their sale in pet shops. Neither major party supported the Bill but, after its success at the 2011 election, the Coalition set up a taskforce to provide advice on companion animal issues, particularly strategies to reduce the high rate of cats and dogs killed. Following the release of a brief discussion paper, the taskforce published a report in October 2012, whose recommendations included establishment of a breeder licensing system.[72] Although the government's response[73] supported most of the 22 recommendations, including in-principle support for a breeder licensing system, follow-up action was mainly in relation to the electorally less controversial recommendations about dangerous dogs, contained in a supplementary report issued in February 2013.[74]

The lack of government action was highlighted in 2015 when the Minister for Primary Industries, Niall Blair, called for a parliamentary inquiry to investigate companion animal breeding practices, following unfavourable media publicity about some commercial puppy breeding operations.[75] Despite the overlap between this inquiry's brief and matters recently investigated by the taskforce, the minister made no mention of the latter's work when announcing the inquiry's establishment to the media.[76] While he adverted to the taskforce in the Legislative Council, he stressed the need not to 'jeopardise the industry' and to have 'a proper system in place – not vigilantes, who trespass' – to rid the pet breeding industry of the 'few rogue operators'.[77] In August 2015, the parliamentary

---

72 NSW Companion Animals Taskforce 2012a.
73 NSW Government, n.d. Response to Companion Animals Taskforce Recommendations.
74 Companion Animals Taskforce 2013.
75 Duff 2015.
76 Blair 2015.
77 NSW, *Parliamentary Debates*, Legislative Council, 12 May 2015, 343 (Niall Blair).

inquiry published its report with 34 recommendations, including the introduction of a breeders' licensing scheme for all commercial cat and dog breeding. With regard to the earlier taskforce, the report of the parliamentary inquiry expressed concern 'that the progress of NSW government agencies in implementing some of the recommendations has been slow or has not met expectations'.[78] Relevantly, it found that the taskforce report continued to be a sound basis for reform and recommended that implementation of its recommendations be a government priority. The government's response, published in 2016, supported the majority of the inquiry's recommendations, although some in part only, with a number of the supported recommendations being the conduct of further reviews.[79] A stand-alone breeders' licensing scheme was not supported because the government believed 'it would place an unnecessary administrative and regulatory burden on the industry without improving compliance or animal welfare outcomes'.[80]

One of the recommendations of both the 2012 taskforce report and the 2015 report of the parliamentary inquiry was that all animals advertised for sale via any medium include an identifying number. In May 2018, the Minister for Primary Industries introduced the Companion Animals and other Legislation Bill into parliament to give effect to this, and other reforms, as part of the government response to the findings of the parliamentary inquiry. As a result, s 23A of the *Prevention of Cruelty to Animals Act* prohibits a person from advertising a dog or cat for sale, or to be given away, without inclusion of an identification number, being either a microchip number, a breeder identification number or a rehoming organisation number. Failure to do so attracts a maximum penalty of 50 penalty units, as does giving an identification number that a person knows, or ought reasonably to have known, is false. As the advertising requirement was an amendment to the *Prevention of Cruelty to Animals Act*, it is enforceable by the RSPCA, the AWL and NSW Police. No extra funding was provided to the

78 Joint Select Committee on Companion Animal Breeding Practices in NSW, Parliament of NSW 2015, [1.54].

79 NSW Government 2016.

80 NSW, *Parliamentary Debates*, Legislative Council, 5 June 2018, 61 (Niall Blair).

RSPCA to enforce the new provisions.[81] Local council officers are not involved although they are responsible for enforcing the *Companion Animals Act*, and the OLG is responsible for managing the NSW Pet Registry. Nearly a year after the commencement of this requirement on 1 July 2019, regular examination of a major online trading site revealed very significant lack of compliance, with many NSW advertisers failing to include an identification number, or including a number that was clearly false. Normally some latitude might be expected for this early period but the minister expressly noted in May 2018 that the implementation of this provision would be delayed for 12 months to allow familiarisation with the required change.[82] While implementation was delayed, it appears that widespread familiarisation had not taken place by the commencement of the provision. More recently, the position with respect to the advertising requirement has improved somewhat but advertisements in breach of the law are still commonplace.

Meanwhile, the increase in the number of people looking for companion animals during the coronavirus pandemic has given rise to another problem: the advertisement of some animals at inflated prices on social media. In response, the NSW government announced additional funding in October 2020 for the RSPCA to investigate and prosecute the 'cowboys' and 'grubs' who are operating 'puppy factories in contravention of the law and also exploiting animals for their own commercial profit'.[83] In addition, the DPI released a consultation paper in November 2021 on the licensing and regulation of cat and dog breeding. The paper proposes the introduction of a licensing scheme for some breeders and considers additional exemptions to the Breeding Code.[84] On 24 November 2021, a Legislative Council select committee was established to inquire into puppy farming in NSW. The committee's terms of reference include the adequacy of the current legislative and enforcement framework and the extent to which the recommendations

---

81 NSW, *Parliamentary Debates*, Legislative Council, 27 August 2020, 14–15 (Emma Hurst).

82 NSW, *Parliamentary Debates*, Legislative Council, 23 May 2018, 252 (Niall Blair). In any case, the requirement to microchip an animal before it is sold, even if it is younger than 12 weeks, has been a longstanding feature of NSW law.

83 Craig 2020.

84 The consultation paper is available at https://bit.ly/3MaWW04.

of the 2015 parliamentary inquiry on companion animal breeding practices have been implemented. Concern about puppy farming was one of the reasons for the establishment of the NSW Companion Animals Taskforce nearly a decade ago, as well as the primary motivation for the NSW parliamentary inquiry into companion animal breeding practices in 2015. That the problem persists raises serious questions about the efficacy of government responses within a policy and legislative framework based on the commodification of animals.

The NSW experience illustrates the difficulty of reforming animal welfare even when evidence of need is abundant. It also reveals how the characteristics of animal welfare regulation identified in Chapter 1 apply to companion animals notwithstanding their enhanced legislative protection. These characteristics include fragmentation of regulatory responsibility, lack of national uniformity, conflict of regulatory interests, inadequate enforcement, difficulty in accessing information about the law's operation, and lengthy delays in effecting reforms. That these issues also define the regulation of companion animals gives some indication of the scope of regulatory flaws in relation to animals in a less favoured legislative position.

Other legal frameworks that impact animal welfare

Other legal frameworks also impact on the welfare of companion animals. Here, too, their property status has relevance. These frameworks include laws governing domestic and family violence, family law disputes and estate planning.

Domestic and family violence

Research into domestic violence 'has demonstrated that animals are often used to control human victims, and that many women who live with animal companions remain in violent relationships due to fears over their animals' fate'.[85] In response, the RSPCA and other agencies have established programs to provide temporary housing and care of

85 Taylor et al. 2019, 1097.

animals caught up in family violence.[86] Recognition of these findings has also led to legislative change, here and overseas. In the US, for example, 35 states have included pets in domestic violence protective orders, as of 2021.[87] In Australia, the following jurisdictions explicitly include harm to animals in definitions of domestic or family violence or other relevant provisions:

- Section 4AB(2)(f) of the *Family Law Act 1975* (Cth) includes intentionally causing death or injury to an animal in the definition of family violence.
- Section 8(2)(c) of the *Family Violence Act 2016* (ACT) includes harming an animal by a person in relation to a family member of the person in the definition of family violence.
- Section 7(1)(c) of the *Crimes (Domestic and Personal Violence) Act 2007* (NSW) was amended in 2020 to include in the meaning of intimidation conduct that causes a reasonable apprehension of harm to an animal that belongs or belonged to, or is or was in the possession of, the person or another person with whom the person has a domestic relationship. Section 36(c) was also amended to include intentionally or recklessly harming an animal in the prohibitions taken to be specified in every apprehended violence order.
- Section 5(b) of the *Domestic and Family Violence Act 2007* (NT) provides that damaging property, including the injury or death of an animal, is domestic violence when committed by a person against someone with whom the person is in a domestic relationship.
- Section 8(2)(g) of the *Domestic and Family Violence Protection Act 2012* (Qld) includes in the meaning of domestic violence causing or threatening to cause the death of, or injury to, an animal whether or not the animal belongs to the person to whom the behaviour is directed, so as to control, dominate or coerce the person.
- Section 8(4)(d) of the *Intervention Orders (Prevention of Abuse) Act 2009* (SA) includes causing the death of, or injury to, an animal in the meaning of an act of abuse against a person resulting in emotional or psychological harm.

86 For examples of these initiatives, see Dam and McGaskill 2020, 4.
87 Wisch 2021.

- Section 5(2)(e) of the *Family Violence Protection Act 2008* (Vic) includes in the definition of family violence causing or threatening to cause the death of, or injury to, an animal, whether or not the animal belongs to the family member to whom the behaviour is directed so as to control, dominate or coerce the family member.
- Section 5A(2)(f) of the *Restraining Orders Act 1997* (WA) includes causing the death or injury to an animal that is the property of the family member as an example of conduct that may constitute family violence.

Note the explicit link between animals and property in the NT and WA legislation. Animals' legal status also has relevance in the case of provisions which lack an explicit reference to animals but include reference to property damage. In this case, however, the provision would only apply if the animal is legally the property of the person requiring protection. Harming an animal may also be covered by other provisions, such as emotional abuse.[88]

In November 2020, Domestic Violence NSW released a major report highlighting the interconnection between the safety and wellbeing of animals and people experiencing domestic and family violence.[89] Confirming the risk to animals in the context of domestic and family violence, the report illustrates different ways that perpetrators use animals as a means of control and the impact of this on both human and non-human animal victims. The report's 12 recommendations include resourcing collaboration between law enforcement and animal welfare agencies, and expanding protections for animals in domestic and family violence laws.[90] Specifically, the report recommended six changes to the *Crimes (Domestic and Personal Violence) Act 2007* (NSW), including adding a reference to animals in the objects clause and in the definition of 'domestic violence offence'. Noting that animals are insufficiently protected from domestic and family violence due to their classification as property, the report also recommended adding a

---

88 National Council to Reduce Violence against Women and their Children 2009, 135.
89 Dam and McCaskill 2020.
90 Ibid, 21.

definition of 'person' which includes animals to s 3.[91] About the same time the report was released, s 7 and s 36 of the *Crimes (Domestic and Personal Violence) Act* were amended, as noted above, by the *Stronger Communities Legislation Amendment (Domestic Violence) Act 2020* (NSW). These amendments commenced on 27 March 2021. This Act also inserted recognition of the intersection between animal abuse and domestic violence in the Act's objects clause, following a successful amendment by the Animal Justice Party in the Legislative Council.

Family law disputes

Despite the reference to animals in s 4AB(2)(f) of the *Family Law Act 1975* (Cth), animals are treated as property if the parties cannot agree about their care when relationships break down.[92] By contrast, a number of foreign jurisdictions have laws requiring the courts to consider the best interests of the animal in determining disputes about them when relationships end. Article 651a of the Swiss Civil Code, for example, provides that the court will award sole ownership to whichever party offers the better animal welfare conditions, with payment of appropriate compensation to the other party at the discretion of the court. This provision does not apply to animals kept for investment or commercial purposes. In the US, the states have jurisdiction over family law matters and disputes about animals have featured in a number of cases. While the courts have typically resolved these disputes on the basis of property ownership, a few cases have acknowledged the special relationship people can have with their companion animals.[93] Some state legislatures have acknowledged the interests of the animal when relationships break down. In 2016, Alaska became the first state to require judicial consideration of an animal's 'wellbeing' in determining disputes about companion animal ownership when marriages end. This law also allows joint ownership of the animal.[94] A similar law was enacted by Illinois in 2017, with a weaker version adopted by California in 2018, which authorises, though doesn't require, the interests of

91 Ibid, 85, 87.
92 Bogdanoski 2013, 94.
93 Pallotta 2017.
94 Pallotta 2019, 168.

animals to be taken into account.[95] In 2021, a Spanish court awarded a divorcing couple joint custody of their dog, describing the couple as the dog's co-caretakers rather than co-owners.[96]

Estate planning

As animals have the legal status of property, they can be gifted by a provision in a will or, if a person dies without a valid will (intestate), any animals they own will be distributed according to the rules of intestacy in state and territory succession legislation. Some jurisdictions expressly include animals in the definition of property in this legislation. For example, s 34A(1) of the *Succession Act 1981* (Qld) defines *household chattels* as:

> all furniture, curtains, drapes, carpets, linen, china, glassware, ornaments, domestic appliances and utensils, garden appliances, utensils and effects and other chattels of ordinary household use or decoration, liquors, wines, consumable stores and domestic animals owned by the intestate immediately before the intestate's death.

Similarly, animals' legal status means they cannot benefit directly under a will so other means of providing for their future care must be considered. One option is provided by legacy programs established by the RSPCA and other animal welfare organisations.[97] Another option is to create a trust.[98] This is a device whereby one person, the trustee, holds the legal title to property on behalf of, and for the benefit of, another person or persons (a private trust) or for a recognised charitable purpose (a charitable trust). To be valid, a private trust requires a beneficiary capable of enforcing its terms, while a charitable trust requires a charitable purpose which benefits the public, either directly or indirectly.[99] A 'pet trust' falls into neither of these categories as it is for a private purpose and animals lack the capacity to enforce it. This is a complex area of law, however, and some older anomalous cases

95 Ibid.
96 Chalmers 2021.
97 For example, Animal Welfare League Queensland's Legacy Pets Program.
98 Law Society of NSW, Young Lawyers' Animal Law Committee 2014, 35.
99 Radan and Stewart 2018, 569.

provide authority for the validity of certain non-charitable purpose trusts, including for the maintenance of specific animals,[100] although the obligation on the trustee is a moral rather than a legal one.[101] In other words, the trustee is entitled to give effect to the terms of the trust but is not bound to do so.[102] The position is more straightforward in some foreign jurisdictions, for example the US where all 50 states now have laws enabling the creation of legally enforceable 'pet trusts'.[103]

More generally, a charitable trust may be created to benefit animal shelters and to prevent cruelty to animals as these purposes 'promote personal and public morality'.[104] Significantly, however, where 'there is no evident connection between an animal-focused disposition or association and a benefit to the human community, it may seem incongruous to conclude that its object is charitable'.[105] In *Murdoch v Attorney-General (Tas)*, for example, Zeeman J held that part of an estate left to a veterinary surgeon 'for the benefit of animals generally' did not create a valid charitable trust because:

> [i]t is the benefit of animals rather than the benefit of the community served by benevolence towards animals that is the expressed object. In some circumstances the achievement of one object will tend to further the achievement of some other object. This is not such a case. Certain things which might be done for the benefit of animals are of no benefit to the community and may even be contrary to the best interests of the community.[106]

Although decided in the late 20th century, this case evokes an earlier era when concern about animal cruelty was confined to its impact on human character, with no direct moral duties owed to animals in their

---

100 *Re Dean* (1889) 41 Ch D 552; *Re Hegarty* [2011] NSWSC 1194, [14]–[22]. The issue did not have to be decided in *Re Hegarty* because the person appointed by the testatrix to care for her animals declined to do so. Accordingly, this case is also a reminder of the importance of securing the informed agreement of any persons appointed by a will to carry out the testator's wishes.

101 Hannah 2009, 68–9.

102 LexisNexis 2018, [430-275] footnote 4.

103 Pallotta 2019, 172.

104 Radan and Stewart 2018, 600; see also Radan 2013, 521–2.

105 Dal Pont 2015, 916.

106 (1992) 1 Tas R 117, 131–2.

own right. It is 'the benefit to the community served by benevolence towards animals' which matters, not the benefit to animals themselves; at the same time, the reference to conflicting human and animal interests invokes the balancing act of the humane treatment principle at the heart of the animal welfare paradigm. In this way, the very technical and apparently unrelated field of trusts takes us back to the large questions about the moral significance of animals with which this book commenced. The limits of the legal classification of animals as property touched on above also compel consideration of alternative conceptions of their status. As it happens, the principles underlying trust law have a role here too.

Legal status of animals: some alternative conceptions

The law of trusts gives expression to the idea that property ownership is capable of division into two different forms of title: legal and equitable. David Favre draws on this idea to propose the concept of equitable self-ownership, whereby humans hold the legal title to animals but animals hold the equitable title to themselves.[107] Just as a trustee has legal obligations to the beneficiary of the trust who holds the equitable interest, so humans would have legal obligations to animals as the equitable title holders of their own lives. Within this proposed framework, animals would be both the subject matter of the legal title and the owner of the equitable title, while the legal title holder would have the responsibilities of a guardian, similar to parents in relation to their minor children.[108] More recently, Favre has extended his concept of equitable self-ownership to the idea of 'living property', a new category of property that recognises that animals 'have interests independent of the humans who own them'.[109] Within this framework, owners would owe legally enforceable duties directly to animals and animals would have the capacity to hold legal rights, with remedies for their breach flowing directly to them.

107 Favre 2004, 240–1.
108 Ibid, 242.
109 Favre 2010, 1022.

Favre's analysis accepts the retention of a form of property status for animals but there is considerable debate among animal law scholars about the significance of animals' legal status as a factor in restricting or effecting change. Robert Garner, for example, argues 'that abolishing the property status of animals is not a sufficient guarantee that they will cease to be exploited'.[110] He further argues that 'whilst the abolition of animals' property status is a necessary step towards the fulfilment of an animal rights agenda, it is incorrect to suggest that significant improvements to animals' wellbeing cannot be achieved from within the existing property paradigm'.[111] By contrast, some legal scholars argue strongly for the abolition of animals' property status as a prerequisite for meaningful change. In Gary Francione's view, the classification of animals as property 'renders meaningless any balancing that is supposedly required under the humane treatment principle or animal welfare laws, because what we really balance are the interests of property owners against the interests of their animal property'.[112] Accordingly, he argues that the 'right not to be treated as the property of others' is 'the precondition for the possession of morally significant interests'.[113]

Among those who seek an end to animals' property status, there are also differences in how to conceptualise its replacement. Maneesha Deckha, for example, situates the personhood debate within an anthropocentric legal system, arguing instead for a 'new legal subjectivity' for animals which pays attention to the characteristics of embodiment, vulnerability and relationality.[114] By contrast, Steven Wise pursues change in the form of legal action to assert the personhood of animals based on their level of practical autonomy.[115] To this end, the Nonhuman Rights Project (NhRP), founded by Wise, engages in litigation in American state courts with the aim of securing the right to bodily liberty for individual captive animals, such as great apes and elephants.[116] The NhRP argues that the characteristics of these animals

110 Garner 2002, 78.
111 Ibid.
112 Francione 2004, 117.
113 Ibid, 124.
114 Deckha 2021.
115 Wise 2002.
116 Nonhuman Rights Project, n.d.

give them the status of 'persons' and entitle them to fundamental rights, such as bodily integrity and liberty, and the protection afforded by the writ of habeas corpus.[117] Although unsuccessful to date, detailed arguments made to various courts about the capacities of animals have received some strong judicial support. In 2015, Justice Jaffe granted a hearing in New York State County Court to determine the lawfulness of the detainment of two chimpanzees, Hercules and Leo. Although denying the petition on the basis of an appellate court precedent, Jaffe J stated that:

> The similarities between chimpanzees and humans inspire the empathy felt for a beloved pet. Efforts to extend legal rights to chimpanzees are thus understandable; some day they may even succeed. Courts, however, are slow to embrace change, and occasionally seem reluctant to engage in broader, more inclusive interpretations of the law, if only to the modest extent of affording them greater consideration. As Justice Kennedy aptly observed in *Lawrence v Texas*, albeit in a different context, "times can blind us to certain truths and later generations can see that laws once thought necessary and proper in fact serve only to oppress."[118]

Subsequent NhRP litigation has brought further judicial acknowledgement of chimpanzees and elephants as autonomous, intelligent creatures, and the injustice of 'a paradigm that determines entitlement to a court decision based on whether the party is considered a "person" or relegated to the category of a "thing"'.[119] In 2020, Justice Tuitt 'regrettably' denied the NhRP's petition for a writ of habeas corpus on behalf of Happy, an elephant captured from the wild but living alone at a zoo since 2006. Basing her decision on precedent, Tuitt J stated that:

---

117 Habeas corpus is a common law writ which commands a person who detains another to bring the detained person before the court to test the lawfulness of the detention.

118 *Nonhuman Rights Project Inc, on behalf of Hercules and Leo v Stanley* (152736/15, 29 July 2015), 32 (reference omitted). For information about this and other NhRP cases, including judgments, see Nonhuman Rights Project, n.d.

119 *Nonhuman Rights Project Inc, on behalf of Tommy v Lavery* 31 NY3d 1054, 1059 (2018), Fahey J.

> [t]his Court is extremely sympathetic to Happy's plight and the NhRP's mission on her behalf. It recognizes that Happy is an extraordinary animal with complex cognitive abilities, an intelligent being with advanced analytic abilities akin to human beings.[120]

An appeal against this decision was heard by the New York Court of Appeals in May 2022, with the outcome expected within six weeks. So far, however, neither courts nor legislatures have been inclined to grant legal personhood to non-human animals, even when they are cognitively and emotionally complex or enjoy the status of a 'beloved pet'.[121] This is despite the law's recognition of 'artificial persons', a legal fiction bestowed on corporations and ships, and a more recent move in some nations to grant a form of legal personality to rivers.[122] On one view, concern about recognising even some animals as persons 'may have less to do with the line separating humans from all other animals, and more to do with the bright line we are invested in keeping firm between companion animals and farmed animals'.[123] If companion animals were granted a status other than property, it might be harder to justify retaining the existing classification for other sentient beings without exposing the contradiction between the current legal framework and its philosophical base. Industry certainly appears keen to maintain the 'bright line' between farmed and companion animals, as submissions to the current review of the Victorian animal welfare legislation illustrate. In relation to the proposed statutory recognition of animal sentience, for example, one agricultural organisation submitted that:

120 *Nonhuman Rights Project Inc, on behalf of Happy v Breheny* (260441/19, 18 February 2020), 16. See Nonhuman Rights Project, n.d.

121 There are some exceptions. In 2016, an Argentinian court declared a chimpanzee a 'nonhuman legal person' and in 2019 a second court in India granted animals the status of legal entity/legal person: Rosalky 2019, 34. In Colombia, non-human animals have standing to litigate to protect their interests. In 2020, a lawsuit was commenced in that country on behalf of hippopotamuses at risk of being killed. In October 2021, a US District Court granted an application by the Animal Legal Defense Fund authorising the plaintiffs to obtain information from experts in the United States. This decision required the US court to recognise the plaintiff hippos as an 'interested person' under the relevant US law: Animal Legal Defense Fund 2021.

122 O'Donnell and Talbot-Jones 2018.

123 Pallotta 2019, 180.

> ... it is not appropriate for sentience to be inserted into regulation in a way that compromises the realities of livestock production. Recognising all animals as sentient does not and should not mean that livestock are synonymous with companion animals.[124]

That the realities of livestock production, not sentience, drive the regulation of farmed animals is the topic to which we now turn.

124 Victoria, Department of Jobs, Precincts and Regions 2021, 9.

4
Farmed Animals

> *Domestic chickens have distinct personalities and exhibit complex cognitive, emotional, communicative and social behaviour.*[1]

> *46% of Australians surveyed think that chickens are sentient, 46% think they are 'somewhat sentient' and 8% think they are not sentient at all.*[2]

> *In the financial year 2019–20, 658 million chickens were slaughtered in Australia producing an estimated 1,246,000 tonnes of chicken meat.*[3]

> *The flock size in relation to egg production as at June 2020 was 28,845,730 (pullets and layers).*[4]

As the above figures illustrate, animals are farmed for food on an industrial scale. On one estimate, over 56 billion farmed animals are killed worldwide every year for food, a number which does 'not include fish and other sea animals whose death numbers are so great they are only measured in tons'.[5] This use of animals is commonly justified on the basis that eating animals is necessary for human health but this belief is

---

1 Marino 2017, 141.
2 Futureye Pty. Ltd. 2018, 6.
3 Australian Chicken Meat Federation, n.d. Facts & Figures.
4 Australian Eggs Limited 2020, 4.
5 Gullone 2017, 34.

increasingly contested. There is now considerable research that not only demonstrates the nutritional adequacy of plant-based diets but also their superiority in terms of health outcomes, as well as their environmental benefits.[6] Vast numbers of animals are also farmed for their fibre and other products. With such enormous numbers, animal agriculture is generally regarded as the biggest single cause of animal suffering in industrialised nations. Arguably, it is responsible for more suffering than all other animal uses put together[7] but the sheer scale of animal agriculture makes reform a herculean task. It also makes it difficult to see animals as individual sentient beings even though the typical farmed animal is no less sentient than the family 'pet'. Given that sentience is 'the reason that welfare matters',[8] how then can we account for the very different treatment of farmed animals the law permits? To answer this question, we need to revisit the concept of animal welfare and the way science, ethical considerations and competing interests all play a part in a complex mix.

Conceptualising animal welfare

In 1986, Professor Donald Broom defined the welfare of an animal as 'its state as regards its attempts to cope with its environment'.[9] Broom's influential work provided the basis for an expanded definition of animal welfare by the World Organisation for Animal Health (OIE),[10] an intergovernmental organisation responsible for improving global animal health, with 182 member countries, including Australia, as of 2018. With a mandate from early this century to take the international lead on animal welfare,[11] the OIE's definition is routinely referenced, including by Australian government publications. As amended, this definition now reads:

6 Willett et al. 2019; Caulfield 2018, 145–63; Gullone 2017, 45–51.

7 See, for example, Rollin 2006 quoted in Gullone 2017, 33.

8 Australia, Department of Agriculture, Water and the Environment 2011.

9 Broom 1986, 524.

10 In 2003, the International Office of Epizootics was renamed the World Organisation for Animal Health but retained its historical acronym OIE (Office International des Epizooties).

11 Schipp and Sheridan 2013, 669.

> Animal welfare means the physical and mental state of an animal in relation to the conditions in which it lives and dies.
>
> An animal experiences good welfare if the animal is healthy, comfortable, well nourished, safe, is not suffering from unpleasant states such as pain, fear, and distress, and is able to express behaviours that are important for its physical and mental state.
>
> Good animal welfare requires disease prevention and appropriate veterinary care, shelter, management and nutrition, a stimulating and safe environment, humane handling and humane slaughter or killing. While animal welfare refers to the state of the animal, the treatment that an animal receives is covered by other terms such as animal care, animal husbandry, and humane treatment.[12]

The guiding principles that accompany the OIE definition incorporate reference to the 'Five Freedoms'. Originally formulated in 1979 by John Webster,[13] the Five Freedoms have become an influential reference point for animal welfare, although they 'define ideal states rather than standards for acceptable welfare'.[14] As modified and formalised by the UK Farm Animal Welfare Council (FAWC) in 1993, the Five Freedoms and their accompanying provisions are:

- *Freedom from thirst, hunger and malnutrition* – by ready access to fresh water and a diet to maintain full health and vigour;
- *Freedom from discomfort* – by providing an appropriate environment including shelter and a comfortable resting area;
- *Freedom from pain, injury or disease* – by prevention or rapid diagnosis and treatment;
- *Freedom to express normal behaviour* – by providing sufficient space, proper facilities and company of the animal's own kind; and
- *Freedom from fear and distress* – by ensuring conditions which avoid mental suffering.[15]

---

12 OIE 2019, art. 7.1.1.
13 Webster 2016, 36.
14 Farm Animal Welfare Council 1993, 3.
15 Ibid, 3–4.

The Five Freedoms paradigm was notable as 'the first to detail the broader dimensions of animal welfare by incorporating subjective experiences, health status and behaviour'.[16] Other approaches since then include the concept of the Five Domains[17] and the tripartite classification of an animal's quality of life over its lifetime: a life not worth living, a life worth living and a good life.[18]

Notwithstanding the 'potentially bewildering complexity' and 'sometimes contradictory ideas about animal welfare', three major orientations (or frameworks) are acknowledged: biological function, affective state and natural living.[19] Biological function emphasises an animal's physical health and wellbeing, and was the dominant orientation in the 1980s. Affective state is concerned with the subjective experiences of animals, both negative states such as pain, hunger and thirst, and positive mental states, such as contentment and playfulness.[20] Natural living refers to an animal's capacity to engage in behaviours 'which are inherent to animals, and typically, which animals are motivated to carry out'.[21] The OIE acknowledges that the assessment of animal welfare involves an holistic consideration of these diverse elements but also notes that the weight given to each is a value-laden process.[22] By way of illustration, scientific committees in Europe and Australia reached opposite conclusions around the turn of the millennium after reviewing the same literature in relation to housing pregnant sows in stalls.[23] At that time, the Australian committee concluded that sow stalls were acceptable on animal welfare grounds, while the European committee did not.[24] For Malcolm Caulfield, the Australian committee's position reflects a continuing focus in this country on animals' physical health and physiological measures at the expense of behavioural indicators, although he observes that this

16 Mellor 2016, 22.
17 Green and Mellor 2011, 264.
18 Farm Animal Welfare Council 2009, ii–iii.
19 Green and Mellor 2011, 263–4.
20 Ibid, 264.
21 Hartcher and Jones 2017, 769.
22 OIE 2019, art. 7.1.2 (4).
23 Hagen et al. 2011, 95.
24 Webster 2005, 8–9.

approach may be changing.[25] Certainly a focus on physical health is at odds with contemporary research which emphasises animals' mental states and the promotion of positive affective experiences.[26]

Case study: development of national poultry standards

Both the importance and limits of science in determining good animal welfare practice are illustrated by the drawn-out process to develop national poultry standards. This process also highlights the pervasiveness of the regulatory characteristics identified in Chapter 1, including conflicts of interest, the dominance of industry stakeholders, lengthy delays, and lack of transparency.

Part of the systematic conversion of the existing model codes of practice, the formal process to develop poultry standards began in 2015, funded by all Australian state and federal governments and major industry organisations. Proposed draft standards and guidelines were initially developed under the direction of the Animal Welfare Task Group which comprises representatives from the senior ranks of Commonwealth, state and territory agriculture/primary industries departments.[27] Responsibility for the contract management of the poultry standards was initially allocated to the NSW DPI. In this context, the DPI's mission to promote primary industries and to drive economic growth assumes a particular significance given that NSW is home to the largest proportion of egg producers in Australia. The DPI was also represented on the initial small writing group, as was Animal Health Australia (AHA).[28] As noted in Chapter 1, AHA is a not-for-profit public company whose membership comprises government agriculture/primary industry departments and major livestock industries. Supporting the writing group was a Stakeholder Advisory Group (SAG). Described as 'widely representative', the SAG included representatives from two animal welfare organisations and 11 industry

25 Caulfield 2018, 89–90; Caulfield 2017, 161.
26 Green and Mellor 2011, 265.
27 Tim Harding & Associates 2017, 22.
28 Zacharin 2017.

bodies.[29] While the Consultation Regulatory Impact Statement (RIS) notes that '[a]ll members of the SAG had an equal opportunity to express their opinions',[30] some interests received substantially greater representation than others.

In November 2017, the proposed draft standards published by AHA as part of the public consultation process included an acknowledgement that they did not necessarily represent the views of all contributing parties. Ironically, in view of their badging as animal welfare standards, it is the two animal welfare organisations represented on the SAG whose dissent is noted; by contrast, industry representatives were broadly supportive, of both the proposed standards and the process that produced them. From the outset, animal welfare organisations were critical of the failure of the Animal Welfare Task Group to undertake an independent review of the science to inform development of the draft standards, with the result that the RSPCA compiled its own review of the scientific literature on layer hen welfare.[31] Similar concerns prompted the Victorian government to commission a review of the scientific literature on the care, management and slaughter of farmed poultry.[32] Meanwhile, the WA Minister for Agriculture criticised the proposed draft standards as not reflecting the latest scientific knowledge or community expectations.[33]

The proposed draft standards comprised option C of the RIS. A notable feature of this option is the lack of any change to the system of housing layer hens in conventional cages,[34] despite acknowledgement that a physically healthy, productive animal may be in a poor state of welfare due to other factors.[35] Indeed, according to the RIS, an animal is 'in a good state of welfare if (as indicated by scientific evidence) it is healthy, comfortable, well nourished, safe, able to express innate behaviour, and it is not suffering from unpleasant states such as

29 Tim Harding & Associates 2017, 22–3.
30 Ibid, 23.
31 Hartcher and Jones 2017.
32 Nicol et al. 2017.
33 Brammer 2017.
34 Also commonly referred to as battery cages.
35 Tim Harding & Associates 2017, vi.

pain, fear and distress'.[36] Having stressed that animal welfare is the principal policy problem that the options sought to address, the RIS then identified the main risks to the welfare of poultry in existing instruments as follows:

- Lack of clear responsibilities for personnel in charge of poultry;
- Lack of freedom of poultry to express innate behaviours;
- Inadequate space allowances for poultry (stocking density);
- Lack of perches, nests and litter for layer hens (production systems);
- Lack of quantitative lighting standards;
- Need for restrictions on routine beak trimming;
- Risky litter management;
- Need to restrict routine use of induced moulting;
- Care of meat chickens and turkeys awaiting slaughtering; and
- Access to water for ducks.[37]

While some of the new standards in option C provide additional welfare measures, taken as a whole there is a significant discrepancy between the animal welfare risks identified by the RIS and the proposed draft standards chosen to address them. For example, there are no proposed new standards that increase the capacity of poultry to express innate behaviours other than very limited changes in relation to nest boxes for breeder poultry and ducks' access to water. There is also no change to stocking densities for most species. Nor is there any general requirement that perches, nests or litter be provided. Some new standards, for example those dealing with lighting, are inconsistent with RSPCA recommendations,[38] while some important welfare measures are only included as non-mandatory guidelines.

In the view of the two animal welfare organisations represented on the SAG, option C is largely representative of current industry practice.[39] How then to explain the discrepancy between this option and the recognition in the RIS that 'a number of current practices' have failed to keep 'pace with animal welfare science and society's expectations'?[40]

36 Ibid, 31.
37 Ibid, vi, 33.
38 RSPCA Australia 2018a, 35.
39 Animals Australia 2018, 2; RSPCA Australia 2018a, 10.
40 Tim Harding & Associates 2017, 28.

First, although the RIS acknowledges the three frameworks – biological function, affective state and natural living – it emphasises narrow measures of animal welfare on the basis that evidence of its broader attributes is indeterminate or lacking. This approach is reinforced by inconsistent references to some aspects of animal welfare. For example, the 'importance' of innate behaviours is said to be 'a matter of contention' notwithstanding the recognition that 'the basic physiological and behavioural needs of poultry include … space to stand, lie and stretch their wings and limbs and perform normal patterns of behaviour',[41] and the inclusion of these needs in the list of existing risks to poultry welfare. This qualified and inconsistent understanding of animal welfare in the RIS reflects the lesser weighting given to animals' mental states and behavioural preferences despite developments in science which indicate that 'animals are potentially much more sensitive to their environmental and social circumstances than was previously thought to be the case'.[42]

As the RIS acknowledges, however, the interpretation of animal welfare science is not a value-free process and different conclusions are possible in relation to the same science.[43] We are told, for example, that:

> … cages provide the least freedom to express natural behaviours but they also have the lowest incidences [*sic*] of feather pecking and cannibalism. Some people might consider that freedom to express natural behaviours is overwhelmingly the most important factor, whilst others might prefer a different weighting.[44]

The choice of option C for the proposed draft standards indicates that the economic consultants responsible for preparing the RIS 'prefer a different weighting' – and one that is consistent with industry preferences. Partiality is also evident in ways that might seem insignificant but are remarkably telling. In the glossary, for example, the meaning of 'cages' includes an additional, evaluative statement about the importance of cage systems as a disease control measure.[45]

---

41 Ibid, 10, 34.
42 Mellor 2015, 17.
43 Tim Harding & Associates 2017, 10.
44 Ibid, 34.
45 This additional statement was omitted from the glossary of the revised draft standards tabled in the Senate in 2021.

By contrast, free-range systems and furnished cages are described in purely factual terms. Further, while it is widely recognised that each of the three farming systems has welfare advantages and disadvantages, no weight appears to have been given to the fact that the disadvantages of other systems can be managed through good husbandry and other practices while the disadvantages inherent in caged farming systems cannot.[46] These welfare disadvantages include fatty liver disease, and increased bone disease and osteoporosis from lack of exercise.[47] As RSPCA Australia observed, the failure to take into account the impact of different practices in terms of their variability, scope and duration is problematic because, for example:

> … the impact of behavioural deprivation on hens in conventional cages is an experience that every hen in the facility faces every day for the duration of their productive lives. It lasts for approximately 18 months and is unchanging. Conversely, incidents of feather pecking are generally sporadic in nature, experienced by a percentage of hens, is highly variable between farms, and its rates of occurrence can be affected by management practices.[48]

RSPCA Australia also criticised the cost–benefit analyses of various options in the RIS for, among other things, relying on 'undisclosed and non-validated data' provided by industry, and on unsupported assumptions about current industry practices.[49]

In relation to society's expectations, the Productivity Commission concluded in 2016 that the existing standard-setting process 'does not adequately value the benefits of animal welfare to the community'.[50] In the case of the poultry standards, a very high level of community interest was evident in the size of the response to the public consultation process, with an estimated 167,000 email and 2,000 hard copy submissions.[51] Common concerns include cage egg production, the conditions in which meat chickens are raised, beak trimming, lighting

46 Caulfield 2018, 75.
47 Nicol et al. 2017, 29–30.
48 RSPCA Australia 2018a, 9.
49 Ibid, 10–11.
50 Productivity Commission 2016, 199.
51 Bray 2018, 2.

and slaughter. Acute value differences in the submissions are illustrated by the issue of housing layer hens in conventional cages, with animal welfare and legal groups and the majority of community submissions opposed to their use, and industry and producer groups tending to support their continuation.[52] In January 2018, the NSW Minister for Primary Industries gave an assurance that the proposed draft standards 'will be changed and updated to reflect the feedback received during consultation'.[53] This assurance, and denial of any industry collusion, was made in response to widespread criticism of the standards development process, including that it had been 'stage-managed' for the benefit of industry.[54] The criticisms were not confined to animal welfare organisations. An email from Victoria's executive director of biosecurity to the NSW DPI in 2016 indicated that the governance and other concerns of RSPCA Australia were shared 'to some extent' by Victoria.[55] Following a damning report on the ABC's *7.30* program, the WA Minister for Agriculture was reported as saying that WA would not adopt the final standards if concerns about both the process and the proposed standards were not adequately resolved.[56]

Nearly seven years after the formal process commenced, the poultry standards have still not been finalised, despite a change in the contract management of the project. With dissenting views unable to be resolved by the SAG, agriculture ministers agreed in October 2019 to appoint an 'independent panel' to supervise the drafting of new poultry standards. Membership of this panel was agreed in February 2020[57] but not made public until December 2020. The department subsequently advised that a draft of the revised standards and guidelines was sent to members of the SAG in March 2021 for comment, with the final version to be presented to the Agriculture Senior Officials Committee in August 2021.[58] Members of the public only gained access to these revised draft standards when they were tabled in the Senate following an order to

52 Ibid, 2–3.
53 Thomas 2018.
54 Ibid. See also Zacharin 2017 for a rebuttal of claims of undue industry influence.
55 Thomas 2018.
56 Thomas and Branley 2017. See also Ellis 2018.
57 Australia, Department of Agriculture, Water and the Environment 2020d.
58 Australia, Department of Agriculture, Water and the Environment 2021a.

produce documents successfully moved by Greens Senator Faruqi on 21 June 2021.[59]

In relation to laying hens, the tabled draft standards prescribe a stocking density for cage systems of 750 square cm per bird if kept in a cage of two or more birds (SB1.11). They also require the provision of a nest area for every seven birds, perching space of 7.5 cm per laying hen and access to a scratch area and/or claw shortening device, unless the birds have access to an outdoor area (SB1.6–10). These revisions to the draft standards represent a move from conventional (battery) cage systems to furnished cage systems for laying hens, although it is anticipated that many egg producers will move to barn-laid systems if these changes are introduced.[60] The revised draft standards provide for these changes to be phased in between 1 July 2032 and 1 July 2036, depending upon the installation date of existing cage systems (SB1.13). There are some other improvements in the revised draft standards for chickens, plus some improvements in the general standards which apply to all poultry species, for example an increase in light intensity to be phased in by 1 July 2025 (SA6.3). Nevertheless, many of the proposed standards are still inadequate and/or remain unchanged. For example, the maximum stocking density for non-caged laying hens remains at 30 kg per square metre (SB1.14) and the maximum stocking density for meat chickens (non-caged systems) is only reduced from 40 to 38 kg per square metre (SB2.5). By contrast, RSPCA Australia recommends a maximum stocking density of between seven and nine birds per square metre for layer hens, for floor-based and tiered systems respectively,[61] and a maximum stocking density of 34 kg per square metre for meat chickens.[62]

As well as the additional delay in the above extension of the process, the finalised standards still have to be endorsed by agriculture ministers and implemented in state and territory legislation before they are enforceable. If the transition period remains as drafted, some

59 Australia, Senate Journals, Australian Animal Welfare Standards and Guidelines for Poultry – Order for production of documents, 21 June 2021, 3634 (Mehreen Faruqi).

60 Bainbridge and Branley 2021b.

61 Equivalent to approximately 14 to 20 kg per square metre depending on the weight of the birds. As per note 66, layer hens kept in caged systems generally weigh less than 2.4 kg.

62 RSPCA Australia 2018a, 45.

conventional cages will be allowed up to 2036, more than 20 years after the formal commencement of the poultry standards review process. But even these very modest reforms are in doubt with the NSW Agriculture Minister reportedly opposed to the phase-out, against the advice of his department.[63] According to documents obtained by animal lawyers under freedom of information laws, the NSW minister indicated in March 2021 that he would not support a phase-out of conventional cages.[64] The NSW position also highlights concerns about industry influence in animal welfare decisions, with a major cage egg producer holding a senior position in the NSW National Party and the responsible minister a National Party MP.[65] Meanwhile, the regulation of poultry welfare continues broadly to reflect the provisions of the 2002 *Model Code of Practice for the Welfare of Animals: Domestic Poultry*. In relation to caged egg production, this code specifies a space allowance of 550 square cm per laying hen, less than the size of an A4 sheet of paper.[66] This contrasts with developments in comparable countries, such as New Zealand, Switzerland, Canada and the European Union (EU), which are currently phasing out conventional cages, where they are not already banned.[67]

By contrast with the tardiness in developing poultry welfare standards, Australian consumers have shown considerable movement in their purchasing preferences. In relation to egg production systems, for example, cage eggs comprised 67.8% of market share by volume in 2008–09[68] compared to 39% of major supermarket chains by volume in 2019–20.[69] Concern about consumer exploitation in this changing environment saw successful enforcement action by the Australian Competition and Consumer Commission against the Australian Chicken Meat Federation and several producers for claiming that meat chickens were 'free to roam' when they were not.[70] Legal action has also been successful against a number of egg producers for

63 Bainbridge and Branley 2021a.
64 Ibid.
65 Ibid.
66 Appendix 1, A1.4 where three or more fowl each weighing less than 2.4 kg are kept in one cage, as is standard industry practice.
67 RSPCA Australia 2018a, 25–6.
68 Australian Egg Corporation Limited 2009, 3.
69 Australian Eggs Limited 2020, 5.
70 Parker et al. 2018, 241.

labelling their products as 'free range', either when the eggs were laid by hens in cages or when hens in practice had no outdoor access on most days.[71] In response to these developments, state and territory consumer affairs ministers agreed to develop a national information standard for free-range-egg labelling, with the objective of enhancing consumer confidence and certainty, not regulating animal welfare.[72] The *Australian Consumer Law (Free Range Egg Labelling) Information Standard 2017* (Cth) commenced in April 2018 and defined free range eggs in s 7(1) as eggs laid by hens that:

(a) had meaningful and regular access to an outdoor range during daylight hours during the laying cycle;

(b) were able to roam and forage on the outdoor range; and

(c) were subject to a stocking density of 10,000 hens or less.

The maximum stocking density of 10,000 birds per hectare is consistent with the preferences of large egg producers but contrary to those of smaller producers, and animal welfare and consumer groups, who supported a maximum outdoor stocking density of 1,500 birds per hectare.[73] It is also inconsistent with Appendix 2.1.4 of the *Model Code of Practice for the Welfare of Animals: Domestic Poultry* which specifies 1,500 birds per hectare, although there is some ambiguity as to whether a higher density is permitted in certain circumstances.[74] While animal welfare regulations in most jurisdictions fail to specify an outdoor stocking density for laying hens, Sch 1 of the *Animal Care and Protection Regulation 2012* (Qld) provides that a person must not keep more than 10,000 laying fowl per hectare in the outdoor area of a free-range system. This is subject, however, to eight conditions if the stocking density exceeds 1,500 per hectare.[75]

---

71 Burgess 2017, 31.
72 Ibid, 9.
73 Australia, Treasury 2016, 32.
74 Parker and De Costa 2016, 910.
75 There is a lack of relevant science with respect to the minimum outdoor space required for the welfare of free-range laying hens.

The broader industry context

As set out in Chapters 1 and 2, the content of codes of practice, standards and guidelines is critical within a regulatory framework which largely exempts farmed animals from the protective reach of animal welfare legislation. While the poultry standards process has been particularly prolonged, other farmed animal standards finalised to date have also been criticised as reflecting industry preferences at the expense of animal welfare. Common concerns across a range of industries include inadequate space allowances, the carrying out of invasive husbandry practices without pain relief, and inadequate regulation of transport and slaughter. These provisions operate within a broader industry context in which animals are selectively bred to maximise their productive efficiency at a cost to their own welfare, with millions of very young animals effectively disposed of every year as by-products of intensive farming systems.

Below we consider some key issues associated with very large animal industries but they are by no means the only farming contexts in which welfare problems arise. Rabbits, for example, are bred for meat in caged housing systems, with the industry characterised by similar regulatory problems, such as lack of transparency.[76] Intensive fish farming is also associated with a variety of welfare problems yet has generated less attention than other intensive animal industries. This may be due in part to the more limited science in relation to fish sentience, an issue to which we return in Chapter 5, as well as concern about the impact of greater regulation given the size of fishing industries.

Breeding, wastage and slaughter: poultry and dairy industries

Public debate around the proposed draft poultry standards focused on egg production systems but these standards also fail to address many other welfare issues, both for hens and other poultry species. An example is the proposed standards for ducks. As a semi-aquatic species, ducks require access to clean water sources which allow full,

76 Lascelles and McEwan 2019, 89–90.

or at least partial, immersion for bathing and wet preening.[77] Under the revised draft standards, however, it is only mandatory to provide facilities which allow ducks to dip their heads under water and showers to allow wet preening, to be phased in by 1 July 2027 (SB4.3). Another example is the conditions in which meat chickens (broilers) are bred and raised. Selectively bred to achieve very high growth rates, by 2011 meat chickens were reaching 2 kg live weight in 35 days compared to 64 days in 1975.[78] The lameness associated with heavy, fast-growing chickens results in pain, limited behavioural expression and an inability to access resources, while genetic selection to increase breast and leg muscle causes other welfare problems.[79] With commercial systems housing thousands of meat chickens in each shed, stocking density also has welfare implications. In illustration of the very limited protection of animal welfare laws, the 'extremely high' stocking densities allowed by the proposed draft poultry standards exceed those under which the majority of the industry are already operating.[80]

Similar welfare problems arise in a range of other industries; for example, the selective breeding of dairy cows to increase milk yield which has doubled over the last three decades.[81] The focus on high milk volume causes the cow metabolic strain, and contributes to health problems, such as mastitis and lameness.[82] To ensure the requisite flow of milk, dairy cows need to give birth every 12–14 months, with the calves typically separated from their mothers on the first day. As only female calves can be used as herd replacements, hundreds of thousands of mainly male calves are sent to slaughter from five days old, every year in Australia. During the development of the *Animal Welfare Standards and Guidelines: Land Transport of Livestock*, the issue of time off feed (TOF) for these 'bobby calves' was a matter of particular contention. As endorsed in 2009, SB4.5 of these standards requires bobby calves to be delivered within 18 hours of their last liquid feed (milk), with no more than 12 hours spent on transports. This provision takes no account

77 Nicol et al. 2017, 178, 182.
78 Australian Chicken Meat Federation, n.d. Infographics.
79 Nicol et al. 2017, 97.
80 RSPCA Australia 2018a, 77.
81 Wicks 2018, 57.
82 Ibid, 62–5.

Figure 4.1. Hundreds of thousands of unwanted calves are sent to slaughter every year from five days old. (Diana Simpson)

of the additional time calves spend awaiting slaughter, which can be considerably longer, including overnight. Despite acknowledging that bobby calves are predisposed to difficulties in coping with transport and handling due to their physiological immaturity, a separate Regulation Impact Statement (RIS) in 2011 recommended the inclusion of a clause in the standards allowing a maximum 30 hours TOF.[83] Although a subsequent meeting of agriculture ministers failed to reach agreement on this recommendation, relevant industry bodies decided to implement the proposed 30-hour limit.[84] This decision is effectively sanctioned by law through the failure of the standards to deal expressly with the issue. Justified in part by an industry-funded scientific study which has

83 Animal Health Australia 2011, 7.

84 Australian Animal Welfare Standards and Guidelines 2020b.

Figure 4.2. Millions of unwanted day old male chicks are killed every year in Australia. (Animals Australia)

been criticised,[85] the outcome coincided with the preferred position of the dairy industry.[86] By contrast, a shorter TOF is supported by animal welfare organisations and, generally, by individual community members, a fact noted by the 2011 RIS in the context of describing bobby calf welfare as 'an emotive issue'.[87] This framing of legitimate concerns about animal welfare as emotive is not uncommon. The same remark was made by the Director-General of the NSW DPI to a parliamentary inquiry in relation to caged egg production.[88] As with the dairy industry, the egg industry also involves 'wastage', but the number of animals involved is many times greater. Because poultry are bred for specific purposes, the male offspring of breeder hens in the egg industry are not considered suitable for eating. The result is an estimated 12 million day-old male chicks 'culled' in Australia each year,[89] either gassed with

85 See, for example, Phillips and Petherick 2015; Caulfield 2017, 164–5.
86 Australian Dairy Farmers and Dairy Australia 2011, 3.
87 Animal Health Australia 2011, 15.
88 Evidence to the Legislative Council Select Committee on the Use of Battery Cages for Hens in the Egg Production Industry, Parliament of NSW, Sydney, 13 August 2019, 2 (Scott Hansen).
89 Burgess 2017, 35.

carbon monoxide or macerated alive, as approved by s 14.1 of the *Model Code of Practice for the Welfare of Animals: Domestic Poultry.*

When very large numbers of animals are involved, as is the case with intensive industries, the risks to their welfare in the course of routine husbandry practices, transportation and slaughter are exacerbated. For example, reports of federal government veterinarians for the period March to August 2019 identified cruelty in the transport of sheep and cattle to Victorian export abattoirs. On arrival, some cattle and sheep 'were unable to bear their own weight and a small number were so debilitated that they died during transportation or had to be put down.'[90] Yet oversight of compliance with animal welfare standards is generally minimal. This is suggested by departmental advice that enforcement of the land transport standards was unlikely to increase government costs significantly.[91] As noted in previous chapters, an informal approach to enforcement tends to be favoured by regulatory agencies but the view that early intervention and other prevention methods work appears to be at odds with the serious animal cruelty uncovered by animal activists. An example is the plunging of still-conscious chickens into boiling water after inadequate stunning in a Melbourne poultry processing plant, the footage of which prompted the food safety regulator, PrimeSafe, to take enforcement action and increase regulatory oversight.[92] PrimeSafe also referred the matter to Agriculture Victoria who enforce the state's animal welfare laws. No further action was taken against the company, however, due to an unwillingness of some witnesses to participate and the remedial action already undertaken as required by PrimeSafe.[93] Notably, the problem only came to the attention of authorities as a result of footage taken secretly by animal activists, despite the fact that the processor had been audited four times in the previous 12 months.[94] Similarly, in 2012, secret footage revealed shocking cruelty to animals in a NSW abattoir even though no problems of that nature had been identified by the regulator during the four inspections in the prior year.[95]

90 Baker 2022.
91 Animal Health Australia 2008, vii.
92 McGrath 2017.
93 RSPCA Australia 2021a, 33.
94 Ibid.
95 Ibid, 18.

In addition to the problems with enforcement, these examples illustrate the fragmentation of regulatory responsibility, with a regulatory role for the federal Department of Agriculture, Water and the Environment in export-registered abattoirs and poultry processors.[96] A further complication is that audits of abattoirs and processing plants are carried out by food safety regulators for compliance with various standards whose principal focus is food hygiene. These include the *Australian Standard for the Hygienic Production and Transportation of Meat and Meat Products for Human Consumption* (AS 4696:2007), Chapter 7 of which deals with animal welfare. This is separate to the 2001 *Model Code of Practice – Livestock at Slaughtering Establishments* whose conversion into national animal welfare standards and guidelines has been delayed since 2012, with the last recorded activity in 2017. Although the Agriculture Ministers' Forum (AGMIN) announced in February 2020 that the process was due to recommence, no significant progress had been made as of January 2021, according to RSPCA Australia.[97] Meanwhile, the lack of mandatory CCTV in all slaughter establishments, as well as the lack of independent monitoring where CCTV is present, is an ongoing animal welfare concern, and in relation to poultry, one not addressed in the proposed draft standards. In 2018, more than 698 million land animals were slaughtered for meat in Australia, of which approximately 93% were poultry (chickens, ducks and turkeys).[98] Given the inherent welfare risks in the slaughter process and the enormous number of animals involved, the need for rigorous and transparent regulation should be self-evident. In March 2021, however, RSPCA Australia released a report identifying major problems with the current regulation of slaughter in Australia. These include a lack of transparency around animal welfare standards and auditing of slaughtering establishments, the failure to progress the conversion of the 2001 model code into national standards, significant jurisdictional inconsistencies in regulatory requirements, compliance

96 See RSPCA Australia 2021a for a detailed account of the regulatory schemes in both domestic and export abattoirs.

97 Ibid, 3. As of March 2022, no information is publicly available as to any further progress in converting the 2001 model code.

98 Food and Agriculture Organization of the United Nations 2018.

and enforcement actions, and the division of responsibility between food safety and animal welfare agencies.[99]

Space allowances: pig industry

Research suggests that pigs are highly sociable and cognitively complex animals, with traits similar to dogs and chimpanzees.[100] Despite this, pig farming is one of the most intensive animal farming industries, with its indoor housing systems characterised by close confinement and a barren environment.[101] As set out in Appendix 3, Table 6 of the 2008 *Model Code of Practice for Animal Welfare – Pigs*, the minimum space requirement for pregnant sows in stalls is 2.2 metres in length and 0.6 metres in width. This size is not much bigger than the pig's body and prevents the sow from turning around. Although s 4.1.5 of the 2008 Pig Code imposed a restriction on the use of sow stalls from July 2017, it still allows sows to be routinely kept in stalls for six weeks in any gestation period. This and other key code provisions have been adopted by regulation in most jurisdictions. In NSW, for example, the *Animal Welfare Code of Practice – Commercial Pig Production* is included in Sch 1 of the *Prevention of Cruelty to Animals Regulation 2012* which means its provisions are enforceable. In other jurisdictions, the equivalent provision has been included directly in the general regulations, for example Sch 2 of the *Animal Care and Protection Regulation 2012* (Qld), or in specific regulations, for example *Animal Welfare (Pig Industry) Regulations 2010* (WA). In Tasmania, however, the *Animal Welfare (Pigs) Regulations 2013* prohibits the confinement of sows in stalls except in more limited circumstances. The ACT has also prohibited the use of sow stalls, although the lack of an intensive pig industry means the move is largely symbolic.

Meanwhile, in response to changing consumer sentiment, the pig industry's peak representative body, Australian Pork Ltd (APL), in 2010 committed its members to a voluntary phase-out of sow stalls by 2017,

99 RSPCA Australia 2021a, 3, 44.
100 Marino and Colvin 2015.
101 Hemsworth et al. 2018, 3.

Figure 4.3. The law permits sows to be housed in farrowing crates for six weeks of their reproductive cycle. (Animals Australia)

although by 2019 only 80% of Australian sows were sow stall free.[102] The industry's move away from using sow stalls contradicts APL's earlier stance that sow stalls were scientifically proven to be good for pig welfare.[103] Pigs are closely confined in other ways also. Again, in relation to sows, s 4.1.7 of the code of practice permits their housing in farrowing crates for six weeks in any one reproductive cycle. Like sow stalls, farrowing crates have metal floors and are barren of any bedding, but at 2 metres by 0.5 metres are even smaller. For sows kept indoors in group housing, the code provides a minimum space allowance of 1.4 square metres per adult, although research funded by APL indicates that 'significant improvements in welfare, in terms of aggression and stress, are likely to be achieved with space allowances for gilts and sows' in the range of 2.0–2.4 square metres per sow.[104] Even with improvements to the conditions of their confinement, intensive pig farming contrasts radically with the way sows live under natural conditions. In the latter

102 Derkson 2019.
103 Caulfield 2018, 140.
104 Hemsworth et al. 2018, 4.

case, sows build nests on hillsides so excrement can run off, forage over large areas each day, and take turns watching piglets with other sows, allowing all sows to forage.[105]

Painful husbandry practices

In Chapter 1, we considered the dehorning of cattle as an example of an invasive husbandry practice which can be carried out without any lawful requirement for anaesthetic or pain relief. Other routine practices include beak trimming of chickens, castration of male calves, piglets and sheep, tail docking, and mulesing of sheep. The 2008 *Model Code of Practice for Animal Welfare – Pigs*, for example, only prohibits surgical castration without anaesthetic on male pigs over 21 days of age (s 5.6.2), despite research which 'indicates that castration in young pigs results in a short-term moderate acute stress response' and 'is likely to be painful for piglets at any age'.[106] The move to replace codes of practice with standards and guidelines, which profess to reflect current scientific knowledge, has to date done little to improve regulation of these practices. In relation to beak trimming, for example, scientific research indicates that it reduces beak function and causes pain to chicks already stressed by sorting and sexing.[107] An alternative approach is the provision of pecking blocks to allow the beak to be gradually blunted, while, if beak trimming is carried out, infrared trimming may have fewer negative effects than hot-blade trimming.[108] Yet the draft poultry standards on beak trimming initially required only the use of 'appropriate tools and methods' (SA9.14) and the removal of no more than one-third of the upper and lower beaks (SA9.15). The non-mandatory guidelines included that beak trimming should be done using an infrared beam within three days of hatching (GA9.13). The tabled draft standards require beak trimming, when undertaken in a hatchery, to be done using an infrared beam within 24 hours of hatching, with a transition

105 Rollin 2019, 154.
106 Hemsworth et al. 2018, 5.
107 Nicol et al. 2017, 55, 58.
108 Ibid, 55.

period up to 1 July 2025 (SA9.16), but allow treatment of up to 40% of the upper and lower beaks (SA9.19).

Animal welfare standards also profess to be based on 'mainstream community expectations' yet the community is typically denied access to knowledge about husbandry practices, as illustrated by the refusal to allow the ABC to broadcast the footage of the dehorning of cattle discussed in Chapter 1. This void may be filled with footage from other sources, such as that shown on Israeli television of cattle having their horns removed without anaesthetic on Western Australian cattle stations.[109] Footage of routine husbandry practices is likely to increase pressure on animal use industries to consider changing their ways. An example is mulesing, which involves the surgical removal of wrinkled skin from the tail and breech area of lambs to reduce the incidence of fly strike. This has traditionally been done without any pain relief despite acknowledgement that it is a very painful procedure with a high degree of tissue trauma.[110] Following a campaign by the People for the Ethical Treatment of Animals for an international boycott of Australian wool, the wool and sheep industry agreed to phase out mulesing by the end of 2010, a deadline subsequently abandoned.[111] During the development of the *Animal Welfare Standards and Guidelines – Sheep*, endorsed in 2016, the cessation of surgical mulesing was strongly supported by the AVA, which noted the availability of alternative methods for the management of fly strike and blowfly control, and advocated the use of approved analgesia until the practice ceased.[112] According to the accompanying RIS, the use of pain relief would provide significant welfare benefits for an estimated 4.86 million lambs each year who are subject to the 'very invasive mulesing procedure'.[113] The endorsed standards, however, allow mulesing without pain relief for sheep under six months of age, once again an outcome generally supported by industry but opposed by animal welfare organisations. Nevertheless, industry practices appear to be slowly changing, with an estimated 80% of sheep now being

109 Wahlquist 2019.
110 Tim Harding & Associates 2014, 40.
111 Sneddon 2011.
112 Sheep Standards and Guidelines Writing Group 2013, 8–9.
113 Tim Harding & Associates 2013, 75.

mulesed with pain relief,[114] although this figure is based on an industry survey, not an independent assessment. Where industry practices are changing, the law tends to follow. In Victoria, for example, cl 8(2) of the *Prevention of Cruelty to Animals Regulation 2019* requires that, from July 2020, pain relief be administered when mulesing sheep with shears.

Live exports

As the example of mulesing suggests, several factors appear to accompany improvements to farmed animal welfare where they are made. The first is increased community awareness of practices which have long been hidden from public scrutiny. Since the advent of digital technology and the widespread use of social media, this information has become much more freely available. A second factor is the pressure brought to bear on animal use industries through consumer purchasing power. The first factor is clearly applicable to live exports. The major animal welfare issues associated with this trade have been known for many decades but it is only in the last ten years or so that they have come to the attention of the wider community, often in a very graphic manner. In relation to the second factor, however, the general public is unable to exert direct pressure on live export companies because the 'product' is not marketed to Australians but is shipped overseas. This makes it even harder for community opinion to effect change, although the severity of the suffering as depicted in media reports has nonetheless wrought some improvements. A third factor influencing governments is the impact of adverse animal welfare events on the way Australia and its products are perceived in international markets. This factor also has relevance for the regulation of the live export trade.

A history of regulatory failure

The export of live animals from Australia dates back to the mid-19th century but the modern live export trade began in the mid-20th century with the mass transit of sheep to the Middle East. By the 1970s, ships

114 Ernst & Young 2019, 66.

were capable of carrying 50,000 sheep[115] and by 1988 over 7 million live sheep were being exported annually.[116] The next 30 years saw a decline in the numbers of sheep exported but the export of live cattle increased from 81,500 head of cattle to over 1 million in the same period, resulting in an increased total value of the live sheep and cattle trade.[117] From 2016 to 2020, over 7.7 million sheep and over 5 million cattle were exported live from Australia, mostly by sea, for feeder and slaughter.[118] While sheep and cattle dominate the trade, other species exported live include goats, buffalo and camels.

Awareness of major animal welfare issues accompanying the trade is longstanding. In 1980, following the death at sea of over 40,000 sheep after the ship caught fire, a report for the Australian Bureau of Animal Health identified multiple deficiencies in the trade's conduct with significant consequences for animal welfare.[119] In 1985, a Senate Select Committee concluded that:

> … if a decision were to be made on the future of the trade purely on animal welfare grounds, there is enough evidence to stop the trade. The trade is, in many respects, inimical to good animal welfare, and it is not in the interests of the animal to be transported to the Middle East for slaughter … The implementation of reforms will help to reduce but not eliminate stress, suffering and risk during transportation of sheep to the Middle East.[120]

As with the Senate Select Committee, more recent reports have acknowledged that the 'livestock export industry is uniquely and inherently risky because it deals with sentient animals along an extended production chain'.[121] Animal welfare issues arise at all points along this chain, including the loading of animals onto ships, the voyage itself, and

115 Senate Select Committee on Animal Welfare, Commonwealth Parliament 1985, 4.
116 Petrie 2019.
117 Ibid.
118 Inspector-General of Live Animal Exports 2021, 19–20.
119 Jones and Davies 2016, 59.
120 Senate Select Committee on Animal Welfare, Commonwealth Parliament 1985, xiii.
121 Keniry 2003, 34; see also Moss 2018, 48.

Figure 4.4. The Middle East is a major destination for live exports from Australia despite the additional significant animal welfare concerns associated with the voyage. (We Animals Media)

transportation and slaughter after arrival at their destinations. Problems during the voyage include heat stress and failure to eat the unfamiliar pelleted feed and are particularly acute on long haul voyages, such as sheep routinely endure to the Middle East. Issues upon arrival at the importing country include extremely rough handling, inappropriate transportation in very hot conditions, and slaughter without stunning, in abattoirs and by individuals outside the supply chain.

Notwithstanding the inherent risks, there was little regulation of the welfare aspects of the live export trade by governments throughout the 20th century. The inclusion of live animals in the provisions of the *Export Control Act 1982* (Cth) brought no substantive change and the enactment of the *Australian Meat and Industry Livestock Act 1997* and its subordinate legislation essentially enabled industry self-regulation.[122] In 2003, the ongoing toll on animal welfare came to prominent attention

122 Caulfield 2018, 182–3.

with the death of 5,691 sheep on the *Cormo Express*, nearly 10% of the sheep loaded. Rejected by Saudi officials at their original destination, the surviving sheep had been on the vessel for 80 days by the time of their discharge at an alternative country.[123] The Keniry Review established in response concluded that the legislative and administrative framework was inadequate for 'such a high-risk trade', with 'key regulatory functions under the control of an industry body'.[124] As a result, there was a regulatory shift from industry to the Commonwealth and the *Australian Standards for the Export of Livestock* (ASEL) were created to cover the conduct of the trade from the domestic sourcing of animals to their disembarkation overseas. Some key recommendations of the review were not implemented, however, including that veterinarians accompany all voyages over ten days and be employed directly by the government, not the exporters.[125] Further, while orders made under the *Australian Meat and Livestock Industry Act 1997* (Cth) required exporters to comply with ASEL, some of the old standards were unchanged in critical ways, for example space allowances.[126]

Regulatory reforms

Meanwhile, investigations by Animals Australia were starting to uncover shocking incidents of cruelty to sheep and cattle after their arrival in the Middle East. Footage from one investigation, of cattle being stabbed and beaten at a Cairo abattoir, was broadcast on the television show *60 Minutes* in 2006.[127] This resulted in the Coalition government banning the export of live cattle to Egypt until 2008.[128] But with the spotlight on the Middle East, animal welfare organisations lacked knowledge of how animals were treated in markets closer to home. In 2009, the Australian government denied a request by RSPCA Australia to observe the treatment of cattle in South-East Asian markets but an industry-organised study into cattle welfare at Indonesian abattoirs concluded

123 Keniry 2003, 29.
124 Keniry 2003, 35, 37.
125 Farmer 2011, 7–8.
126 Caulfield 2018, 183–4.
127 Carleton 2006.
128 Petrie 2019, 18.

that it was 'generally good'.[129] On 30 May 2011, the reality of that treatment was broadcast on *Four Corners*, in a program aptly titled 'A Bloody Business'.[130] In response to the footage and the resulting public outcry, the Labor government immediately suspended the live cattle trade to 11 Indonesian abattoirs, extending it to all Indonesian abattoirs on 8 June 2011. The suspension was lifted on 6 July 2011 when stricter export controls were introduced under a new regulatory framework, the Exporter Supply Chain Assurance System (ESCAS).[131] In an attempt to impose requirements on the handling of Australian animals in foreign jurisdictions, ESCAS was based on the following principles:

- control by the exporter of the whole of the supply chain;
- individual animals to be traceable at any point in the supply chain;
- all elements of the supply chain must meet OIE animal welfare standards; and
- exporter engaged third party auditing of the supply chain.

These principles were set out in the 2011 Farmer Review which recommended that they be developed for all markets for feeder and slaughter (not breeder) live animals,[132] a recommendation implemented by January 2013.[133] By contrast, the recommendation for a comprehensive review of ASEL as a matter of priority[134] was not acted upon. New draft standards were proposed by a departmental committee in 2013 but not implemented and it would take nearly a decade before a new version, ASEL 3.0, commenced operation on 1 November 2020. While acknowledging some improvements, the new standards were criticised by RSPCA Australia as falling short on key animal welfare issues, such as stocking densities.[135] Even so, the Minister for Agriculture amended the new standards just days before they were due to take effect to allow

129 Jones and Davies 2016, 26, 29.
130 Ferguson 2011.
131 Petrie 2019, 21.
132 Farmer 2011, 92.
133 Petrie 2019, 25.
134 Farmer 2011, xv.
135 RSPCA Australia 2019b.

the export of cattle under 'a reduced pen space allocation subject to ongoing performance and welfare outcomes'.[136]

ESCAS and ASEL are now incorporated into the live export regulatory framework by the *Export Control (Animals) Rules 2021* and the *Export Control Act 2020*. Although ESCAS has led to some improvements in animal welfare, extreme cruelty continues to occur as evidenced by the regulatory compliance and mortality investigations listed on the Department of Agriculture's website.[137] Most of the incidents of noncompliance have come to light through investigations by Animals Australia and other advocacy groups (and the resulting pressure on exporters to self-report), not through the work of the regulator. Behind the bland departmental references to noncompliance, the images provided by animal advocates reveal the true nature and extent of animal suffering.[138] In 2015, the government admitted that 'it is not known how well the recorded non-compliance rate reflects the true non-compliance rate' or 'what proportion of non-compliance is detected and reported'.[139] In 2018, the Moss Review noted that the regulator lacked oversight of significant aspects of the supply chain, with considerable reliance on animal welfare organisations to alert the department to instances of noncompliance.[140] In any case, compliance with ESCAS does not ensure the absence of suffering. While ESCAS requires exporters to meet OIE animal welfare standards (guidelines), these are minimal and do not, for example, mandate pre-slaughter stunning.

Nor has the introduction of ESCAS prevented major animal welfare problems arising at earlier points in the supply chain. In April 2018, graphic footage filmed by a whistleblower was broadcast on *60 Minutes* showing sheep cooking alive and dying slowly in their own excrement on voyages to the Middle East during the northern hemisphere summer of 2017.[141] One of these voyages had already been the subject of an investigation by the Department of Agriculture because, under

136 Australia, Department of Agriculture, Water and the Environment 2020a.

137 Australia, Department of Agriculture, Water and the Environment 2021c; Australia, Department of Agriculture, Water and the Environment 2021d.

138 Animals Australia n.d.

139 Commonwealth of Australia 2015, 17.

140 Moss 2018, 30, 35.

141 Bartlett 2018.

Figure 4.5. Documented by a crew member turned whistleblower, footage of sheep suffering on five separate voyages to the Middle East in 2017 led to public outrage and some regulatory changes. (Animals Australia)

ASEL, the government must be notified if the mortality rate is equal to or greater than the reportable level. At the time of the voyage, the reportable level for sheep was 2% and the mortality rate on the voyage was 3.76%. According to the department's original investigation report, the sheep had been prepared and transported consistently with ASEL, with the high death rate attributed to heat stress. At that time, the only consequence for the exporter, Emanuel Exports, was a requirement to review and comply with a heat event management plan for their next consignment of sheep to the Middle East using the same vessel.[142]

In response to the graphic footage and the subsequent public outcry, the government introduced a series of measures, including a review into the regulatory capability and culture of the Department of Agriculture and Water Resources (the Moss Review) and another into the conditions for the export of sheep to the Middle East during the

142 Australia, Department of Agriculture, Water and the Environment 2017. Note, the original report has been updated. For a copy of the original version, and other useful documentation, see Vets Against Live Exports n.d.

northern hemisphere summer by a former industry-employed vet (the McCarthy Review). In August 2018, the Department of Agriculture cancelled the live export licence of Emanuel Exports and, a month later, the licence of its wholly owned subsidiary, EMS Rural Exports,[143] a rare step for a regulator characterised by its failure to impose meaningful sanctions.[144] These licence cancellations were challenged by the export companies in the Administrative Appeals Tribunal. In November 2021, the tribunal set aside the decisions to cancel the licences and replaced them with decisions to suspend the licences from the date of their original suspension (prior to their cancellation) in 2018 until 3 December 2021. The tribunal found that Emanuel Exports breached its licence conditions and that its 'conduct, through its previous managing director, showed bad faith and a serious lack of integrity', with consequent harm to thousands of sheep. Nevertheless, the tribunal was satisfied that Emanuel Exports 'has implemented the policies and systems necessary to redeem itself and satisfy us that it is a body corporate of integrity and competence'.[145]

Meanwhile, in 2019 the WA Department of Primary Industries and Regional Development charged Emanuel Exports and two of its directors with cruelty to animals under the *Animal Welfare Act 2002* (WA).[146] The prosecution followed an 18-month investigation and advice from the State Solicitor's Office that the operation of the state law can co-exist with federal live export laws.[147] In a preliminary hearing in June 2021, the magistrate ruled that application of the state's animal welfare laws is not necessarily inconsistent with Commonwealth laws in relation to live exports.[148] At the federal level, the Moss Review found that the Department of Agriculture's focus on facilitating trade and industry deregulation appeared to have

143 *Emanuel Exports v Department of Agriculture* [2021] AATA 4393, [3].

144 Inspector-General of Live Animal Exports 2020, 39; Jones and Davies 2016, 176.

145 *Emanuel Exports v Department of Agriculture* [2021] AATA 4393, [380]–[381].

146 Western Australia, *Parliamentary Debates*, Legislative Council, 6 August 2019, 4899 (Alannah MacTiernan).

147 Ibid.

148 MacTiernan 2021; *Department of Primary Industries and Regional Development v Emanuel Exports*, unreported, Magistrates Court of Western Australia (Criminal Jurisdiction), Shackleton M, 3 June 2021.

had a negative impact on its regulatory culture and recommended, among other things, the creation of an Inspector-General of Live Animal Exports to oversee its work.[149] This office was subsequently established by the *Inspector-General of Live Animal Exports Act 2019* (Cth). Notably, however, appointment to the position is made by the agriculture minister and an amendment by the Greens in the Senate was required before reference to animal welfare was included in the objects clause of the legislation. In addition, while the Moss Review acknowledged that the role of Australian Government Accredited Veterinarians (AAVs) 'appears to be inherently conflicted' due to their employment by the exporters, only a requirement for AAVs to make an annual declaration of any personal conflict of interest was recommended.[150]

The McCarthy Review's recommendations included moving away from a risk assessment based on mortality to one based on animal welfare, reducing the reportable level for sheep travelling to the Middle East from 2% to 1%, an increase in space allocation, and adjustments to the heat stress risk assessment (HSRA) model.[151] In response, the government said that it would work to implement the McCarthy Review recommendations, subject to further testing and consultation in relation to HSRA matters,[152] for which purpose an expert Technical Reference Panel was convened. The panel's final report recommended a revised HSRA model, whose implementation would effectively prevent live sheep exports to the Middle East between 1 May and 31 October.[153] The AVA also repeatedly advised the government that sheep exported to the Middle East between May and October inclusive remain susceptible to heat stress and die, regardless of stocking density.[154] Further, inadequate reductions in stocking densities and a failure to prevent voyages to the Middle East between May and October were among criticisms of the McCarthy Review by the RSPCA.[155] Nevertheless, the *Australian Meat*

149 Moss 2018, xi–xii.

150 Moss 2018, ix, 54.

151 McCarthy 2018, 8–11.

152 Australia, Department of Agriculture and Water Resources 2018.

153 Independent Heat Stress Risk Assessment Technical Reference Panel 2019; Daly 2020.

154 See, for example, Australian Veterinary Association 2019, 2.

155 RSPCA Australia 2018c.

and Live-stock Industry (Prohibition of Export of Sheep by Sea to Middle East – Northern Summer) Order 2020 (the Northern Summer Order) made under s 17 of the *Australian Meat and Livestock Industry Act 1997* prohibited these exports only for the period 1 June to 14 September, with a slightly longer period for voyages to Qatar and Oman.

In its first year of operation, the utility of the Northern Summer Order as an animal welfare measure was put to the test via s 11 which allows an application for an exemption from the prohibition period. On 2 June 2020, the Department of Agriculture rejected an application to export 56,000 sheep when the original voyage was delayed due to an outbreak of Covid-19 among crew members. A second application, however, was granted to the same exporter by the department's deputy secretary on 13 June. Subject to various conditions which reduced the number of sheep, this shipment was authorised to load until midnight on 17 June. Despite the acknowledged animal welfare risk, greater weight was given to the 'significant financial and ongoing trade impact' on the business operations of the exporter and associated entities, the exporter's relationship with its trading partners, Australia's trade relations with Kuwait and the Gulf region, and even the impact on Kuwaiti food security.[156] By contrast, while the deputy secretary 'gave some weight' to the submissions from Animals Australia, RSPCA Australia, the AVA and animal welfare expert Professor Phillips, he did not consider them to be 'representative of the community as a whole'; nor did he believe that 'granting an exemption two months after the Northern Summer Order commenced would, in and of itself, undermine public confidence in the regulatory framework, the Department's administration of that framework, and the live animal export industry'.[157] In relation to animal welfare, the deputy secretary found that the cumulative impact of measures proposed by the exporter and other conditions would result in a risk of heat stress commensurate with that posed by voyages departing in May 2020.[158] In his review of the department's progress in implementing the recommendations of the Moss Review, the Inspector-General of Live Animal Exports noted that the heat stress scores during

156 Australia, Department of Agriculture, Water Resources and the Environment 2020b, 9.

157 Ibid, 5.

158 Ibid, 9.

the exempted voyage 'appear to confirm that exporting sheep to the Middle East during the northern summer prohibition period results in a poor animal health and welfare outcome for many of the animals, despite the additional risk mitigations undertaken by the exporter'.[159]

In December 2021, the Department of Agriculture released a draft report which reviewed live sheep exports by sea to, or through, the Middle East during the northern hemisphere summer. The draft recommendations increase the absolute prohibition periods for Persian Gulf destinations, other than Kuwait, but decrease these periods for Red Sea destinations and Kuwait.[160] In addition, the draft recommendations include a conditional prohibition period for most destinations which would allow the export of sheep during absolute prohibition periods provided additional conditions are met. In relation to Kuwait, for example, it is proposed to reduce the current prohibition period (1 June to 14 September) by seven days (1 June to 7 September), with a conditional prohibition from 1 June to 14 June.[161] Kuwait is one of Australia's largest export markets for live animals and in 2020–21 was the destination of 52% of all exported sheep.[162] The draft report was released for public consultation eight days before Christmas with a closing date of 28 January 2022. The Department justified this holiday timeframe by the need to 'give farmers, exporters and customers certainty and enable them to plan for the 2022 Northern Hemisphere summer'.[163]

Reform or rationalisation?

Regulatory changes since 2011 have brought some improvement to the welfare of the millions of animals exported live every year from Australia. But these changes have occurred only after evidence of terrible suffering has come to public attention through the work of animal advocates and whistleblowers; even then, the resulting reforms have departed in significant ways from the recommendations of scientists and failed to ensure animal welfare in a trade still recognised

159 Inspector-General of Live Animal Exports 2020, 47.
160 Department of Agriculture, Water and the Environment 2021f, 9.
161 Ibid, 14–15.
162 Livecorp, Industry Overview n.d. https://livecorp.com.au/industry.
163 Australia, Department of Agriculture, Water and the Environment 2021e.

as inherently risky.[164] The limited nature of the regulatory reforms is exemplified by the last-minute amendment to ASEL 3.0 and the developments in relation to live sheep exports during the northern hemisphere summer. The reasoning of the deputy secretary in granting the second application for an exemption provides stark illustration of the conflict of interests when responsibility for regulating animal welfare resides with departments of agriculture. His belief that the concerns of animal welfare organisations are not widely shared is not supported by the evidence. Following the broadcast of 'A Bloody Business', the Department of Agriculture noted a 556% increase in the volume of ministerial correspondence, most of it related to live exports.[165] In 2019, the department acknowledged that the footage shown in April 2018 had 'shocked the Australian community and undermined public confidence in the live export trade'.[166] Surveys provide further evidence of strong community concern, notwithstanding some differences in results. A nationwide survey commissioned by RSPCA Australia in April 2018 found that around three out of four Australians want live exports to end,[167] while research commissioned by the Department of Agriculture found that poor animal welfare in live export ships was the 'top driver' of community concern about farming in Australia.[168]

The deputy secretary's statement of reasons also highlights the cumulative effect of reforms which fall short of measures originally promised. Even without the granting of an exemption, the prohibition of voyages between 1 June and 14 September in the Northern Summer Order fails to give effect to the advice of the Technical Reference Panel and other experts. Accordingly, an assessment that the risk of heat stress is commensurate with that posed by voyages departing in May is scarcely reassuring, even if accurate. The exemption also jars with the department's own conclusion in 2019 that the welfare benefits of additional space allowances are limited if 'ambient temperatures are

---

164 Moss 2018, 48. For a comprehensive and readable account of the history and politics of Australian live exports and its animal welfare failures, see Jones and Davies 2016.

165 Australia, Department of Agriculture, Fisheries and Forestry 2012, 37.

166 Australia, Department of Agriculture 2019b, 9.

167 RSPCA Australia 2018d. See also Sinclair et al. 2018.

168 Futureye Pty. Ltd. 2018, 33.

very hot, as they can be during June to September (inclusive)'.[169] Meanwhile, in response to the *60 Minutes* footage, the government had implemented a policy of requiring independent observers to accompany live export voyages. On 17 March 2020, this initiative was suspended due to the coronavirus pandemic, although an independent observer was placed on the exempted voyage. Even when activated, however, this policy's utility is limited because the observers are not required to accompany every voyage and they are employees of the Department of Agriculture, not independent animal welfare experts. In addition, only brief summary reports are published, often after lengthy delays, with the department denying RSPCA Australia access to relevant video footage on the basis that it could lead to 'unfounded or unwarranted adverse criticism of the live animal export industry as a whole'.[170]

Even with these limitations, the summary reports provide evidence of continuing significant animal welfare problems, as illustrated by a detailed analysis of the independent observer summaries on live cattle export voyages to China between July 2018 and December 2019.[171] The findings of the analysis include:

- food shortages and limited food access in 27% of voyages, including food deprivation resulting from breaches of ASEL or ASEL deficiencies;
- water supply issues in 43% of voyages, including problems with water quality and water deprivation;
- cattle exposed to extreme temperatures in 51% of voyages, with heat stress specifically noted in 38% of the summary reports;
- poor pen conditions and insufficient space in 81% of voyages, with insufficient bedding under ASEL on 41% of voyages;
- health issues on all voyages, including eye disease, pneumonia and lameness; and
- instances of poor animal welfare and/or mortality at discharge in 54% of voyages.[172]

---

169 Australia, Department of Agriculture 2019a, 20.
170 Bourke 2019.
171 Hing et al. 2021.
172 Ibid, 4–14, 17.

The analysis also highlights other significant concerns, such as the lack of a shipboard veterinarian on nearly 60% of the voyages and the routine conclusion in summary reports that no negative effects on health or animal welfare were observed despite the frequency of the kind of impacts listed above.[173] In addition, the analysis illustrates the fallacy of equating low mortality with good animal welfare. In the case of one voyage, the summary report documented extreme suffering due to food and water deprivation, heat stress and poor pen conditions yet the mortality was relatively low.[174]

Government and industry response

A degree of regulatory reform has been embraced by an industry keenly aware, as is the Department of Agriculture, that more footage of animal suffering like that shown in 2018 risks the future viability of the live export trade.[175] In December 2018, the Australian Live Exporters Council announced its intention to implement a voluntary moratorium on the sheep trade to the Middle East during June, July and August 2019, five months before it was legislated by government. This initiative has since been used by industry to protest its animal welfare credentials, even as it sought to contravene its own prohibition.[176] Similarly, the regulatory framework imposed after the broadcast of 'A Bloody Business' is now incorporated into a narrative that industry cares about animal welfare.[177] Where cruelty is exposed, it is framed as an exception to a system that otherwise functions well, even, for example, in the case of thousands of sheep brutally slaughtered in Pakistan in 2012 which was described as a 'hiccup in the system'.[178] Another more recent example is footage allegedly showing Australian cattle being cruelly slaughtered in

173 Ibid, 14.
174 Ibid, 12.
175 See, for example, Australia, Department of Agriculture 2019a, 21.
176 Kelly 2020.
177 See, for example, Jones and Davies 2016, 186.
178 Ellis 2013b, 359. This shipment was the subject of another *Four Corners* program, 'Another Bloody Business', broadcast on the ABC on 5 November 2012. In 2018, a former manager of the live export company responsible for the shipment was sentenced for falsifying documents critical to the animal welfare outcomes: AAP 2018.

export-approved Indonesian abattoirs in 2020, nearly a decade after the *Four Corners* exposé led to the introduction of ESCAS. Once again, the footage was obtained by Animals Australia, not the industry regulator; once again, industry leadership described the images as 'distressing' while characterising the 'unfortunate' situation as an exception.[179] This complaint is still under investigation by the Department of Agriculture, as is another lodged in June 2021 by People for the Ethical Treatment of Animals who obtained 'shocking' footage of cruelty to cattle in Indonesian facilities.[180]

Despite continuing critical breaches of ESCAS, the regulatory response remains muted. Following a report in July 2021 of noncompliance at a Jordanian abattoir, RSPCA Australia called for the export company's licence to be stripped in light of its record of 44 previous breaches of ESCAS over the past eight years.[181] The 2021 report is still under investigation but the Department of Agriculture 'did not require any further immediate action' for breaches involving the same company in 2020, also in relation to sheep in Jordan. Instead, the company was simply required 'to develop and implement a more robust management plan' for 2021, even though the breaches constituted 'critical non-compliance'.[182] Meanwhile, the expansion of live export markets has been aggressively pursued, including in countries with poor animal welfare standards.[183] At the same time, the government seeks to avoid accountability through the adoption of a narrative which frames the Department of Agriculture as an independent regulator. Concerns directed to the responsible minister about animal welfare are routinely referred to the 'independent' regulator, in defiance of both the department's manifest conflict of interests and the doctrine of ministerial responsibility. This narrative is also at odds with the eleventh-hour amendment to ASEL 3.0 which deprived cattle of access to the slightly increased space allowance; although a decision of the

179 Daly 2020.

180 Barrett 2021; Australia, Department of Agriculture, Water and the Environment 2021d.

181 RSPCA Australia 2021b.

182 Australia, Department of Agriculture, Water and the Environment 2021d, Report #179, 6–8.

183 Humphries and Goodfellow 2016.

minister, it was left to the department to announce the change.[184] Having regard to all of the above, regulatory improvements over the last decade arguably provide an example of Francione's view that 'reforming exploitation through welfarist means will simply facilitate the indefinite perpetuation of such exploitation'.[185]

Contested concepts, competing values

Weak standards, inadequate enforcement and lack of transparency characterise all farmed animal welfare, whether in relation to live exports or other domestic industries. Underpinning these issues is the lack of independent regulation which enables the privileging of certain industries over the concerns of animal welfare experts and the broader public.[186] Despite the Productivity Commission's recommendation to establish an independent animal welfare commission, any conflict is routinely denied by those with an interest in existing arrangements. In 2019, in evidence to a Legislative Council inquiry into animal cruelty laws, representatives of the NSW Farmers Association first emphasised their support for the principle of regulatory impartiality, then strongly opposed the creation of an independent office of animal welfare in favour of the DPI's continuing administrative responsibility. This anomalous position was achieved by linking partiality with political advocacy or public campaigns, while describing the DPI as having a vested interest in animal welfare, not a conflict of interests.[187] A similar alignment of interests was evident in a 2020 parliamentary inquiry in Victoria into the impact of animal rights activism on agriculture.[188] This inquiry was

184 Australia, Department of Agriculture, Water and the Environment 2020a.

185 Francione 1995, 257.

186 The selective nature of this support is illustrated by the export of thousands of sheep under the exemption to the Northern Summer Order at the same time that WA abattoirs were threatened with closure due to the critically low level of the state's sheep flock: Mercer and Edwards 2020.

187 Evidence to the Legislative Council Select Committee Inquiry into Animal Cruelty Laws, Parliament of NSW, Sydney, 13 February 2020, 12 (James McDonald), 17 (Annabel Johnson).

188 Legislative Council Economic and Infrastructure Committee, Parliament of Victoria 2020.

conducted by the Legislative Council's Economy and Infrastructure Committee which stated that:

> The Committee understands that Agriculture Victoria's two roles of promoting the industry and enforcing animal welfare standards could be seen as contradictory. However, it agrees with Agriculture Victoria that the roles often complement each other. There is no evidence showing that Agriculture Victoria has put the economic interests of the animal agriculture industry ahead of the welfare interests of animals.[189]

The belief that the roles of industry promotion and animal welfare regulation are complementary rests in part on the assertion that 'animal welfare and economic health are strongly linked', as Agriculture Victoria submitted to the inquiry.[190] Echoing the opinion of the Director-General of the NSW DPI,[191] this view is asserted despite scientific evidence that animals can maintain their productivity while in a poor state of welfare.[192] In this way, the justification of regulatory preferences by industry and government returns us to the concept of animal welfare and the complex role of science with which the chapter commenced. Different understandings of animal welfare inform different kinds of research, the purpose for which it is undertaken, and by whom, as well as the weight attached to various findings.[193] Veterinary ethicist Bernard Rollin is emphatic: '*sound science does not determine your concept of welfare; rather, your concept of welfare determines what counts as sound science!*'[194] In turn, concepts of animal welfare are influenced by normative assumptions and ethical frameworks,[195] all of which operate within a broader socio-economic and political context.

---

189 Ibid, 108.

190 Ibid, 107.

191 Evidence to Legislative Council Select Committee on the Use of Battery Cages for Hens in the Egg Production Industry, NSW Parliament, Sydney, 13 August 2019, 4 (Scott Hansen).

192 See, for example, Veit and Browning 2021, 13; Tim Harding & Associates 2017, vi; Webster 2005, 9.

193 See Caulfield 2018 for a critique of the use of science by Australian animal industries.

194 Rollin 2019, 159. Emphasis in the original.

195 Schmidt 2011, 167.

As the prolonged process of developing welfare standards for poultry highlights, science provides necessary and important data but cannot of itself resolve inherent value conflicts. For this reason, we will return to ethical considerations in the final chapter when we reflect on some of the regulatory issues encountered here through the lens of various theories about the moral significance of animals.

5
Animals Used for Entertainment, Sport and Recreation

> *Being a hunter and fisherman, the idea of sentience goes too far and gives certain groups the ability to attempt to shut down hobbies such as fishing, horse racing and hunting.*[1]

Animals are used for entertainment, sport and recreation in a variety of settings, including some in which gambling is an integral part. These activities involve native and exotic animals, domesticated animals and wild animals. They are regulated by a confusing array of provisions and enforced by a wide range of agencies, including those with conflicting functions. Regulatory inconsistencies abound, both intrastate and interstate. Within jurisdictions, the extent of animal protection depends upon the species of animal and the activity regulated, while some activities are banned in some jurisdictions but allowed in others, for example recreational duck hunting. Below we consider some key welfare problems associated with using animals for entertainment, sport and recreation, and identify some of the deficiencies in the regulation of these settings. Once again, these weaknesses reflect regulatory characteristics found across all animal use sectors. The significant animal welfare

1 Survey respondent. Victoria, Department of Jobs, Precincts and Regions 2021, 9.

issues associated with many recreational and sporting animal uses also highlight the problematic nature of the concept of necessity which forms the basis of animal welfare legislation.

Exhibited animals

The National Implementation Plan for the (now defunct) AAWS stated that national standards for zoo animals were due for completion in 2011 and expected to be referenced in state and territory legislation in 2012.[2] It was only in April 2019, however, that the Agriculture Ministers' Forum endorsed the *Australian Animal Welfare Standards and Guidelines: Exhibited Animals – General*, plus five separate standards and guidelines for specific animal groups. The purpose of these standards is the specification of uniform national welfare standards to replace the existing laws governing exhibited animals which differ between the states and territories.[3] As with the standards for farmed animals, the national standards are intended to be adopted or incorporated by regulation in each jurisdiction but this has not yet occurred.[4] Moreover, while the endorsed standards and guidelines apply to all vertebrate animals kept at facilities for exhibition purposes, such as zoos and wildlife parks, they do not apply to circuses, mobile exhibits or animals kept for racing and sporting events. Despite significant support for the inclusion of circuses and mobile exhibits, the RIS advises that this request was 'outside the scope of the standards development process'.[5] Accordingly, even after the adoption of the endorsed national standards by all jurisdictions, assuming this occurs, the regulation of some exhibited animals will continue to lack uniformity.

---

2 Australia, Department of Agriculture, Water and the Environment 2011.
3 Harding and Rivers 2019, 1.
4 For a progress report on their implementation, see Australian Animal Welfare Standards and Guidelines, Exhibited Animals at http://www.animalwelfarestandards.net.au/exhibited-animals/.
5 Harding and Rivers 2019, 13.

Inconsistent and fragmented regulation

Pending adoption of the national standards in each jurisdiction, the welfare of exhibited animals is regulated by state and territory laws which differ widely in their content, application and status. Licensing systems in most jurisdictions separately regulate the keeping of native and exotic animals, the former under nature conservation laws and the latter under vertebrate pest management legislation.[6] In two jurisdictions, specific exhibited animals legislation has been enacted which covers native and exotic species. In addition, the principal animal welfare Acts apply generally to exhibited animals but, as with other animal use sectors, there may be relevant exemptions and defences. Some jurisdictions have codes of practice or standards governing exhibited animals but their coverage is mostly not comprehensive and their legal status varies. The following brief reference to key state and territory legislative instruments illustrates the extent of regulatory fragmentation and inconsistency.

In the ACT, animals kept for exhibition purposes are covered by the general provisions of the *Animal Welfare Act 1992* and *Animal Welfare Regulation 2001*. Under ss 52–53 of the Act, it is an offence to conduct a circus or travelling zoo without a permit or to use a prohibited animal, defined by s 51 as a bear, elephant, giraffe, primate (other than a human) or feline (other than a domestic cat) or an animal prescribed by regulation. The effect of this and cognate provisions is to ban exotic animals in circuses in the ACT, the only jurisdiction to do so. In South Australia, the *Animal Welfare Regulations 2012* mandate compliance with the *South Australian Code of Practice for the Welfare of Animals in Circuses 1997* which is a prescribed code of practice for the purposes of s 43 of the *Animal Welfare Act 1985*. This section provides that nothing in the Act renders unlawful anything done in accordance with a prescribed code of practice. In Western Australia, cl 6(1) of the *Animal Welfare (General) Regulations 2003* includes the code of practice for exhibited animals and the code of practice for the conduct of circuses in the list of codes adopted under s 94(2)(d) of the *Animal Welfare Act 2002*. Compliance with these codes of practice provides a defence to a charge of animal cruelty under s 19(1) of the WA Act.

---

6 Ibid, 6.

According to their prefaces, these WA codes are based, respectively, on the *General Standards for Exhibiting Animals in New South Wales* and the *Standards for Exhibiting Circus Animals in New South Wales*. These, and other relevant NSW standards, are made under s 14 of the *Exhibited Animals Protection Act 1986* and cl 8 of the *Exhibited Animals Protection Regulation 2021*. Under the proposed NSW reforms, however, the provisions governing exhibited animals would be incorporated into a single legislative framework for animal welfare. The only other jurisdiction to have separate legislation covering exhibited animals is Queensland, with the *Exhibited Animals Act 2015* and the *Exhibited Animals Regulation 2016*. Also, as noted above, some jurisdictions have relevant regulations or codes of practice under legislation primarily concerned with other matters, such as nature conservation. In Tasmania, for example, the *Wildlife (Exhibited Animals) Regulations 2010* are made under the *Nature Conservation Act 2002*.

Justifications

In addition to inconsistencies in and between the existing regulatory frameworks, the RIS identified significant gaps in animal welfare standards in all or most jurisdictions in a wide range of matters, including enclosures, dietary and water requirements, health and wellbeing, and euthanasia.[7] As the RIS notes, providing an appropriate environment for some animals can be very costly;[8] at the same time, the risks to animal welfare are increased by commercial pressures which encourage facilities to keep a wider range of exotic animals and to introduce interactive programs for visitors.[9] While the RIS acknowledges the heightened risk in exhibiting non-domestic animals who 'have evolved to survive in a particular environment' to which they are highly adapted,[10] the endorsed national standards are predicated on the appropriateness of keeping both domestic and wild animals captive for exhibition purposes. In a nod to the broader debate, the RIS refers to 'an ethical argument that "The continued existence of zoos

7 Ibid, 23.
8 Ibid, 22.
9 Ibid, 23.
10 Ibid, 22.

and their good purposes such as conservation, science, education and recreation can be ethically justified only if zoos guarantee the welfare of their animals"'.[11] In fact, the quote incorporated in this statement is taken from the abstract of an article on zoo animal welfare in which the author posits that the '[e]thical justification for the existence of zoos is questionable'.[12] Nevertheless, the reference to 'good purposes' suggests the need to examine a range of claims about the contributions of animal exhibits, in addition to animal welfare issues.

According to the RIS, the exhibition of animals benefits the wider public, as well as individual visitors, because of its contributions to the economy, conservation, education and biosecurity.[13] In summarising the benefits, however, the RIS relies on the findings of a 2009 consultant's report commissioned by the former Australasian Regional Association of Zoological Parks and Aquaria (now the Zoo and Aquarium Association).[14] In turn, these findings draw heavily, though not exclusively, on zoo survey data and/or information gathered from zoo visits in relation to 30 of the total 107 zoos in Australia at that time.[15] While the participating zoos represented a wide cross-section of Australian exhibits, the non-participants were mainly small-scale, privately owned zoos which 'make a minimal contribution to the total conservation, education and other economic and social output of the total zoo sector'.[16] Accordingly, the reliance in the RIS on this data underplays the extent of the exhibited animal industry which contributes little or nothing in the way of public benefits.

This is not the only problem with the incorporation of the 2009 data. The finding that more Australians visit zoos than any other form of cultural entertainment except movies[17] suggests their popularity as a recreational activity but reveals nothing about their educational value. The consultant's report, however, notes a 'very strong commitment to student and visitor education' in all but one of the zoos visited and cites

11 Ibid, 21.
12 Wickins-Drazilova 2006, 27.
13 Harding and Rivers 2019, 18–19.
14 Harding and Rivers 2019, 19; Aegis Consulting Australia and Applied Economics 2009.
15 Beri et al. 2010, 193.
16 Ibid.
17 Aegis Consulting Australia and Applied Economics 2009, 3.

a zoo survey which 'indicates that 83% of visitors discovered new things they didn't know about before visiting the zoo'.[18] While it might seem surprising if it were otherwise, these further findings tell us nothing about the educational content or value of zoo visits or the formal school programs some zoos develop, in terms of animal welfare or conservation. On the contrary, the consultant's report notes that 'education program evaluation is not highly developed amongst zoos', both in Australia and globally.[19] Although the 2009 report claims investment by Australian zoos in new research in relation to conservation education,[20] the RIS cites no references in support of this despite its publication a decade later. The lack of information about the educational activities, if any, of those animal exhibits which declined to participate in the consultant's study is a further troubling omission.

In addition to education, wildlife conservation has increasingly become a justification for zoos. According to the RIS, the significant value the community places on conservation is reflected in the Australian government's ratification of international treaties concerning biodiversity and endangered species, as well as state and federal regulation of threatened species and habitat protection.[21] Yet as we will see in Chapter 6, these state and federal laws fail to protect native wildlife in significant ways,[22] which suggests that governments have to date placed little value on conservation as a public benefit. Nevertheless, some zoos do engage in conservation programs, and in some cases have successfully claimed these activities as evidence that their purposes are not primarily commercial. In the *Asian Elephants* case,[23] for example, three animal welfare organisations challenged the decision of the federal Minister for Environment and Heritage to issue permits for the importation by Melbourne Zoo and Sydney's Taronga Zoo of eight Asian elephants from Thailand. Under Part 13A of the EPBC Act it is an offence to import certain species without a permit, which must not be

18 Ibid, 5.
19 Ibid, 5, 52.
20 Ibid, 5.
21 Harding and Rivers 2019, 20.
22 See, for example, Samuel 2020; Australian Conservation Foundation 2020.
23 *Re International Fund for Animal Welfare (Australia) Pty Ltd and Minister for Environment and Heritage* (2005) 41 AAR 508; (2006) 42 AAR 262.

issued unless the minister is satisfied as to certain matters set out in the Act and Regulations. The case was heard by the Administrative Appeals Tribunal, which, among other things, had to determine:

- whether the zoos were suitably equipped to manage, confine and care for the animals, including meeting their behavioural and biological needs (the welfare requirement); and
- whether the elephants were being imported for the purposes of conservation breeding or propagation and not primarily for commercial purposes.

In its judgment, the tribunal acknowledged that the welfare requirement was the matter which caused it the greatest difficulty.[24] The expert evidence was conflicting, with different perspectives put forward according to whether the expert witness had been employed in zoos or involved with animals in the wild or in larger wildlife parks. While the tribunal conceded at [72] that elephants 'walk long distances on a daily basis in the wild', they found at [93] that the space available in the zoos, while not large, was adequate to satisfy the statutory requirements, having regard to the proposed training and enrichment programs. In so deciding, the tribunal took into account at [4] 'that the welfare requirement implies care and management in circumstances of confinement' and 'that the phrase "meeting the behavioural and biological needs of the animals" does not require natural conditions but assumes captivity and the meeting of the needs other than by reproducing the conditions found in nature'. In relation to the purposes of the importation, the tribunal had regard to the objects and functions of the zoos, as set out in the statutes which established them, as well as to their operating costs, to conclude at [112] that:

> … we do not think that the primary activities of the zoos involve commercial purposes. Their purposes are education, research, breeding and so on. Education involves exhibition … The fact that zoos seek to defray their costs and even to maximise, by earning income, the amount of grant money they can use to further their

---

24 *Re International Fund for Animal Welfare (Australia) Pty Ltd and Minister for Environment and Heritage* (2005) 41 AAR 508, 524, [62].

> objects, including the exhibition of animals, does not seem to us to make any part of their activities, let alone the import of animals which will be exhibited, a commercial purpose.

While accepting that part of the zoos' motivation for importing the elephants was the likely increase in visitor numbers, the tribunal at [114] was 'satisfied that the importing of the elephants is not primarily motivated by earning more income at all' but substantially for the purpose of the breeding program. Having come to these conclusions, and with regard to other relevant matters, the tribunal decided that replacement permits should be issued, with some additional conditions in relation to the elephants' welfare.[25] Apart from the merits or otherwise of the tribunal's assessment of the animal welfare requirement, this decision suggests the irony of the significance attached to the ratification of international treaties in the RIS in relation to zoos' conservation function. This is because Part 13A was inserted into the EPBC Act in 2001 to ensure Australia's compliance with the *Convention on International Trade in Endangered Species of Wild Fauna and Flora*.[26] In a subsequent, detailed analysis, junior counsel for the applicant animal welfare organisations in the *Asian Elephants* case exposes the way in which an apparently rigorous regulatory regime, like that created by the EPBC Act, can fall short of its legislative objects.[27]

Questions also arise about the relevance of education, research and conservation purposes in the case of other animal exhibits. In cetacean displays, for example, captive dolphins live in very different conditions from their natural environment although they are intelligent, self-aware and emotionally complex animals with a capacity for self-recognition similar to humans and great apes.[28] According to RSPCA Australia, these highly restrictive settings limit the utility of studies relating to captive dolphins and there are 'no formal scientific research programs associated with dolphinariums in Australia'.[29] While the ongoing captivity of rescued dolphins might be necessary if they are genuinely

---

25 *Re International Fund for Animal Welfare (Australia) Pty Ltd and Minister for Environment and Heritage* (2006) 42 AAR 262.

26 Allars 2007, 329.

27 Ibid.

28 RSPCA Australia 2019a, 9.

29 Legislative Council Portfolio Committee No 4, Parliament of NSW 2020, 48–9.

unfit to be released after rehabilitation, breeding from captive dolphins cannot be justified on the basis of conservation as bottlenose dolphins are not endangered in the wild.[30] In evidence to a NSW parliamentary inquiry into the exhibition of exotic animals, the managing director of Dolphin Marine Conservation Park stated that they had ceased breeding dolphins and did not oppose legislation to prohibit future breeding.[31] In February 2021, the *Biodiversity Conservation Regulation 2017* was amended to prohibit the import or breeding of cetaceans in NSW. This leaves only one dolphin breeding facility in Australia, in Queensland.

In the case of circuses, there is no evidence of public benefits, particularly in relation to the exhibition of non-domestic species. As White puts it, '[i]f the ethical justifications for zoos are at least arguable, they are difficult to discern at all in relation to circuses using wild animals'.[32] This view is supported by a comprehensive study of the science and literature commissioned by the Welsh government to determine whether travelling circuses and other travelling animal shows meet the legislated animal welfare requirements for their captive wild animals.[33] The study found that 'the overall contribution of travelling circuses and mobile zoos to conservation and/or education is likely to be marginal, and any potential benefits are likely to be outweighed by the negative impressions generated by using wild animals for entertainment'.[34] Based on the scientific evidence, the researchers also concluded that captive wild animals do not achieve their optimal legislated animal welfare requirements in these conditions.[35] In their submission to the NSW parliamentary inquiry into the exhibition of exotic animals, RSPCA Australia referred to the Welsh study and other research to conclude that 'the requirements of circus life are not compatible with the physiological, social and behavioural needs of most animals' and that 'standards are not sufficient to adequately safeguard the welfare

30 RSPCA Australia 2019a, 16; Gray 2017, 204–5.
31 Evidence to Legislative Council Portfolio Committee No 4, Parliament of NSW, Sydney, 13 August 2020, Inquiry into Exhibition of Exotic Animals in Circuses and Exhibition of Cetaceans in NSW, 22 (Terry Goodall).
32 Cao et al. 2015, 265.
33 Dorning et al. 2016, 9.
34 Ibid, 25.
35 Ibid, 46.

of exotic animals'.[36] In July 2020, the Welsh parliament voted to ban the use of wild animals in travelling circuses from December 2020, joining an estimated 45 countries, nations or states which have taken this action.[37] Apart from the ACT, no Australian state or territory has banned circuses with exotic animal species, although over 30 councils have prohibited their use of council parklands[38] in acknowledgement of the animal welfare issues and changing community opinion. While the exhibition of exotic animals in circuses in Australia has declined, there are still two circuses in NSW in possession of exotic animals (another is authorised to display them but not currently doing so), plus two interstate-based circuses with Arabian camels authorised to travel to NSW.[39] While the NSW Legislative Council inquiry found 'that exotic animals in circuses and cetaceans exhibited in New South Wales meet the welfare requirements as set out in the current legislative and regulatory framework', it recognised that 'these welfare requirements are outdated and do not meet all community expectations'.[40]

Enforcement

Jurisdictions without comprehensive standards for exhibited animals may experience enforcement problems due to the lack of defined animal welfare requirements or because there are no departmental officers with relevant expertise.[41] Even where standards are incorporated, they may be weak and out of date, for example the *Standards for Exhibiting Circus Animals in New South Wales*. These standards have been in operation for 30 years and allow animals to be held in much smaller enclosures when travelling, which can be for up to 11 months per year.[42] A lion, for example, can be kept in a 20 square metre enclosure when travelling compared to 300 square metres in off-display housing in line with the

36 RSPCA Australia 2019a, 6.
37 RSPCA UK 2020.
38 RSPCA Australia 2019a, 6.
39 NSW Department of Primary Industries 2019, 2.
40 Legislative Council Portfolio Committee No 4, Parliament of NSW 2020, 27.
41 Harding and Rivers 2019, 33–4.
42 Evidence to Legislative Council Portfolio Committee No 4, Parliament of NSW, Sydney, 13 August 2020, Inquiry into Exhibition of Exotic Animals in Circuses and Exhibition of Cetaceans in NSW, 3–4 (Peter Day, Scott Hansen).

requirements for zoos, the rationale for the space reduction being the daily interaction and engagement of travelling circus animals with their trainers, as well as their performances.[43] This limited space takes the form of an annexe to the animal's wagon in which it can be confined for up to 18 hours each day.[44] Yet the adoption of more contemporary, mandatory national standards, while necessary, is not sufficient to guarantee animal welfare. Apart from any issues with the content of standards, their efficacy depends upon how and by whom they are regulated. In NSW, for example, the exhibited animals legislation is administered and enforced by the DPI, which advises online that routine audits, as distinct from inspections in response to a complaint, are generally carried out on an announced basis.[45] The same webpage provides no information about audit results or corrective action taken, either in response to audits or public complaints, nor is this information available under the DPI's other webpages related to exhibited animals. Where standards are weak and routine inspections prearranged, it is unsurprising if animal exhibits are generally found to be compliant.[46] While the Director-General of the DPI is assisted by an Exhibited Animals Advisory Committee established by s 6 of the *Exhibited Animals Protection Act 1986*, only one of its six members is a nominee of an animal welfare organisation.

Additionally, with the focus of public concern on larger exhibits and the display of exotic animals, smaller and less formal settings may not be a priority in terms of compliance monitoring. Mobile animal exhibits in NSW, for example, are required to comply with various matters set out in the *Standards for Exhibiting Animals at Mobile Establishments in New South Wales* (Mobile Establishment Standards), as well as the *General Standards for Exhibiting Animals.* Clause 11(1) of the Mobile Establishment Standards requires the provision of educational value which promotes appreciation of and respect for the animals and their

43 Ibid, 2 (Scott Hansen).
44 Clause 7(4) *Standards for Exhibiting Circus Animals in New South Wales.*
45 NSW Department of Primary Industries n.d. Zoo, Circus and Other Exhibited Animals.
46 Evidence to Legislative Council Portfolio Committee No 4, Parliament of NSW, Sydney, 13 August 2020, Inquiry into Exhibition of Exotic Animals in Circuses and Exhibition of Cetaceans in NSW, 10 (Peter Day). See also Gotsis 2018, 6.

environment. In the author's observation, however, it is common for no or minimal educational information to be provided by small mobile exhibits such as 'petting zoos' which are a staple of local fairs; where it is provided, the less savoury but more realistic aspects of the life of farmed animals are omitted. Animal welfare standards also appear to be breached by many of these exhibits. For example, animal enclosures have frequently been observed in hot and noisy areas of street fairs and/or with no or inadequate refuge spaces provided within the exhibit for small animals to escape constant handling by children. These practices breach cl 8(7) and (8) of the Mobile Establishment Standards.

Racing

In an echo of the live export trade, the necessity for regulatory change in the exhibited animal industry is emphasised as a means of ensuring its viability in a changing public environment. According to the RIS:

> Compliance with the proposed mandatory community-endorsed national standards is likely to reduce risks to the future viability of the industry from complaints and campaigns about poor animal welfare, loss of social licence and further regulatory restrictions on industry access to exotic animals. ... These non-financial risks to future viability of the industry are likely to be significantly greater than the minor financial costs proposed. It is apparent that the majority of the industry sees compliance with such standards as being beneficial to the industry's future viability.[47]

Concern about loss of social licence and industry viability have also featured in the racing industry, particularly in relation to greyhounds. In the case of both the greyhound racing and horse racing industries, the catalyst for regulatory change has come from the public exposure of major animal welfare issues. As with the live export trade, the revelations of cruelty have resulted from the work of animal advocates not the designated regulatory agencies.

47 Harding and Rivers 2019, 68.

Greyhound racing

NSW and Victoria are the two largest greyhound racing jurisdictions in Australia, which is one of only eight countries in the world with a commercial greyhound racing industry.[48] On 16 February 2015, horrific cruelty in the Australian industry was exposed by the ABC's *Four Corners* program.[49] Against a backdrop of the industry's public rejection of live baiting, the footage showed piglets, possums and rabbits attached live to lures and spun around trial tracks multiple times, to be chased and mauled by greyhounds. In one scene, those participating joke about an animal still alive at the end of this process; in another, a baby possum is cruelly killed, amid laughter and joking, as its mother watches on, tied to the lure. The activities covered by the *Four Corners* program spanned three states – NSW, Queensland and Victoria – and involved prominent participants in the greyhound racing industry. Significantly, the practices came to light as a result of investigations by Animals Australia and Animal Liberation Queensland, although the practice of live baiting had previously been drawn to the attention of regulators. In NSW, for example, evidence of live baiting was put before a Legislative Council Select Committee in 2014,[50] as well as information about other significant animal welfare issues in the greyhound racing industry, including overbreeding and the consequent 'wastage' of greyhounds. At the time, the Select Committee only made some minor recommendations with respect to these issues, while concluding overall that 'the incidence of greyhound cruelty and neglect is minimal'.[51]

Following the *Four Corners* program, however, there was a very different response, as events in NSW illustrate. The board members and CEO of Greyhound Racing NSW (GRNSW) resigned and a Special Commission of Inquiry was established, headed by former High Court justice Michael McHugh, to investigate governance, integrity and animal welfare issues in the NSW industry. Despite the illegality of live baiting, the commission found that a significant number of trainers engaged in the practice, and that even non-participants must have

48 McHugh 2016, 107–8.

49 Meldrum-Hanna 2015.

50 Legislative Council Select Committee on Greyhound Racing in NSW, Parliament of NSW 2014, 111–12.

51 Ibid, 99.

known it was occurring.[52] But this was by no means the only problem. The commission concluded that the industry had lost the trust of the community and other stakeholders because, as set out in its report, it:

- has implicitly condoned as well as caused, the unnecessary deaths of tens of thousands of healthy greyhounds;
- has failed to demonstrate that in the future it will be able to reduce the deaths of healthy greyhounds to levels the community could tolerate;
- has engaged in the barbaric practice of live baiting;
- has caused and will continue to cause injuries to greyhounds that range from minor to catastrophic;
- has treated greyhounds as dispensable commercial commodities;
- has deceived the community concerning the extent of injuries and deaths caused during race meetings;
- has preferred the commercial interests of the industry to the animal welfare interests of greyhounds;
- has exported greyhounds to race in places such as Macau where animal welfare standards are very poor; and
- has ignored or failed to recognise that the industry has obligations to the community that go beyond its strictly legal obligations.[53]

As a result, the commission recommended that 'the Parliament of New South Wales should consider whether the industry has lost its social licence and should no longer be permitted to operate in NSW'. In the event of the continuation of the industry, however, the commission made a further 79 recommendations as to its regulation.[54] In response to these findings, the then NSW Premier Mike Baird announced that greyhound racing would be banned in NSW from July 2017, with an assistance package to be provided to industry. In August 2016, the Greyhound Racing Prohibition Bill was passed by the NSW Parliament, despite opposition from some National MPs, the Labor Party and the Shooters, Fishers and Farmers Party. Two months later, however, Premier Baird reversed the decision to ban greyhound racing, claiming

52 McHugh 2016, 57–8.
53 Ibid, 18.
54 Ibid, 22–9.

that community feedback indicated he had got it wrong.[55] In fact, surveys mostly showed majority community support for the ban but this was no match for the vocal opposition of the greyhound racing industry, sections of the media, and some members of the National Party.[56] The latter included the then leader of the federal National Party and Deputy Prime Minister, Barnaby Joyce, notwithstanding his admission that he had not read the report of the Special Commission of Inquiry and did not intend to do so.[57]

Having decided not to proceed with the ban, the NSW government instead established a Greyhound Industry Reform Panel 'to recommend a new regime that would allow the industry to continue while applying the strictest animal welfare standards in the country',[58] even though the Special Commission of Inquiry had already dealt extensively with these issues. The resulting report of the panel recommended the separation of greyhound racing's commercial and regulatory functions, a comprehensive animal welfare plan, including an enforceable code of practice, whole of lifecycle tracking and care of greyhounds, a new licensing and accreditation scheme, and stronger penalties and new offences.[59] Most of these recommendations were given effect by the *Greyhound Racing Act 2017*, which also repealed the *Greyhound Racing Prohibition Act 2016*. Other key jurisdictions also held inquiries and introduced reforms, although only the ACT effectively abolished the industry through the combined effect of the *Domestic Animals (Racing Greyhounds) Amendment Act 2017* and *Racing (Greyhounds) Amendment Act 2017*. Among other changes, Victoria established a Racing Integrity Board and Commissioner to provide independent oversight of integrity issues and Queensland established a Racing Integrity Commission responsible for all racing codes in that state.[60]

While these developments are welcome, problems persist. These include the number of greyhounds bred, ongoing track injuries and

---

55 Australian Broadcasting Corporation 2016.
56 Ellis 2016.
57 Bettles 2016.
58 NSW, *Parliamentary Debates*, Legislative Assembly, 28 March 2017, 62 (Paul Toole).
59 Iemma et al. 2017.
60 Greyhound Welfare and Integrity Commission 2019, 5.

deaths, and the conditions in which racing greyhounds are kept. The Special Commission of Inquiry found that 40% of greyhounds whelped are considered unsuitable for the racetrack, while greyhounds who do race are retired within a few years despite a natural lifespan of between 12 and 15 years of age.[61] The result is more greyhounds than available homes, with rehoming policies unable to address a problem which is inherent in the economics of the racing industry.[62] Although there was a drop in the number of greyhounds bred following the *Four Corners* program,[63] there is no breeding cap on the industry as a whole. An amendment moved by the Greens to the Greyhound Racing Bill 2017 (NSW) to mandate an annual breeding cap of 2,000 greyhounds failed to win support, even though the industry had written to the government in 2016 just before the Greyhound Racing Prohibition Bill was passed, guaranteeing a controlled breeding program, including a cap of 2,000 greyhounds annually for racing purposes.[64] Further, while whole of life tracking was a key recommendation of the NSW, Queensland and Victorian inquiries in order to monitor greyhound welfare over the course of their lives, its implementation has been problematic. In NSW, for example, welfare and integrity functions are now the province of a new body, the Greyhound Welfare and Integrity Commission (GWIC), separate from the industry's commercial arm, but still responsible to the Minister for Better Regulation and Innovation, whose portfolio includes racing and gambling. Under the *Greyhound Racing Act 2017*, the GWIC's functions relate to greyhounds owned or kept in connection with racing, raising concerns that it is unable to track the welfare of dogs transferred to non-racing members of the public. According to the GWIC, it 'has no lawful right to intervene in any way' in relation to greyhounds who are sold, retired or given away to non-industry participants.[65] In February 2021, the NSW government announced a new technology, to be implemented in the second half of the year, to make it easier to track the whereabouts of NSW greyhounds but this applies to greyhounds

61 McHugh 2016, 1–2.
62 Ibid, 3.
63 Riga 2018.
64 NSW, *Parliamentary Debates*, Legislative Council, 5 April 2017, 56–7 (Mehreen Faruqi).
65 Lind 2020.

registered under the *Greyhound Racing Act 2017*. The GWIC advises that connecting this technology 'to the new NSW Pet Registry, which the NSW Government is also investing in, will also be explored'.[66] The report on the statutory review of the *Greyhound Racing Act 2017* published in April 2021 noted that submissions from animal welfare organisations 'expressed concern about greyhounds not being tracked after leaving the industry'.[67] The review, however, only recommended an expansion of reporting on greyhound rehoming and retirement 'to include additional information and data from independent rehoming and rescue organisations, where practical'.[68]

According to the GWIC's Annual Report, 3,935 pups were born in NSW in 2019–20, while 1,405 greyhound retirements were notified.[69] Of the notified retirements, 37% were retained by the owner or trainer, 2% went to another registered participant as a pet and 17% were rehomed to a non-participant by the owner or trainer. Only 18% of the retired greyhounds were accepted by the industry rehoming program, Greyhounds As Pets, and 27% by another animal adoption or rescue agency.[70] While the GWIC has confidently asserted that retired greyhounds 'usually become pets or are retained in the industry for breeding',[71] it is difficult to see how racing industry participants are able to retain such large numbers of greyhounds, or rehome them privately, on an ongoing basis. Certainly, others are much less sure of their fate.[72] Even if homes are found for all unwanted and retired greyhounds, the regular rehoming of large numbers of greyhounds has serious consequences for the thousands of other dogs in animal rescue agencies waiting to be adopted.

Greyhounds also experience serious welfare problems during their racing careers, with the risk of injury and death a constant hazard. In 2019–20, 2,447 of the greyhound starters in NSW suffered injuries requiring a stand-down period, including catastrophic racing injuries

66 Greyhound Welfare and Integrity Commission 2021, 21.
67 NSW Government 2021, 25.
68 Ibid, 26.
69 Greyhound Welfare and Integrity Commission 2020, 44.
70 Ibid, 47.
71 Greyhound Welfare and Integrity Commission 2019, 43.
72 Cockburn 2020.

leading to sudden death or euthanasia in the case of 52 dogs.[73] Australia-wide, there were 9,861 track injuries and 202 track-related deaths in 2020, according to the Coalition for the Protection of Greyhounds, which monitors national deaths and injuries on an ongoing basis.[74] Off the track, there are other welfare issues. Kennel inspections are a key feature of the GWIC's welfare strategy, but it is worrying that numerous verbal instructions and written directions have to be issued for very basic matters. These include seek veterinary advice for fleas and ticks and advanced dental disease, address kennel hygiene (such as remove built-up faeces and urine), replace or clean bedding and provide shade in outdoor yards.[75] According to the Minister for Better Regulation and Innovation, the Greyhound Welfare Code of Practice published by the NSW government in 2020 'signals to the broader community the collective resolve of the greyhound racing industry to establish and maintain the highest standards of welfare and care in Australia'.[76] Although this Code contains welcome improvements, it falls badly short in some areas, such as housing. The Code commenced on 1 January 2021 but standard 1.6 provides that all existing greyhound housing areas are deemed compliant with the minimum housing requirement in standard 5.9 until 31 December 2030, with the possibility of an extension for a further five years in certain circumstances. In practice, therefore, greyhounds can be kept in substandard housing for up to 15 years from the Code's commencement, and up to 20 years from the *Four Corners* program which was the catalyst for major change.

In addition to regulatory reforms, the *Four Corners* exposé had consequences for numerous individual participants in the Australian industry, including life bans and criminal convictions for some of the industry's most respected figures.[77] Even so, the process has not been straightforward. In Queensland, for example, nine of 22 trainers had

73 Greyhound Welfare and Integrity Commission 2020, 46.
74 Coalition for the Protection of Greyhounds 2020.
75 Greyhound Welfare and Integrity Commission 2020, 20.
76 NSW Government 2020, 2. As noted by RSPCA NSW, the inclusion of the statement 'Securing a prosperous industry by improving welfare and integrity' in the footer is inappropriate given the Code's objectives to protect the welfare and promote the wellbeing of greyhounds: RSPCA NSW 2020b, 1. The same statement is included in the footer of the GWIC's Annual Reports.
77 Branco 2016.

their life bans reduced to between five and ten years on appeal to the Queensland Racing Disciplinary Board.[78] In NSW, two trainers were jointly charged with serious animal cruelty under s 530(1) of the *Crimes Act 1900* (NSW) in relation to alleged live baiting but applied at their District Court trial to have key prosecution evidence excluded pursuant to s 138 of the *Evidence Act 1995* (NSW). This section provides that evidence obtained improperly or in contravention of an Australian law, or in consequence of such an impropriety or contravention, is inadmissible unless the desirability of admitting the evidence outweighs the undesirability of admitting evidence that has been obtained in that way. In this case, there were three categories of evidence in dispute: seven covert recordings of activities at a Sydney property made by a photographer acting on behalf of Animals Australia, in contravention of s 8(1) of the *Surveillance Devices Act 2007* (NSW); material obtained by RSPCA inspectors as a result of a search warrant executed after receiving copies of the recordings; and admissions allegedly made by one trainer to the photographer who later posed as a greyhound owner. After a decision by the trial judge to exclude all three categories of evidence, the prosecution appealed to the NSW Court of Criminal Appeal which found that the difficulty of lawfully obtaining the surveillance evidence without more than an anonymous complaint tipped the balance in favour of admitting the first recording but not the remaining ones.[79] The Court of Criminal Appeal also held that the search warrant evidence and the alleged admissions were admissible, having regard to material differences in the way they were obtained and other matters.[80] On appeal to the High Court, however, all of the recordings were held to be inadmissible, although the other categories of evidence were allowed.[81]

With important competing public interests to weigh, the exercise of judicial discretion in relation to illegally or improperly obtained evidence is a complex matter. Nevertheless, this case illustrates the difficulty of securing evidence and prosecuting alleged offenders in animal cruelty cases. With respect to the above matter, Animals Australia acted in

78 Ibid.
79 *R v Grech; R v Kadir* [2017] NSWCCA 288, [111].
80 *R v Grech; R v Kadir* [2017] NSWCCA 288, [127]–[142].
81 *Kadir v The Queen; Grech v The Queen* (2020) 276 CLR 109.

response to an anonymous tip-off in an industry where there was already some evidence that live baiting was occurring.[82] At the same time, an anonymous complaint to RSPCA NSW would have been insufficient to support a request by that organisation to the police to apply for an optical surveillance warrant, while investigation of such a complaint by the RSPCA would include liaison with GRNSW.[83]

Horse racing

The critical role of undercover surveillance activities was demonstrated yet again in 2019 with the public exposure of the suffering endured by retired racehorses sent for slaughter. Horses being killed for human consumption are sent to abattoirs, and to smaller establishments, called knackeries, if being killed for consumption by other animals. Despite the racing industry's claim that only 0.4% of retiring Australian racehorses end up at abattoirs or knackeries each year (about 34 animals), a special investigation by the ABC's *7.30* program revealed that more than 40 former racehorses were slaughtered in just one day at Meramist abattoir in Queensland.[84] As with the greyhound racing exposé, the ABC program highlighted a huge problem of 'wastage' in the racing industry, including the harness racing industry, as well as major discrepancies between industry assurances and the reality of life for large numbers of animals.[85] While the slaughter of racehorses is not illegal, the program noted that it is counter to the industry's animal welfare strategy to minimise wastage and defies Racing Australia's traceability rule to track thoroughbreds from birth to retirement. Further, in rules introduced by Racing NSW following the greyhound racing exposé, retired racehorses must not be sold at a livestock auction not approved by the regulator, or sent to an abattoir or knackery, breaches of which were revealed by the *7.30* program.[86] In addition to these failings, the program exposed

82 Legislative Council Select Committee on Greyhound Racing in NSW, Parliament of NSW 2014, 111–12.
83 *Kadir v The Queen; Grech v The Queen* (2020) 276 CLR 109, 130 [26].
84 Meldrum-Hanna and Donaldson 2019.
85 Australian Broadcasting Corporation 2019.
86 In another connection between the two industries, the slaughter of retired racehorses at knackeries helps to prop up greyhound racing by providing mince to feed the racing dogs.

the appalling cruelty to which multiple horses were subject before and during the slaughter process, including being beaten, kicked, shocked and ineffectively bolted. In yet another damning indictment of regulatory failure, this cruelty was once again only brought to light by covert footage supplied to the ABC after an undercover investigation.

Following the ABC exposé, the federal Department of Agriculture, Water and the Environment conducted a regulatory investigation into the Meramist abattoir but the media statement announcing its finalisation provided scant information. Noting that noncompliance with the Australian Meat Standard had been identified, the department stated that it 'has directed Meramist to amend its approved arrangement to better ensure its operations adhere explicitly to the Industry Animal Welfare Standards for Livestock Processing Establishments'. It further stated that the department will continue its 'ongoing oversight' of the abattoir's export operations and 'may seek to undertake further regulatory action' should further noncompliances be identified.[87] While the media release sought to reassure the public that the department 'takes animal welfare breaches seriously', the lack of detail in the statement provides no grounds for confidence.

By contrast, the state government's inquiry into the management of retired thoroughbred and standardbred horses in Queensland was independent, transparent and extensive. The resulting report (the Martin Report) noted that the existing *Model Code of Practice for the Welfare of Animals: Livestock at Slaughtering Establishments* 2001 is voluntary and lacks standards relevant to horse slaughter.[88] The Martin Report was also scathing about the current process to convert this Model Code of Practice into animal welfare standards and guidelines. Referring to the most recent draft standards and guidelines, the Martin Report stated that the process:

> … has been under review for years and much more time will pass before the review is complete … the delay is unacceptable. However, delay is not even the main problem … Similar to the Code it is to replace, the draft sets out slaughter establishment design standards

87 Australia, Department of Agriculture, Water and the Environment 2020c.
88 Martin and Reid 2020, 63.

> which are vague generalisations, in no way species-specific, and otherwise repetition of basic animal welfare obligations.[89]

Problems were also identified in relation to the *Australian Animal Welfare Standards and Guidelines: Land Transport of Livestock* (LTL Standards). These were the first finalised standards in the broader project to convert voluntary codes of practice into enforceable national standards but, as discussed in Chapter 3, the LTL Standards typically offer less protection than equivalent provisions governing companion animals. Again, the Martin Report did not mince words, describing the defects in these standards with respect to horses, as regulated by the Queensland Code of Practice for the Transport of Livestock, as 'staggeringly obvious' and noting that any changes to the national standards could be years away.[90]

In addition, major failings were identified in the enforcement of both the transport standards and the *Animal Care and Protection Act 2001* (Qld) (ACAP Act). In the case of abattoirs licensed to export meat for human consumption, enforcement of animal welfare is complicated by the dual role of the Commonwealth and state governments. As set out in the Martin Report, the very poor animal welfare at the Meramist abattoir illustrates significant problems with this regulatory regime. Under approved arrangements with the Commonwealth, an export abattoir must appoint an animal welfare officer who is responsible for completing an incident report when animal welfare issues are observed. Export abattoirs are also required to have an on-plant veterinarian whose role includes monitoring overall compliance with animal welfare standards.[91] Any animal welfare incidents observed by the animal welfare officer must be notified to this veterinarian, who in turn reports to the federal Department of Agriculture. Among other powers, the federal department's auditors can issue a Corrective Action Request (CAR), as can the on-plant veterinarian for noncompliance with legislative requirements.[92] The federal department's usual response to an animal welfare incident is to issue a CAR rather than to take other regulatory

---

89 Ibid, 6–7.
90 Ibid, 80.
91 Ibid, 59.
92 Ibid.

action.[93] Biosecurity Queensland is required to be notified of animal welfare incidents observed by the on-plant veterinarian or animal welfare officer[94] and has responsibility for enforcing the ACAP Act and the transport standards but has no powers to enter without consent or prior notice to routinely monitor animal welfare at abattoirs.[95] Instead, it acts on complaints from the public and in response to notification of an animal welfare incident report from the on-plant veterinarian or the federal department.[96] Prior to the broadcast of the *7.30* program, Biosecurity Queensland appears to have received no complaints about the treatment of the horses as depicted, either because the incidents were not recorded in an incident report or the reports were not shared with the state regulator.[97] Most of the animal welfare incidents reported to Biosecurity Queensland in 2019 by the federal Department of Agriculture in relation to Meramist concerned transportation of horses – either the unfit loading of emaciated and injured horses or shocking injuries sustained during transport. In some of these cases, Biosecurity Queensland's response was to shift responsibility to the relevant interstate authority even when the drivers were subject to the state's animal welfare law.[98] Biosecurity Queensland also failed to undertake any analysis 'to determine whether the frequency and severity of the incidents disclosed welfare issues of a systemic nature'.[99] In relation to the Queensland knackery, there is no routine welfare monitoring, with oversight dependent upon complaints by members of the public, including activists, and, perhaps, food safety auditors if they observe an animal welfare incident.[100]

As with the greyhound racing controversy, exposure of the treatment of retired racehorses has had consequences for some industry participants and acted as a catalyst for regulatory change. In 2020, Biosecurity Queensland charged three people with a number of offences, including animal cruelty; they were fined a combined total of less

93 Ibid, 74.
94 Ibid, 59.
95 Ibid, 62.
96 Ibid, 59.
97 Ibid, 73.
98 Ibid, 75.
99 Ibid.
100 Ibid, 66.

than $7,000 after pleading guilty.[101] In February 2020, the Queensland government responded to the Martin Report by stating its support, or support in principle, for its 55 recommendations. The extent of their implementation, and the timeframe for action remain to be seen but some changes are afoot. In 2020, the *Animal Care and Protection Regulation 2012* (Qld) was amended by the insertion of cl 6A to prescribe an electrical prod for horses, thus making it a cruelty offence to use this device on a horse (though not on other livestock such as calves). Earlier that year, the Queensland Agriculture Minister committed to installing CCTV cameras in the state's slaughterhouses by 31 October at the latest.[102] As of January 2021, however, RSPCA Australia noted the lack of any CCTV use in Queensland abattoirs, poultry processing plants and knackeries.[103] At a national level, a Senate committee recommended that the federal Department of Agriculture establish a national horse traceability working group to progress the development and implementation of a national horse traceability register.[104] At the AGMIN forum in February 2020, agriculture ministers agreed to establish a working group for this purpose, in consultation with industry, and co-led by Queensland and Victoria.[105] In November 2021, a Thoroughbred Aftercare Welfare Working Group established by industry published a report with 46 recommendations to improve horse welfare.[106]

But the fate of retired racehorses is not the only animal welfare problem associated with this industry. In late 2016, Harness Racing Australia decided that racing would be 'whip free' from September 2017, but this plan was subsequently put on hold, citing safety concerns, with a move to 'wrist-only' whip use instituted instead.[107] Whip use is also still allowed in the thoroughbred racing industry, subject to certain restrictions. The Australian Rules of Racing permit use of an approved padded whip and specify its manner of use, as well as the frequency of its

101 Siganto 2020.
102 Crockford and Layt 2020.
103 RSPCA Australia 2021, 37–9.
104 Senate Standing Committee on Rural and Regional Affairs and Transport, Parliament of Australia 2019, xiii.
105 Australia, Department of Agriculture, Water and the Environment 2020d.
106 Thoroughbred Welfare Initiative 2021.
107 Australian Harness Racing 2017. A 'wrist only' flicking motion was mandated in 2020 by an amendment to Australian Harness Racing Rule 156(2).

use prior to the final 100 metres of a race, after which it can be wielded at the rider's discretion, subject to the other rule requirements.[108] An earlier observational study, however, cast doubt on the ability of racing stewards to enforce whip rules,[109] and there is evidence that the use of padded whips does not obviate pain.[110] While industry representatives dispute that whip use is painful,[111] research in 2020 commissioned by the RSPCA and carried out by veterinary experts found that the outer, pain-sensitive layer of skin is similar in both horses and humans, which means that horses and humans are hurt by whips in a similar way.[112] Further, a recent comparison of whipping-free and whipping-permitted races found 'no evidence that the use of whips contributed to steering, reduced the likelihood of interference, improved the safety of horse or jockey or made horses run faster overall'.[113] With global pressure mounting to reconsider whip use,[114] Racing Victoria is advocating reform but its proposals were not adopted at the Racing Australia board meeting in November 2020.[115]

Other animal welfare problems revealed by research include the high incidence of bone injuries suffered by racehorses. This is consistent with ongoing bone fatigue and suggests 'that the current frequency and duration of rest periods is insufficient to prevent bone damage'.[116] A more visible welfare issue is the number of horses who die on the racetrack or soon after, with between 116 and 149 deaths every racing year in Australia for the period 2014 to 2021.[117] These numbers do not include horses who die from racing-related injuries off the track after being raced or in training.[118] Deaths and injuries are even higher in jumps racing. In recognition of an inherent conflict between this activity and animal welfare, a Senate Select Committee formed the majority

108 *Australian Rules of Racing*, AR 132.
109 McGreevy et al. 2012.
110 Newby 2015.
111 Ibid; Fox Koob 2019.
112 Tong et al. 2020.
113 Thompson et al. 2020, 1995.
114 McGreevy and Jones 2020.
115 Tatnell 2020.
116 RSPCA Australia 2018e, 2.
117 Coalition for the Protection of Racehorses 2021, 10.
118 Ibid, 4. NSW is the only state which sometimes reports on deaths in trackwork and training but not all of these deaths are reported: 11.

view that state governments should phase out jumps racing over the next three years.[119] That finding was published in 1991 but jumps racing still occurs in South Australia and Victoria, with NSW the only state to expressly ban it.[120] In 2016, a South Australia Select Committee on Jumps Racing recommended that it not be banned despite conceding that the risk of injury and fatality to horses is unquestionably greater than in flat racing.[121] Instead, the committee recommended a range of improvements in relation to animal welfare and industry transparency and accountability.[122] Although the recommendations included measures to address overbreeding and wastage, these issues were to feature prominently three years later in the *7.30* program on the fate of former racehorses. In October 2021, Racing SA announced that jumps racing would not be scheduled in the racing calendar as of 2022, not for reasons of animal welfare but because the industry is no longer sustainable due to declining participation levels and horse numbers.[123]

Rodeos

Rodeos are permitted in all Australian jurisdictions except the ACT where they are banned by s 18 of the *Animal Welfare Act 1992*. Paradoxically, the two jurisdictions which host jumps racing, South Australia and Victoria, have the strongest protections for animals in rodeo events. In particular, these two jurisdictions effectively prohibit calf roping (a rope and tie event) by specifying a minimum body weight for animals of 200 kilograms. Calf roping is permitted in the other states and the Northern Territory despite opposition from animal welfare organisations and research evidence of the risk to animal welfare. An Australian study which assessed both the behaviour and physiology of calves before and after two major components of a roping event recommended further research after detecting an acute stress response

119 Senate Select Committee on Animal Welfare, Parliament of Australia 1991, 24.
120 Select Committee on Jumps Racing, Parliament of South Australia 2016, 49–50.
121 Ibid, 5.
122 Ibid, 10–11.
123 Racing SA 2021.

Figure 5.1. Calf roping is still legal in some jurisdictions despite serious animal welfare concerns. (Animals Australia)

in the calves.[124] In 2020, research by Australian veterinary scientists found that calves in roping events experience negative emotions such as agitation, anxiety, fear, confusion and stress, raising 'serious concerns as to the continuation of these events on welfare grounds'.[125] Other rodeo events which raise animal welfare concerns include steer wrestling, with its attendant risk of serious injury, and bronco-riding, where metal spurs and a strap tightened around the horse's sensitive flanks and underbelly are used to encourage it to react. As well as the risk of injury and death, these events cause animals fear, distress and pain.[126]

As calf roping illustrates, there is a high degree of inconsistency between jurisdictions in the regulation of rodeos. Any protections afforded animals are typically incorporated by regulation, with relevant codes of practice prescribed in some jurisdictions. Even here, however,

124 Sinclair et al. 2016, 38.
125 Rizzuto et al. 2020, 128.
126 RSPCA Australia 2020a.

there is no uniformity. In NSW, cl 36 of the *Prevention of Cruelty to Animals Regulation 2012* specifies the 1988 *Code of Practice for the Welfare of Animals Used in Rodeo Events*, compliance with which exempts a person from the operation of the prohibition on the activities contained in ss 18(1), 18A and 20 of the *Prevention of Cruelty to Animals Act*. In Tasmania, s 11A of the *Animal Welfare Act 1993* mandates compliance with any prescribed code of practice for rodeos; cl 5 of the *Animal Welfare (General) Regulations 2013* prescribes the *NCCAW Code of Practice – Standards for the Care and Treatment of Rodeo Livestock*. This refers to the code of practice developed by the now defunct National Consultative Committee for Animal Welfare and published by the federal Department of Agriculture, Fisheries and Forestry in 2006. In WA, the *Animal Welfare (General) Regulations 2003* include the *Code of practice for the conduct of rodeos in Western Australia*, based on the NCCAW Standards, in cl 6(1). As a result, it is a relevant code of practice for the purposes of the *Animal Welfare Act* and can be used as a defence under s 25, although compliance with it is not mandatory. These various codes of practice were developed some time ago and are therefore unlikely to reflect either contemporary animal welfare science or community expectations. There is no code of practice in SA and Victoria but relevant clauses in the general regulations, particularly in Victoria, generally offer a higher standard of animal protection than the code provisions.[127] In Queensland, animal welfare rodeo standards and guidelines finalised in December 2021 continue to allow calf roping despite strong public opposition to this activity.[128] As of 1 January 2022, these standards form the basis of a mandatory rodeo code of practice under the Qld Act. More generally, provisions on the handling and management of cattle in the *Australian Animal Welfare Standards and Guidelines for Cattle*, endorsed in 2016, have some relevance for rodeo events where they have been regulated.

127 RSPCA Australia 2020b.
128 Claughton 2022.

Recreational hunting and fishing

As Gullone argues, 'we are conditioned to accept certain aggressive behaviours, such as "recreational" shooting, bullfighting or rodeos, as entertainment or sport when they are targeting particular species … and others as antisocial when they are targeting other species, such as companion animals'.[129] Recreational hunting, for example, is typically exempt from the application of the animal welfare Acts despite the considerable animal suffering it causes. That the pursuit and killing of some species for pleasure is not only regarded as a legitimate activity but sufficiently important to outweigh the attendant suffering illustrates the highly problematic nature of the balancing act inherent in the animal welfare paradigm. Although the lawfulness of hunting is restricted to certain species and may be tied to compliance with a code of practice or be subject to the proviso of no unnecessary suffering, the ambiguity of this concept, the limited protections contained in codes and the lack of enforcement render these qualifications effectively meaningless.

Of the many different animals hunted for sport in Australia, most are introduced species, with 'pest' or 'feral' animal control often given as a justification, an issue we return to in Chapter 6. Hunting of some native species is also permitted, for example native waterbirds. Subject to certain restrictions, such as bag limits, recreational duck and quail hunting is legal in South Australia, Tasmania, Victoria and the Northern Territory for declared species during specified seasons. By contrast, this activity was banned in Western Australia in 1990, in NSW in 1995, and in Queensland in 2005.[130] When announcing the Queensland ban, the premier told parliament that '[t]his is not an appropriate activity in contemporary life'. He further stated that 'the likely rate of wounding instead of direct kills was unacceptable, leading to unreasonable pain and suffering' and that 'few modern hunters viewing a bird in flight are able to distinguish a species which can be shot from one which is protected'.[131] Although difficult to quantify with precision, the RSPCA estimates that

129 Gullone 2017, 41.

130 Duck shooting may be allowed for other purposes, such as those permitted by the NSW Native Game Bird Management Program.

131 Queensland, *Parliamentary Debates*, Legislative Assembly, 10 August 2005, 2246–7 (Peter Beattie).

approximately 26% of birds shot will be wounded or maimed/crippled, with the likely outcome a slow and painful death.[132] In 2019, the Victorian Game Management Authority (GMA) commissioned a survey of licensed game hunters to establish their level of understanding of game hunting laws, good hunting practice and safety.[133] In relation to the specific questions for duck hunters, only 13% answered correctly about the dispatch of downed ducks and only 37% correctly answered questions about minimising wounding.[134] As the GMA notes, the majority of game licence holders are not required to undergo any knowledge testing before obtaining a recreational licence, provided they have the appropriate authorisation to use their chosen hunting method, although game duck hunters must successfully complete a waterfowl identification test.[135] It is of significant concern that, despite this requirement, only 20% of duck hunters identified game ducks correctly.[136]

As with the exhibited animal industry, hunting organisations lay claim to conservation and research objectives, among the justifications for their members' activities. Field and Game Australia, for example, bills itself as 'Australia's most surprising conservationists', with the benefits of membership including 'increased opportunities to play a role in vital wetland habitat conservation, restoration and preservation, as well as contribute to scientific research into our wonderful waterfowl'.[137] The notion of duck hunting as conservation is also promoted by regulatory authorities, as are its economic benefits. On its website, the GMA refers hunters to its Duck WISE education video on YouTube;[138] the Tasmanian Department of Primary Industries, Parks, Water and Environment also advises applicants for a game hunting licence to study this video[139] which begins as follows:

132 RSPCA Australia 2020e, 12–13.
133 Victoria, Game Management Authority 2020b, 2.
134 Ibid, 22 Table 9.
135 Ibid, 5.
136 Ibid, 22.
137 Field & Game Australia Inc. n.d.
138 Victoria, Game Management Authority 2020c.
139 Tasmania, Department of Primary Industries, Parks, Water and Environment, Wildlife Management 2021.

> Recreational duck hunting is a traditional cultural pastime that attracts visitors to regional Australia, supporting local businesses and the economy. For many hunters, it's their chance to enjoy some of the most beautiful parts of the country and share quality time in the company of friends and family. Duck hunting creates an incentive to conserve and protect wetlands and waterways and hunters spend countless hours restoring wetlands and controlling pest animals. The value placed on waterfowl and their habitat ensures their conservation and the long-term viability of duck hunting. Recreational duck hunting is a significant economic contributor. Game hunting generates hundreds of millions of dollars in economic activity and annually creates thousands of jobs across Australia.[140]

The Victorian GMA is an independent statutory authority but its members are appointed by the Minister for Agriculture to whom it reports. When the Bill establishing the GMA was introduced in the Victorian Parliament, the government was at pains to stress its role as a regulator not a promoter of hunting.[141] This emphasis was unsurprising in view of the abolition of the NSW Game Council in 2013 due to its inherent conflict of interests, a matter to which we return in Chapter 6. Notwithstanding the rhetoric in the Victorian Parliament, the GMA's regulatory competence came under sustained criticism following events on the opening weekend of the 2017 duck hunting season at the Koorangie State Game Reserve. Described in parliament as 'nothing short of a relentless massacre of birds', more than 800 dead waterbirds were recovered by duck rescuers, including protected, rare and threatened species who had been shot and left to die.[142] The Coalition Against Duck Shooting also released footage of two pits containing a total of almost 200 birds, suggesting that birds had been dumped because hunters were exceeding their bag limit.[143] Despite the significant noncompliance with game laws observed by GMA staff and other authorised enforcement officers, only one infringement notice was issued for shooting before the legal time, with four hunters

140 Victoria, Game Management Authority 2014.

141 See, for example, Victoria, *Parliamentary Debates*, Legislative Assembly, 12 December 2013, 4671–2 (P.L. Walsh).

142 Victoria, *Parliamentary Debates*, Legislative Council, 22 March 2017, 1518, 1557 (Sue Pennicuik).

143 Day 2017.

subsequently issued with infringement notices for failing to retain a wing on a game duck (for identification purposes); by contrast, 11 protesters were issued with banning notices.[144] The subsequent independent review into the GMA found that it had failed to deliver its compliance and enforcement responsibilities effectively, with unsanctioned breaches of the law widespread and commonplace.[145] Among other things, the review also documented the tension in the GMA's allocated roles, noting that it 'appears to have exacerbated these tensions and is sometimes perceived as playing, and occasionally slides into, advocacy and promotional roles'.[146] While the GMA states that 19 of the 21 supported recommendations directed at the GMA have been fully implemented, with work in progress on the remaining two,[147] the Duck WISE education video extract above suggests that its role confusion continues.

Although recreational fishing also gives rise to animal welfare issues,[148] it attracts far less controversy than duck hunting. The reasons for this arguably include the popularity of this pastime and its integration into the cultural fabric. As Balcombe notes, '[w]hile the unsustainability and cruelty of commercial fishing are increasingly recognized, recreational fishing retains a benign and beloved place in our culture'.[149] Other reasons for the apparent lack of concern about the welfare aspects of this activity include the way different species are regarded by the community, a lack of knowledge about the capacities of fish, and the continuing debate about fish sentience. Compared to mammals, fish lack recognisable facial expressions and other attributes which attract human empathy[150] and do relatively badly when assessed for sentience by the general public. In the research commissioned by the Department of Agriculture referred to in Chapter 4, fish were viewed as sentient by only 23% of people, somewhat sentient by 52% and not sentient by 25%. This contrasts with the findings for cattle, for example, which were 56%,

144 Victorian Game Management Authority's Review of the 2017 duck season opening weekend. Report to the Minister for Agriculture cited in Fisher and Davey 2017, 38.

145 Fisher and Davey 2017, vii.

146 Ibid, 14.

147 Victoria, Game Management Authority 2020a, 5.

148 See, for example, Huntingford et al. 2007.

149 Balcombe 2016, 225.

150 Brown 2015, 2.

38% and 6% respectively.[151] After reviewing the scientific research, Black acknowledged that 'a scientific consensus may not yet have been reached' but concluded that 'the weight of evidence supports the view that fish are sentient and a precautionary approach would therefore require that fish interests be accorded due consideration'.[152] Another review of the science found 'extensive evidence of fish behavioural and cognitive sophistication and pain perception', suggesting that 'best practice would be to lend fish the same level of protection as any other vertebrate'.[153] More recently, Sneddon reviewed the empirical evidence to conclude that it is 'highly likely' that fish experience pain, making it 'vital that we seek to minimize and alleviate pain in fish when logistically possible'.[154]

In fact, fish receive very little protection under Australian laws. As noted in Chapter 2, fish are included in the definition of 'animal' in the principal animal welfare statutes of most, though not all, jurisdictions. Even where included, however, provisions apply which effectively exempt fishing from the operation of the legislation, for example s 24(1)(b) of the *Prevention of Cruelty to Animals Act 1979* (NSW). As a result, fish uses covered by animal welfare legislation are largely confined to aquaculture, and to fish used as companion animals or for science, but even in these contexts cruelty offences are 'almost impossible to establish'.[155] Various aspects of recreational fishing, for example bag and size limits, are regulated under fisheries legislation which is typically administered by authorities within primary industries departments but this legislation is not typically directed at fish welfare. In Western Australia, s 191A of the *Fish Resources Management Act 1994* provides that a fisheries officer may exercise the powers conferred by the *Animal Welfare Act 2002* on general inspectors under that Act for the purpose of enforcing s 258(1)(va) and (vb) of the *Fish Resources Management Act 1994*. In broad terms, s 258(1)(va) and (vb) authorise the making of regulations to prevent cruelty to fish and to provide for fish welfare, including the adoption of codes of practice, but to date no regulations

151 Futureye Pty. Ltd. 2018, 6.
152 Black 2013, 262. See also Balcombe 2016, 85. For a different view, see Browman et al. 2019.
153 Brown 2015, 1.
154 Sneddon 2019, 374, 379.
155 Black 2013, 253.

have been made pursuant to these provisions.[156] Accordingly, the *Code of Practice for Recreational Fishers in WA* has only voluntary status, as does the *National Code of Practice for Recreational and Sport Fishing* developed by Recfish Australia, on which it is based. In 1997, the ACT approved the document *We Fish for the Future – The National Code of Practice for Recreational and Sport Fishing* under s 22 of the *Animal Welfare Act 1992* but not as a mandatory code under s 23.

Limited guidance about fish welfare is provided by some government departments in the form of advice about such matters as the humane 'dispatch' of fish and how to handle them to minimise fish injury and trauma. Some government agencies also provide online fishing resources for children which include reference to environmental matters impacting fish welfare, such as litter on waterways and risks to fish from abandoned tackle.[157] In the case of NSW, a smiling cartoon crustacean accompanies the online information about the DPI's schools educational program. Along with smiling fish, this image also appears on the department's online activity sheets available for children to download to 'learn more about fish and the fishy environment'.[158] Whether intentional or not, the message conveyed to young children by the department responsible for administering NSW's animal welfare laws is that aquatic species are happy to be caught and killed. We return to the important role that messaging plays in constructing the limits of animal protection in the next chapter, in the context of the very different level of protection afforded wild animals when labelled as 'pests'.

---

156 Western Australia, Department of Primary Industries and Regional Development 2020, 23. The Independent Review of the WA Act recommends the inclusion of vertebrate fish and cephalopods in the definition of 'animal' for the purposes of Part 2 of the *Animal Welfare Act*.

157 For example, the NSW DPI's Get Hooked ... it's Fun to Fish educational program for primary school children, NSW Department of Primary Industries n.d., Recreational fishing.

158 Ibid.

6
Animals in the Wild

In 2020, an independent review of the *Environment Protection and Biodiversity Conservation Act 1999* (Cth) (the Samuel Review) found that:

> Australia is losing biodiversity at an alarming rate and has one of the highest rates of extinction in the world. More than 10% of Australia's land mammals are now extinct and another 21% are threatened and declining. Populations of threatened birds, plants, fish and invertebrates are also continuing to decrease and the list of threatened species is growing.[1]

This is happening despite the fact that threatened native animal species receive the most favourable legal treatment of all animals living in the wild, with common native animals less well protected and introduced animals receiving almost no protection at all.[2] This hierarchy of legal response provides stark illustration of one of the key themes of animal welfare regulation: context and setting, not sentience, determine the level of protection that the law affords. The legal framework is further complicated by the application of environmental and conservation legislation in the case of some animals, and legislation regulating hunting and 'pest' animal control in the case of others. These state

1 Samuel 2020, 40 (reference omitted).
2 Thiriet 2013; White 2009b.

and territory regulatory schemes are additional to the principal animal welfare Act in each jurisdiction, as well as a direct legislative role for the Commonwealth in the form of the EPBC Act. With a wide range of agencies involved in the administration and enforcement of these disparate laws, this chapter also illustrates the fragmentation of regulatory responsibility, the lack of independent oversight, and the difficulty in accessing data which characterise all animal welfare regulation. These similarities pervade the regulation of wild animals notwithstanding the difference in their legal status.

Legal status

As described in earlier chapters, domestic animals are legally classified as property. The position with respect to wild animals is different, and more complicated. The longstanding common law position distinguishes between domestic animals and animals in their wild state – the former constitute property, the latter do not. Nevertheless, at common law, when wild animals are killed by the owner of land on which they are found, or by another with the owner's authority, they become that person's absolute property; if reclaimed live from the wild, ownership is qualified because their property status is lost if animals regain their natural state.[3] Some jurisdictions, however, have enacted legislation which vests ownership of specified categories of wild animals in the Crown. In NSW, for example, s 2.18(2) of the *Biodiversity Conservation Act 2016* (BC Act) provides that a protected animal (other than an excluded animal) is, until lawfully captured and killed, deemed to be the property of the Crown. The degree of ownership conferred by this kind of provision is questionable.[4] In *Yanner v Eaton*, the High Court considered the meaning of s 7(1) of the *Fauna Conservation Act 1974* (Qld) which provided that all fauna, save fauna taken or kept otherwise than in contravention of this Act during an open season with respect to that fauna, is the property of the Crown and under control

3 *Blades v Higgs* [1865] EngR 593.
4 McEwen 2011, 251. See also White 2009b, 231–4.

of the Fauna Authority.[5] By majority, the High Court held that the Act did not confer on the Crown 'full beneficial, or absolute, ownership' of the fauna but vested in the Crown 'no more than the aggregate of the various rights of control by the Executive that the legislation created'.[6] In other words, the statutory vesting of 'property' in the Crown reflects a state's power 'to preserve and regulate the exploitation of an important resource' through, for example, limits on what, and how, fauna might be taken.[7] Each jurisdiction has enacted a licensing scheme under nature conservation legislation which regulates these kinds of activities.

Legal and regulatory framework

Animal welfare legislation

Wild animals are encompassed by the general definition of 'animal' in the principal animal welfare Act in each jurisdiction. While provisions which impose obligations on a person in charge are necessarily inapplicable to wild animals, except in contexts where they are cared for by humans, such as zoos or wildlife rehabilitation centres, the general cruelty prohibitions nominally apply to all animals. In other words, it is an offence under the animal welfare Acts for a person to be cruel to a wild animal where the relevant statutory criteria are met. As with most other animal settings, however, the application of the general cruelty provisions is subject to significant qualification. First, various exemptions and defences exclude some wild animals from the operation of the cruelty provisions. In NSW, for example, s 24(1)(b)(i) of the *Prevention of Cruelty to Animals Act 1979* provides a defence if the relevant act or omission occurs in the course of, and for the purpose of, hunting, shooting, snaring, trapping, catching or capturing the animal in a manner that inflicted no unnecessary pain. In addition, the prohibition against poisoning animals in s 15 is restricted

5 The *Fauna Conservation Act 1974* has been repealed. Section 83(1) of the *Nature Conservation Act 1992* (Qld) provides that, subject to various exceptions, all protected animals are the property of the state.
6 (1999) 201 CLR 351, 370, [30] (Gleeson CJ, Gaudron, Kirby and Hayne JJ).
7 Ibid, 369–70 [28] (reference omitted).

to domestic animals. Another example is s 42 of the *Animal Care and Protection Act 2001* (Qld), which exempts an act to control feral or pest animals that does not involve the use of a prohibited trap or spur and when done in a way that causes as little pain as is reasonable, and complies with any prescribed conditions. In addition, s 6A(3) provides that, with limited exceptions, a person does not commit an offence under the *Animal Care and Protection Act 2001* for an act or omission authorised under the *Nature Conservation Act 1992*. In Victoria, s 6 of the *Prevention of Cruelty to Animals Act 1986* provides that the Act does not apply, *inter alia*, to the following activities relevant to wild animals: the killing, hunting, shooting, catching, trapping or netting of animals (other than farm animals) carried out in accordance with a code of practice; anything done in accordance with the *Catchment and Land Protection Act 1994*; and, except for Part 3 dealing with scientific procedures, to anything done in accordance with the *Wildlife Act 1975*. In combination with other legislation relevant to wild animal welfare, these kinds of provisions have the effect of creating a hierarchy of protection according to the status of the animal: threatened native, common native or introduced species.[8] Where the cruelty prohibition does apply, it is difficult to prove beyond reasonable doubt that an act or omission caused *unnecessary* harm or suffering, for the reasons discussed in earlier chapters, and further illustrated below. In the case of animals living in the wild, this difficulty is exacerbated by the problems associated with law enforcement in non-domestic settings, for example hunting activities that occur in remote and rural areas, often at night.[9]

A further difficulty arises from the limited rights of third parties to initiate court proceedings in public interest litigation. As noted in Chapter 2, some jurisdictions restrict the traditional right to institute a private prosecution for an alleged breach of the criminal law. In addition, unless authorised by statute, an ordinary member of the public lacks standing to sue to restrain a breach of the law, or to compel the performance of a public duty, if they have no special interest in the matter beyond that of any other member of the public in upholding the law.[10] An example is the injunction sought by Animal Liberation

---

8 Thiriet 2013, 227; White 2013b.
9 Thiriet 2009, 280.
10 *Australian Conservation Foundation v Commonwealth* (1980) 146 CLR 493.

in 2007 to restrain the proposed aerial shooting of goats and pigs in NSW nature reserves on the grounds that the operation was likely to breach the *Prevention of Cruelty to Animals Act 1979*. The application was dismissed because the court held that Animal Liberation lacked standing; Hamilton J also held that even if it were otherwise, the evidence 'does not show a sufficient likelihood of the infliction of cruelty' to justify the relief sought.[11] The same judge had granted an interlocutory injunction in proceedings in 2003 initiated by Animal Liberation and involving the aerial shooting of goats but distinguished that case both on the quality of the evidence and the lack of the defendant's objection to the plaintiff's standing on that occasion.[12] In 2014, an international animal protection organisation, Animals' Angels, was granted standing on appeal to the Full Federal Court of Australia in an action for judicial review of a departmental decision in relation to a live export company. Kenny and Robertson JJ held that 'standing requires a sufficient interest, not one which is a unique interest or the strongest interest compared with others who may have an interest'.[13] In deciding that Animals' Angels had the requisite special interest, Kenny and Robertson JJ had regard to the appellant's objects, its activities in Australia, the nature of the decision sought to be reviewed and the department's recognition of the organisation's particular status in the area of live animal export.[14] The substantive grounds of the appeal, however, were not made out.

Nature conservation legislation

In the case of some conservation legislation, provisions allow third parties who meet the statutory criteria to take court action to remedy or restrain a contravention of the Act. An example is s 475 of the EPBC Act which enabled the legal action by Friends of Leadbeater's Possum Inc against VicForests, discussed later in this chapter. This section

11 *Animal Liberation Ltd v Department of Environment and Conservation* [2007] NSWSC 221, [9].
12 Ibid, [3].
13 *Animals' Angels eV v Secretary, Department of Agriculture* (2014) 228 FCR 35, 72, [121].
14 Ibid, 71–2, [119]–[120].

was also relied on by the Australian Brumby Alliance (ABA) in court proceedings to restrain Parks Victoria from trapping and removing brumbies from the Alpine National Park. In that case, the Federal Court accepted that the ABA had standing but rejected the argument that the proposed action constituted a contravention of the EPBC Act.[15] In addition, some government decisions affecting animals are reviewable by administrative tribunals whose relatively broad standing provisions allow third parties, including non-government organisations, to bring proceedings in public interest matters. As illustrated below with respect to the killing of kangaroos, these proceedings nevertheless face significant obstacles.

Some protection for individual native animals is included in state and territory nature conservation legislation. An example is s 2.1 of the NSW BC Act which makes it an offence to harm, or attempt to harm, an animal that is of a threatened species, part of a threatened ecological community, or a protected animal (amphibians, birds, mammals and snakes native to Australia or that occasionally migrate to Australia). The extent of wildlife protection provided by conservation laws is limited, however. For example, a recent review of the Victorian legislative framework identified 'a confusing mix' of laws in addition to the *Wildlife Act* which 'are out of date and do not meet current community expectations'.[16] In any case, the purpose of conservation legislation is environmental protection rather than animal protection, with a consequent focus on whole species not individual animals. Indeed, subject to consideration of ecological issues, conservation legislation enables the exploitation of some native animals as a resource and their lethal and nonlethal control where they are deemed to cause damage to the environment or to private property. This is achieved through licensing systems, with acts done in accordance with an authorised licence or permit typically providing a defence against conduct which would otherwise constitute an offence. Adding to the complexity is the lack of national consistency in state and territory conservation legislation and the role of the Commonwealth in some cases. Those jurisdictions which allow the large-scale, commercial killing of kangaroos also have management plans which meet the requirements of s 303FO of the

15 *Australian Brumby Alliance Inc v Parks Victoria Inc* [2020] FCA 605.
16 Environmental Justice Australia 2020, 6.

EPBC Act because a proportion of the resulting animal products are exported and thus subject to federal regulation in addition to state law.[17]

The complexity of conservation regulation may be illustrated by reference to the position in NSW. The *National Parks and Wildlife Act 1974* contains a number of sections, for example s 56 and s 70, which make it an offence to harm animals in various sites, such as national parks, nature reserves and wildlife refuges. These provisions are subject to numerous exceptions, however, including if the person proves that the relevant act was done in accordance with a licence granted under sections of the Act repealed by the BC Act. As noted above, the BC Act also makes it an offence to harm native animals but s 2.10 provides a defence to a prosecution if the act that constitutes the offence was authorised by, and done in accordance with, a biodiversity conservation licence. Section 2.14(2)(a) includes minimum standards relating to the humane treatment of animals as conditions that may be imposed on a licence, and s 2.14(4) makes it an offence to contravene a licence condition. Section 2.9 authorises the provision of additional defences by regulation and the making and publication by the minister of codes of practice relating to animals or plants. Clause 2.9 of the *Biodiversity Conservation Regulation 2017* creates a defence to a prosecution for relevant offences if the person charged establishes that the act was authorised by, and done in accordance with, a code of practice made, or adopted, by the minister. Clause 2.31 of the Regulation provides for the making or adoption of a management plan in relation to the conservation of native animals that may be adversely affected by any commercial activity. Under cl 2.26, any relevant management plan may be taken into consideration in determining a licence application and compliance with the plan may be required by the licence (cl 2.33). The *NSW Commercial Kangaroo Harvest Management Plan 2017–2021* made under this legislation requires all licensed 'harvesters' to comply with the *National Code of Practice for the Humane Shooting of Kangaroos and Wallabies for Commercial Purposes* published by the Australian government. This Code is also referenced in cl 9A.05 of the *Environment Protection and Biodiversity Conservation Regulations 2000*. The *NSW Commercial Kangaroo Harvest Management Plan 2017–2021* was

17 Thiriet 2013, 229.

approved by the federal Minister for the Environment and Energy on 13 December 2016 for the purposes of the EPBC Act whose objects relevantly include the promotion of the humane treatment of wildlife.

Native animals and commercial purposes: kangaroo killing

Both the size of the commercial kangaroo industry and the iconic status of kangaroos would suggest the existence of stringent animal welfare regulation. In fact, however, there are major problems both with the content of regulatory tools and with their enforcement. Considered to be the 'world's largest commercial kill of land-based wildlife',[18] the most recent available national statistics show that 1,570,473 kangaroos and wallaroos (macropods) were killed for commercial purposes in NSW, Queensland, South Australia and Western Australia in 2019.[19] This figure does not include the very substantial number of joeys who are killed or left to die as collateral damage.[20] The commercial killing of kangaroos also occurs on a smaller scale in Victoria, while two species of wallaby are killed commercially in Tasmania.[21] As the principal regulatory instrument, the *National Codef Practice for the Humane Shooting of Kangaroos and Wallabies for Commercial Purposes* (Commercial Kangaroo Code) contains minimum requirements and operates in conjunction with relevant legislation in each jurisdiction. The most recent edition of the Commercial Kangaroo Code was published in November 2020 following a review of the 2008 edition. The review was led by AgriFutures Australia, the trading name for the Rural Industries Research and Development Corporation established under the *Primary Industries Research and Development Act 1989* (Cth). According to its website, at 12 May 2021, AgriFutures Australia represents 'the interests and aspirations of farmers and rural communities' and its 'vision is to grow the long-term prosperity of Australian rural industries'. The project team responsible for conducting the review and preparing a

18 Boom et al. 2013, 1.
19 Australia, Department of Agriculture, Water and the Environment 2020e.
20 Boom and Ben-Ami 2013, 162.
21 Australia, Department of Agriculture, Water and the Environment n.d.

revised version of the code consisted of two research scientists from the NSW DPI's Vertebrate Pest Research Unit.[22]

The scope of the Commercial Kangaroo Code 'is to ensure that the shooting of kangaroos and wallabies for commercial purposes is carried out in a manner to minimise, to the fullest extent possible, pain, distress and suffering',[23] but its provisions make clear that only 'an achievable standard of humane conduct'[24] is required. For example, while the Commercial Kangaroo Code acknowledges that orphaned dependent young-at-foot 'are likely to experience severe suffering and have a poor chance of survival',[25] there is no prohibition on the shooting of their mothers (or female kangaroos generally); on the contrary, the advice contained in the 2008 code to avoid shooting females with obvious pouch young or young-at-foot has been removed.[26] This was because '[f]eedback from harvesters and landholder surveys revealed an overwhelming opposition to a "male only-harvesting strategy". An unintended consequence of this strategy is that kangaroo welfare is now at even more risk from non-commercial shooting and illegal killing'.[27] Also removed is the requirement to shoot dependent young-at-foot as soon as possible; instead, s 3.5 only requires shooters to 'make every reasonable effort' to kill dependent young-at-foot 'whenever practically possible'.[28] In relation to pouch young, s 3.4 of the Commercial Kangaroo Code prescribes a concussive blow to the head for partially furred to fully furred young, considered the 'most suitable method' currently available.[29] The terminology 'concussive blow to the head' has replaced 'blunt trauma', for consistency 'with euthanasia and slaughter guidelines, and to avoid negative public perception of the term blunt trauma'.[30] Earlier research by the project team is cited as

---

22 Sharp and McLeod 2020.
23 *National Code of Practice for the Humane Shooting of Kangaroos and Wallabies for Commercial Purposes* 2020, 2.
24 Ibid, 1.
25 Ibid, 14.
26 Sharp and McLeod 2020, 22, 80.
27 Ibid, 22.
28 Ibid.
29 *National Code of Practice for the Humane Shooting of Kangaroos and Wallabies for Commercial Purposes* 2020, 32.
30 Sharp and McLeod 2020, 22.

Figure 6.1. The Commercial Kangaroo Code prescribes a concussive blow to the head as the method for killing pouch young. (iStockphoto)

evidence for the acceptability of killing partially and fully furred pouch young by hitting the rear of the joey's head against a large, unmoving solid surface such as the tray of a utility vehicle, although it is noted that the 'humaneness of this method depends on the operator's skill and determination'.[31] If the procedure is incorrectly performed, 'it is likely that the animal will suffer prior to death'.[32] This method is also prescribed by s 3.6 for young-at-foot animals up to approximately 5 kg bodyweight. As recommended,[33] more specific detail as to best practice application of the required methods has been included in the 2020 Commercial Kangaroo Code, but there is no requirement for shooters to demonstrate their competency in relation to the killing of pouch young. Apart from the testing requirements for shooting accuracy, the provisions under the heading 'Harvester responsibility and competency' are expressed in terms both general and awkward. Section 1.1 provides that 'A person conducting commercial harvesting must exercise a duty of care to ensure kangaroos and wallabies are harvested humanely and they understand and comply with the requirements of this Code'; s 1.2 provides that 'Harvesters must be competent to perform their required tasks and can be supervised by a competent person'. These are the kind of 'vague generalisations' heavily criticised by the Martin Report when reviewing livestock standards and guidelines relevant to horses,[34] as discussed in Chapter 5.

Acknowledging that the 'use of blunt trauma to the head is a somewhat controversial method of killing animals', McLeod and Sharp argue that it 'can be a humane method of euthanasia for in-pouch joeys as long as it is applied correctly', with the operator's skill and confidence 'a significant influence on welfare'.[35] The authors distinguish between a *good* death and a *humane* one with regard to the commercial killing of kangaroos:

> ... the termination of the life of dependent young should more accurately be described as 'humane killing' rather than euthanasia. This is because it may not be possible to provide the 'good' death

31 *National Code of Practice for the Humane Shooting of Kangaroos and Wallabies for Commercial Purposes* 2020, 32.

32 Ibid.

33 McLeod and Sharp 2014, 28.

34 Martin and Reid 2020, 6–7.

35 McLeod and Sharp 2014, 22, 24.

> that could potentially be given if the animals were domestic pets or laboratory animals. Under the circumstances where kangaroo young are killed, that is, in remote areas by a single operator at night time, the killing methods need to be practical.[36]

Yet it is precisely the circumstances under which kangaroos are killed which make it difficult to know whether the required methods are being correctly applied, or indeed at all. With a lack of monitoring at point of kill, the extent of compliance with code provisions cannot be accurately assessed although there is evidence of noncompliance. In Sharp and McLeod's study, for example, researchers accompanied 14 professional shooters over 15 nights between 2011 and 2013 to observe how they killed young kangaroos. Significantly, the number of shooters who agreed to participate in the project 'was disappointingly low', despite a small financial incentive and assurance of confidentiality.[37] Of the 24 young-at-foot observed during this research, only one was shot in accordance with the 2008 Commercial Kangaroo Code; another was shot at twice but escaped unwounded, while one was believed by the shooter to be large enough to survive on its own. In all other cases, there was no attempt to kill the young animals, even though eight of them remained still and calm after the shooting of the female. Of those young-at-foot who took flight, none were pursued by the shooter; nor did any spend time searching for young animals when the shot female had a long teat which indicated the likelihood of still dependent young.[38] That professional shooters act in this way while being observed raises serious questions about the extent of noncompliance when no one is watching.

Another major welfare issue where noncompliance has been identified is the failure to kill kangaroos with a shot to the head as required in order to produce a rapid death. To determine how many kangaroos had been shot commercially in compliance with code requirements, RSPCA Australia inspected a total of 24 processors and

36 Ibid, 29. Note also Broom's argument that the term 'euthanasia' should be reserved for killing an animal for its benefit: 2017, 16. While dependent young kangaroos are killed to spare them suffering, this is only necessary because the adult female on whom they depend has been deliberately killed.

37 McLeod and Sharp 2014, 16.

38 Ibid, 19.

two tanneries across four states, mostly during 2000.[39] Although the percentage of kangaroos head-shot had increased, from 86% in 1985 to 95.9% in 2000–02, this still left an estimated 112,578 kangaroos not shot in accordance with requirements.[40] As noted by the RSPCA report, this statistic is a conservative estimate because only carcasses and skins at processors were inspected, thus excluding noncompliant shootings of animals left in the field and animals shot and injured but not retrieved.[41] State government agencies tasked with regulating the kangaroo industry also rely on inspections of chillers and processors, and occasionally shooters' vehicles, to identify compliance breaches.[42] Research into enforcement in the commercial kangaroo industry up to 2011 found that the majority of detected offences related to breaches of reporting requirements, with offences typically dealt with by way of warning letters, written cautions and infringement notices.[43] As with other areas of animal welfare, finding and updating enforcement data is difficult and time-consuming due to the diverse state legislative frameworks, fragmented regulatory responsibility and lack of a national database. As an example of more recent statistics, however, a total of 124 matters were investigated by compliance teams in NSW in 2019 resulting in 47 'compliance response outputs', 34 of which related to a non-head-shot. Of these, 21 received an advisory letter, official caution or warning letter and 13 received a penalty infringement notice. No licences or registrations were cancelled during 2019 and there were no prosecutions.[44] In 2020, one prosecution was commenced and the department issued three show cause notices to 'harvesters' as to why their licences should not be cancelled. One licence was cancelled, another expired before further action was taken and the third was not cancelled. No details are provided about the reason for the show cause notices or the nature of the offence prosecuted.[45]

39 RSPCA Australia 2002, [4.2.1], [4.2.1.1].
40 Ibid, [4.4.1].
41 Ibid.
42 Boom et al. 2012, 45–8.
43 Ibid, 49–61, 71.
44 NSW, Department of Planning and Environment 2020a, 18.
45 NSW, Department of Planning and Environment 2021a, 22.

In comparison with the commercial industry, fewer kangaroos are killed for non-commercial purposes, although the number is still significant[46] and has increased in recent times.[47] Enforcement of compliance with the *National Code of Practice for the Humane Shooting of Kangaroos and Wallabies for Non-Commercial Purposes*, endorsed in 2008, is considered to be 'extremely poor', even though the level of cruelty is generally thought to be higher for a number of reasons, including different testing requirements.[48] Under s 1.3 of the Commercial Kangaroo Code, for example, shooters must pass a recognised (or approved shooting) accuracy test at least every five years.[49] Under the non-commercial code, however, s 3.1 provides that '[t]here is no competency testing regime for non-commercial kangaroo and wallaby shooters nor is there an intention to introduce a regime'. Even so, testing requirements for commercial shooters are not without problems. In the Commercial Kangaroo Code, for example, Appendix 1 specifies assessment requirements for shooting accuracy and testing, including that testing must not be conducted when it is windy or when visibility is poor. However, the standard operating procedure for shooting kangaroos and wallabies in Appendix 4 only specifies that shooters avoid shooting during adverse weather that would affect the accuracy of the shot.

The report of a NSW parliamentary committee published in 2021 documented significant problems with both the commercial and non-commercial killing of kangaroos. The committee accepted the inadequacy of chiller inspections for monitoring possible animal cruelty and found that there 'is a lack of monitoring and regulation at the

46 In NSW, for example, non-commercial 'culling' is typically up to 10% of the commercial harvest. NSW Office of Environment and Heritage 2018a, 4.

47 McLeod and Hacker 2019, 571.

48 RSPCA Australia 2020c. See also Animal Defenders Office 2021.

49 Requirements may also be imposed in the form of licence conditions. In NSW, for example, current licence conditions for professional kangaroo harvesters include possession of a Category B Firearms licence and a Firearms Accreditation for Kangaroo Harvesters provided by a Registered Training Organisation: NSW, Department of Planning and Environment 2020b.

point-of-kill during both commercial and non-commercial killing'.[50] It noted the 'unarguable' severe impact of the 2017–19 drought on kangaroo numbers in NSW and found that the methodology used to produce population estimates lacks transparency.[51] With serious concerns about the compatibility of a commercial kangaroo management program with the objectives of the *Biodiversity Conservation Act 2016*, the committee recommended a review of the Kangaroo Management Plan's objectives by the NSW Auditor-General in regards to the requirements of that Act and the federal EPBC Act.[52] In relation to non-commercial killing, the committee expressed 'grave concern' at the inability of the National Parks and Wildlife Service to provide accurate numbers of kangaroos killed under non-commercial licences, viewing it as 'indicative of lax monitoring and oversight across the board'.[53] Following release of the committee's report, allegations of cruelty and unnecessary killing of kangaroos by private landholders were aired by the ABC but rejected by a pastoralist on the basis that cruelty is 'a very, very small percentage of what happens'.[54] The ABC also documented concerns among some staff in the NSW Department of Planning, Industry and Environment about its policing of the commercial kangaroo industry. These include the impossibility of establishing the accuracy of the number of 'processed' carcasses, as well as a lack of compliance action, with no licence suspensions or prosecutions between 2015 and 2019, and a fivefold decrease in infringement notices over that period.[55]

Problems with the regulation of kangaroo killing are typical of the broader themes in animal welfare regulation, including weak and generally expressed minimum standards, fragmented and ineffective compliance monitoring and enforcement, and slow progress in revising codes of practice. As with the standard-setting process in general, the kangaroo codes are developed within a framework that privileges

---

50 Legislative Council Portfolio Committee No. 7 – Planning and Environment, Parliament of NSW 2021, 82.
51 Ibid, 56–7.
52 Ibid.
53 Ibid, 69.
54 Hambrett et al. 2021.
55 Ibid.

stakeholders with interests other than animal welfare.[56] Although the project team for the Commercial Kangaroo Code recommended an auditing program to ensure high levels of compliance, this was in the context of the need to maintain public confidence in the industry and its regulation.[57] As with other animal industries, the Commercial Kangaroo Code assumes the legitimacy of certain practices and relies heavily on general terms such as 'reasonable efforts' and 'whenever practically possible'. In combination with the definition of 'humane' methods of killing as 'those which *minimise* pain, suffering and distress' (emphasis added), the Commercial Kangaroo Code reflects the key attribute of all animal welfare legislation: harming animals is only prohibited where it is considered unjustifiable or unnecessary.

This qualified understanding of animal welfare has also found expression in the reasoning of the Administrative Appeals Tribunal (AAT). The Wildlife Protection Association of Australia (WPAA) sought a review in the AAT of the decision by the federal Minister for the Environment and Heritage in 2006 to approve the NSW Commercial Kangaroo Harvest Management Plan 2007–2011 (the Plan). One of the issues the AAT had to determine was whether the Plan satisfied the requirement of humane treatment of kangaroos imposed by the EPBC Act and the *Environment Protection and Biodiversity Conservation Regulations 2000*. The AAT accepted that instantaneous death by head-shot was not achieved on occasions, resulting in a period of suffering for the wounded animal, and in some instances a lingering death, but concluded that:

> … those instances, whilst unfortunate, do not detract from our conclusion that the Plan does all that can be done to promote the humane treatment of wildlife. Any management plan that involves the commercial killing of free-ranging animals will involve a risk that perfection will not always be achieved. What is required is that the Plan achieve as near to perfection as human frailty will

56 See Sharp and McLeod 2020 for details of the review process for the Commercial Kangaroo Code.

57 Ibid, 73.

> permit. We are satisfied that the system of accreditation, licensing and compliance management achieves that object.[58]

In relation to the treatment of orphan joeys, the AAT accepted:

> … that there will be a very small number of instances where young at foot die in this way, but we do not regard the fact, even in combination with the instances where an instantaneous killing of the adult is not possible, as leading to the conclusion that the Plan does not satisfy the object of promoting the humane treatment of wildlife. We are satisfied that it does meet that object.[59]

With respect to the fate of the joeys, the AAT found it unnecessary to resolve the conflicting evidence but provided no basis for its finding that young-at-foot die in 'a very small number of instances'.[60] In relation to the shooting of adult kangaroos, the tribunal had regard to the 2002 study by RSPCA Australia to conclude that death other than by head-shot only occurs in a 'small percentage of cases'.[61] As Thiriet observes, this ignores both the problematic survey sampling of that study and the very large number of kangaroos not head-shot.[62] The framing of the issue in terms of percentages, not raw numbers, not only underplays the extent of suffering but contributes to the construction of a particular understanding of animal welfare, an issue to which we return in Chapter 8.

Although ultimately unsuccessful, the WPAA was able to litigate because under the EPBC Act the minister's decision to approve the Plan was reviewable by the AAT. Under s 27 of the *Administrative Appeals Tribunal Act 1975*, an application for review of a decision may be made by any person whose interests are affected by the decision, including an organisation or association, if the decision relates to a matter included in its objects or purposes. Similarly, in 2009, Animal Liberation was able to challenge the killing of kangaroos by the Department of Defence on land in Canberra used as a military training facility because the

58 *Wildlife Protection Association of Australia Inc and Minister for Environment, Heritage and the Arts* [2008] AATA 717, [50].
59 Ibid, [51].
60 Ibid.
61 Ibid, [48].
62 Thiriet 2013, 230.

Nature Conservation Act 1980 (ACT) allowed an application to the ACT Civil and Administrative Tribunal (ACAT) for review of the grant of the licence by any person whose interests are affected.[63] At the initial hearing, Animal Liberation was found to fall within the definition of 'a person whose interests are affected' under s 22Q of the *ACT Civil and Administrative Tribunal Act 2008* (ACT).[64] The organisation was also initially successful in obtaining an interlocutory injunction to suspend the kangaroo killing but at the final hearing the ACAT confirmed the regulator's decision to approve the cull.[65]

The above cases illustrate the difficulty of persuading a tribunal on the merits of the issues where animal welfare conflicts with other interests. The AAT case also suggests the way a pattern of litigation by non-government organisations may lead to constriction of statutory rights of review, for example the removal of the right to seek review of certain decisions made personally by the minister under the EPBC Act. This amendment of the law by the *Environment and Heritage Legislation Amendment Act (No 1) 2006* (Cth) followed a series of challenges to ministerial approval of management plans in the AAT by conservation and animal welfare organisations.[66]

Native animals and non-commercial purposes

As the killing of kangaroos illustrates, an animal's native status does not necessarily protect it from the infliction of lawful harm. In addition to commercial purposes, the lawful killing of protected species may be authorised for non-commercial reasons, such as land management and mitigation of crop damage, subject to licence or permit conditions. By contrast with killing for commercial purposes which is described as 'harvesting', the killing of animals for non-commercial purposes is generally referred to as 'culling'. In the ACT,

63 See now the *Nature Conservation Act 2014* (ACT).

64 *Animal Liberation ACT v Conservator of Flora and Fauna* (Administrative Review) [2009] ACAT 9, [11].

65 *Animal Liberation ACT v Conservator of Flora and Fauna* (Administrative Review) [2009] ACAT 17, [125].

66 Thiriet 2013, 231.

for example, the government has carried out an annual kangaroo cull in nature reserves for over a decade. Despite conflicting evidence as to its necessity on conservation grounds,[67] the ACAT has indicated that it prefers the evidence in support of the culls. In an application by Animal Liberation ACT in 2014 to review decisions to grant licences to kill 1,606 kangaroos in eight nature reserves, the ACAT appeared to accept that the 'eventual death of a number of semi-independent young at foot would be a probable consequence of a cull, and that this was an undesirable outcome'.[68] Nevertheless, and despite acknowledging some potential for conflict of interest,[69] the ACAT preferred the evidence of the respondent's witnesses and accepted it as sufficient to justify the grant of the licences.

But kangaroos are not the only native animals permitted to be killed for non-commercial purposes. A wide range of other native species in Australia may be subject to authorised control measures, including birds, possums, snakes, flying foxes and wombats. These measures may be lethal or nonlethal. In NSW, information on the Public Register of Licences to Harm includes the species harmed, the maximum number to be harmed and the permitted control method. The most frequently authorised control method is shoot (firearms).[70] In Victoria, 4,254 authorities to control wild animals (ATCWs) were issued in 2018 for a total of 230,844 animals.[71] This data refers to the total number of authorisations issued for lethal and nonlethal methods and the maximum number of animals authorised, not the actual number controlled. Some more detailed information is now available following the establishment of the Office of the Conservation Regulator, as noted below. Of the 2,653 ATCWs issued between 1 January and 31 December 2021, 2,584 were for lethal control.[72]

Apart from the number of animals affected, the extent of damage caused by animals, the animal welfare impact and the need for lethal

67 Taylor 2017.
68 *Animal Liberation ACT v Conservator of Flora and Fauna* (Administrative Review) [2014] ACAT 35, [48].
69 Ibid, [41].
70 NSW, Department of Planning and Environment 2021c.
71 Victoria, Conservation Regulator 2018.
72 Victoria, Conservation Regulator 2022.

control methods are contentious issues. In Queensland, for example, damage mitigation permits to shoot flying foxes were reintroduced in response to rural interests by the Liberal and National Party Coalition (LNP) following the 2012 state election despite a ban on shooting as a control method in 2008 on animal welfare grounds.[73] Under cl 164(2) of the *Nature Conservation (Animals) Regulation 2020* (Qld), the killing must be in accordance with the *Code of Practice – Ecologically sustainable lethal take of flying foxes for crop protection* made under the *Nature Conservation Act 1992* (Qld). This Code covers three species, including the grey-headed flying fox, listed as vulnerable under the EPBC Act though not the *Nature Conservation (Animals) Regulation 2020* (Qld). As set out in s 1.1, the Code's purpose incorporates the formulaic reference to the minimisation of pain and suffering, with other key provisions similarly vague. Before granting a permit, for example, the chief executive must be satisfied that a *reasonable* attempt has been made to implement nonlethal deterrence methods and that the applicant *may* suffer 'significant economic loss', this being defined as *any* loss that *may* impact on the commercial viability of the crop for the grower.[74]

Another example of contentious government-sanctioned killing of native animals for damage mitigation purposes was the issue of a permit in 2020 to cull southern hairy-nosed wombats in South Australia. This decision was criticised by the Humane Society International, which pointed to alternative nonlethal solutions to prevent damage.[75] This example also illustrates the lack of public data in some jurisdictions about the number and type of wildlife authorised to be killed for damage mitigation and other non-commercial purposes. If data is not readily available, interested persons may need to resort to freedom of information legislation with its attendant delay and cost; even then, access to documents may be refused or granted in part only.[76] Where information about the authorised control of wild animals is published,

73 Thiriet 2013, 233–4.
74 Sections 3.2–3.4. Emphasis added.
75 Wahlquist 2020.
76 For example, SA Department for Environment and Water Disclosure Log, Disclosure Document F0003011604, 28 April 2020 in relation to an application for information about the number of destruction permits issued for southern hairy-nosed wombats. See https://www.environment.sa.gov.au/about-us/freedom-of-information/foi-disclosure-log/DEW-disclosure-log.

much more detailed data may be needed to enable effective evaluation of the regulatory schemes. As part of a review of the Victorian Authority to Control Wildlife (ATCW) system, for example, the Department of Environment, Land, Water and Planning noted stakeholder suggestions for improving information provision, including data on matters such as the number of ATCWs issued for nonlethal control, the number of applications rejected and the proportion issued to different land use sectors.[77] A subsequent review of Victorian wildlife protection laws prepared for the Humane Society International found that the system for authorised control of wildlife contains little accountability and lacks transparency.[78] While the assumption of responsibility for this system by the recently created Office of the Conservation Regulator (OCR) is a positive development, the OCR lacks a legislative base and statutory independence.[79] Also lacking transparency is s 7A of the *Wildlife Act 1995*, which provides for the declaration, by executive order, of protected wildlife as 'unprotected', subject to any specified conditions, on the recommendation of the minister. In 1984, this provision was used to 'unprotect' wombats in Victoria; while this status has recently changed, other native species which remain subject to 'unprotection' orders include brushtail possums, dingoes and sulphur-crested cockatoos.[80]

Wildlife trade

State and territory conservation laws also create licensing regimes for other commercial and non-commercial purposes, including the keeping and trading of some live native animals. In NSW, for example, the commercial wildlife trade is regulated by Part 2 of the BC Act. Although s 2.5 of the Act creates an offence of dealing in, or attempting to deal in, a native animal, s 2.11 provides that the Environment Agency Head may grant a biodiversity conservation licence to authorise the doing of an act that would otherwise constitute an offence under that provision. Under s 2.14, the licence may be granted subject to conditions, including

77 Victoria, Department of Environment, Land, Water and Planning 2018, 27.
78 Environmental Justice Australia 2020, 11.
79 Ibid, 18.
80 Ibid, 12.

minimum standards relating to the humane treatment of animals, with contravention of a licence condition constituting an offence.

The requirement to hold a licence is, however, subject to exemptions in the case of some native species. Clause 2.22 of the *Biodiversity Conservation Regulation 2017* (NSW) (the BC Regulation) provides that the offence of dealing in, or attempting to deal in, an animal in s 2.5 of the Act does not apply to the 41 bird species listed in that clause. These exemptions, plus the bird and reptile species that can be traded by a licensed animal dealer, are set out in the *Commercial trade of native animals policy* published by the NSW Office of Environment and Heritage in 2018.[81] Under Part 4 of this policy, the commercial trade of live native mammals and amphibians is not permitted, and the business must be conducted at the premises specified on the dealer's registration certificate. The policy states that grant of a licence requires demonstration by the applicant of 'appropriate knowledge and skills in keeping native animals' but does not specify what this entails. Some further detail is provided by the licence conditions available online, although these are not without problems. Under the current licence for dealing in live birds in NSW, birds must be kept at the registered premises and must comply with 'the mandatory requirements and conditions' in the *Animal Welfare Code of Practice No 4 – Keeping and Trading of Birds* published in 1996 (Bird Keeping and Trading Code).[82] In fact, however, the provisions in this Code are expressed almost exclusively in non-mandatory terms. Under the current licence for dealing in live reptiles,[83] all reptiles must be kept in the care of a person who can demonstrate they have at least three years' relevant experience. Other animal welfare conditions for reptiles include compliance with heating and lighting requirements, and with the minimum enclosure sizes specified in Attachment 2 of the licence. Under the *Commercial trade of native animals policy*, a licence to trade native reptiles will only be issued to a dealer who conducts their business in a pet shop and who can demonstrate compliance with the

81 NSW, Office of Environment and Heritage 2018b.

82 NSW, Department of Planning and Environment 2019. Animal dealer (live bird) licence, Schedule B. Presumably it is the licensees not the birds who are required to comply with the code.

83 NSW, Department of Planning and Environment 2021b. Animal dealer (live reptile) licence, Schedule A.

Animal Welfare Code of Practice – Animals in Pet Shops published in 2008 (Pet Shop Code).[84] Both these Codes are given legal force by Part 4 of the *Prevention of Cruelty to Animals Regulation 2012* (NSW) (POCTA Regulation), which provides that proprietors, managers, employees and workers of prescribed animal trades must comply with the provisions of each relevant code of practice listed in Sch 1 in relation to the relevant prescribed animal trade. The Bird Keeping and Trading Code and the Pet Shop Code are listed as relevant codes for the prescribed animal trade, pet shop, which is defined as a business in the course of which an animal is kept in a shop, or any booth or stall in a market or at a fair, for the purposes of sale.

As with many animal settings, the mass of regulatory detail in each jurisdiction, combined with the lack of national uniformity, makes it difficult to find information and to evaluate the extent to which animal welfare is addressed. Even a cursory examination, however, suggests familiar failings: fragmented regulation, exemptions from legislative requirements, outdated codes of practice and weak protections which reflect a narrow understanding of animal welfare. These problems may be illustrated by reference to the provisions governing the trading of live native birds in NSW, in particular, the requirements for their accommodation. At first glance, bird trading appears to be abundantly regulated with relevant provisions in the BC Regulation, the Bird Keeping and Trading Code, the POCTA Regulation and the Pet Shop Code. As noted above, however, the BC Regulation exempts 41 species of native birds from the offence of dealing in an animal under s 2.5 of the Act. According to RSPCA NSW, the exemption of these species from the licensing system 'poses unacceptable risks to the birds involved as there is no tracking system to identify their source (i.e. verification they have not been caught from the wild), their existence and whereabouts or to monitor the adequacy of their husbandry and care'.[85] In addition, current licensing requirements do not address online trading by animal keepers,

84 Draft standards and guidelines for pet shops and breeding dogs and cats to supersede the existing codes of practice were released by the NSW DPI for public consultation in 2018. An updated *Code of Practice – Breeding Dogs and Cats* was published on 30 August 2021 but an updated code for pet shops is yet to be finalised.

85 RSPCA NSW 2018a, 9.

an omission acknowledged by the regulatory agency.[86] In the view of RSPCA NSW, it should be a mandatory requirement for anyone dealing in native animals online or through any other medium, whether as a hobby or a business, to be licensed and to provide the licence number in any advertisement for sale or transfer to assist with traceability, transparency and accountability.[87] With respect to the Bird Keeping and Trading Code, as already noted, its provisions are expressed almost wholly in non-mandatory terms, for example s 5.1, which states that each species *should* be accommodated according to its need. By contrast, the Pet Shop Code incorporates mandatory provisions, including special requirements for birds in s 15, for example the requirement to provide sufficient perches and environmental enrichment. In terms of cage size, s 5.1.1.3 of the Pet Shop Code provides that all animal enclosures must meet the minimum requirements set out in Appendix 1. By way of example, the specified indoor cage size for the large sulphur-crested cockatoo (one of the 41 exempt species) is 6,000 square cm minimum floor area and 100 cm minimum height for three birds. While s 15.2.8 of the Pet Shop Code refers to the provision of freedom of movement and capacity for exercise or flight, as appropriate to the species, this provision is not mandatory. Clause 26(3)(e) of the POCTA Regulation also addresses space requirements but the terminology lacks specificity, requiring each animal to be provided with 'sufficient space within which to rest, stand, stretch, swim, fly or otherwise move about'. This kind of provision is capable of wide interpretation. In this context, it is notable that s 9(1A)(b) of the *Prevention of Cruelty to Animals Act* exempts an animal of a species which is usually kept in captivity by means of a cage from the requirement to provide adequate exercise. Although s 9(3) requires the cage to allow the animal a reasonable opportunity for adequate exercise, this provision, like the regulation, is open to wide interpretation. Section 9(1A)(b) is also a stark example of the way in which usual practice dictates the limits of animal protection the law affords.

Any ambiguity in wildlife provisions is unlikely to be tested by under-resourced enforcement agencies, a position further complicated by the fragmentation of responsibility that characterises most animal

86 NSW Office of Environment and Heritage 2018c, 33–4.
87 RSPCA NSW 2018a, 5.

welfare regulation. In the case of the above example of native bird trading in NSW, contravention of a licence condition constitutes an offence under the BC Act administered by the NSW Department of Planning and Environment, while the RSPCA has responsibility for enforcing the prevention of cruelty legislation, including compliance with the two relevant codes of practice. In addition to state agencies, the Commonwealth has an important role in the regulation of the wildlife trade, both legal and illegal. As well as exposing animals to serious health and welfare risks, the illegal trade in wildlife is a major cause of biodiversity loss.[88] Apart from the work of federal agencies in detecting and prosecuting the illegal movement of wildlife, the Commonwealth regulates the lawful import and export of wildlife under the EPBC Act. The *Asian Elephants* case, considered in Chapter 5, is an example of the regulation of wildlife imports under Part 13A of that Act. Exports of live native animals are regulated under the same legislation. The objects of Part 13A are set out in s 303BA and include ensuring that Australia complies with its obligations under the *Convention on International Trade in Endangered Species of Wild Fauna and Flora* (CITES) and promoting the humane treatment of wildlife. Under Part 13A, the minister must not issue a permit authorising the export of a live native bird unless satisfied, *inter alia*, that the proposed export would be for an eligible non-commercial purpose. In 2020, the federal Environment Minister ordered an independent investigation into departmental approval of the export of hundreds of native parrots between 2015 and 2018, including threatened species, following media reports that the birds were being sold not exhibited.[89]

Conflicting government interests

As with other animal settings, regulatory authorities responsible for enforcing nature conservation and environment legislation may favour relatively soft regulatory approaches over the exercise of more formal enforcement options. Once again, however, detailed information about

88 RSPCA Australia 2017, 1–2. For an interdisciplinary analysis of global wildlife trafficking issues, see McEwan and Turley 2021.

89 Cox 2020a; KPMG 2020.

regulatory activities is difficult to obtain. Further, inter-jurisdictional comparisons are problematic because of legal and regulatory differences, while even within the same jurisdiction enforcement functions may be fragmented. In NSW, for example, enforcement of the BC Act is carried out by local authorised officers and by the Special Investigations Unit which deals with the more serious matters. There is no centralised database of local investigations and the data held by the Special Investigations Unit is not publicly available. According to the then Department of Planning, Industry and Environment, however, there have been 20 formal investigations and 'numerous' penalty notices issued by the Special Investigations Unit for the s 2.1(1) offence of harming animals in the three years since the Act's commencement but no prosecutions have taken place.[90] Detailed information is also difficult to obtain in Victoria but the OCR's initial *Year in Review* reports five prosecutions with 45 charges for cruelty to or disturbance of wildlife in 2019–20. The OCR also undertook six prosecutions for illegal possession and trade of wildlife, and issued 14 infringements and 39 warnings, although it is unclear what activities the latter relate to.[91] Meanwhile, several highly publicised wildlife protection controversies led to the announcement by the Victorian Environment Minister in May 2020 of a review of the *Wildlife Act*.[92] These controversies included the failure to prosecute a landowner under that Act despite evidence of his involvement in the killing of hundreds of wedge-tailed eagles.[93] At the federal level, the reliance on a weak and inadequate collaborative approach to compliance and enforcement was one of the factors in the Samuel Review's finding that the EPBC Act is ineffective.[94] Among

90 Email from Peter Stathis, Manager, Biodiversity and Wildlife, NPWS, NSW Department of Planning, Industry and Environment to author, 10 November 2020.

91 Victoria, Conservation Regulator 2020, 11. Regulating wildlife was not included in the office's four priorities for 2019–20 but is listed as the final regulatory priority for 2020–21.

92 Environmental Justice Australia 2020, 5.

93 The sentence of 14 days' imprisonment imposed on the farm worker who pleaded guilty to killing the wedge-tailed eagles is the only custodial sentence ever imposed for the destruction of wildlife in Victoria. The worker was also fined $2,500: Environmental Justice Australia 2020, 7.

94 Samuel 2020, 21.

the problems noted were a failure to take serious enforcement action when warranted, inadequate penalties, a fragmented and disparate data collection and information system, limited transparency of compliance and enforcement functions, and no overarching framework to support evaluation of the Act.[95]

Enforcement may be particularly complicated when another government agency is responsible for alleged breaches. Documents obtained under freedom of information laws, for example, show that the federal environment department became aware of the clearing of a significant number of stringybark trees by the Victorian Department of Environment, Land, Water and Planning without approval under the EPBC Act.[96] These trees are a food source for the endangered south-eastern red-tailed black cockatoos. According to a media report, the matter was investigated but no action taken although similar cases involving private landowners resulted in the imposition of penalties.[97] Another Victorian government authority was initially restrained from conduct damaging to wildlife by the actions of an environmental group. In 2017, Friends of Leadbeater's Possum Inc commenced action in the Federal Court to stop logging by the Victorian statutory authority, VicForests, in 66 areas which constitute critical habitat for two threatened species of possum, the critically endangered Leadbeater's Possum and the vulnerable Greater Glider.[98] In her judgment, Mortimer J noted the 'inherent contradiction' under which VicForests operates, being required to perform its commercial forestry function in Victoria's native forest while doing so 'in a way which avoids and mitigates adverse impacts on a wide range of biodiversity values'.[99] Under s 18 of the EPBC Act, it is an offence to engage in conduct which has, will have or is likely to have a significant impact on a listed threatened species. However, under s 38 of the EPBC Act, forestry operations conducted in accordance with a regional forest agreement (RFA) are exempt from this provision.

95 Ibid, 21–3, 147–50.
96 Cox 2020b.
97 Ibid.
98 *Friends of Leadbeater's Possum Inc v VicForests (No 4)* [2020] 704.
99 Ibid, [12].

In 2020, for complex reasons set out in a lengthy judgment,[100] the court found that VicForests had not acted in accordance with the relevant RFA in the areas already logged and that its scheduled operations in the remaining areas were not likely to be conducted in accordance with the RFA. As a result, none of the areas logged or proposed to be logged were subject to the s 38 exemption. The court further held that s 18 has been contravened and/or is engaged because of the likely significant impact of VicForests' past and proposed forestry operations on the Greater Glider and/or the Leadbeater's Possum.[101] On 10 May 2021, the Full Federal Court allowed an appeal by VicForests. The court held that Mortimer J's finding that the actual conduct of forestry operations must be undertaken in accordance with the contents of the relevant RFA – that is, in accordance with any restrictions, limits, prescriptions or contents of the Code – in order to secure the benefit of the exemption in s 38(1) cannot be sustained'.[102] On 7 June 2021, Friends of Leadbeater's Possum filed an application for special leave to appeal this decision in the High Court on the grounds that the Full Court erred in its construction of key provisions of the EPBC Act and the *Regional Forest Agreement Act 2002* (Cth).[103] The application was refused by the High Court on 10 December 2021.

Control of introduced animals

Permission to kill kangaroos and other native wildlife on the basis of damage mitigation illustrates that these animals are not immune from the lawful infliction of harm when classified as pests. Legal protection in relation to non-native species living in the wild is even more limited. Although introduced into Australia through human agency, sometimes accidentally but mostly by design,[104] it is nonetheless animals who pay

100 The Federal Court's summary of the case is available at https://www.judgments.fedcourt.gov.au/judgments/Judgments/fca/single/2020/2020fca0704/summary/2020fca0704-summary.
101 The principal findings of the court are summarised in the judgment at [6].
102 *VicForests v Friends of Leadbeater's Possum Inc* [2021] FCAFC 66, [130].
103 Friends of Leadbeater's Possum Inc. 2021.
104 Franklin 2006; White 2013b, 461.

the price: native animals through the impact on their lives and habitat; introduced animals through persistent attempts to eradicate or contain them. Methods of control include shooting, trapping, poisoning, gassing, and the introduction of disease, as well as nonlethal methods such as exclusion fencing. Traditionally, there has been little if any regard for animal welfare in relation to the control of introduced animals despite the large numbers of animals affected.[105] In recognition of this failing, a workshop hosted by RSPCA Australia, the Animal Welfare Science Centre and the Vertebrate Pests Committee in 2003 led to the publication in 2008 of *A model for assessing the relative humaneness of animal pest control methods* (the relative humaneness model).[106] A second edition was published in 2011, following establishment of a panel to apply the model to selected existing methods of animal control.[107] While expressly acknowledging 'a worldwide trend towards ethical and moral concern for welfare of animals regardless of their status', the relative humaneness model also makes clear that 'welfare is just one of the issues to be considered' in assessing the suitability of a control method, along with such matters as effectiveness, cost, target specificity and practicality.[108] As 'an enabler not an inhibitor', the ranking process encourages the use and development of more humane techniques but does not compel them.[109]

The above development was part of a broader process to improve the humaneness of vertebrate pest control. The few existing codes of practice (COPs) and standard operating procedures (SOPs) for controlling animals considered pests were reviewed and the process to develop new COPs and SOPs outlined.[110] Initially covering ten animal species, each COP classified the control methods as *acceptable*, *conditionally acceptable* or *not acceptable*. In 2007, all jurisdictions agreed to phase out those methods listed as not acceptable,[111] with 31 December 2009 the recommended deadline for implementation.[112]

105 Thiriet 2007a, 418.
106 Sharp and Saunders 2011, 3–4.
107 Ibid, 4.
108 Ibid, 6, 34.
109 Ibid, 6.
110 Saunders and Sharp 2008, 158.
111 Ibid.
112 Ibid, 159.

The control methods identified in the COPs as *not acceptable* were: steel-jawed traps (rabbits, foxes, dogs, cats), strychnine baiting (foxes, dogs), chloropicrin fumigation of warrens (rabbits), warfarin baiting (pigs) and yellow phosphorus (CSSP) baiting (pigs).[113] Writing in 2007, RSPCA Australia's chief scientist noted that the phase-out of these methods is 'long overdue' and 'could be achieved 12 months earlier than the suggested deadline'.[114]

Over a decade later, there is no publicly available information about the status of the phase-out agreement but the PestSmart website, managed by the Centre for Invasive Species Solutions, documents the continued use of *not acceptable* control methods as of 2012. According to the 2012 model code of practice for the humane control of feral pigs, for example, CSSP was one of the poisons being used at that time for feral pig control in Australia, with warfarin trialled for this use under an experimental permit.[115] With numerous statutes in each jurisdiction relevant to pest control, it is difficult to establish the current position in every case but at least some methods listed as not acceptable continue to be permitted in some parts of Australia. For example, cl 8(1) of the *Animal Welfare (General) Regulations 2003* (WA) permits the use of an unpadded metal-jawed leghold trap in certain circumstances for the purpose of wild dog control. Clause 8(2) provides that the jaws of the trap must be bound with cloth containing strychnine. While the purpose of this requirement is to ensure a rapid death for any animal caught in the trap, the use of strychnine was also listed as a not acceptable method. In addition, methods which cause considerable suffering but were listed as conditionally acceptable continue to be lawfully used. An example is the use of baits poisoned with 1080, assessed by the relative humaneness model as causing hours of moderate to severe suffering when ingested by foxes.[116] In an echo of departmental investigations into reports of noncompliance in the live export trade, the technical language of relative humaneness blunts appreciation of the actual experience of the animals involved. In a moving account of the suffering endured by a

113 Braid and Buller 2007, 18.
114 Letter from Bidda Jones to Chris Buller, 20 November 2007.
115 Sharp 2012, 4–5.
116 Sharp and Saunders 2011, 97–8.

cat deliberately poisoned with 1080 in laboratory research, the biologist Clive Marks writes that:

> This should not happen. Reams had been written and careers built upon fragile facts. According to the government websites carnivores do not suffer when they are poisoned with 1080. Yet, in truth, very few had ever seen the outcomes of using this poison on cats. We all knew that this was because no one really wanted to see.[117]

To the extent that the above COPs and SOPs offer some protection to the management of introduced animals, they have not been given legal force by animal welfare legislation and merely provide guidance for the animals' more humane control. This is despite the support of RSPCA Australia in 2007 for the formal adoption of the COPs under state and territory laws[118] and the lack of protection for animals considered pests in animal welfare legislation. As previously noted, most of the animal welfare Acts include defences or exemptions to cruelty provisions for hunting or harming introduced animals considered as pests. Indeed, in the context of land management, the killing of some introduced species may be legally required. An example is s 20(1)(f) of the *Catchment and Land Protection Act 1994* (Vic) which provides that a landowner must take all reasonable steps to prevent the spread of, and as far as possible, eradicate, established pest animals, as defined by s 67. There is also a lack of national uniformity in relation to those provisions which do provide some protection, for example the use of steel-jawed traps referred to above which are prohibited in some jurisdictions but only partially prohibited or allowed in others.

Species membership is no guarantee of protection from legal harm when an animal is characterised as a pest. In *Brighton v Will*, the owner of a mobile petting zoo had his convictions for serious animal cruelty quashed on appeal to the Supreme Court of New South Wales. As set out in the judgment,[119] the charges arose from the appellant's actions in 2016 following the discovery of an attack by two dogs on a camel he owned, causing it significant injuries. Having captured one of the dogs,

117 Marks 2013, 55.
118 Letter from Bidda Jones to Chris Buller, 20 November 2007.
119 [2020] NSWSC 435, [11]–[17].

the appellant stabbed it at least six times with a pitchfork although by then the dog was subdued and tied to a tree. He then left the pitchfork in the dog while he sought medication from a vet for the injured camel. Finding the dog still alive on his return, he suspended it from a tree and beat it across the head with a mallet between six and eight times. In the Local Court, the magistrate found him guilty of two counts of serious cruelty to an animal in contravention of s 530(1) of the *Crimes Act 1900* (NSW) and sentenced him to a term of imprisonment. Under s 530(2)(b), a person is not criminally responsible for a s 530 offence if the conduct occurred in the course of or for the purposes of routine agricultural or animal husbandry activities, recognised religious practices, the extermination of pest animals or veterinary practice. In the Supreme Court, Rothman J upheld the appeal on the grounds that the magistrate had erred in holding that the dog was not a 'pest animal' and its killing was not an 'extermination'.[120] This case illustrates the great difficulty in successfully prosecuting animal cruelty and the court's very literal interpretation of s 530(2)(b) has been strongly criticised.[121] In the event, the RSPCA sought leave to appeal to the Court of Appeal which held that 'the primary judge erred in concluding that the defence in s 530(2)(b) was made out. Whilst the primary judge was correct to conclude that the dog was a "pest animal", its killing did not occur "in the course of or for the purposes of … the extermination of pest animals"'.[122] However, because the magistrate at first instance 'did not express his understanding as to the meaning of the requirement of intention and did not make any express finding as to the respondent's intention in respect of each charge', the matter was remitted to the Local Court to be determined in accordance with law.[123]

The gaps in protection afforded by animal cruelty laws are compounded by the variety of agencies with some responsibility for controlling introduced species. This regulatory fragmentation was remarked upon by a 2017 Victorian parliamentary inquiry. Noting

---

120 Ibid, [186]–[188].
121 Riley 2020a.
122 *Will v Brighton* (2020) 104 NSWLR 170, 190, [97] (Bell P).
123 Ibid, 190, [99] (Bell P); *Will v Brighton (No 2)* [2021] NSWCA 8. Note that s 530(1A) which governs the reckless infliction of severe pain was inserted into the *Crimes Act 1900* only in 2017.

that all three levels of government are involved in managing 'invasive' animal species, with multiple regulatory sources and overlapping policies and responsibilities, the Victorian inquiry concluded that the legislative framework is 'convoluted and confusing'.[124] At the level of local government, councils are responsible for the control of introduced animals on the public lands they manage,[125] while state and territory governments have legislated extensively across multiple domains, including nature conservation, biosecurity, pesticide use, agriculture, natural resources, land management, hunting and biological control. The Commonwealth also has a legislative role under the EPBC Act which provides for the ministerial listing of key threatening processes (s 183) and the making or adoption of a threat abatement plan (s 270B). In addition, the federal government has a significant national policy and co-ordination function through initiatives such as the development of the Australian Pest Animal Strategy.[126] This strategy is implemented by the Environment and Invasives Committee (previously the Invasive Plants and Animals Committee), whose membership is comprised of representatives of all Australian state and territory primary industry and environment departments and chaired by a member of the National Biosecurity Committee.

A package of reforms proposed by an independent panel tasked with reviewing the Australian regulatory framework for pesticides and veterinary medicines also has implications for animal welfare. Acknowledging growing concern about the treatment of pest animals, the panel proposed 'that the humaneness of pest animal control methods be assessed and displayed on the product label so that users can make an informed decision regarding humaneness of a (vertebrate pest control product)'.[127] If adopted, this welcome proposal 'would place the Australian pesticides and veterinary medicines regulatory system in a world-leading position'.[128] As with the information standard for

124 Environment, Natural Resources and Regional Development Committee, Parliament of Victoria 2017, 49.

125 Invasive Plants and Animals Committee 2016, 11.

126 Invasive Plants and Animals Committee 2016. The Australian Pest Animal Strategy 2017–27 lists the Australian Animal Welfare Strategy as a national related strategy at [11] even though the AAWS was already effectively defunct.

127 Matthews et al. 2021, 100.

128 Ibid, 101.

free range eggs, however, this regulatory approach relies on informed consumers as the driver of change, with user choices shaping decisions made by product developers and acting as an incentive for investment in more humane technologies.[129] Reflecting an awareness of the need to maintain social licence for vertebrate pest control tempered by pragmatism, the independent panel considered the proposal to be 'an opportunity to advance animal welfare objectives, at minimal cost, and without sacrificing users' decision-making prerogatives'.[130] It would also involve 'little regulatory impact as the regulator will not be required to assess any additional data; additional data requirements can be collected during existing trials and there are no additional obligations for users'.[131]

Case study: controlling cats

Current issues in cat control highlight the problematic nature of regulatory approaches to introduced animals. In 1999, 'predation by feral cats' was listed as a key threatening process under the EPBC Act, triggering the development of a threat abatement plan (TAP) which establishes a framework for a national response.[132] The first TAP for cats was published in 1999 and replaced in 2008 and 2015. As the TAP notes, cats were not only brought to Australia by colonists as early as the 18th century but were deliberately dispersed into the wild in the 19th century in order to control introduced house mice and rabbits.[133] The TAP is supported and complemented by Australia's first Threatened Species Strategy (TSS) published in 2015 whose targets 'to measure success' include killing two million feral cats by 2020.[134] 'Feral' cats are defined as those living and reproducing in the wild and surviving by hunting and scavenging, as opposed to owned domestic cats, or stray cats found

129 Ibid, 100, 101.
130 Ibid, 100.
131 Ibid.
132 Australia, Department of the Environment 2015a, 4–5. Prior to 1999, predation by feral cats was listed as a key threatening process under the *Endangered Species Protection Act 1992* (Cth).
133 Australia, Department of the Environment 2015b, 5.
134 Australian Government 2015, 11. The process for developing a new TSS began with a public survey on 30 October 2020.

in and around populated areas, including rural properties, who may depend on some human-provided resources.[135]

While introduced animals contribute significantly to biodiversity loss, the focus on this issue and the priority given to the lethal control of feral cats has been widely criticised, on animal welfare and other grounds. Wallach et al. argue that '[s]etting a conservation goal by the number of animals killed, rather than by a recovery target of any particular endemic species, defines the good by the act of killing', excluding nonlethal options from consideration 'even if they would provide better outcomes'.[136] Doherty et al. argue that the target to cull two million cats lacks a sound basis in science because of the unreliable estimates on which it is based, the difficulty of reliably measuring progress, and the lack of an explicit link between the target and direct conservation outcomes, such as measured increases in populations of threatened species.[137] Pointing out that feral cats are mentioned more than 70 times in the TSS, while habitat loss is rarely mentioned and land clearing not at all, the authors conclude that the focus on feral cats and the very visible and symbolic culling target may distract from other more politically sensitive threats to biodiversity.[138] Similarly, the identification in 2017 by the retiring Threatened Species Commissioner of feral cats as the number one threat to biodiversity[139] has been strongly disputed by some scientists and conservationists, with habitat loss, mostly through land clearing, viewed as the main driver of species extinction.[140] The inadequacy of some state land clearing laws has been widely documented,[141] while at the federal level, analysis of the EPBC Act has shown the legislation to be ineffective at halting habitat loss for terrestrial threatened species.[142]

The combined effect of habitat loss and other threats to biodiversity was highlighted by a NSW parliamentary inquiry into koala populations

135 Australia, Department of the Environment 2015b, 6.
136 Wallach et al. 2018, 1257.
137 Doherty et al. 2019.
138 Ibid, 4.
139 Borschmann 2017.
140 See, for example, Wintle and Bekessy 2017; Ward et al. 2019, 2.
141 See, for example, WWF Australia and Nature Conservation Council of NSW 2018.
142 Ward et al. 2019, 12.

and habitat. The inquiry found that the 'ongoing destruction of koala habitat through the clearing of land for agriculture, development, mining and forestry has severely impacted most koala populations in the state over many decades'.[143] The committee also found 'that climate change is having a severe impact on koalas, not only by affecting the quality of their food and habitat, but also by compounding the severity and threats of other impacts'.[144] In conjunction with the scale of loss caused by the 2019–20 bushfires, the committee concluded that the koala will become extinct in NSW before 2050 without urgent government intervention.[145] Almost three billion native vertebrates are estimated to have been impacted by the extreme bushfires in Australia in 2019–20.[146] The subsequent Royal Commission into National Natural Disaster Arrangements acknowledged the role of climate change in the frequency and intensity of extreme weather, with natural disasters 'expected to become more complex, more unpredictable, and more difficult to manage'.[147] Yet research commissioned by the Australian Conservation Foundation in relation to the management of critically endangered species under the EPBC Act found that climate change impacts are commonly omitted in conservation documents. Even where included, 'climate threat analysis tended to be brief and generalised', with limited recommendations to mitigate climate impacts'.[148]

The importance of addressing the complex causes of biodiversity loss was raised in submissions to a parliamentary inquiry established in 2020 to examine 'the problem' of feral and domestic cats in Australia.[149] Using data from the cat TAP to compare the multiple threats faced by vulnerable and endangered species, Riley et al. concluded that human action accounts for almost 60% of the total risks with 37.5% due to the impact of other

---

143 Legislative Council Portfolio Committee No. 7 – Planning and Environment, Parliament of NSW 2020, x.

144 Ibid.

145 Ibid, 11–12. In February 2022, the listing of koalas in NSW, Queensland and the ACT under the EPBC Act was upgraded from 'vulnerable' to 'endangered'.

146 World Wide Fund for Nature Australia 2020.

147 Royal Commission into National Natural Disaster Arrangements 2020, 22.

148 Reynolds et al. 2021, 4–5.

149 House of Representatives Standing Committee on the Environment and Energy, Parliament of Australia 2020.

species.[150] A wide range of other issues were also highlighted. The AVA noted that the TSS 2019 Progress Report failed to report on outcomes for the four key priorities, with publicly available detail 'particularly lacking' in relation to the target to kill two million feral cats.[151] RSPCA Australia's submission[152] referred to a recent study which estimated the Australian feral cat population as fluctuating between 1.4 and 5.6 million, depending on climate variables, with a further estimated 0.7 million unowned cats living in 'highly modified environments' such as urban areas, intensive farm sites and rubbish dumps.[153] In evidence to the inquiry, the Threatened Species Commissioner acknowledged that 'subsequent research' shows the number of cats 'isn't quite as high' as the 18 to 20 million estimate on which the two million target cull was based.[154] More generally, attention was drawn to the choice of terminology by an inquiry whose terms of reference omit any mention of animal welfare. RSPCA Australia, for example, noted the contribution of language to the 'demonisation of cats as aggressive predators', expressing concern that their labelling as 'pests' encouraged 'a lack of consideration for their welfare and, in the most extreme cases, deliberate inhumane treatment'.[155] Similarly, the inquiry's reference to the cat 'problem' rather than the 'impact' of cats serves to polarise community attitudes 'which can significantly affect support for control measures as well as lead to inhumane treatment of cats'.[156]

Hunting

Recreational hunting is commonly cited by hunters and their representative organisations as a means of controlling 'pest' animals but its efficacy as a control mechanism is not borne out by research.

---

150 Riley 2020b, 17–19. See also Riley et al. 2021.
151 Australian Veterinary Association 2020, 10.
152 RSPCA Australia 2020f, 5.
153 Legge et al. 2017, 299.
154 Evidence to House of Representatives Standing Committee on the Environment and Energy, Parliament of Australia, Canberra, 26 August 2020, 2 (Sally Box).
155 RSPCA Australia 2020f, 13.
156 Ibid, 2.

Indeed, there is a risk that recreational hunters exacerbate the problem through their choice of target animals, the dispersal of animals into new areas or the deliberate release of animals for hunting purposes.[157] According to the Invasive Species Council, more than 50% of the population of many species must be killed every year just to maintain a stable population, and even a large cull may 'result in perverse outcomes of expanded distributions and increased densities of targeted and non-targeted feral animals'.[158] While Bengsen and Sparkes found insufficient evidence to support or disprove the effectiveness of recreational hunting programs on public lands as a control mechanism, they note that the best information available suggests it 'is unlikely to provide a sufficient source of mortality to suppress many introduced mammal populations continually'.[159] Between 2014 and 2017, NSW National Parks and Wildlife Service managed a trial supplementary pest control program in national parks and other conservation reserves using volunteers from the Sporting Shooters Association. Despite a total cost of the trial of $5.9 million, an evaluation by the NSW Natural Resources Commission (NRC) was unable to 'draw firm conclusions on the conservation benefits for threatened species and ecological communities, due to the limited scale of the trial and limitations of the ecological monitoring'.[160] The NRC concluded, nevertheless, 'that volunteer ground shooting has the potential to be an effective supplementary pest control technique ... if used as part of an integrated pest management program under controlled conditions'.[161] As part of its evaluation, the NRC commissioned a systematic literature review of ground-based shooting by the Invasive Animals Cooperative Research Centre. Noting that there are situations where ground shooting can be useful, the review concluded that 'there are major limitations' on its ability 'to contribute to pest management objectives, and poor application of ground shooting methods can potentially cause more harm than good'.[162] In relation to animal welfare, the NRC evaluation reported that 18% of volunteers achieved

157 Booth 2009, 8; RSPCA Australia 2020e, 6.
158 Booth 2009, 2.
159 Bengsen and Sparkes 2016, 297, 306.
160 NSW Natural Resources Commission 2017, 1.
161 Ibid.
162 Bengsen 2016, 21.

only an average or poor rating for marksmanship and shot placement, a less satisfactory rating than for firearm safety and some other issues.[163] Nevertheless, and perhaps unsurprisingly, all of the volunteers agreed that 'operations were always implemented in accordance with required animal welfare standards'.[164]

Where shooting is not part of a managed program, or where other hunting methods are employed, the risk to animal welfare is significant. While there is the usual lack of national uniformity, in broad terms whether and what type of licence is required depends on the species hunted, where the activity takes place and the reason for hunting. Even when a licence is required, there is no or inadequate assessment of a hunter's competency in relation to animal welfare. In general terms, hunting methods include firearms, bows and arrows, and knives, and a hunting licence may be obtained by children. Some hunting activities, for example the use of dogs to hold pigs, are banned in some jurisdictions but allowed in others. Reference to the *Game and Feral Animal Control Act 2002* (NSW) (GFAC Act) illustrates these deficiencies. No licence is required to hunt cats, dogs (other than dingoes), goats, foxes, hares, rabbits, pigs, deer, and certain birds on private land (Sch 3). A restricted licence is required to hunt game animals (other than native game birds) on public land or to kill native game birds on private land under the authority of a native game bird management licence (s 15(2)). Grant of a restricted game hunting licence requires membership of an approved hunting club or organisation and completion of 'adequate training' (s 19). According to the NSW DPI, however, the training requirement is satisfied by completion of the restricted licence accreditation course conducted by hunting clubs and involving an open-book, multiple choice test, with the Hunter Education Handbook supplied at the venue.[165] The only reference to training in the current application for a general licence is the need to pass a Waterfowl Identification Test if authorised to hunt under the native game birds management program.[166] Children as young as 12 are eligible for a standard hunting licence or visitor's

163 NSW, Natural Resources Commission 2017, 24.

164 Ibid, 23.

165 NSW Department of Primary Industries n.d. R-Licence Accreditation Course.

166 NSW Department of Primary Industries, FORM B1: Application for a NSW General Game Hunting Licence, April 2015.

hunting licence, subject to adult supervision and the need to hold a minor's firearms permit if a firearm is used (cl 13; Sch 1 of the GFAC Regulation). This provision contrasts with the prohibition on the sale of companion animals in NSW to those under 18, presumably on the basis that children lack the skills or maturity to make responsible decisions about animal welfare.[167] Up to five dogs may be used to locate, hold or bail pigs on public land, subject to the requirements in Sch 1, Part 3 of the GFAC Regulation. The booklet about 'responsible' pig dogging published by NSW DPI makes no mention of animal welfare, in relation to either the pigs or the dogs.[168]

Other provisions relevant to animal welfare are also problematic. Although s 6 of the GFAC Act provides that nothing in the Act affects the operation of the *Prevention of Cruelty to Animals Act*, remember that s 24(1)(b)(i) of that Act provides a defence if the manner of hunting inflicted no unnecessary pain. Section 24 of the GFAC Act makes compliance with the mandatory provisions of an approved code of practice a condition of a game hunting licence, and s 23 makes contravention of a licence condition an offence. Mandatory provisions are contained in Sch 2 of the GFAC Regulation and include conditions relevant to animal welfare. As so often, however, they are expressed in very general terms; for example, an animal must not be inflicted with *unnecessary* pain and must be shot within the *reasonably* accepted killing range, and the firearm, bow and arrow or other thing used must be such as can *reasonably be expected* to humanely kill the target animal. Section 29 of the GFAC Act provides for the suspension or cancellation of a licence in certain circumstances, including if the holder contravenes any mandatory provision of the code of practice, or is found guilty of an animal cruelty offence, or the offence of releasing animals for the purpose of hunting.

In 2014, administration of the GFAC Act was transferred to the Game Licensing Unit (GLU) in the NSW DPI following an independent review which found that the then Game Council had 'not been able to

167 See, for example, para 9.1.1.2 of the NSW *Animal Welfare Code of Practice Breeding Dogs and Cats* 2021. As originally drafted, the GFAC Regulation would have allowed children to obtain a licence to hunt unsupervised but this clause was removed following strong public opposition: Ellis 2013a, 44.

168 NSW Department of Primary Industries 2016c.

resolve the inherent conflict of interest associated with its functions to both represent the interests of hunters, and to regulate their activities'.[169] Although the GLU's regulatory and enforcement policies emphasise the need to ensure transparency of operations and to maintain public confidence in the administration of game hunting legislation,[170] very little information is available online about its compliance and enforcement activities and none of it is specific to animal welfare.[171] No further information is available directly from the GLU about these matters. Notably, however, the GLU's enforcement policy only specifies licence cancellation if there are four or more breaches of a mandatory code provision or four or more offences in the past 12 months. Where the regulator becomes aware that a licence holder has been found guilty of a s 29 offence involving harm to animals, personal violence, damage to property or unlawful entry into land, the policy states that the penalty applied in relation to the offence should guide the GLU's response when considering licence suspension or cancellation.[172] As noted in earlier chapters, however, there are major obstacles to enforcing animal cruelty laws and even when matters are prosecuted penalties are typically low. In any case, the provisions in the GFAC Act regarding animal welfare only apply to licensed hunters; even then, in Caulfield's view they 'are unenforceable, unenforced and easily circumvented'.[173]

Traditional hunting

As we have seen, hunting for recreation and animal control often involves cruelty, yet the application of animal welfare legislation is inconsistent and limited. Some traditional hunting activities fall into the same category. In 2007, in an article headed 'Out of the "too hard basket" – Traditional hunting and animal welfare', Thiriet acknowledged the sensitivity of the subject, as well as the paucity of material in relation

169 Dunn et al. 2012, 3.
170 NSW Department of Primary Industries 2016a, 2016b.
171 NSW Department of Primary Industries n.d. Game Licensing Unit Outcomes.
172 NSW Department of Primary Industries 2016a, 14.
173 Caulfield 2018, 258.

to the animal welfare dimension.[174] This remains largely the case today. Nevertheless, with evidence that some hunting activities regarded as traditional cause considerable cruelty,[175] it is important to consider the relevant law in a context where the state-sanctioned cruelty of non-Indigenous practices has been widely acknowledged.

Traditional hunting activities are recognised as falling within the bundle of rights which constitute native title. Section 223(2) of the *Native Title Act 1993* (Cth) includes hunting and fishing in the definition of native title rights and interests in s 223(1). Section 211 preserves certain native title rights and interests, including hunting and fishing, by removing native title holders from any prohibition or restriction imposed under Commonwealth, state or territory law in the form of a licence, permit or other instrument where the activity is carried on:

(a) for the purpose of satisfying their personal, domestic or non-commercial communal needs; and

(b) in exercise or enjoyment of their native title rights and interests.

Section 211(2) of the *Native Title Act* includes a note that native title holders are subject to laws of general application in carrying on the relevant activity or gaining access to the land or waters for the purpose of carrying on the activity. While s 211 and s 223 have been the subject of judicial consideration by the High Court in relation to hunting and fishing,[176] determination of the relevant issues in these cases has not required consideration of any animal welfare provisions.

Some jurisdictions make specific reference to traditional hunting practices in their animal welfare legislation. Prior to 2012, s 8 of the *Animal Care and Protection Act 2001* (Qld) exempted acts or omissions by Aboriginal people under Aboriginal tradition and by Torres Strait Islanders under Island custom from the operation of the Act, subject to any conditions prescribed by regulation. The Act was subsequently amended by the newly elected LNP government to give effect to a policy commitment made after graphic footage of a turtle being butchered alive

174 Thiriet 2007b, 61.
175 Thiriet 2013, 238–9; Thiriet 2004.
176 *Yanner v Eaton* (1999) 201 CLR 251; *Karpany v Dietman* (2013) 252 CLR 507.

and a dugong being towed to its death was shown on the ABC.[177] The footage was obtained covertly, a means of exposure strongly criticised by the same political interests in the context of other animal settings. As noted by the parliamentary committee tasked with considering the amending legislation, the resulting Bill left intact other exemptions from cruelty offences, including cruelty associated with fishing and religious slaughter.[178] Another matter noted by the committee, and raised at public hearings and in subsequent submissions, was the lack of consultation with communities affected by the amendments before the Bill's introduction.[179] Nevertheless, the committee recommended the Bill's passage, subject to certain assurances and the inclusion of clear examples of permissible hunting methods.[180] Section 8 of the *Animal Care and Protection Act* now provides:

> A person does not avoid liability to be prosecuted for an offence under this Act only because the act or omission that constitutes the offence happens in the exercise or enjoyment of native title rights and interests.

Section 8 is qualified, however, by s 41A. This section provides an offence exemption for killing an animal under Aboriginal tradition, Island custom or native title provided that the act is done in a way that causes the animal as little pain as is reasonable. Section 41A(3) specifies the following acts or omissions as not falling into that category:

> (a) injuring the animal to stop it escaping after it has been caught;

177 Dingle and Robinson 2012.

178 Agriculture, Resources and Environment Committee, Parliament of Queensland 2012, 4. The concern to protect dugongs and turtles also contrasts with the reintroduction by the same government of damage mitigation permits to shoot flying foxes despite the known animal welfare issues.

179 Ibid, 5–7. See also Sowry 2015, 160–1.The rush to amend this provision contrasts sharply with the characterisation of the political response to other serious animal cruelty exposed by the media, with both the suspension of live exports to Indonesia in 2011 and the proposed NSW ban on greyhound racing in 2016 commonly denounced as 'kneejerk' reactions.

180 Ibid, 14–15.

(b) injuring the animal or prolonging its life to attract another animal;

(c) taking flesh from the animal for human consumption before the animal is dead;

(d) doing a thing or omitting to do a thing that causes the animal to die from dehydration or starvation.

The Northern Territory is another jurisdiction that addresses traditional hunting in its animal welfare legislation. As originally drafted, cl 110(2) of the Animal Protection Bill 2018 replicated s 79(2) of the existing *Animal Welfare Act 1999* (NT) to provide that it is not a defence to a prosecution for an offence against this Act that the conduct constituting the offence was in accordance with cultural, religious or traditional practices. In relation to cl 110(2), the Legislative Assembly Committee responsible for considering the Bill had regard to a number of matters raised in submissions to its inquiry. These included concerns about inconsistencies with existing Commonwealth and territory legislation, as well as with the *United Nations Declaration on the Rights of Indigenous Peoples*, the privileging of customs expressed in written codes, and the potential impact on the already disproportionately high rate of Indigenous incarceration.[181] Although acknowledging that there had been no prosecutions against traditional hunters under the existing law, nor any constitutional challenges, the committee was persuaded to recommend the Bill be changed to include a provision similar to s 41A of the Queensland legislation.[182] As enacted, s 110(1) of the *Animal Protection Act 2018* (NT) recognises the right of Aboriginal communities to conduct cultural practices and hunting and fishing activities in accordance with their traditional laws and customs; s 110(2) provides that it is a defence to a prosecution for an offence of cruelty or aggravated cruelty, other than an offence under s 24(3), if the person is an Aboriginal person and the conduct complied with Aboriginal traditional law or custom. More generally, s 111(2) provides that, subject to s 110, it is not a defence to a prosecution that the conduct was in accordance with cultural, religious or

181 Legislative Assembly Social Policy Scrutiny Committee, Parliament of the Northern Territory 2018, 50–3.

182 Ibid, 52–3.

traditional practices. The *Prevention of Cruelty to Animals Act 1986* (Vic) also includes a reference to traditional activities in s 6 which deals with the application of the Act. This section was amended in 2016 by insertion of the following provision:

> (1C) If a traditional owner group entity has an agreement under Part 6 of the **Traditional Owner Settlement Act 2010**, nothing in this Act prevents any member of the traditional owner group who is bound by the agreement from carrying out an agreed activity in accordance with the agreement and on land to which this agreement applies.

The definition of 'agreed activities' in s 82 of the *Traditional Owner Settlement Act* includes hunting and taking animals. Asked in the Victorian Parliament about this amendment, the government stated that it provides equivalence to existing exemptions in the *Prevention of Cruelty to Animals Act* for people who have recreational fishing or game hunting licences.[183]

Where animal welfare legislation lacks specific reference to Indigenous practices, traditional hunting is likely to receive the same treatment as other forms of hunting.[184] This includes the application of defences where relevant, such as s 24(1)(b)(i) of the NSW Act, already noted, and s 22 of the *Animal Welfare Act 2002* (WA) which provides a defence for an act authorised by law. While these defences are qualified – requiring proof that the act was done without the infliction of unnecessary pain or in a humane manner – the ambiguity of these terms and the difficulties they create for enforcement has previously been noted. Apart from animal welfare legislation, various other statutes contain provisions which exempt Aboriginal persons engaged in traditional activities from certain requirements respecting animals, for example s 17(1)(c) of the GFAC Act (NSW), s 68D of the *National Parks and Wildlife Act 1972* (SA) and s 182 of the *Biodiversity Conservation Act 2016* (WA).

183 Victoria, *Parliamentary Debates*, Legislative Council, 8 November 2016, 5861 (Steven Herbert).

184 Thiriet 2013, 240.

Uncertainty about the relationship between animal welfare laws and legally recognised traditional practices was highlighted in 2019 after a video of an off-duty Aboriginal police officer stoning a wombat was posted on social media.[185] The wombat was subsequently killed with a traditional hunting stick and eaten.[186] In response to widespread outrage, the South Australian Police Commissioner ordered both a criminal and internal disciplinary investigation into the officer's conduct, with an undertaking to report publicly on the outcomes. When doing so, the Police Commissioner agreed that some of the content of the video was 'disturbing', saying that he took 'personal displeasure in seeing any animal distressed, or being killed as the wombat was killed'. Nevertheless, the investigation established that the officer had the appropriate permit to hunt wombats for food, that his 'actions were not inconsistent with traditional hunting practices', and that the Director of Public Prosecution's office had advised that 'there would be no reasonable prospect' of a criminal conviction.[187]

In view of the jurisdictional inconsistencies, the complexity of federal native title legislation and the existence of relevant international instruments, the application of animal welfare laws to traditional hunting practices requires clarification. It is most important that any changes necessary to protect animals be developed in full consultation with Aboriginal and Torres Strait Islander communities.[188] They must also be part of a broader reform agenda in which the suffering caused by many non-Indigenous practices is acknowledged and similarly addressed. The latter includes activities commonly justified by reference to tradition and culture, such as recreational duck hunting, as well as that other practice in the 'too hard basket', religious slaughter. Culture or tradition cannot justify animal cruelty but to target traditional hunting while ignoring the suffering caused by non-Indigenous practices would be to perpetuate injustice, both to Australia's First Peoples and to the animals.

185 Kotzmann 2020b.
186 Smith 2019.
187 Stevens 2019.
188 Kotzmann 2020b; Sowry 2015, 161.

Complex issues, ethical debates

The complexity of regulatory issues in relation to animals in the wild reminds us of the need for ethical debates and broader theorising to inform the development of the law. In relation to introduced species, one recent strand of theorising emphasises the synergies between conservation and animal protection[189] and seeks to promote programs that benefit both individuals and species.[190] Known as compassionate conservation, this approach would extend the precautionary principle to animal regulation, with potentially harmful practices banned until proven safe.[191] Those who reject this approach stress the impact of introduced animals on native species and believe that it is not feasible at present to control them over large areas without lethal methods.[192] For this reason, the Invasive Species Council advocates the continuing use of 1080 despite acknowledging the suffering and distress it causes.[193] Although the Invasive Species Council also recommends giving priority to the development of more humane replacements and other nonlethal control methods,[194] the use of animals in scientific research involves its own ethical difficulties, as we will see in Chapter 7. In any case, securing adequate funding is an ongoing challenge, with the development of humane control methods readily dismissed on the basis of difficulty or cost.[195] Whatever the complexities, however, this much is clear: the use of control methods that cause moderate to severe suffering stands in contradiction to our knowledge of animal sentience. The focus on controlling animals rather than addressing human causes of biodiversity loss is also an abdication of our responsibility and leaves animals to bear the burden of problems created by us.

189 Ramp et al. 2013, 308.
190 Wallach et al. 2018, 1258–9.
191 Ramp et al. 2013, 309.
192 Booth 2020, 10.
193 Ibid, 16.
194 Ibid, 10.
195 See, for example, Saunders and Sharp 2008, 160.

7
The Use of Animals in Research and Teaching

The use of animals in research and teaching is regulated somewhat differently to other animal settings but is characterised by the same invisibility and lack of transparency. There is no public access to facilities where animals are used or kept and very little publicly available information about regulatory action. Nor is there a national database with information about the number of animals used, or their species, the purposes of the use, the severity of the procedures to which the animals are subjected, or their fate at the conclusion of the research. There is not even mandatory public reporting in each state and territory; where data is publicly available, the absence of any standardised format means there are inconsistencies within and between jurisdictions, as well as variable timeframes in which data is released. For these reasons, it cannot be stated with precision how many animals are used in Australia each year for research or teaching purposes or how many are subjected to the most harmful procedures. According to the Australian and New Zealand Council for the Care of Animals in Research and Teaching (ANZCCART), about six million animals are used each year in Australia, with a very significant proportion of these used in observational studies only with little or no interference,[1] but no reference is given in support of the figure cited.

Animal use statistics

ANZCCART is an independent body whose main role, as described on its website, is 'to provide leadership in developing community consensus on ethical, social and scientific issues relating to the use and wellbeing of animals in research and teaching'. In the absence of any national database, ANZCCART's website refers readers to Humane Research Australia (HRA) and those jurisdictions that publish animal use statistics. A not-for-profit organisation which challenges the use of animals in research and promotes humane alternatives, HRA collates Australian statistics from the limited information available. Due to the reporting deficiencies noted above, these statistics are estimates only but the numbers are viewed as conservative.[2] The latest available HRA statistics at the time of writing show that 20,160,469 animals were used by five jurisdictions (NSW, Queensland, Tasmania, Victoria and Western Australia) in 2017[3] compared to approximately 11,736,081 for the same jurisdictions in 2016.[4] The picture is complicated, however, by the much greater number of animals used in Queensland and, to a much lesser extent, Western Australia in that year for non-invasive research or research falling into the least harmful category: observational studies involving minor interference. The position is further complicated by the failure of Queensland to provide data by purpose or severity of procedure.[5] If the Queensland data is excluded, the number of animals used by NSW, Tasmania, Victoria and Western Australia in 2017 is 6,861,728, of which 3,879,872 animals were used

1 Australian and New Zealand Council for the Care of Animals in Research and Teaching 2018, 3.
2 Merkes and Buttrose 2019, 228.
3 Humane Research Australia 2017.
4 Humane Research Australia 2016.
5 HRA lodged a freedom of information application to determine the purpose and category of the large number of animals used by Queensland in 2017: Humane Research Australia 2017.

for observational studies involving minor interference. In 2016, the same four jurisdictions used a total of 7,216,611 animals, with 5,415,983 listed in the least harmful category. In NSW, this is described as not involving interaction with animals or, where there is interaction, it is not expected to compromise the animal's welfare any more than handling, feeding, etc., and with no pain or suffering involved.[6] While it is important to acknowledge that a significant proportion of animals are used in the least harmful way, this should not overshadow the very large number of animals who are subjected to other procedures with greater impact, including those that involve severe pain and suffering. Based on the above figures, for example, 2,981,856 animals in NSW, Tasmania, Victoria and Western Australia were subjected to other procedures in 2017, an increase over the 1,800,628 animals used by the same jurisdictions for these procedures in 2016. This is in addition to the animals used for research and teaching in the other jurisdictions, including Queensland, which reported the use of 4,519,470 animals in 2016 but provided no breakdown of this number by procedure severity. Because of the difficulty in cross-jurisdictional comparisons, we will consider the NSW statistics in detail when we examine the principles governing the regulatory framework.

As well as the lack of transparency, the absence of national, up-to-date statistics typifies a problem endemic to all animal use settings: the interminable delay in addressing issues relevant to animal welfare. In 1989, the Senate Select Committee on Animal Welfare recommended the annual publication of comprehensive statistics about animal experimentation.[7] In 1998, the NSW Parliamentary Research Service reported that 'a national scheme is underway to establish a comprehensive national database of animal use statistics, in order to develop an accurate, clear and simple mechanism to obtain meaningful data relating to animal use in research and teaching'.[8] More than 20 years later, this national scheme has failed to eventuate. In 2018, ANZCCART noted that it is working with state and territory governments and relevant

6 NSW Department of Primary Industries 2020b, 105. Wildlife field research can still involve some harm to animals: Marston 2015.

7 Senate Select Committee on Animal Welfare, Parliament of Australia 1989, Recommendation 2.30.

8 Figgis and Griffith 1998, 22.

organisations to address problems with consistency and accuracy in Australian animal use statistics,[9] but it is unclear what progress, if any, has been made in this respect. More recently, ANZCCART has prepared a draft openness agreement, 'a voluntary pledge that can be signed by organisations wishing to demonstrate commitment to greater transparency in their use of animals for research or teaching'.[10] Several countries have implemented formal openness agreements, with one published in New Zealand in 2021.[11]

Legal and regulatory framework

Consistent with nearly all other animal use settings, the states and territories are primarily responsible for the regulation of animal use for the purpose of research and teaching. As set out below, most jurisdictions include extensive provisions in their principal animal welfare Acts while NSW regulates this field with separate legislation. Note, however, that the proposed NSW reforms incorporate the regulation of animal research into a single animal welfare statute.

- *Animal Welfare Act 1992* (ACT) Part 4
- *Animal Research Act 1985* (NSW)
- *Animal Protection Act 2018* (NT) Part 4
- *Animal Care and Protection Act 2001* (Qld) Chapter 4
- *Animal Welfare Act 1985* (SA) Part 4
- *Animal Welfare Act 1993* (Tas) Parts 4 and 5
- *Prevention of Cruelty to Animals Act 1986* (Vic) Part 3
- *Animal Welfare Act 2002* (WA) Part 2

Although there are jurisdictional differences, all state and territory frameworks create a licensing or authorisation regime, require the establishment of an animal ethics committee (AEC), incorporate the

9 Australian and New Zealand Council for the Care of Animals in Research and Teaching 2018, 3.
10 Australian and New Zealand Council for the Care of Animals in Research and Teaching n.d.
11 Australian and New Zealand Council for the Care of Animals in Research and Teaching, 2021.

Australian Code for the Care and Use of Animals for Scientific Purposes (the Scientific Code) in some manner, and create an inspectorate, with sanctions for legislative breaches.[12] In addition, the legislative frameworks typically cover the breeding and/or supply of animals used in connection with research.

In NSW, for example, s 4 of the *Animal Research Act* authorises the regulations to prescribe a code of practice with respect to the conduct of animal research and the supply of animals for this use. Clause 4 of the *Animal Research Regulation 2021* prescribes the Scientific Code for this purpose. Under Part 4 of the Act, research establishments are accredited and licensed, and individuals issued with authorities to carry out animal research. It is unlawful to carry on the business of animal research unless licensed (s 46) or to engage in animal research without an animal research authority (s 47). Among other things, an animal research authority does not authorise the carrying out of animal research otherwise than with the approval of an animal ethics committee (AEC) and in accordance with the Scientific Code (s 26(2)). Other key parts of the Act are Part 4 which deals with the supply of animals, Part 6 which provides for the appointment and powers of inspectors, and Part 2 which creates the Animal Research Review Panel (ARRP) whose functions include evaluation of the efficacy of the Scientific Code and investigation of complaints. Note that the offences created by the *Animal Research Act* relate to the regulatory framework it establishes not to animal cruelty *per se*. Under s 47(2), however, it is an offence to carry out animal research otherwise than as authorised by the animal research authority, and s 26(2) prohibits the authorisation of research, *inter alia*, other than in accordance with the Scientific Code which addresses animal welfare.

Similar frameworks operate in those jurisdictions which regulate this field through provisions in their principal animal welfare Act and Regulations, although there are some legislative differences. In Queensland, for example, Chapter 4 of the *Animal Care and Protection Act 2001* requires registration to use an animal for a scientific purpose and this use must be approved by an AEC and comply with the Scientific Code. Similarly, in Victoria, Part 3 of the *Prevention of Cruelty to*

12 Timoshanko et al. 2016, 325.

Animals Act 1986 makes it an offence to carry out scientific procedures unless licensed and procedures must be carried out in compliance with any conditions prescribed by regulation or imposed by the department head. Compliance with the Scientific Code and matters relevant to the operation of AECs are included in the conditions prescribed by the *Prevention of Cruelty to Animals Regulations 2019*.

Most jurisdictions include provisions in their principal animal welfare legislation which effectively exempt procedures on animals carried out in accordance with these regulatory requirements from the application of cruelty offences. This objective is achieved in various ways. Under s 24(1)(e) of the *Prevention of Cruelty to Animals Act 1979* (NSW), for example, it is a defence to an offence under that Act or its regulations if the accused person satisfies the court that the act or omission occurred in the course of, and for the purpose of, carrying out animal research or supplying animals for use in connection with animal research in accordance with the provisions of the *Animal Research Act*. In Queensland, s 40 of the *Animal Care and Protection Act 2001* provides an offence exemption for acts or omissions which comply with the Scientific Code. In the ACT, relevant cruelty offences in Part 2 of the *Animal Welfare Act 1992* do not apply to conduct in accordance with an approved code of practice (s 20) and the Scientific Code is an approved code for the purposes of s 22. Some jurisdictions include provisions which exempt medical or surgical procedures for scientific research purposes, for example s 8(2)(h)(ii) of the *Animal Welfare Act 1993* (Tas).

Certain research procedures are regulated by provisions in the relevant Act or Regulation in some jurisdictions. In NSW, s 56A of the *Animal Research Act* requires establishments to keep a record of lethality tests and provide a copy to the ARRP, which may cause the information, other than the name of the establishment, to be made available to the public. A lethality test is defined as an animal research procedure in which any material or substance is administered to animals for the purpose of determining whether any animals will die or how many animals will die. Lethality tests include the LD 50 test (Lethal Dose 50 test) whose name derives from the dose of an administered substance required to cause the death of 50% of the target species. Section 26(4)(a) of the *Animal Research Act* prohibits approval by an AEC of the carrying out of the LD 50 test for the purpose of product testing, except with the concurrence of the minister on the recommendation of the ARRP. Section 26(4)(b) prohibits the Draize test, in which a substance is applied to the eye of an animal to determine its irritancy, unless carried out for the sole purpose of establishing that prophylactic or therapeutic eye medications are not eye irritants. In Queensland, s 92 of the *Animal Care and Protection Act 2001* prohibits, *inter alia*, the Draize test and the LD 50 test without the chief executive's written approval. In South Australia, these tests are limited to those purposes set out in cl 11 of the *Animal Welfare Regulations 2012*. In Victoria, cl 115(3) of the *Prevention of Cruelty to Animals Regulation 2019* prohibits the conduct of a scientific procedure involving the eye of any animal to determine irritancy of a chemical or biological agent unless carried out under terminal anaesthesia, while cl 115(4) requires, *inter alia*, ministerial approval for lethality tests.

Australian Code for the Care and Use of Animals for Scientific Purposes

Although the Scientific Code has no legal status in itself, its adoption by the regulatory framework in each jurisdiction gives it legal force and consequently its provisions substantially dictate the requirements for animal use in research and teaching throughout Australia. First produced in 1969 by the National Health and Medical Research Council (NHMRC), the main funding body in Australia of research using animals,[13] the Scientific Code is currently in its 8th edition, published in 2013. The NHMRC is a statutory body whose functions include advising and making recommendations to the Commonwealth, the states and the territories on public health and medical research. An Animal Welfare Committee has been established as a working committee under s 39 of the *National Health and Medical Research Council Act 1992* (Cth), with members appointed by the NHMRC CEO to advise on issues relevant to the use of animals in research. In reviewing the 7th edition of the Scientific Code, the NHMRC's Animal Welfare Committee and Code Reference Group undertook public consultation on the

13 Caulfield 2018, 218.

proposed revisions, as required by s 13 of the Act. As is usual now in revising codes of practice, animal welfare organisations are considered stakeholders in the review process but, as with other animal settings, their representation is outnumbered by stakeholders whose primary interest lies elsewhere. Unsurprisingly then, the resulting 8th edition has been criticised for its failure to address major concerns expressed in submissions, such as the need for greater transparency.[14]

Scope of the Scientific Code

The Scientific Code applies to the care and use of all live non-human vertebrates and cephalopods for scientific purposes. Accordingly, it applies to a wider range of species than the animal welfare Acts in some jurisdictions. Scientific purposes are defined broadly at [5] as:

> ... all activities conducted with the aim of acquiring, developing or demonstrating knowledge or techniques in all areas of science, including teaching, field trials, environmental studies, research (including the creation and breeding of a new animal line where the impact on animal wellbeing is unknown or uncertain), diagnosis, product testing and production of biological products.

As originally restructured for the 8th edition, the Scientific Code comprised the following six sections:

1. Governing principles.
2. Responsibilities.
3. Animal wellbeing.
4. The care and use of animals for the achievement of educational outcomes in science.
5. Complaints and noncompliance.
6. Independent external review.

In June 2021, the 8th edition was updated to incorporate a new Section 7 to ban the use of animals for cosmetic testing. Section 7.3 provides that the AEC must not approve a project or activity involving the use of animals for testing of finished cosmetic products, and s 7.5 prohibits

14 Merkes and Buttrose 2013.

investigators from using animals to test finished cosmetic products. Note, however, that a chemical ingredient contained in cosmetic products may still be tested on animals where the proposed use of animals is justified by a purpose other than use in a cosmetic, and it conforms to the other Code requirements.[15] The addition of Section 7 complements new federal legislation which impacts the importation and manufacture of cosmetic products tested on animals. The *Industrial Chemicals Act 2019* (Cth) prohibits the use of animal test data obtained from tests conducted on or after 1 July 2020 to support the import or manufacture in Australia of chemicals for an end use solely in cosmetics (s 168). Animal test data is defined in s 9 to mean data or information of a kind prescribed by the rules that relates to tests conducted on:

(a) any live vertebrate animal (other than a human being or other animal prescribed by the rules);
(b) any animal prescribed by the rules.

Clause 9 of the *Industrial Chemicals (General) Rules 2019* (Cth) prescribes cephalopods for the purposes of paragraph (b) of this section and kinds of data or information that relate to tests conducted on animals are prescribed by cl 8.[16]

Governing principles

The governing principles of the 8th edition, set out in Section 1, are referred to and elaborated on throughout the document:

1.1 Respect for animals must underpin all decisions and actions involving the care and use of animals for scientific purposes. This respect is demonstrated by:

 (i) using animals only when it is justified

 (ii) supporting the wellbeing of the animals involved

15 Sections 7.2(ii), 7.4 and 7.6.

16 For further information about the ban, see Australia, Department of Health 2021.

(iii) avoiding or minimising harm, including pain and distress, to those animals

(iv) applying high standards of scientific integrity

(v) applying Replacement, Reduction and Refinement (the 3Rs) at all stages of animal care and use:

(a) the *Replacement* of animals with other methods

(b) the *Reduction* in the number of animals used

(c) the *Refinement* of techniques used to minimise the adverse impact on animals

(vi) knowing and accepting one's responsibilities.

1.2 The care and use of animals for scientific purposes must be subject to ethical review.

1.3 A judgment as to whether a proposed use of animals is ethically acceptable must be based on information that demonstrates the principles in Clause 1.1, and must balance whether the potential effects on the wellbeing of the animals involved is [sic] justified by the potential benefits.

1.4 The obligation to respect animals, and the responsibilities associated with this obligation, apply throughout the animal's lifetime, including acquisition, transport, breeding, housing, husbandry, use of the animal in a project, and provisions for the animal at the conclusion of their use.

These requirements are further developed in the following Section 1 provisions:

- Use animals only when justified (cll 1.5–1.7).
- Support the wellbeing of animals (cll 1.8–1.9).
- Avoid or minimise harm, including pain and distress, to animals (cll 1.10–1.14).
- Apply high standards of scientific integrity (cll 1.15–1.17).

- Apply Replacement, Reduction and Refinement (the 3Rs) at all stages (cll 1.18–1.30).
- Accept responsibilities (cll 1.31–1.32).

The 8th edition also inserted a new Section 3 on animal wellbeing. This is defined at [6] as an animal who 'is in a positive mental state and is able to achieve successful biological function, to have positive experiences, to express innate behaviours, and to respond to and cope with potentially adverse conditions'. The governing principles which introduce Section 3 reinforce the requirements set out in Section 1. These include that the wellbeing of animals must be considered in terms of the cumulative effects of the animal's lifetime experience (cl 1.8) and that unless there is evidence to the contrary, it must be assumed that procedures and conditions that would cause pain and distress in humans cause pain and distress in animals (cl 1.10). As Caulfield notes, these and other provisions incorporate a precautionary principle and are far more extensive than any included in animal welfare statutes.[17] In terms of the Scientific Code's substantive provisions, however, very little has changed,[18] despite the emphasis on respecting animals and the active promotion of their wellbeing.

Animal ethics committees

Institutions must ensure, through the operation of an animal ethics committee (AEC), that all activities involving the care and use of animals comply with the Code (cl 2.1.2). As AECs are the cornerstone of the regulatory system, it is important to consider their functioning in detail. Clause 2.3.1 provides that the primary responsibility of an AEC is to ensure, on behalf of the institution for which it acts, that all activities relating to the care and use of animals are conducted in compliance with the Code. Key functions include reviewing applications for projects, conducting follow-up review of approved projects, and monitoring the care and use of animals (cl 2.3.2). The AEC must only approve those projects that are ethically acceptable and conform to the requirements

17 Caulfield 2018, 232.
18 Dandie 2013, 2.

of the Code. As set out in cl 1.3, whether a proposed use of animals is ethically acceptable must be based on information that demonstrates the principles in cl 1.1, and must balance the potential effects on the wellbeing of the animals involved against the potential benefits of their use.

Given these weighty responsibilities, the composition of AECs is critical. The core membership requirement is set out in cl 2.2.4, as reproduced in part below:

> Institutions must ensure that membership of the AEC comprises at least one person from each of four categories of membership:
>
> (i) Category A – a person with qualifications in veterinary science that are recognised for registration as a veterinary surgeon in Australia, and with experience relevant to the institution's activities or the ability to acquire relevant knowledge.
>
> (ii) Category B – a suitably qualified person with substantial and recent experience in the use of animals for scientific purposes relevant to the institution and business of the AEC.
>
> (iii) Category C – a person with demonstrable commitment to, and established experience in, furthering the welfare of animals, who is not employed by or otherwise associated with the institution, and who is not currently involved in the care and use of animals for scientific purposes.
>
> (iv) Category D – a person not employed by or otherwise associated with the institution and who has never been involved in the use of animals in scientific or teaching activities, either in their employment or beyond their undergraduate education.

In theory, Category C and D members bring a measure of independence and public accountability to AEC decision making but in practice their impact is limited. First, the Scientific Code also requires the appointment of a chairperson and this appointment may be additional to Category A to D members. While cl 2.2.3 provides that institutions should consider appointing a chairperson who is independent of the care and use of animals for scientific purposes, cl 2.2.2 provides that institutions should consider appointing a chairperson who holds a senior position in the institution. In addition, cl 2.2.5 recommends that institutions appoint to the AEC a person responsible for the routine care of the institution's animals, while cl 2.2.6 provides that institutions may appoint additional members with skills and background of value to the AEC. Where there are more than four members, categories C and D must together represent at least one-third of the AEC membership (cl 2.2.8). In other words, AECs can be, and probably usually are, lawfully dominated by those with an institutional or professional allegiance to using animals in research. The significance of this dominance is made clear by cl 2.3.11 which provides:

> Decisions should be made on the basis of consensus. Where consensus cannot be reached after reasonable effort to resolve differences, the AEC should explore with the applicant(s) ways of modifying the project or activity that may lead to consensus. If consensus is still not achieved, the AEC should only proceed to a majority decision after members have been allowed a period of time to review their positions, followed by further discussion.

This is not the only problem, however. As has been widely acknowledged, it can be hard for research institutions to find interested and suitable members of categories C and D.[19] Once appointed, they are subject to various pressures within AECs, as are other members, not least of which is the dependence on project approval to secure institutional research funding.[20] Further, it may not be easy, some would say impossible,[21] for lay members to critically evaluate proposals, notwithstanding the requirement in cl 2.4.12 for applications to be written in plain English and for investigators 'to ensure that all AEC members are provided with sufficient information to participate effectively in the assessment of the application'. The AEC must be satisfied that the research is justified on the basis that the potential benefits outweigh its costs but there is considerable debate about the efficacy of using animals, including among the scientific community. Major questions include the degree to which animal models have predictive value for outcomes in the

19 See, for example, Animal Research Review Panel 2019, 18; Russell 2012, 132.
20 Timoshanko et al. 2016, 329.
21 Caulfield 2018, 236.

human population and the extent to which research using animals has resulted in benefits.[22] In such hotly contested and uncertain terrain, those members with qualifications and experience in science or related disciplines are likely to heavily influence AEC findings as to key Scientific Code requirements.[23] These include whether the proposed project has potential benefit for humans, animals or the environment, whether the use of animals is essential to achieve the stated aims, whether the project involves the minimum number of animals required to obtain valid data and whether alternatives to animal use are available.

Lack of transparency

Under cl 2.3.5 of the Scientific Code, the AEC may approve only those projects and activities that are ethically acceptable and conform to the requirements of the Code. One means of assessing the efficacy of the regulatory framework might be to examine the number of protocols rejected by AECs or approved only subject to major modification. Another might be identification and consideration of those projects approved by a majority of AEC members where consensus proved elusive. While there is some evidence that outright rejection of proposals is rare,[24] relevant information about the work of AECs is not accessible to the public even though it is collected. Clause 2.2.30 requires institutions to maintain records related to AEC business, including minutes that record decisions and other aspects of the AEC's operation. Under cl 2.3.28, the AEC must submit a written report on its operations at least annually, advising on the matters set out in cl 2.3.29, including the numbers and types of projects and activities assessed, and approved or rejected. Notably, however, these reports must be submitted to the governing body of the institution(s) for which it acts, the same institution whose work the AEC is responsible for overseeing. These institutions have not demonstrated a readiness to make any of the information in these reports more widely available. According to

22 See, for example, Herrmann and Jayne 2019; Shanks et al. 2009.

23 Johnson 2014, 19.

24 Russell 2012, 135. In relation to the operation of committees in Sweden, Canada, the UK and the US, see Rose 2013, 10–14.

HRA, a request for the annual AEC reports of all major Australian universities for a range of years was ignored, or refused, in all but one case, while requests for even redacted versions of project applications, progress reports and final reports were also unsuccessful.[25]

The secrecy extends to the requirements imposed on institutions to monitor and review compliance with the Scientific Code. Clause 2.1.9 mandates the conduct of an independent external review at least every four years to assess the institution's compliance with the Code and the continued suitability, adequacy and effectiveness of its procedures. Although the review must be conducted by people with appropriate qualifications and/or experience who are independent of the institution and its activities, arrangements for the review are the responsibility of the institution (cl 6.2). In addition, the process for the manner in which the review is to be conducted must be developed in consultation with the institution, and the findings and recommendations from the review are reported to the institution's governing body (cl 6.5). Institutions are also obliged to conduct an annual review of the AEC's operation and the effectiveness of its processes regarding complaints and noncompliance (cl 2.1.9). Despite submissions during the review of the draft 8th edition calling for increased transparency,[26] cl 2.1.10 merely provides that institutions 'should consider' making publicly available an annual report of compliance with the Code and a summary of the independent external review report. As far as can be ascertained, however, institutions have failed to act on this recommendation. Notably, in response to an inquiry about this matter, the NHMRC recommended contacting relevant state and territory regulatory authorities. Yet the regulatory authority in NSW advises that the information sought is not held by the department because cl 2.1.10 recommends making these reports and summaries publicly available but does not mandate it.

This lack of transparency is reinforced by the following provisions in the Scientific Code applicable to institutions, AEC members and those conducting the independent external review:

25 Merkes and Buttrose 2019, 230.
26 Merkes and Buttrose 2013.

- Before appointment, all AEC members must acknowledge in writing their acceptance of any institutional requirements for confidentiality (cl 2.2.11).
- Members must maintain confidentiality regarding the content of applications and the deliberations of the AEC, in accordance with institutional requirements (cl 2.2.17).
- Institutions must establish procedures for the governance and operation of the AEC, including confidentiality (cl 2.2.20).
- Institutions should develop policies for maintaining confidentiality regarding the content of applications and the deliberations of the AEC (cl 2.2.22).
- Institutions must ensure that members of the (external) review panel are advised of requirements for confidentiality (cl 6.2).
- Members of the (external) review panel must adhere to confidentiality requirements regarding the review (cl 6.4).

Noting that less information is publicly available in Australia about animal research than in EU countries, Merkes and Buttrose propose that the following existing information be made available as a first step towards increased transparency: records of AEC meetings; AEC annual reports; institutions' annual reports to their state/territory government; and institutions' reports of the external reviews. They further propose that non-technical, plain language summaries be published online in Australia, as they are in the EU, clearly describing what happens to the animals used.[27] Nevertheless, the same authors noted that, as of 2019, improved transparency requirements in the EU since 2010 had not led to better implementation of the 3Rs nor seen an overall reduction in the number of animals used in research.[28]

Animals' fate at the conclusion of research

Another aspect of the use of animals for research and teaching that lacks public documentation is the fate of animals when no longer needed for

27 Merkes and Buttrose 2019, 238.
28 Ibid, 239.

the purpose originally approved. As set out in cl 3.4.1 of the Scientific Code in the section on animal wellbeing, the authorised options are:

(i) rehousing (rehoming)

(ii) return to normal husbandry conditions or natural habitat

(iii) humane killing

(iv) reuse

(v) tissue sharing.

Clause 3.4.2 provides that opportunities to rehome animals 'should be considered wherever possible'. An animal must not be released to a person at the conclusion of their use unless approved by the AEC (cl 3.4.3). There is no national data, however, about the number or proportion of animals who are rehomed or returned to normal husbandry conditions or their natural habitat. Nor is there any information about which species have been rehomed. According to the *NSW 2018 Animal Use in Research Statistics*, published by the DPI, some NSW establishments voluntarily reported on the fate of animals for the 2018 reporting year but only in relation to animals used for the research purpose: environmental study, with the fate of all animals being: remain free living in the wild or released to the wild.[29] Reporting on the fate of animals is mandatory in NSW from 2019 but only for domestic cats and dogs. In 2018, the *Animal Research Regulation* was amended to provide that in the case of a domestic dog or cat, the annual report to the department must include information as to whether the animal has been retained for research use or dealt with in some other way, for example euthanased or rehomed (cl 24(4)). While the *Research Animal Rehoming Guidelines* developed by the ARRP and published in 2020 has a broader application, its provisions are voluntary not mandatory.[30]

The lack of appropriate species-specific retirement facilities for some animals used in research, for example primates, has obvious relevance to their fate. The *Principles and guidelines for the care and use*

29 NSW Department of Primary Industries 2020b, 51.
30 Animal Research Review Panel 2020.

of non-human primates for scientific purposes developed by the NHMRC states that retirement must be considered as an option at the conclusion of their use 'if suitable in terms of the health and temperament of the animal, and space and resources are available at a facility that can meet their species-specific physical, social and behavioural needs'.[31] The same document acknowledges that:

> The complex and highly social behaviour and advanced cognitive capacity of many non-human primates make it difficult to adequately provide for their needs in a captive environment or research setting. In addition, many non-human primates have long lifespans and are often used in long-term research programs or re-used in multiple experiments over the course of their lives, presenting additional challenges for their care and welfare.[32]

Despite this recognition, the NHMRC guidelines sanction the keeping of primates in conditions antithetical to their complex needs. For example, non-human primates may be kept in individual cages when this is 'unavoidable' (cl 5.9) and may be held for up to six weeks without access to an outside enclosure. This period may be longer in some conditions or where the approval of the AEC has been obtained and the NHMRC notified (cl 5.14). These provisions are considered to accord with current best practice (cl 5.2). Further, while NHMRC-funded research using non-human primates must comply with that body's guidelines, the NHMRC appears to rely on the work of institutional AECs to monitor compliance, and it is unclear what consequences, if any, accompany any detected breaches. When asked during Senate Estimates how animal medical research is monitored and reported on, the NHMRC deferred to the regulatory responsibility of state and territory governments and noted the requirements of the Scientific Code. Although the inquiry was made in the context of the use of primates for research purposes, no mention was made of the additional requirement to comply with the NHMRC guidelines for primate research funded by that body.[33]

---

31 National Health and Medical Research Council 2016, 6.

32 Ibid, 1.

33 Parliament of Australia, Senate, Community Affairs Committee, Health Portfolio, Answers to Additional Estimates Questions on Notice, Budget Estimates 2019–2020 (Reference No. SQ20-000320).

This kind of incomplete response sits awkwardly with the NHMRC's assertion of 'national leadership on the use of animals for scientific purposes' and its references to transparency and accountability as 'key principles underpinning high-quality research'.[34]

Species used

In February 2020, the escape of three baboons while being transported from a NSW research facility put the spotlight on the use of non-human primates in research.[35] Under the NHMRC's guidelines, the use of great apes (gorillas, orangutans, chimpanzees and bonobos) for scientific purposes is only permitted when it will not have any appreciable negative impact on the animals or will potentially benefit the individual animals and/or their species.[36] Some jurisdictions also include provisions which regulate the use of gorillas, orang-utans, chimpanzees and bonobos, for example the *Prevention of Cruelty to Animals Regulation 2019* (Vic), cll 116 and 128 of which prohibit their use unless approved by the minister. Approval requires determination by the minister that it is in the best interests of that animal, or of the genus to which it belongs, and the benefits are not outweighed by the likely harm, or it is necessary to protect human health and the objective cannot be achieved by any other scientific means. The final condition is broader than the NHMRC guidelines and thus allows wider use of these animals by Victorian licence holders in projects not funded by the NHMRC.[37]

Other non-human primates which can be used in Australia for research are macaques, marmosets, night monkeys and baboons. While details are limited, some state and federal parliamentarians have sought to shed light on the use of these animals. In 2020, in response to a question on notice from Greens Senator Faruqi, the Health Minister advised that three projects which involve the use of non-human primates were approved by the NHMRC in 2019 (to commence in 2020), with 318 non-human primates proposed for use in research projects currently funded

34 Ibid.

35 Nguyen 2020.

36 National Health and Medical Research Council 2016, 4.

37 Humane Research Australia 2019.

by the NHMRC.[38] Another question from Senator Faruqi was directed to the NHMRC during 2020 Senate Estimates. Asked how many baboons were used for research purposes from July 2017 to March 2020 and how many were killed or harmed from 2018 to 2020, the NHMRC stated that it is the responsibility of the states and territories to collect statistics on animals used for research. It did, however, provide data on the number of baboons proposed for use in NHMRC-funded research submitted in the years 2017–19, with ten baboons proposed for use in 2017, 30 in 2018 and none in 2019.[39] In 2020, NSW Animal Justice Party MLC Emma Hurst moved a motion in the NSW Legislative Council for production of documents relating to the Australian National Baboon Colony in NSW.[40] The documents produced in response were accompanied by a claim of privilege identifying documents which are available for inspection by members of the Legislative Council only.[41] Documents classified as non-privileged can be viewed at the NSW Parliament or supplied by an MP to members of the public or the media. More documents were classified as privileged than non-privileged, however, including the Animal Research Review Panel Site Inspection Report of the Australian National Baboon Colony at Wallacia.[42] On 3 December 2021, a NSW Legislative Council inquiry was established to inquire into the use of primates and other animals in medical research in NSW.

Despite the lack of national data, the NSW Animal Use in Research Statistics provide some indication of which species are used. These statistics indicate that 44 primates were used in research in NSW in 2018, of whom nine were used for one of the most invasive procedures: major surgery with recovery.[43] More generally, the data indicates that

38 Parliament of Australia, Senate, Answers to Questions on Notice, Health Portfolio, 24 August 2020 (Reference No. SQ 1738).

39 Parliament of Australia, Senate, Community Affairs Committee, Health Portfolio, Answers to Additional Estimates Questions on Notice, Budget Estimates 2019–2020 (Reference No. SQ20-000320).

40 NSW, *Parliamentary Debates*, Legislative Council, 5 August 2020, 74–6.

41 NSW, *Parliamentary Debates*, Legislative Council, 26 August 2020, 62; 16 September 2020, 70.

42 Email from Tess Vickery, policy adviser to Emma Hurst, to author, 12 January 2021.

43 NSW Department of Primary Industries 2020b, 13, 26, 31.

the number of animals from various species groupings used in NSW between 2010 and 2018 inclusive is as follows:

Native mammals	10,716,840
Aquatic animals	6,531,762
Laboratory mammals	4,582,268
Birds (includes poultry)	3,948,493
Domestic mammals	1,267,627
Amphibians	730,784
Reptiles	150,697
Exotic feral mammals	88,820
Primates	649
Exotic zoo animals	530

The picture is complicated, however, by annual variations and the large number of some species used in some years for environmental or other studies involving the least harmful procedure: observation involving minor interference. In 2017, two projects in this category used almost 775,000 fish, while in 2015 and 2016, there was a large increase in animals used mainly due to two projects involving the aerial counting of bats.[44] The *2018 NSW Animal Use in Research Statistics* show that the most frequently used species groupings for all procedures were aquatic animals, laboratory mammals, birds (mainly poultry) and domestic mammals, in that order. In relation to the most harmful procedures, the most frequently used species in that year were mice, aquatic animals, poultry, rats, sheep and guinea pigs. Other species used in these procedures include rabbits, pigs, cattle and dogs.[45]

The 3Rs: a progress report

With their inclusion in the governing principles of the Scientific Code, the 3Rs (Replacement, Reduction and Refinement) are integral to the

44 Ibid, 4.

45 Ibid, 9–50. As discussed further below, the most harmful procedures are major surgery with recovery, major physiological challenge, death as an endpoint and production of genetically modified animals.

regulatory framework in Australia. First articulated by a zoologist, William Russell, and a microbiologist, Rex Burch, in 1959, the 3Rs are recognised internationally as the key principles which should inform the use of animals in research.[46] The concept had its origins in a project initiated by the Universities Federation for Animal Welfare in 1954 and the subsequent publication by Russell and Burch of *The Principles of Humane Experimental Technique*,[47] in which the authors demonstrated 'the total correlation between humaneness and scientific efficacy'.[48] Six decades later and with the 3Rs endorsed by regulatory regimes around the world, it is not unreasonable to expect considerable progress with their implementation. There is evidence, however, that the number of animals used for scientific purposes worldwide is increasing.[49] This appears to reflect the situation in Australia also, although the lack of relevant data means it is impossible to assess the position with precision. An increase in the overall number of animals used would be less problematic if there was clear evidence that they were being used for research in the least harmful categories. As we will see, however, the evidence from NSW does not support this. The lack of progress has been recognised by the European Parliament. In September 2021, it passed a resolution calling on the European Commission 'to establish an EU-wide action plan with ambitious yet achievable targets and milestones to accelerate progress in phasing out the use of animal methods in scientific research and education'.[50]

At the 2013 ANZCCART Conference, Bain and Debono reported that they had 'been unable to find a national statistics compilation that systematically reports on the degree of 3Rs implementation'.[51] In acknowledgement of the limited evidence, the NHMRC published an Information Paper in 2019 with the aim of presenting information about the implementation of the 3Rs, promoting informed discussion of

46 Gerber 2009, 214.
47 Russell and Burch 1959. A special edition, republished in 1992, is available at https://caat.jhsph.edu/principles/the-principles-of-humane-experimental-technique.
48 Russell 2009, 277.
49 Taylor and Alvarez 2019; Herrmann 2019, 4.
50 Humane Research Australia 2021.
51 Bain and Debono 2014, 25.

the issues and guiding recommendations for improvement if required.[52] Based on a literature review and a survey of investigators, AEC members and institutional representatives, the Information Paper includes some interesting findings but lacks specific information or statistical data about the uptake of the 3Rs. In relation to current practices, the literature review 'highlighted the paucity of peer-reviewed publications during the period 2007–2017 about the acceptance, uptake and/or implementation of the 3Rs in Australia' but noted findings which 'suggest that the 3Rs may not have been fully implemented and adopted'.[53] While the survey responses demonstrate a longstanding awareness of the 3Rs on the part of AEC members and investigators, they also reveal areas of poor understanding in relation to these principles.[54] Further, the lack of scientific or technological innovation was identified by all participant groups as the primary barrier to implementation of the 3Rs, with insufficient funding also identified by representatives of research institutions as a key factor.[55] This reflects a global problem. With the development of replacement methods 'limited most by the availability of funds', the redirection of funding is considered 'essential for the paradigm change towards advanced, animal-free science'.[56] Although a separate fund for research into alternatives to animal experimentation in Australia was recommended in 1989 by the Senate Select Committee on Animal Welfare,[57] no dedicated funding is provided through the NHMRC for the development of alternatives to animal use.[58]

While the numbers vary from year to year and the information available is limited, there appears to be no downward trend in the overall number of animals being used for research in Australia. On the contrary, animal use appears to be increasing, including for the most harmful procedures. More generally, there is concern that the emphasis on Refinement over Replacement not only reverses the order set out by Russell and Burch but may be used as justification for the continuing

52 National Health and Medical Research Council 2019, 5.
53 Ibid, 12.
54 Ibid, 14–15.
55 National Health and Medical Research Council 2019, 18.
56 Herrmann 2019, 31, 35.
57 Senate Select Committee on Animal Welfare, Parliament of Australia 1989, Recommendation 5.49.
58 Merkes 2019, 237.

use of animals.[59] The problems may be illustrated by reference to NSW, which provides a relatively detailed picture of animal use in research, including reference to the implementation of the 3Rs. The *2018 NSW Animal Use in Research Statistics* break down the number of animals used for different procedures in each of the calendar years 2010 to 2018 inclusive. Extrapolating the data for those categories with the greatest impact on animals, it indicates that the total use of animals has increased for these categories over this nine-year period. Table 7.1 sets out the number of animals used for three categories: major surgery with recovery, major physiological challenge and death as an endpoint. These categories are defined as follows:[60]

> **Major Surgery with Recovery**: Animal is rendered unconscious with as little pain or distress as possible. A major procedure such as abdominal or orthopaedic surgery is carried out and the animal allowed to recover. Post operative pain is usually considerable and at a level requiring analgesia.
>
> **Major Physiological Challenge**: Animal remains conscious for some or all of the procedure. There is interference with the animal's physiological or psychological processes. The challenge causes a moderate or large degree of pain/distress which is not quickly or effectively alleviated. Examples given include major infection, arthritis studies with no pain alleviation and isolation or environmental deprivation for extended periods.
>
> **Death as an Endpoint**: This category only applies in those rare cases where the death of the animal is a planned part of the procedures and animals die but are not euthanased, for example lethality testing.[61]

---

59 Gerber 2009, 217.

60 NSW Department of Primary Industries 2020b, 106–7.

61 As the definition in the Scientific Code at [4] makes clear, the death of the animal is deliberately used to evaluate biological or chemical processes, responses or effects and the investigator will not intervene to kill the animal humanely before death occurs.

Table 7.1. NSW 2018 Animal Use in Research Statistics*

	Major surgery with recovery	Major physiological challenge	Death as an endpoint	Total
2010	25,823	22,625	17,465	**65,913**
2011	19,643	28,614	17,767	**66,024**
2012	19,514	54,411	17,445	**91,370**
2013	18,105	42,647	15,997	**76,749**
2014	28,592	103,859	16,351	**148,802**
2015	16,722	34,489	16,771	**67,982**
2016	16,082	29,148	15,741	**60,971**
2017	28,436	77,292	13,982	**119,710**
2018	20,872	34,121	15,551	**70,544**
Total	193,789	427,206	147,070	**768,065**

* NSW Department of Primary Industries 2020b, 8. The final column is the total number of animals used for these three categories. The *2019 NSW Animal Use in Research Statistics*, published after this chapter was written, reveal that a total of 70,497 animals were used in 2019 for the same three categories: NSW Department of Primary Industries 2020a, 8.

Although there is considerable annual variation, the total number of animals used each year in NSW for these three categories only dipped below the 2010 starting point once, while several years show very significant increases, mainly due to substantially greater numbers of animals subjected to procedures involving major physiological challenge. The fact that 147,070 animals were subjected to procedures with death as an endpoint for the period 2010 to 2018 also calls into question the accuracy of the description of this category as only applicable in 'rare cases'.

In addition to the above categories, the number of animals used for the production of genetically modified animals has increased very substantially, from 98,386 in 2010 to 369,034 in 2018.[62] As advised by the DPI, 'animals in this category may be subjected to both minor *and* major physiological challenges *and* surgical procedures'.[63] When the animals in this category are added to those above, the total number of animals used in all four categories in NSW increased from 164,299 in 2010 to 439,578 in 2018.[64]

Under the heading 'Examples of methods used to implement the 3Rs', the *NSW 2018 Animal Use in Research Statistics* also include 'practical examples' of implementation strategies, as reported by research establishments.[65] Running to 46 pages, this impressive-looking list bears closer examination. Some of the examples are informative, and some specify the number of animals affected, but many are expressed in very general terms or simply reflect or restate the principles of the 3Rs or the strategies set out in the Scientific Code. Even where specific techniques are reported, there is typically no information as to the actual reduction in the number of animals used, or replaced, while the description of the strategies is often qualified. The following are just a few examples taken from the 2018 statistics, with the relevant page number noted, in order to illustrate the above limitations.

In relation to the principle of *Replacement*, listed examples include:

> *Encouragement of researchers to undertake literature and systematic reviews.* 57
>
> *Models for anatomical and clinical examinations are being reviewed constantly. Where appropriate these are used to replace the use of animals.* 58
>
> *On a regular basis researchers are implementing methods that partially replace the use of animals in their projects. Often the*

62 In 2019, 426,302 animals were used in this category: NSW Department of Primary Industries 2020a, 8.

63 NSW Department of Primary Industries 2020b, 107. Emphasis in the original.

64 Ibid, 8.

65 Ibid, 57.

> *establishment gets to hear about these through annual reports or expiry reports submitted by researchers.* 59

In relation to the principle of *Reduction*, listed examples include:

> *We have used in vitro models wherever possible and use cell lines and tissue culture wherever possible.* 65

> *Researchers are encouraged to share tissues wherever possible.* 70

> *Researchers are asked to use longstanding and well-established procedures in their research to ensure the minimum number of animals used.* 73

> *Using only minimum number of animals – discussion with researchers about their proposed AEC project.* 79

> *Close scrutiny of the numbers of animals requested in applications and progress reports to the Committee.* 79

Many examples claim a reduction in the number of animals used by exposing the same animals to multiple procedures. While cl 1.22 of the Scientific Code authorises the reuse of individual animals as a means of reduction, it refers to 'appropriate' reuse and requires the benefits of reusing animals to be balanced against any adverse effects on their wellbeing. Clause 1.24 states that reducing the number of animals should not result in greater harm to the animals used. In the listed examples, however, there is no or only oblique reference to these requirements:

> *Multiple tissues were collected from individual animals to enable analysis of as many parameters as possible from each animal.* 74

> *Re-use of animals, where appropriate, after extended recovery interval.* 76

Further, some examples reflect the application of basic methodologies that might be expected for any scientific procedure, or simply describe an unexpected outcome:

> *To reduce and refine our animal experiments, we analyse results of an experiment before starting the next experiment.* 72

> *The number of mice used in the project was reduced as the number of tumour cells required were less than expected.* 75

Of the three principles, *Refinement* has the largest number of entries in the 2018 list but many of the examples simply represent longstanding responsibilities of institutions and researchers, as required by the Scientific Code:

> *Suitable pain relief is always used for any intensive or surgical procedure.* 80
>
> *Trained personnel only administer treatments and collect samples on commercial farms.* 80
>
> *Use of analgesic after surgery.* 83
>
> *To reduce adverse impacts on animals, the AEC reviews each procedure carefully and may require more information to be provided.* 91
>
> *The establishment management continues to enforce the requirement of AEC applications being written in 'lay terms' and including definitions of medications.* 93
>
> *Continued emphasis on environmental enrichment.* 95
>
> *Animals are given appropriate rest periods.* 100
>
> *Following animal welfare procedural guidelines.* 100
>
> *Proper use of analgesics and anaesthetics.* 101

In highlighting the limits of many of the entries, the point is not to deny any institutional progress or to suggest that individuals who use or care for the animals are not concerned with their welfare. Some of the examples will have resulted in the use of fewer animals, while the wellbeing of animals will have been enhanced in some cases. It is also noteworthy that NSW provides considerably more information about animals used in research and teaching than some jurisdictions and should be commended for doing so. In the form presented, however, the information reveals little about how, and to what extent, the 3Rs are being implemented. It is also puzzling that the ARRP describes these lists as 'initiatives in replacement, reduction and refinement'[66] when many of the examples simply constitute a restatement of key Scientific Code principles or the requirement to provide animals with a basic level of care. Further, any suggestion that the reported strategies represent progress over time is contradicted by the raw data which indicates an increase in the number of animals used, including for the most harmful procedures. In combination, these difficulties leave the regulator open to the charge that inclusion of the list of strategies is largely a public relations exercise.

The NHMRC Information Paper is similarly problematic. For example, the identified 'areas of strength' in the 'implementation of the 3Rs' include 'Consideration of the 3Rs by AEC members when reviewing an application' and 'Consideration of the 3Rs by investigators during the design, conduct and review of animal care and use'.[67] Yet AEC members must have regard to the governing principles of the Scientific Code, including the 3Rs, in deciding whether to approve proposed animal use, and investigators must apply these principles in all aspects of the care and use of animals, including planning, conducting and reviewing projects. To characterise compliance with regulatory obligations as the implementation of the 3Rs is to confuse the ethical framework with the achievement of its objectives. That the NHMRC views as 'extremely positive' the finding that 90% of investigators reported that they consider the 3Rs when designing an experiment is troubling indeed.[68] Given that this course of action is mandated by section 2.4 of the Scientific Code, the NHMRC's response seems to suggest a very low expectation of regulatory compliance.

Compliance and enforcement

With the key role played by institutional actors and minimal government oversight, the regulatory framework is sometimes described as one of

66 Animal Research Review Panel 2019, 19.
67 National Health and Medical Research Council 2019, 19.
68 Ibid.

co-regulation or, more commonly, enforced self-regulation.[69] Although each jurisdiction creates an inspection regime to oversee the institutional self-regulation, little is known about the compliance and enforcement activities of these inspectorates. Again, the position in NSW may be used to illustrate issues familiar from other animal use settings. Part 4 of the *Animal Research Act* (ARA) provides a formal mechanism for the making of complaints against an accredited research establishment, the holder of an animal research authority, and the holder of an animal supplier's licence (ss 22, 28 and 42). In each case, complaints must be in writing and lodged with the Director-General who is to refer them to the ARRP for investigation. After consideration of the resulting ARRP report, the Director-General has the power to suspend or cancel the accreditation, authority or licence which is the subject of the complaint (ss 24, 28B and 44). Any person who is dissatisfied with a determination of the Director-General under Part 4 that affects them may apply to the NSW Civil and Administrative Tribunal for administrative review of the determination (s 45). The Director-General's powers are consistent with the view of the NSW Minister for Agriculture and Fisheries when the Animal Research Bill was debated that '[e]nforced self-regulation depends ultimately upon the power of the licensing authority to suspend or cancel a license'.[70] Information about complaints is included in the annual reports of the ARRP but no suspensions or cancellations are reported for the years for which annual reports are available online (2002–03 to 2018–19). This may be attributable, in part at least, to the infrequency of formal complaints. According to the 2018–19 ARRP Annual Report, for example, no formal complaints were received that year although three informal complaints were considered.[71] The annual reports for the preceding two years each note one complaint, while the Annual Report for 2015–16 records the receipt of two complaints.[72] It is unclear whether the complaints received in the period 2015–18 were formal or informal; in any case, no information is provided about

69 Timoshanko et al. 2016, 326.

70 NSW, *Parliamentary Debates*, Legislative Council, 13 November 1985, 9403 (J.R. Hallam).

71 Animal Research Review Panel 2019, 19.

72 Animal Research Review Panel 2018a, 13; Animal Research Review Panel 2018b, 14; Animal Research Review Panel 2017, 13.

the outcomes of any of these complaints, in contrast to earlier years. A small number of complaints is unsurprising, however, given the secrecy of animal research and the cultural and institutional pressures on those who are in possession of the relevant knowledge.

In relation to prosecutions, s 57 of the ARA provides that proceedings for an offence against the Act or Regulations can only be instituted by the Director-General or a person authorised by the Director-General. In 1997, the NSW Regulation Review Committee observed that no prosecutions had been initiated under the NSW animal research legislation[73] and only two prosecutions have occurred since then.[74] One prosecution was in relation to the supply by a council pound of dogs and cats to research establishments; the other in relation to the collection of blood from sheep and the sale of the serum by a company without authorisation under the ARA to do so.[75]

With respect to the application of the *Prevention of Cruelty to Animals Act 1979* (NSW) (POCTAA), the defence provided by s 24(1)(e) has already been noted. This defence only applies to research carried out 'in accordance with the provisions' of the ARA but the interaction of the two statutes, in combination with the secrecy surrounding the use of animals in research, effectively curtails a broader operation of the animal welfare legislation. Under s 24D(3) of the POCTAA, an inspector may not exercise enforcement powers 'in relation to animal research carried out in accordance with the *Animal Research Act 1985* on designated land within the meaning of that Act unless the inspector is also an inspector within the meaning of that Act.' This provision is ambiguous as there would be no need for enforcement powers to be exercised in relation to animal research carried out in accordance with the provisions of the ARA due to the operation of s 24(1)(e). That leaves open the possibility that an inspector appointed under the POCTAA could exercise enforcement powers in relation to conduct by an accredited research establishment not in accord with the provisions of the ARA. Very strong evidence would be required to warrant an investigation, however, and without

73 Figgis and Griffith 1998, 54.

74 Email from Lynette Chave, Leader, Animal Research, Animal Welfare, NSW Department of Primary Industries to author, 4 February 2021.

75 Animal Research Review Panel 1999, 25; Animal Research Review Panel 2008, 18.

routine access to research establishments, the necessary evidence would be difficult to obtain. On another interpretation, s 24D(3) is intended to describe research governed by the ARA and to prevent investigation by non ARA inspectors of an accredited research establishment regardless of compliance with the requirements of that legislative scheme. This interpretation is supported by the minor textual difference between s 24(1)(e) and s 24D(3). Either way, it appears that s 24D(3) was intended to preclude the investigation by POCTAA inspectors of research carried out at licensed establishments, unless the inspector is also appointed under the ARA.[76] Departmental advice, as of 2021, confirms there are no inspectors who are appointed under both Acts. This omission is particularly problematic given the administration and enforcement of the ARA by the NSW DPI, which is also a major player in the animal research industry.[77] Accordingly, regulation of animals used in research gives rise to the same problem of a conflict of interests which characterises other animal use settings.

The heart of the problem

In 1997, in a short piece recommended by ANZCCART two decades later, a longstanding category D member, Graham Nerlich, highlighted two key issues about the operation of AECs, with the aid of a fictional device in each case.[78] The first issue concerns the importance of good lay descriptions; the second, the need for the record to show that the AEC and the researcher have fulfilled their duties and acted responsibly. To illustrate that researchers can produce excellent lay descriptions of complex matters, Nerlich noted that *human* ethics committees

76 The debate on the Animal Research Bill in the Legislative Council in 1985 noted the view of the NSW RSPCA that the proposed legislation would prevent the authorised entry into research establishments of its officers: NSW, *Parliamentary Debates*, 13 November 1985, 9408 (J.H. Jobling); 9413 (Elisabeth Kirby).

77 NSW, Parliamentary Debates, Legislative Council, 13 November 1985, 9424 (J.R. Hallam).

78 *Australian and New Zealand Council for the Care of Animals in Research and Teaching News* 1997, 10 (2) reproduced in Australian and New Zealand Council for the Care of Animals in Research and Teaching 2018, 33–4.

always reject a researcher's information sheet unless it 'fully, and intelligibly' informs the potential human subjects about the reasons for the experiment and what will happen to them if they participate. Accordingly, a 'helpful fiction' for researchers using animals is to pretend that the lay description is an information sheet and imagine 'that one has to explain to the subject of the experiments its aims, the value of its results and just what is to be done to the subject'. With respect to the question of record, 'another useful fiction' was suggested: 'to imagine the protocols and the minutes of meetings as being later perused and evaluated'.

While good lay descriptions and comprehensive records are unquestionably important, these fictional devices, employed without a hint of irony, highlight the conundrum at the heart of animal experimentation. As Nerlich notes, human subjects who don't understand what's involved are less likely to participate '[s]o the pressure to make things plain in lay terms comes partly from the subjects themselves'. Yet no animal consents to procedures involving major physiological challenge or death as an endpoint; nor would human subjects do so no matter how clear the explanation. Instead, lacking any autonomy as research subjects, animals must rely on the institutional AEC to balance the impact of the proposed research on their lives against its 'potential' benefit to humans, other animals or the environment. These decisions are made within a framework which accepts the deliberate infliction of severe harm on sentient beings without their consent for a potential benefit to others despite the profound moral questions this raises. Even within this paradigm, however, the reliance on AECs as the lynchpin of the regulatory framework is problematic. As we have seen, AECs are accountable to the institution they serve and their membership is open to domination by those with an institutional or professional alignment with the researcher. Nor are AECs transparent because members are bound by confidentiality agreements and protocols and minutes are only perused by the relevant institution, apart from the requirement for an external review every four years. External reviews were introduced after Nerlich's piece was written and were mandated by the current edition of the Scientific Code, although ANZCCART wrongly refers to this as the 'triennial review process'.[79] As discussed, however, this process is also compromised in terms of independence and lacks transparency. Accordingly, the useful fiction about exposing AEC minutes to broader scrutiny also rings hollow.

79 Australian and New Zealand Council for the Care of Animals in Research and Teaching 2018, 34. An external triennial review was recommended by cl 2.1.2 of the 2004 Scientific Code but the external review mandated by the 2013 edition is only required every four years.

8

(Re)telling the Animal Law Story

In May 2018, a Northern Territory parliamentary committee reported on its inquiry into the Animal Protection Bill 2018. Two matters raised at the start illustrate how much work remains to be done if animals are to be afforded greater legal protection. First, the Northern Territory Cattlemen's Association (NTCA) submitted that changing the law's title, from the existing 'animal welfare' to 'animal protection', was a matter of concern because:

> The term 'Animal Protection' suggests *animal rights* rather than *animal welfare* is the priority of the legislation, which changes the intent of the Bill altogether. The proposed title has the connotation that in the NT animals need to be 'protected' and that 'care' of animals is not currently adequate. From an industry's perspective, the change to the title of the Bill suggests that 2.1 million head of cattle will require to be 'protected' under the Bill.[1]

The committee rejected that argument. It was satisfied that, given the Bill's objects and provisions, it could not be construed as giving priority to animal rights.[2] The second matter under consideration was whether

1 Legislative Assembly Social Policy Scrutiny Committee, Parliament of the Northern Territory 2018, 18 (emphasis in original).

2 Ibid, 19.

recognition of animal sentience should be included in the Bill's objects, as recommended by a number of major submissions to the inquiry but opposed by the Department of Primary Industry and Resources. The department noted that 'the content of the Bill and intention would remain the same with or without that recognition' and that 'the adding of sentience as a specific statement did not add to the intent of the legislation or enhance compliance' with it.[3] The General Manager of Fisheries and Product Integrity in the department further advised that:

> ... an Act is there to provide something that is clear and enforceable so symbolism was not a necessary step and it would not enhance the provisions of the Act and how they are applied in the field. I think the other factor is that we would be keen to see where this progresses nationally too in terms of – there is a lot of work going on nationally about how to harmonise some of these things and understanding around animal welfare and a whole range of associated legislation.[4]

In response, the committee expressed itself satisfied with the department's advice, stating that recognition of sentience 'is implicit in the Bill and does not need to be explicitly stated' in the Bill's objects.[5]

Legal recognition of sentience

It is telling that two decades into the 21st century, the peak industry body for Northern Territory pastoralists finds the idea of protecting animals too radical to legislate, while the department responsible for administering the law considers explicit recognition of animal sentience unnecessary. In any event, long before the NT legislation actually commenced, things *had* progressed nationally. As previously noted, recognition of sentience was included in the ACT legislation in 2019 and will feature in at least some of the other jurisdictions currently undergoing legislative reviews. In Victoria, for example, the reform

3 Ibid, 20.
4 Ibid.
5 Ibid.

process acknowledges that animals are sentient beings with 'the ability to feel, perceive and experience what happens to them in a negative or positive way', including physical pain and emotions such as happiness, fear and distress.[6] Accordingly, the government has committed to recognising animal sentience in its new animal welfare legislation, with a reference to sentience in the new Act's objects, or in the definition of animals, or in a set of legislative principles.[7] In another recent development, the Free Trade Agreement signed by Australia and the UK on 17 December 2021 recognises that animals are sentient beings.[8]

Even so, Australia is lagging behind a number of foreign jurisdictions which recognised animal sentience some years ago. The EU first recognised animal sentience in 1997 in the *Treaty of Amsterdam* and, again in 2007, in the *Treaty of Lisbon* which superseded it.[9] Article 13 of the current *Treaty on the Functioning of the European Union* (TFEU) states:

> In formulating and implementing the Union's agriculture, fisheries, transport, internal market, research and technological development and space policies, the Union and the Member States shall, since animals are sentient beings, pay full regard to the welfare requirements of animals, while respecting the legislative or administrative provisions and customs of the Member States relating in particular to religious rites, cultural traditions and regional heritage.

In 2015, the long title of the *Animal Welfare Act 1999* (NZ) was amended to recognise that animals are sentient. In the same year, the Civil Code of Québec was amended to provide that animals are not things but sentient beings. The 2015 legislation also enacted the *Animal Welfare and Safety Act* with the following preamble:

> AS the condition of animals has become a social concern;
> AS animals contribute to the quality of life in Quebec society;

---

6 Victoria, Department of Jobs, Precincts and Regions 2020, 17.
7 Ibid, 17–18.
8 Article 25.1. The Agreement is available at https://www.dfat.gov.au/trade/agreements/not-yet-in-force/aukfta/australia-uk-fta-official-text.
9 Broom 2017, 26.

> AS the human species has an individual and collective responsibility to ensure animal welfare and safety;
> AS animals are sentient beings that have biological needs;
> AS the State considers it essential to intervene in order to establish an effective legal and administrative regime to ensure animal welfare and safety.

Other countries or regions with explicit legal recognition that animals are not things include France, Columbia, Brussels and Slovakia.[10] As art. 13 of the TFEU exemplifies, however, these provisions may be qualified. France provides further illustration. While the 2015 recognition of animal sentience in the French Civil Code was seen as historic, some categories of animals are excluded, and animals are still 'subject to the regime of goods'.[11] That the force feeding of ducks and geese for foie gras production remains legal in France illustrates the limits of express recognition of sentience.[12]

Notwithstanding these limits, legal recognition of sentience is a small but important step in improving animal protection. Apart from any potential to influence statutory interpretation, explicit recognition of animal sentience contributes to the framing of the human and non-human animal relationship through law's symbolic function.[13] Its recognition in law can take more than one form. In the UK, for example, the government introduced the Animal Welfare (Sentience) Bill into the House of Lords on 13 May 2021. This Bill provides for the establishment of an Animal Sentience Committee to report on whether, or to what extent, the government is having, or has had, all due regard to the effect on the welfare of sentient beings when formulating or implementing its policies. In Australia, the summary of the findings of the public consultation for the review of the *Prevention of Cruelty to Animals Act 1986* (Vic) noted that 60% of survey respondents supported recognising animal sentience in the new legislation.[14] This proposal was also supported by most submissions but opposed by seven of the nine

10 Kotzmann 2020a, 287; Pallotta 2018.
11 World Animal Protection 2020b, 1.
12 Ibid.
13 Kotzmann 2020a, 309–10.
14 Victoria, Department of Jobs, Precincts and Regions 2021, 9.

agricultural organisations that provided feedback. According to the summary report, opponents believe that 'explicit recognition will not achieve any practical benefits for animals' but also that 'it has potential to be used to impact currently lawful activities'.[15] An MP's comments during the parliamentary debate in the ACT on the amendment which included explicit recognition of sentience in the *Animal Welfare Act 1992* are also instructive:[16]

> I must confess that, in some ways, this was something I had to grapple with, because the law and our community have historically treated animals as property, and sentience and reason were reserved for humans. This bill challenges the norm, and it is natural that we should question and be cautious about such a big step in our legislative framework.

It is surprising that explicit recognition of sentience not only attracts industry opposition but is still regarded by some as 'such a big step' and a challenge to 'the norm'. After all, animal sentience is an established fact, not a matter of opinion.[17] Long recognised by science, it is the acknowledged basis of existing animal welfare laws; indeed, it is the reason that the use of animals is mediated by the concept of humaneness. Perhaps the caution is because, as the MP's comments suggest, formal recognition of sentience exposes the incongruity of animals' property status. Or perhaps it is because the concept of sentience also grounds other approaches to the moral significance of animals which have much more far-reaching implications. Whatever the explanation, these considerations return us to ethical questions and those philosophical distinctions which so exercised the minds of the Northern Territory pastoralists.

15 Ibid.
16 ACT, *Parliamentary Debates*, Legislative Assembly, 26 September 2019, 3948–9 (Nicole Lawder).
17 Western Australia, Department of Primary Industries and Regional Development 2020, 18.

Moral significance of animals revisited

The equation by the NTCA of animal protection with animal rights is confused on two counts. First, as Broom puts it, '[w]elfare is a characteristic of an individual animal whilst animal protection is a human activity'.[18] In this sense, a law regulating the human use of animals may fairly be described as animal protection whether the legislation imposes obligations consistent with the animal welfare paradigm (although the adequacy of the protection may be open to critique) or much more extensive requirements. The second source of confusion is the conflation of animal protection with animal rights. A rights framework is based on the belief that animals are individuals in possession of inherent value, with an equal right to respectful treatment as an act of justice and independent of their utility.[19] By contrast, the welfarist ethic is underpinned by the use of animals as a human resource, with harming animals sanctioned by law where it is considered justifiable or necessary. As the NT parliamentary committee correctly identified, the Animal Protection Bill (now the *Animal Protection Act*) embodies an animal welfare ethic not an animal rights one, irrespective of its title.

As Peter Singer notes, however, the 'language of rights is a convenient political shorthand',[20] one that is commonly used to describe any approach which accords animals greater protection than at present. Although Singer's seminal work, *Animal Liberation*, is often characterised as an animal rights' tract, it is not an argument based on rights but on a form of utilitarian moral philosophy which places value on maximising the satisfaction of preferences and minimising pain.[21] Within this utilitarian tradition, Singer elaborates the principle of equality, better known in the context of sexism and racism, in relation to our treatment of animals. This principle requires like interests to be accorded equal consideration, with the treatment of other beings on

18 Broom 2016, 47.
19 Regan 1983, 280.
20 Singer 1995, 8.
21 Called preference utilitarianism, this is the form of utilitarianism Singer held at the time. He has more recently moved to a more classical form of utilitarianism based on the maximisation of the surplus of happiness over suffering. These different forms of utilitarianism often lead to the same result. The Panpsycast Philosophy Podcast 2018.

the basis of arbitrary and irrelevant criteria morally indefensible. The question thus arises: with respect to animals, what constitutes like interests? Acknowledging Bentham's pioneering 19th century work, Singer identifies the relevant interests as the capacity of animals to experience pleasure and pain and says:

> If a being suffers, there can be no moral justification for refusing to take that suffering into consideration. No matter what the nature of the being, the principle of equality requires that the suffering be counted equally with the like suffering – in so far as rough comparisons can be made – of any other being.[22]

As animals have a like interest in avoiding suffering and pursuing pleasure, a failure to give equal consideration to these interests in the utilitarian moral calculus is to engage in speciesism. Coined by Richard Ryder, and popularised by Singer's work, the term speciesism refers to 'a prejudice or attitude of bias in favour of the interests of members of one's own species and against those of members of other species'.[23] Avoiding speciesism does not mean treating animals the same as humans as Singer is careful to specify: the extension of the principle of equality to non-human animals 'does not require equal or identical *treatment*; it requires equal consideration. Equal consideration for different beings may lead to different treatment and different rights'.[24] Singer acknowledges that the impact of any given action may vary between animals and humans, or between different animal species, and that it is the same amount of pain (or pleasure) which requires equal consideration.[25] While precise comparisons of suffering between different species are probably impossible, radical changes to the way we treat animals would result even if we only prevented suffering when it was certain that the interests of animals would be affected to a much greater extent than the interests of humans.[26]

Singer's work is an example of consequentialist theorising which looks to the results of action to determine right and wrong. By contrast,

---

22 Singer 2011, 50.
23 Singer 1995, 6.
24 Ibid, 2.
25 Ibid, 15–16.
26 Ibid, 16–17.

Tom Regan's influential work, *The Case for Animal Rights*, reflects a deontological approach to ethics which denies 'that moral right, wrong, and duty depend *only* on the value of consequences of what we do'.[27] According to a rights view, certain individuals have moral rights and these 'are more basic than utility and independent of it'.[28] In Regan's analysis, certain individuals have inherent value and are due equal respect, regardless of whether they are moral agents or moral patients.[29] Moral agents are individuals whose sophisticated abilities enable them to make moral choices for which they should be accountable unless circumstances dictate otherwise; by contrast, moral patients lack the capacity 'to control their own behavior in ways that would make them morally accountable for what they do'.[30] The latter category includes some humans, for example young children, and animals. For Regan, both moral agents and moral patients have inherent value when they are the 'subject-of-a-life'. Individuals, whether human or non-human, fit this criterion if they:

> ... have beliefs and desires; perception, memory, and a sense of the future, including their own future; an emotional life together with feelings of pleasure and pain; preference- and welfare-interests; the ability to initiate action in pursuit of their desires and goals; a psychophysical identity over time; and an individual welfare in the sense that their experiential life fares well or ill for them, logically independently of their utility for others and logically independent of their being the object of anyone else's interests.'[31]

---

27 Regan 1983, 143. Regan notes that some deontological theories 'hold that the value of consequences is entirely irrelevant' to the determination of what we ought to do, while others 'hold that, though the value of consequences is relevant, other things are relevant too'.

28 Ibid, 145.

29 Ibid, 232–3.

30 Ibid, 152.

31 Ibid, 243.

In relation to animals, Regan conservatively attributes these capacities to all mammals aged one year or older.[32] Accordingly, the 'respect principle' requires the inherent value of these animals to be taken into account as a matter of justice.[33] Consistently with this, they are due to be treated with respect and not as 'renewable resources having value only relative to human interests'.[34] This applies to the premature termination of their lives in deference to our interests, even if the animals have otherwise been treated humanely.[35] A more recent development within a rights framework is the work of lawyer Gary Francione. Grounding the moral significance of non-human animals in sentience alone,[36] Francione maintains that because animals' property status will always preclude equal consideration of their interest in not suffering, the most basic right of animals is the right not to be regarded as property.[37] Personhood status for animals is central to taking their interests seriously because persons 'are precisely those beings who have interests that *cannot* be traded merely for consequential reasons alone'.[38] Criticising animal advocacy which does not effectively challenge animals' property status, Francione argues that acceptance of the personhood of non-humans goes hand in hand with the abolition of institutionalised animal exploitation.[39] By contrast, some rights proponents adopt an interest-based conception of rights and argue that abolition of animals' property status is not necessary to achieve justice for animals.[40]

---

32 Ibid, 77–8. Regan notes the difficulty in drawing the line between animals who do and do not satisfy his subject-of-a-life criterion and that many animals who do not meet it are nevertheless conscious and capable of experiencing pain. Given our ignorance, Regan argues that 'it is not unreasonable to give these animals the benefit of the doubt, treating them as if they are subjects, due our respectful treatment, especially when doing so causes no harm to us': 1983, 367.

33 Ibid, 248.

34 Ibid, 394.

35 Ibid.

36 Francione 2008, xiii.

37 Ibid, 38, 189.

38 Ibid, 193.

39 Ibid, 21, 23.

40 See, for example, Cochrane 2009.

Utilitarian and rights theories have dominated contemporary animal ethics discourse[41] but there are also other approaches based on different criteria. Virtue ethics, for example, is a strand of theorising which 'directs us to think about the rights and wrongs of our treatment of non-human animals in terms of virtues and vices rather than in terms of consequences, or rights and duties'.[42] Virtues 'are not just morally good character traits but *excellent* character traits', capable of supporting virtuous action, that is, action 'informed and shaped by reason'.[43] These attributes are necessary because morally good character traits, such as kindness and compassion, provide no clear answer in the case of moral dilemmas and can also inhibit right action in some circumstances, for example the need to kill a bird which has been mauled by a cat.[44] More generally, a concern with compassion, and other feeling states, distinguishes some of the more recent theorising from the rationality of the dominant approaches and their denial of the relevance of emotions to animal ethics.[45] Rejecting the reliance on abstract principle, Cora Diamond, for example, invites us to reflect on the idea of animals 'as our fellows in mortality, in life on this earth' and how this relates not just to moral concepts like justice but to other central concepts, such as pity.[46] A feminist ethic of care also favours a more nuanced, contextualised and relational approach to the human–animal relationship than the rational, abstract and universal nature of utilitarian and rights theorising.[47] Within this ethic of care, sympathy is not an irrational or sentimental response but an emotional and cognitive exercise,[48] one that involves 'an imaginative construction of the reality of another which is logically anterior to justice'.[49] Importantly, because attention must be paid not just to the individual suffering animal but also 'to the political and

41 While theorising about animal ethics has attracted renewed attention since the last quarter of the 20th century, it has a much longer history: Donovan and Adams 2007, 4. See also Bruce 2018, 2.
42 Hursthouse 2011, 119.
43 Ibid, 126–8.
44 Ibid, 126–7.
45 Donovan 2007, 59.
46 Diamond 2004, 102.
47 White 2013a, 45–6.
48 Donovan 2007, 179–80.
49 Ellis 2009, 373.

economic systems that are causing the suffering', political analysis is central to a feminist ethic-of-care approach to animal ethics.[50] Another alternative approach is found in the theorising of Martha Nussbaum. Her capabilities approach starts with 'a basic wonder at living beings' and a wish to provide a world in which different types of creatures flourish in their diversity and their particularity.[51] Acknowledging the differences between species, this approach seeks to create the conditions that allow animals to live a dignified existence and to flourish according to their different capabilities.

All of the above, and other relevant theories, are more complex than presented here and all are subject to significant discussion and critique in the literature. While it is beyond the scope of this work to engage in philosophical debate, it is important to acknowledge the breadth and depth of theorising which supports an enhanced view of animals' moral worth, as well as the practical implications of different theories. A key difference, for example, is that approaches based on a rights framework oppose any use of animals, or at least any use which denies animals the respect they are due, while utilitarianism accepts some use of animals provided that equal consideration is given to their interests. Animal experimentation is commonly used to illustrate the implications of these different ethical positions. Rights theorising rejects the use of animals in research because it 'assumes that their value is reducible to their possible utility relative to the interests of others';[52] by contrast, utilitarianism would accept animal experimentation 'if the benefit were sufficiently great, the probability of achieving that benefit high enough and the suffering to the animals sufficiently small'.[53]

Relevance of theories

Notwithstanding some very real differences, a wide range of philosophical approaches accord animals greater moral significance than they currently enjoy. This is because they view the lives of sentient

50 Donovan 2007, 3.
51 Nussbaum 2004, 306.
52 Regan 1983, 384.
53 Singer 2011, 58.

Figure 8.1. Bobby calves receive very different protections to companion animals. (Animals Australia)

beings as valuable in and of themselves, not as an adjunct to the satisfaction of human preferences. To give effect to this belief, regardless of its philosophical base, would require considerable change to the legal and regulatory framework. This may be illustrated by reflecting on issues previously covered in this book from a range of theoretical perspectives. You will recall, for example, that current laws allow the routine transport to slaughter of five-day-old calves without liquid feed for up to 30 hours and the live maceration of millions of male chicks every year because they cannot lay eggs and don't meet the requirements of the chicken meat industry. These practices are unacceptable from an animal rights perspective because they defy the respect principle, and from a utilitarian perspective because the interests of the animals have not been accorded equal consideration. But equally, these practices might be disavowed because they do not constitute virtuous action, or because they fail to recognise our fellowship with other vulnerable creatures, or because they deny animals any opportunity for their diverse capabilities to flourish, or because they exhibit a human failure to exercise moral imagination and occur in a context which lacks any political analysis.

Apart from their practical implications, some knowledge of different theories can bring a fresh perspective to animal protection issues, while suggesting related lines of inquiry. Again, this may be illustrated by reference to matters previously considered. The 2005 codes of practice for humane pest animal control included the AVA's 1997 definition of humane as:

> … causing the minimum pain, suffering and distress possible. To be humane is to show consideration, empathy and sympathy for an animal, an avoidance of (unnecessary) stress, and the demonstration of compassion and tenderness towards our fellow creatures.

In 2007, a decision was made to delete this definition as it was considered to be 'an inappropriate starting point for defining humane methods of pest control'.[54] Some repudiation of affective states is also apparent in the regulation of the commercial kangaroo industry. In their research on kangaroos for the Rural Industries Research and Development Corporation, McLeod and Sharp note that animals are sometimes not killed in the most humane way out of deference to human feelings. In this context, they cite Rollin's example of injured horses killed at the racetrack by means of an injection of succinylcholine 'because the public got upset when they saw blood if horses were shot',[55] even though the latter method is more humane for the animals. In relation to the killing of in-pouch kangaroos, McLeod and Sharp submit that, provided it is correctly performed, the duration and extent of animal suffering from blunt trauma to the head is much less than from other methods. While it 'may be unpleasant to perform' and 'may be seen as cruel and violent by observers', the researchers argue that 'the advantage of causing the least animal suffering outweighs the disadvantage of being aesthetically unpleasant'.[56] Accordingly, they recommend educating the public about

54 Sharp and Saunders 2011, 18; Braid and Buller 2007, 14.
55 McLeod and Sharp 2014, 29; Rollin 2009, 1084.
56 McLeod and Sharp 2014, 29.

the relative humaneness of this method of killing in-pouch young.[57] The research also established a discrepancy between the intention of shooters to euthanase dependent young-at-foot and how often they actually did this. In accounting for this disparity, one relevant factor was described as an 'internal head versus heart conflict': most shooters reported 'a strong desire to reduce the suffering of joeys' but also a dislike of killing them and a belief that in doing so they are taking away the joeys' 'chance at life'.[58]

McLeod and Sharp make an important point about the need to put the interests of animals before the sensibilities of humans in determining the manner of their death. Notably absent, however, is any teasing out of the shooters' feeling states, despite recognition 'that affect (or sentiment) is likely to be an important factor' in their decisions.[59] The researchers acknowledge that 'vulnerable young animals can have a significant emotional impact on humans, creating an innate drive to protect them' and that 'harvesters could experience strong emotions when faced with killing a joey'.[60] Their recommendations, however, focus on educating shooters about the welfare impact on orphaned young-at-foot, with consistent messaging required about the need for euthanasia.[61] Brief reference is subsequently made to the need for further research to investigate the discrepancy between shooter intention and behaviour.[62] In similar vein, the acknowledgement that forcefully hitting the heads of joeys against a large, unmoving solid surface is 'aesthetically unpleasant for both operators and observers'[63] prompts only limited reflection on why this might be so and no analysis of the potentially brutalising effect of this manner of killing. A similarly narrow approach is taken to the incorporation of Rollin's example about racetrack deaths: no mention is made of the likely reason for not wishing to 'upset' the public, namely the need to keep hidden the dark side of an industry in order to preserve its viability.

57 Ibid, 137.
58 Ibid, 121–2.
59 Ibid, 106.
60 Ibid, 121.
61 Ibid, 122.
62 Ibid, 139.
63 Ibid, 24.

Different dimensions emerge when these matters are viewed through the lens of alternative approaches to animal ethics. A feminist ethic of care, for example, might interrogate the shooters' concern that animals should have a 'chance at life', as well as the researchers' apparent lack of curiosity about this ambivalence. The reference to 'aesthetically unpleasant' killing might also prompt broader lines of inquiry: on whom does society depend to perform other 'aesthetically unpleasant' work and what is its impact on their lives and wellbeing? The independent inquiry into the slaughter of former racehorses in Queensland, considered in Chapter 5, accepted Animals Australia's submission that '[i]ndividuals who work in fast-paced commercial abattoirs must develop an emotional distance from animals being processed as a coping mechanism, and this disconnect increases the likelihood of deliberate cruelty occurring'.[64] Notwithstanding the different context, routine killing in the kangaroo industry also raises questions about the impact on those involved and the ramifications for animal welfare.

These reflections on emotional distancing might in turn lead to questions about the determination to keep animal suffering hidden from the public, whether in abattoirs, on the racetrack or elsewhere. As Adams argues, 'individuals are insulated from exposure to animal suffering, though their consequent emotional upset would be both valid and a valid foundation for theorizing'.[65] This insulation comes not only from the invisibility of much animal use but also from a cultural construction in which animals are not 'seen as possessing individual identities',[66] as we saw in Chapter 4 in the context of animal agricultural industries. In the live export industry, for example, the routine deaths of very large numbers of animals during transport are reduced to a percentage below which mortality is considered acceptable. Moreover, images of animal suffering obtained in connection with regulatory investigations are kept from the public as part of deliberate departmental policy:

> The department will not be publically [sic] releasing any footage relating to the above investigations. The department does not publish video or still images of cruelty to animals on its website.

64 Martin and Reid 2020, 62.
65 Adams 2007, 210.
66 Ibid, 211.

> This is because publication of this type of content may fall outside generally accepted community standards and can cause distress. The department has a responsibility to people, especially children, who may access information on our website. We want to ensure they do not inadvertently see images that they may find upsetting or disturbing.[67]

Applying Adams' theorising to the above policy might lead us to ask: is the department more concerned with the sensibilities of children or with the validity of the community's 'consequent emotional upset'? And why might *publication* of images of animal cruelty fall outside accepted community standards while support for the industry responsible for the cruelty apparently does not? Significantly, the department's policy not only keeps animal cruelty hidden from public view but frames its absence as a virtuous act. In the case of the live export industry, professed concern about public distress is used to justify a lack of transparency; in the case of the commercial kangaroo industry, the public must be educated as to the irrationality of their response. In each case, the focus on managing public emotion deflects attention from the industry, its underlying assumptions and whether the suffering involved is 'necessary'. Animal suffering is also kept hidden from the public by legislation. Ag-gag laws are the most obvious mechanism, but even public order legislation can have a chilling effect. In *R v Radunz*, the defendant was found guilty of committing a public nuisance under s 6 of the *Summary Offences Act 2005* (Qld) for standing in a public place holding a television playing silent footage of standard practices in Australian slaughterhouses.[68] During the trial, the court observed 'that a reasonable person is likely to have a serious, adverse, emotional reaction to the images and that reaction will seriously impact on their enjoyment of that public place'.[69] In this case, the footage depicted lawful practices but was still considered too offensive for public consumption.[70]

Theorising then is useful because it helps us to think systematically about our relationship with non-human animals and to question the

67 Australia, Department of Agriculture, Water and the Environment 2021d.
68 Rutledge-Prior and Ward 2021.
69 Ibid, 47.
70 Ibid, 49–50.

assumptions on which it is based. It also shapes the research in which we engage, enhances our analysis of existing problems and sets priorities for needed change. Although some theories advocate reform within existing legal and political frameworks, others deny that the interests of animals can be meaningfully addressed without abolishing all animal exploitation.[71] While acknowledging the difficulties, this chapter will nevertheless consider key reform proposals which arguably have the potential both to improve the wellbeing of animals and to contribute to changing ideas about their moral significance.

The international context

Before examining the scope for domestic reform, it is useful to situate the Australian position within a broader international context. In 2014, World Animal Protection (WAP) established the Animal Protection Index (API) which ranks 50 countries according to ten animal welfare indicators grouped into four goals: recognition of animal sentience and prohibition of animal suffering; presence of animal welfare legislation; establishment of supportive government bodies; and support for international animal welfare standards.[72] The latest edition, published in 2020, gave Australia an overall grade of D (where A is the highest score and G is the weakest). With a grade of B, the highest ranked countries were Austria, Denmark, the Netherlands, Sweden, Switzerland and the UK. Most European countries received an overall grade of C, with EU legislation having enhanced some aspects of animal welfare in that region. Key EU reforms have included a directive in 1999 prohibiting the installation of new battery cages for laying hens from 2003 and the use of existing battery cages from 2012.[73] In relation to pigs, a 2001 directive prohibited the installation of any new sow stalls from 2003 and the use of existing stalls from 2013.[74] While these are important changes, their limits should also be noted, although some member states have gone

71 See, for example, Francione and Garner 2010.
72 World Animal Protection n.d.
73 Stevenson 2009, 311.
74 Ibid.

further in banning or phasing out cages.[75] In the case of pigs, sows may still be kept in stalls for the first four weeks of gestation and for one week before the expected birth, and at other times kept in group housing.[76] Similarly, the ban on battery cages does not prohibit the confinement of laying hens but requires that any cages used must be enriched, with a nest, litter and perch, and a minimum space requirement of 750 square cm for each hen.[77] In any case, many other EU animals kept in enormous numbers continue to experience severe welfare problems that are only somewhat ameliorated or not covered at all by EU legislation.[78] Broom nominates broiler chickens as falling into the first category and disorders of high-producing dairy cows in the second, with fish, rabbits and ducks among other commonly kept animals who experience major welfare problems not covered by EU legislation.[79] Where regulations exist, their efficacy depends on their enforcement, the adequacy of which may be lacking. An audit of EU farm animal welfare, for example, found that tail docking is widespread in intensive pig farms in most member states, although routine use of this practice is prohibited by legislation.[80] Taking into account that animals in Europe generally receive more extensive protection than in large parts of the world, the magnitude of global animal suffering is immeasurable.

Adding to the problem is that a country which imposes more stringent animal welfare measures on its producers is at risk of being swamped by cheaper imports from countries with very different standards. Banning or otherwise discriminating against less welfare-friendly products may be difficult, however, due to the effect of international agreements aimed

---

75 European Commission 2021, 3.

76 *Council Directive 2008/120/EC of 18 December 2008 on Laying down minimum standards for the protection of pigs* [2008] OJ L 47/5, art. 3.4.

77 *Council Directive 1999/74/EC of 19 July 1999 on Laying down minimum standards for the protection of laying hens* [1999] OJ L 203/53, art. 6.1. But see notes 111–12 below in relation to the European Citizens' Initiative 'End the Cage Age'.

78 Broom 2017, 49–50.

79 Ibid, 49–51.

80 European Court of Auditors 2018, 42.

at reducing tariffs and other trade barriers.[81] Article III of the *General Agreement on Tariffs and Trade* (GATT), for example, requires World Trade Organization (WTO) member states to treat imported goods no less favourably than like goods produced domestically.[82] While it may be argued that animal products produced by different farming methods are not 'like' goods, there has been a 'marked reluctance' on the part of the GATT to permit distinctions on the basis of the way in which goods are produced.[83] A country found to have breached art. III, or art. XI which prohibits the imposition of bans or restrictions on imports or exports, may seek to rely on the exceptions contained in art. XX. Three of these have potential relevance to animal welfare: art. XX(a) measures necessary to protect public morals, art. XX(b) measures necessary to protect human, animal or plant life or health and art. XX(g) measures relating to the conservation of inexhaustible natural resources. The WTO's historically narrow approach to the interpretation of these exceptions may have influenced past government animal welfare policies.[84] In 2009, Stevenson argued that governments may be 'taking too cautious a view of the GATT restrictions and using them as an excuse for not making more meaningful changes to benefit the welfare of animals'.[85] Any such caution may be even less appropriate in light of the WTO's decision in the EU Seal Regime case. The case was initiated by Canada and Norway over EU Regulations banning the importation and sale of seal products on animal welfare grounds, subject to certain exceptions. In 2013, the WTO Panel determined that the objective of the EU Seal Regime falls within the scope of art. XX(a) and is provisionally deemed necessary to protect public morals within

81 The privileging of free trade policies also impacts animal welfare in a domestic context. An attempt by the ACT in 1997 to ban the sale of caged eggs was frustrated by the operation of the *Mutual Recognition Act 1992* (Cth). Adopted by each state and territory, this Act aims to promote the free movement of goods and service providers throughout Australia. While each jurisdiction is free to regulate the production of goods within its own boundaries, the sale of goods produced in other parts of the country cannot, with some exceptions, be banned without the concurrence of all the states and territories.

82 See generally Kawharu 2013.

83 Stevenson 2009, 319.

84 Ibid, 330.

85 Ibid, 331.

the meaning of art. XX(a), findings upheld by the WTO Appellate Body in 2014.[86] With respect to certain other aspects of the Regulations, the EU was requested to bring its measures into conformity with its obligations under the GATT.[87]

Animal welfare measures which impact WTO rules may also be upheld where nation states are carrying out the requirements of another multilateral treaty,[88] at least where it has been ratified by all parties to a dispute.[89] At present, however, there is no global treaty on animal welfare. In the case of wildlife, existing international treaties are mostly concerned with the conservation of endangered or commercially valuable species not the welfare of individual animals,[90] and there is no international treaty at all on the welfare of domestic animals. Various proposals since the 1980s have sought to establish a mechanism to fill this gap but as yet nothing concrete has eventuated. One initiative, led by the World Society for the Protection of Animals (now WAP), is in the form of a proposed Universal Declaration on Animal Welfare (UDAW). According to indicator 11 on WAP's API, the UDAW is 'a proposed formal international acknowledgement of a set of principles giving animal welfare due recognition among governments and the international community'. A draft UDAW, revised in 2005, has received significant international support, including from Australia,[91] but at this stage has not been adopted by the UN. Even if adopted, the UDAW is limited by the qualified nature of its standards and the fact that declarations are not enforceable against signatories.[92] Meanwhile, the World Organisation for Animal Health (OIE) appears to be positioning itself as the most likely intergovernmental organisation to achieve an international animal

---

86 Appellate Body Reports, *European Communities – Measures Prohibiting the Importation and Marketing of Seal Products*, WT/DS400/AB/R; WT/DS401/AB/R (22 May 2014) [6.1(c)]. This decision and a summary of key findings by the Panel and Appellate Body are available at https://www.wto.org/english/tratop_e/dispu_e/cases_e/ds400_e.htm.

87 These changes were implemented by the EU in 2015: World Trade Organization 2015.

88 Favre 2016, 96.

89 White 2013c, 396–7.

90 Favre 2016, 92–3.

91 World Animal Protection 2020a.

92 White 2013c, 395.

protection agreement,[93] with its Global Animal Welfare Strategy adopted by all member countries in May 2017.[94] As White notes, however, there are several reasons to be cautious about the OIE's capacity to provide an effective animal protection framework. These include the aspirational and non-binding nature of its existing welfare standards, with animal welfare subsidiary to the OIE's focus on facilitating animal agriculture and trade.[95] In a notable echo of domestic agencies with responsibility for the regulation of animal welfare, this focus is given expression by the Global Animal Welfare Strategy's assertion that the 'ethical and economic drivers of animal welfare are complementary'.

An alternative, and preferable, means of achieving a global framework is an international animal welfare treaty with provisions binding on contracting parties. With this in mind, an umbrella treaty, the International Convention for the Protection of Animals,[96] was drafted in 1988 but has been unable to attract an international sponsor.[97] Thirty years later, the Global Animal Law Association released a first draft of its proposed UN Convention on Animal Health and Protection.[98] More recently still, the coronavirus pandemic has heightened awareness of the interconnectedness of all life forms. In this context, the American Bar Association passed a resolution in February 2021 urging 'all nations to negotiate an international convention for the protection of animals that establishes standards for the proper care and treatment of all animals to protect public health, the environment and animal wellbeing'. It further resolved to encourage 'the US State Department to initiate and take a leadership role in such negotiations'.[99] The backdrop to these initiatives is a growing recognition 'that virtually all aspects of (commodified) human–animal interactions (ranging from food production and

93 Ibid, 394.
94 OIE, World Organisation for Animal Health 2017.
95 White 2013c, 394–5.
96 Animal Legal & Historical Center n.d.
97 Favre 2016, 97, 100.
98 Global Animal Law n.d.
99 The resolution and further information are available at Lewis & Clark Law School, Center for Animal Law Studies, https://law.lclark.edu/live/news/45294-american-bar-association-calls-for-the-negotiation.

distribution, working animals, animal use in research, to breeding and keeping of pets) possess a transboundary dimension'.[100]

One important attribute of an international convention is that conformity with its requirements is an expectation of membership.[101] Problems can still arise, however, as the dispute between Australia and Japan about whaling illustrates. This dispute has a long and complex history. For more than ten years, a non-government organisation, the Humane Society International (HSI), engaged in litigation in Australian courts in relation to Japanese whaling activities in waters over which Australia has a territorial claim. In 2008, the HSI obtained an injunction in the Federal Court ordering that a Japanese whaling company be restrained from killing, injuring, taking or interfering with any Antarctic minke, fin or humpback whale in the Australian Whale Sanctuary in contravention of the EPBC Act.[102] Due to complex political and legal considerations, including the lack of recognition by some nations of Australia's territorial claim in Antarctica,[103] the injunction was not enforced. In 2015, in further Federal Court proceedings initiated by the HSI, the Japanese vessel responsible for continued whaling was held to be in contempt of court for breaching the 2008 injunctions and fined a total of $1,000,000.[104] Meanwhile, with no resolution of the issue, Australia initiated proceedings in the International Court of Justice (ICJ) in 2010 challenging Japan's whaling activities in the Antarctic on the grounds that they breached Japan's obligations under the *International Convention for the Regulation of Whaling* (ICRW) and other international obligations. Originally created to conserve whaling stocks for the orderly development of the industry, the ICRW established the International Whaling Commission (IWC) in 1946. Exhibiting a gradual change in focus, the IWC decided in 1982 that commercial whaling should be paused from the 1985–86 season. Commonly referred to as the commercial whaling moratorium, this decision remains in place today.[105] In the Australian challenge to its

100 Peters 2016, 16.

101 Favre 2016, 89.

102 *Humane Society International Inc v Kyodo Senpaku Kaisha Ltd* (2008) 165 FCR 510.

103 Hatten 2013, 292, 296.

104 *Humane Society International Inc v Kyodo Senpaku Kaisha Ltd* [2015] FCA 1275.

105 International Whaling Commission n.d.

whaling activities in the Southern Ocean heard by the ICJ, Japan relied on an exception to the moratorium contained in art. VIII of the ICRW. This article provides that notwithstanding anything in the Convention, any contracting government may grant a special permit authorising the taking and killing of whales for the purposes of scientific research, subject to certain conditions. In 2014, the ICJ held, by majority, that taken as a whole Japan's JARPA II whaling program in the Antarctic was not authorised by art. VIII as the special permits granted were not for the purposes of scientific research.[106] Following this decision, Japan resumed whaling under a new program, New Scientific Whale Research Program in the Antarctic Ocean (NEWREP-A) Research Plan, and subsequently disputed the IWC's jurisdiction over whaling matters.[107] On 26 December 2018, Japan announced that it would withdraw from the ICRW effective from 30 June 2019. It further announced the resumption of commercial whaling within Japan's territorial sea and exclusive economic zone, and the cessation of whaling in the Antarctic Ocean/Southern Hemisphere.[108]

Reforming the domestic legal and regulatory framework

Developments in foreign jurisdictions illustrate that courts, as well as legislatures, have a part to play in improving animal welfare. Some further examples are worth noting. In 2003, the Supreme Court of Israel held, by majority, that regulations allowing the force feeding of geese to produce foie gras breached Israel's animal welfare legislation. As a result, the court decided to annul the regulations but also to suspend the annulment until 31 March 2005 in order to allow amendment of the current situation.[109] In June 2020, in an application for judicial review brought by the New Zealand Animal Law Association and the animal advocacy organisation Save the Animals from Exploitation, the High

106 *Whaling in the Antarctic (Australia v Japan; New Zealand intervening)* [2014] ICJ Rep 226.

107 Press and Hodgson-Johnston 2015.

108 Japan, Ministry of Foreign Affairs, Agriculture, Fisheries and Forest 2018.

109 *Noah (The Israeli Federation of Animal Protection Organisations) v Attorney General* (2003) HCJ 923/01, [25]–[27]. For further details of this case, see McEwen 2011, 255–60.

Court of New Zealand ruled that two regulations governing the use of farrowing crates and mating stalls were invalid. This was because their failure to provide for the transition or phasing out of the practice and use of these crates and stalls was contrary to parliament's intention and the purposes of the *Animal Welfare Act 1999* (NZ). Two minimum standards in the 2018 Animal Welfare (Pigs) Code of Practice were also held to be invalid on the same grounds.[110] Commenced by animal protection organisations, these cases also demonstrate the importance of public advocacy in bringing about change. In another example, a European Citizens' Initiative, 'End the Cage Age', garnered 1.4 million signatures from across every member state inviting the European Commission to propose legislation to prohibit the use of cages for farmed animals, including hens, rabbits, ducks, sows and calves.[111] In response, the European Commission stated that it:

> … intends to put forward a legislative proposal by the end of 2023 to phase out and finally prohibit the use of cages for all the animal species and categories referred to in the initiative … as part of the planned revision of EU animal welfare legislation, under conditions (including the length of the transition period) to be determined based on (European Food Safety Authority) opinions, the results of an impact assessment and a public consultation.[112]

Recent legislative changes in foreign jurisdictions include the mandatory use of CCTV in abattoirs in England, Scotland and France.[113] In Australia, the mandatory use of CCTV is likely to be considered during the conversion into national standards and guidelines of the *Model*

110 *New Zealand Animal Law Association v Attorney-General* [2020] NZHC 3009, [8]. The court held (at [88]) that amendments to the *Animal Welfare Act 1999* in 2015 were plainly intended to ensure that practices authorised by regulation which did not fully meet the Act's animal welfare obligations, other than those relating to a religious or cultural practice, 'were to be time limited up to 10 years and ultimately phased out. Any extension of that time was to be limited to up to five years once only'.

111 European Parliament 2019–2024, Motion for a Resolution, B9-0296/2021, 25 May 2021, 2.

112 European Commission 2021, 15.

113 Legislative Council Economic and Infrastructure Committee, Parliament of Victoria 2020, 102.

Code of Practice for the Welfare of Animals: Livestock at Slaughtering Establishments. That such a relatively basic matter is yet to receive national consideration illustrates the failure of existing frameworks and the significant difficulty in effecting change. As noted in Chapter 4, the conversion of this model code has been delayed since 2012, with little progress in the last decade. Other examples of the national standards development process are scarcely less problematic. Nearly four years after the close of public consultation for the draft poultry standards, there remains no resolution of major issues despite overwhelming support from animal welfare organisations and the broader public for significant change. While some improvements have resulted from the relatively independent panel's work, the draft standards are yet to be endorsed by agriculture ministers despite the very lengthy transition period proposed for the infrastructure changes. A further problem is that even finalised standards lack consistent implementation due to the political exigencies within jurisdictions, as the failure to regulate the sheep and cattle standards in NSW illustrates. In any case, regulated standards typically provide little protection for the most vulnerable animals, as the land transport standards in relation to bobby calves exemplify. According to the first edition of these standards published in 2008, government and industry were 'firmly committed to improving calf welfare outcomes' within two years; a subsequent version of the standards published in 2012 made an identical claim. As of 2021, however, these 'animal welfare' standards remain unchanged.

The need for independent regulation

One roadblock to progressing animal protection in the domestic context is the lack of national leadership. As previously noted, the Commonwealth withdrew from an active coordination role in 2013 when it ceased funding the AAWS. Apart from any direct regulatory impact, the lack of a national framework is one reason for Australia's D ranking in the global API.[114] It also signals to the community that animal protection is a low priority for governments, despite

114 World Animal Protection 2020a.

evidence of considerable community concern.[115] Crucially, however, the problem is not simply the absence of national leadership but the lack of any *independent* national policy or regulatory framework. Although legislative attempts to establish an independent office of animal welfare have been unsuccessful to date, even when the scope of proposed reforms has been modest,[116] the contents of this book provide compelling evidence in support of major change. Advocated for over a decade by animal lawyers and other interested parties,[117] the case for a federal independent animal welfare body has also been recognised by those whose primary interests lie elsewhere. In its 2016 report into the regulation of Australian agriculture, the Productivity Commission recommended the establishment of a stand-alone statutory organisation, the Australian Commission for Animal Welfare (ACAW), to develop new standards for farmed animal welfare and to publicly assess the effectiveness of their implementation and enforcement by state and territory governments.[118] While this proposal does not make the line of accountability explicit, the additional suggested function for the ACAW in relation to live exports includes making recommendations to the federal Minister for Agriculture.[119] Members of ACAW would be appointed by the Australian government after consultation with state and territory governments, with the AGMIN forum or an intergovernmental agreement providing a mechanism for intergovernmental co-operation.[120] In relation to the states and territories, the Productivity Commission proposed that animal welfare monitoring and enforcement be separated from agriculture policy matters, that the former matters be reported on publicly and transparently, and that adequate resourcing be made available for the effective discharge of these functions.[121]

---

115 See, for example, Futureye Pty. Ltd. 2018.

116 See, for example, the Voice for Animals (Independent Office of Animal Welfare) Bill 2015 introduced by the Greens.

117 See, for example, Caulfield 2008, 17. For further discussion of alternative governance arrangements, see Goodfellow 2015 and White 2016a.

118 Productivity Commission 2016, 238.

119 Ibid.

120 Ibid, 237–8.

121 Ibid, 245.

The Productivity Commission correctly identified a range of problems with respect to the national standards process, as well as the need to include the states and territories within the scope of regulatory reforms.[122] As McEwen argues, however, it is 'fundamental' that a national animal welfare authority not be 'subject to appointment by or the dominion of the Commonwealth Department of Agriculture'.[123] Even with appropriate safeguards in the enabling legislation, genuine independence would remain elusive were members to be appointed on the advice of, and/or required to report to, the Minister for Agriculture.[124] The need to separate governance arrangements from industry interests is just as urgent with respect to the states and territories. It is no more reasonable to have animal welfare regulated by state and territory primary industries and agriculture departments than it would be to have agricultural industries regulated by animal welfare agencies. Indeed, if the latter were to occur, industry bodies would soon shed their faith in the complementarity of animal welfare and industry promotion and productivity. Further, the problems of competing priorities, conflicting interests and cultural indifference are reduced but not resolved by placing responsibility for animal welfare in a separate unit of agriculture departments or in another government department, such as the environment. What is required instead is the establishment in each state and territory of an independent statutory authority to assume responsibility for the administration and enforcement of animal welfare legislation. In each case, members of these authorities should be

---

122 As White argues, the ideal would be the creation of a new federal agency with primary responsibility for national animal protection legislation: 2016a, 317. The Commonwealth appears reluctant to test the extent of its constitutional powers with respect to animal welfare, however, and the states are unlikely to cede theirs: Goodfellow 2015, 282 and White 2007, 348.

123 McEwen 2011, 232. McEwen made this point when arguing for a national statutory authority responsible for all animals. Citing the political realities of the reform process, a more pragmatic approach was taken by him in evidence to the Senate Rural and Regional Affairs and Transport Legislation Committee 2015 Inquiry into the Voice for Animals (Independent Office of Animal Welfare) Bill 2015, Canberra, 14 September 2015, 11–13.

124 Goodfellow highly recommends that ministerial responsibility for statutory animal welfare bodies be given to a portfolio separate to agriculture but maintains that the functions of these bodies could be protected with appropriate statutory safeguards regardless of the portfolio chosen: 2015, 277.

appointed by, and accountable to, a senior minister with no conflicting interests. The Attorney-General has been suggested both in relation to a federal office of animal welfare and independent state authorities.[125]

This primary reform is linked to the efficacy of others. It may be, for example, that the use of CCTV will eventually be made mandatory in slaughter establishments but without routine monitoring by an agency free of competing interests the benefits for animals might be marginal. As noted by RSPCA Australia, there is at present 'little to no transparency around animal welfare standards or auditing of slaughtering establishments' and no public reporting of outcomes in most jurisdictions when investigations do occur.[126] The need for greater regulatory transparency in relation to animal protection was recognised by the Productivity Commission and thrown into sharp relief by the writing of this book. Although some government and industry bodies provided helpful information, some requests for regulatory detail, or even basic information, were met with silence. In some cases, agencies responded but were unable to help due to the inadequacy of data collection systems; in other cases, information was provided but its publication prohibited as a matter of policy. This experience, across a wide range of animal sectors, contrasts starkly with government and industry rhetoric about the value placed on transparent animal welfare regulation. It is a deficiency which independent statutory bodies would be well placed to address. Detailed information collected and published by state and territory authorities could be collated and analysed by a national statutory office and disseminated publicly via an accessible national database. The national office would also be responsible for commissioning independent research and scientific advice to complement the regulatory data, as well as providing detailed public information, including images, about routine animal practices. *If* properly resourced, these two fundamental reforms – fully independent statutory bodies and much greater transparency about animal use and regulation – have synergistic potential. Ready access to detailed information and independent advice would expand the terms of the animal protection debate and prompt consideration of important

125 Productivity Commission 2016, 234; Senate Rural and Regional Affairs and Transport Legislation Committee 2015, 12; McEwen 2011, 232; Legislative Council Select Committee on Animal Cruelty Laws in New South Wales 2020, 57.

126 RSPCA Australia 2021a, 3.

matters unlikely to be addressed under the current framework. An example is the function of offence exemptions in current animal welfare legislation. As White suggests in the context of farmed animal regulation in Queensland, removal of the blanket exemption for compliance with codes of practice would have the 'practical consequence' of drawing into sharper relief the qualified language of terms such as 'reasonable', 'justified' and 'necessary'.[127] In other words, by addressing one key issue we begin to expose the interlocking fragility of the whole legislative edifice.

Perhaps the potential for far-reaching effect is one reason that governments have shown little support for the creation of statutory animal protection bodies. In 2020, a NSW Legislative Council committee recommended, by majority, that responsibility for animal welfare be moved out of the Department of Primary Industries and that an independent statutory office be established to oversight the animal welfare framework.[128] The government response, in the form of advice from the Minister for Agriculture, unsurprisingly failed to support these recommendations.[129] In 2013, the federal Labor government flagged an intention to develop an independent office of animal welfare at federal level as a statutory authority outside the agriculture portfolio. The proposed office would manage the development of national policy, facilitate harmonised outcomes by the states and territories and oversee the Commonwealth's live export responsibilities.[130] In July 2013, however, the government announced a modified measure: an independent statutory office holder, the Inspector-General of Animal Welfare and Live Animal Exports, reporting directly to the Minister for Agriculture.[131] In any event, with Labor's subsequent election loss this proposal was not implemented.[132]

127 White 2016a, 306–7.

128 Legislative Council Select Committee on Animal Cruelty Laws in New South Wales, Parliament of NSW 2020, 30, 60.

129 Marshall 2020a.

130 Australia, *Parliamentary Debates*, House of Representatives, 11 February 2013, 745 (Melissa Parke).

131 Fitzgibbon 2013.

132 As noted in Chapter 4, the coalition government established an Inspector-General of Live Animal Exports in 2019 in accordance with the recommendations of the Moss Review.

The power of stories

Twenty years ago, Radford wrote that seeking to change legislation affecting animals 'is a political act; achieving such an objective is an expression of power'.[133] Where power lies in Australia today is evident in the weak legal protections for animals, the choice of primary industries and agriculture departments to administer them, the seemingly endless delay in effecting even relatively minor reforms, and the high degree of secrecy that surrounds animal use and its regulation. But power has other, more subtle, manifestations: in order to control change, narratives about animal protection and the law must also be managed. Official narratives are on display in routine government assertions that Australia has high standards of animal welfare, administered and enforced by impartial agencies; less obvious is the intersection of these and other narratives to form a powerful political story. This can be demonstrated by the report of the parliamentary inquiry into the impact of animal rights activism on Victorian agriculture.[134] While many of the committee's views are contradicted by the facts, these are in turn countered by reference to other narratives. As illustrated below, with relevant page numbers noted, the result is a kind of self-referential loop, apparently impervious to challenge despite its many factual failings.

Critical to the committee's findings is the view that the Victorian animal agriculture industry is already subject to extensive oversight with high animal welfare standards (82–3). In fact, as we have seen, animal agriculture is largely exempt from animal welfare legislation. According to the committee, however, 'animal rights stakeholders' are wrong to say that the *Prevention of Cruelty to Animals Act 1986* (Vic) does not apply to animal production because the Act does apply when relevant activities are not carried out in accordance with codes of practice (92). In fact, as we have seen, these codes of practice contain very weak protections for animals and are largely reflective of industry practices. But, notes the committee, these codes are written 'after usually fairly substantive consultation', including with animal welfare groups and the broader community (91). In fact, as we have seen, industry

133 Radford 2001, 192.

134 Legislative Council Economic and Infrastructure Committee, Parliament of Victoria 2020.

stakeholders dominate the development process and the final codes typically privilege their interests over the concerns of animal welfare organisations and the broader community.

Similarly, while the committee acknowledges concerns around transparency and regulatory conflicts of interest, the discussion is heavily qualified and dismissed by reference to counter narratives. Activists 'argue' there is a lack of transparency (xv), there is a 'perceived' lack of transparency in the animal agriculture industry (73–4), there are 'accusations' of a lack of transparency or poor animal welfare standards (80); moreover, 'it is not known how much illegally taken footage is not made public because the footage does not reveal acts of cruelty' (74); and, in contradiction of the last point, some footage conflates 'standard practices with illegal animal cruelty' which is 'dishonest and misleading to consumers' (84); in any case, industry 'is committed to stamping out any "rogue" operators and stopping animal cruelty when it becomes known' (87). In fact, the idea of animal cruelty[135] as the preserve of rogues and outliers is enabled by the lack of application of the general cruelty laws noted above and sustained by the invisibility of animal use industries. According to the committee, however, it is a 'misperception that the animal agriculture industry operates in secrecy' because 'there is a large deal of oversight' by the regulators Agriculture Victoria and PrimeSafe (82). In fact, as we have seen, government regulation of animal welfare is under-resourced in terms of both funding and expertise, with a heavy reliance on soft enforcement options and animal welfare a low priority. But, says the committee, the low number of prosecutions does not indicate 'a lack of action regarding animal welfare. Rather, it reflects Agriculture Victoria's "compliance continuum" approach' (106), an approach with which the committee agrees (87). Further, the Victorian Farmers Federation has a 'different take on the issue of transparency',

135 As Hursthouse notes, the terminology of cruelty is ambiguous. An act of cruelty can 'mean an act from the character trait of cruelty, or a characteristic of a cruel person' but it can also mean an act which 'is nothing but the infliction of unnecessary suffering': 2011, 134. Given the alignment of necessity with social acceptability, Gullone suggests that animal cruelty is '[b]ehaviour that causes suffering, or distress to, and/or the death of an animal for instrumental purposes': 2017, 33.

one which identifies 'a need to increase urban communities' awareness of contemporary animal agriculture practices' (83).

The committee understands 'that there is a level of misinformation among the wider community regarding animal agriculture practices and the laws governing them' (84), including a failure to understand the regulatory compliance continuum (87). 'Agriculture Victoria is ideally placed to correct this misinformation' by explaining standard industry practices and relevant legislation and regulations on its website (84). In fact, while much more information about routine husbandry practices and regulatory activities is sorely needed, explanations by regulatory agencies are problematic because of the inherent conflict in their dual roles of promoting industry and safeguarding animal welfare. But, says the committee, this conflict of interest is merely a 'perception among activist stakeholders' (86); the roles are complementary and there is 'no evidence showing that Agriculture Victoria has put the economic interests of the animal agriculture industry ahead of the welfare interests of animals' (108). In fact, the view of Agriculture Victoria that 'animal welfare and economic health are strongly linked' (107) is consistent with industry views that 'engaging in cruel practices reduces the quality of the product and, therefore, profits' (87). Ironically, given the clear scientific evidence that animal welfare and productivity don't always align, the assertion of their complementarity is evidence in itself of the very conflict of interest which the committee denies.

But official narratives are not confined to regulatory measures, as this report also illustrates. Throughout the report, the committee explicitly chooses '[f]or the sake of simplicity' to use the terms 'animal rights activists' and 'animal rights stakeholders', despite acknowledgement that evidence was received 'from the complete spectrum of people concerned about how animals are treated in our society' (xiv). By choosing this terminology, the report arguably fuels the idea that concern about the treatment of animals is in some sense extreme or only relevant at the margins of society. These notions were in vogue over a century ago when 'heightened concern' about animals was diagnosed as a 'form of mental illness'.[136] With women considered especially susceptible, this 'imputation of illness was a double slander on both animals and women'.[137] Today, the

136 Linzey and Linzey 2019, v.
137 Ibid, v–vi.

label of mentally ill has fallen out of favour, but concern about animal treatment is commonly characterised as sentimental, emotive or plain uninformed. Or worse in some cases. In relation to legitimate concerns about farm trespass, a constructive policy response would be to enforce existing laws and address the underlying regulatory problems, such as the lack of transparency, as recommended by lawyers.[138] Instead, political leaders not only favour the introduction of new offences with very harsh penalties but some use the opportunity to label those involved as 'virtue-signalling thugs' and 'domestic terrorists'.[139] With no evidence to date of violence among animal activists engaged in trespass in Australia,[140] rhetoric of this kind is perhaps intended to promote the idea that any strong concern about animals is extreme and a threat to the social order. As Linzey and Linzey observe, however, '[w]hen those expounding the rational case for the ethical treatment of animals are outrageously labelled, we do well to invite some historical reflection'.[141]

As this analysis suggests, official narratives about animal protection are powerful and pervasive but fail to tell a complete or accurate story about the role of the law. While regulatory problems also occur in other sectors, the need for fundamental reform in the case of animals is particularly strong. Animal protection is a unique regulatory field because animals are not 'things', regardless of their status in law, but sentient beings who are nevertheless used as human resources. With no power to assert their own interests in regulatory contexts, animals are wholly dependent on human agency for their most basic needs. Even within the limited terms of the animal welfare paradigm, however, the law is failing to protect animals, as the contents of this book illustrate. The conflicting interests and lack of transparency which characterise the current regulatory framework are also an affront to the fundamental democratic principles of openness and accountability. Documented failings of other regulatory settings, such as the aged care sector, demonstrate that these principles are vital when power is exercised over the vulnerable. In the case of non-human animals, the

138 See, for example, Law Institute of Victoria 2019, 18–24.

139 Barilaro 2019.

140 Legislative Council Economic and Infrastructure Committee, Parliament of Victoria 2020, 39.

141 Linzey and Linzey 2019, vi.

Figure 8.2. Current laws contribute to the invisibility of many animals and the failure to see them as the individual, sentient beings they are. (Teya Brooks Pribac)

acute vulnerability associated with their use by humans is exacerbated by animals' property status which means they lack legal personality and the concomitant right to legal representation of their interests.[142]

To begin to address these concerns, this book has focused on two key reforms which have both a material and an ideational operation. The first relates to the need for much greater transparency about animal use and regulation. Comprehensive information is not only essential for informed decision making but, if readily and openly available, contributes to the evolution of thinking about the human and non-human animal relationship. Including images in this information would also give animals a small but important voice by insisting on their visibility. The second key reform is genuinely independent regulation. As long as responsibility for

142 Kotzmann 2020a, 305; Pallotta 2019, 180.

animal protection is retained by agriculture departments, or indeed any existing government agency, the worth of animals is framed in merely adjunctive terms; by contrast, to shift responsibility to independent statutory bodies is to acknowledge officially that animals are important in their own right. In other words, it not only opens up the possibility of better decision making and legislative reform but makes a profound public statement about the moral significance of animals. Implementation of these changes would reflect advances in scientific knowledge, start to address deep community concern about our current treatment of animals, and allow a constructive role for law in a very different version of the non-human animal story.

Bibliography

Acil Allen Consulting. 2018. *Regulatory Impact Statement for the Companion Animal Regulation 2018*, 13 March 2018.

Adams, Carol J. 2007. "Caring About Suffering: A Feminist Exploration." In *The Feminist Care Tradition in Animal Ethics*, edited by Josephine Donovan and Carol J. Adams, 198–226. New York: Columbia University Press.

Aegis Consulting Australia and Applied Economics. 2009. *Report on the Economic and Social Contribution of the Zoological Industry in Australia*. Mosman, NSW: Australasian Regional Association of Zoological Parks and Aquaria.

Agriculture, Resources and Environment Committee, Parliament of Queensland 2012. *Animal Care and Protection and Other Legislation Amendment Bill 2012*. Report No. 5, July 2012.

Allars, Margaret. 2007. "To Breed or to Exhibit?: The Asian Elephants Case and Reasons for Regulatory Failure." *Environment Planning and Law Journal* 24 (5): 329–45.

Animal Defenders Office. 2021. Submission No 234 to Legislative Council Portfolio Committee, Parliament of NSW, *Inquiry into the Health and Wellbeing of Kangaroos and other Macropods in NSW*, 26 April 2021. https://www.parliament.nsw.gov.au/committees/inquiries/Pages/inquiry-details.aspx?pk=2707#tab-submissions.

Animal Defenders Office. 2019. Submission No 135 to Legislative Council Select Committee, Parliament of NSW, *Inquiry into Animal Cruelty Laws in NSW*, 6 December 2019. https://www.parliament.nsw.gov.au/committees/listofcommittees/Pages/committee-details.aspx?pk=263#tab-submissions.

Animal Health Australia. 2020. *Strategic Plan 2020–2025*. https://www.animalhealthaustralia.com.au/who-we-are/about/.

Animal Health Australia. 2014. *Australian Animal Welfare Standards and Guidelines for Cattle. Public Consultation Response Action Plan*, May 2014. Canberra: Animal Health Australia.

Animal Health Australia. 2013. *Proposed Australian Animal Welfare Standards and Guidelines, Cattle. Consultation Regulation Impact Statement*. Version 1.0, 1 March 2013. Canberra: Animal Health Australia.

Animal Health Australia. 2011. *Australian Animal Welfare Standards and Guidelines – Land Transport of Livestock, Proposed Amendment to the Land Transport of Livestock Standards (SB4.5), Bobby Calves Time Off Feed Standard. Decision Regulation Impact Statement*. Version 1, 6 July 2011. http://www.animalwelfarestandards.net.au/land-transport/bobby-calf-post-public-consultation-process/.

Animal Health Australia. 2008. *Australian Animal Welfare Standards and Guidelines – Land Transport of Livestock. Regulatory Impact Statement*. March 2008. http://www.animalwelfarestandards.net.au/land-transport/consultative-process/.

Animal Legal & Historical Center. n.d. "International Convention for the Protection of Animals." Michigan State University. https://www.animallaw.info/treaty/international-convention-protection-animals. Accessed 3 November 2021.

Animal Legal Defense Fund. 2021. "Animals Recognized as Legal Persons for the First Time in U.S. Court." Press Release, 20 October 2021. https://aldf.org/article/animals-recognized-as-legal-persons-for-the-first-time-in-u-s-court/.

Animal Liberation Queensland. 2019. "Animal Activists Call on Qld Premier and Agriculture Minister to Prohibit Calf Roping, Ahead of National Rodeo Finals in Warwick." Media Release, 24 October 2019. https://alq.org.au/content/animal-activists-call-qld-premier-and-agriculture-minister-prohibit-calf-roping-ahead.

Animal Research Review Panel. 2020. *Research Animal Rehoming Guidelines*. NSW Department of Primary Industries. December 2020. https://www.animalethics.org.au/policies-and-guidelines/animal-rehoming.

Animal Research Review Panel. 2019. *Annual Report 2018–19*. NSW Department of Primary Industries. December 2019. https://www.animalethics.org.au/annual-reports.

Animal Research Review Panel. 2018a. *Annual Report 2017–18*. NSW Department of Primary Industries. November 2018. https://www.animalethics.org.au/annual-reports.

Animal Research Review Panel. 2018b. *Annual Report 2016–17*. NSW Department of Primary Industries. January 2018. https://www.animalethics.org.au/annual-reports.

Animal Research Review Panel. 2017. *Annual Report 2015–16*. NSW Department of Primary Industries. March 2017. https://www.animalethics.org.au/annual-reports.

Animal Research Review Panel. 2008. *Annual Report 2006–07*. NSW Department of Primary Industries. https://www.animalethics.org.au/annual-reports.

Animal Research Review Panel. 1999. *Annual Report 1997–98*. NSW Agriculture.

Animal Welfare League Queensland. 2018. *G2Z, Australian Cat Action Plan, A Practical Guide for Government and Non-government Sectors to Improve the Management and Welfare of Domestic Cats*. June 2018. https://www.g2z.org.au/national-cat-action-plan.html.

Animals Australia. 2018. Submission No 65. Proposed Draft Australian Animal Welfare Standards and Guidelines for Poultry. Version Public Consultation, 12 March 2018. http://www.animalwelfarestandards.net.au/poultry/poultry-submissions/.

Animals Australia. n.d. "Live Export Investigations." https://www.animalsaustralia.org/investigations/live-export-investigations.php. Accessed 3 November 2021.

Animals Medicine Australia. 2019. *Pets in Australia: A National Survey of Pets and People*. Newgate Research. https://animalmedicinesaustralia.org.au/report/pets-in-australia-a-national-survey-of-pets-and-people/.

Arlinghaus, Robert, Steven J. Cooke, Alexander Schwab and Ian G. Cowx. 2007. "Fish Welfare: A Challenge to the Feelings-based Approach, with Implications for Recreational Fishing." *Fish and Fisheries* 8: 57–71. http://doi.org/10.1111/j.1467-2979.2007.00233.x.

Australia. Department of Agriculture. 2019a. *Live Sheep Exports to or Through the Middle East – Northern Hemisphere Summer. Draft Regulation Impact Statement*. Live Animal Export Division. Commonwealth of Australia.

Australia. Department of Agriculture. 2019b. September 2019. *Middle East Sheep Exports Policy Options Discussion Paper*. Live Animal Exports Division. Commonwealth of Australia.

Australia. Department of Agriculture, Fisheries and Forestry. 2012. *Annual Report 2011–12*.

Australia. Department of Agriculture, Fisheries and Forestry. 2005. *The Australian Animal Welfare Strategy*.

Australia. Department of Agriculture and Water Resources. 2018. *Regulator's Response to the McCarthy Review into the Export of Sheep to the Middle East During the Northern Hemisphere Summer*. https://www.agriculture.gov.au/sites/default/files/sitecollectiondocuments/biosecurity/export/live-animals/response-mccarthy-review.pdf.

Australia. Department of Agriculture, Water and the Environment. 2021a. "Australian Animal Welfare Standards and Guidelines for Poultry." Last updated 21 July 2021. https://www.agriculture.gov.au/animal/welfare/standards-guidelines/poultry.

Australia. Department of Agriculture, Water and the Environment 2021b. *Exporter Supply Chain Assurance System Regulatory Performance Report*, 1 October to 31 December 2020, February 2021. https://www.awe.gov.au/biosecurity-trade/export/controlled-goods/live-animals/livestock/regulatory-framework/compliance-investigations/investigations-regulatory-compliance/escas-reg-performance-rep-oct-dec-2020.

Australia. Department of Agriculture, Water and the Environment. 2021c. "Investigations into Mortalities." Last updated 8 September 2021. https://www.awe.gov.au/biosecurity-trade/export/controlled-goods/live-animals/livestock/regulatory-framework/compliance-investigations/investigations-mortalities.

Australia. Department of Agriculture, Water and the Environment. 2021d. "Regulatory Compliance Investigations." Last updated 16 August 2021. https://www.awe.gov.au/biosecurity-trade/export/controlled-goods/live-animals/livestock/regulatory-framework/compliance-investigations/investigations-regulatory-compliance.

Australia. Department of Agriculture, Water and the Environment. 2021e. "Review of Live Sheep Exports by Sea During the Northern Hemisphere Summer: Public Consultation on Draft Report." Media Statement, 17 December 2021. https://www.awe.gov.au/about/news/media-releases/review-of-live-sheep-exports-by-sea.

Australia. Department of Agriculture, Water and the Environment. 2021f. *Review of Live Sheep Exports by Sea to, or Through, the Middle East During the Northern Hemisphere Summer*. Draft Report, December 2021. https://haveyoursay.awe.gov.au/nhs-prohibition-review.

Australia. Department of Agriculture, Water and the Environment. 2020a. "ASEL 3.0: Performance-based Access to an Alternative Minimum Pen Space Allocation." Media Statement, 27 October 2020. https://www.awe.gov.au/about/news/media-releases/media-statement-asel-30-performance-based-access-alternative-minimum-pen-space-allocation.

Australia. Department of Agriculture, Water and the Environment. 2020b. *Public Statement of Reasons*, 13 June 2020. https://www.agriculture.gov.au/sites/default/files/documents/public-statement-of-reasons-20200613.pdf.

Australia. Department of Agriculture, Water and the Environment. 2020c. "Regulatory Investigation into Meramist Abattoir Finalised." Media Statement, 24 February 2020. https://www.awe.gov.au/about/news/media-releases/regulatory-investigation-meramist-abattoir.

Australia. Department of Agriculture, Water and the Environment. 2020d. *Agriculture Ministers' Forum*, 21 February 2020, Launceston. https://www.awe.gov.au/news/stay-informed/communiques/ag-ministers-forum-february-2020.

Australia. Department of Agriculture, Water and the Environment. 2020e. "Macropod Quotas and Harvest for Commercial Harvest Areas in NSW, QLD, SA and WA – 2020." https://www.environment.gov.au/biodiversity/wildlife-trade/natives#a3.

Australia. Department of Agriculture, Water and the Environment. 2017. *Sheep Exported by Sea to Kuwait, Qatar and the United Arab Emirates in August 2017.* Mortality Investigation Report 69. https://www.awe.gov.au/biosecurity-trade/export/controlled-goods/live-animals/livestock/regulatory-framework/compliance-investigations/investigations-mortalities/sheep-qatar-kuwait-uae-report-69.

Australia. Department of Agriculture, Water and the Environment. 2011. *Australian Animal Welfare Strategy (AAWS) and National Implementation Plan 2010–2014.* https://www.agriculture.gov.au/animal/welfare/aaws/australian-animal-welfare-strategy-aaws-and-national-implementation-plan-2010-14#part-2-national-implementation-plan.

Australia. Department of Agriculture, Water and the Environment. n.d. "Sustainable Harvest of Australian Native Wildlife." https://www.environment.gov.au/biodiversity/wildlife-trade/natives#a3. Accessed 3 November 2021.

Australia. Department of the Environment. 2015a. *Background Document for the Threat Abatement Plan for Predation by Feral Cats.* https://www.awe.gov.au/environment/biodiversity/threatened/publications/tap/threat-abatement-plan-feral-cats.

Australia. Department of the Environment. 2015b. *Threat Abatement Plan for Predation by Feral Cats.* https://www.awe.gov.au/environment/biodiversity/threatened/publications/tap/threat-abatement-plan-feral-cats.

Australia. Department of Health. 2021. "Ban on the Use of Animal Test Data for Cosmetics." Last updated 5 July 2021. https://www1.health.gov.au/internet/main/publishing.nsf/Content/ban-cosmetic-testing-animals.

Australia. Treasury. 2016. *Free Range Egg Labelling. Decision Regulation Impact Statement.* Consumer Affairs Australia New Zealand March 2016. https://obpr.pmc.gov.au/published-impact-analyses-and-reports/free-range-egg-labelling-0.

Australian and New Zealand Council for the Care of Animals in Research and Teaching. 2021. *Openness Agreement on Animal Research and Teaching in New Zealand.* July 2021. https://anzccart.org.nz/business-consultancy-on-the-edge/openness-agreement/.

Australian and New Zealand Council for the Care of Animals in Research and Teaching. 2018. *Information Package for Members of AECs.* Ver. 9.1 January 2018. https://anzccart.adelaide.edu.au/resources#resources-for-australian-animal-ethics-committee-aec-members.

Australian and New Zealand Council for the Care of Animals in Research and Teaching. n.d. "Public Consultation for an Australian Openness Agreement on Animal Research." https://anzccart.adelaide.edu.au/openness-agreement-public-consultation. Accessed 6 May 2022.

Australian Animal Welfare Standards and Guidelines. 2020a. *Australian Animal Welfare Standards and Guidelines for Cattle*. http://www.animalwelfarestandards.net.au/cattle/.

Australian Animal Welfare Standards and Guidelines. 2020b. "Bobby Calf Time off Feed Standard." Page reviewed December 2020. http://www.animalwelfarestandards.net.au/land-transport/bobby-calf-time-off-feed-standard/.

Australian Animal Welfare Standards and Guidelines. 2020c. "Cattle Background." Page reviewed December 2020. http://www.animalwelfarestandards.net.au/cattle/background/.

Australian Animal Welfare Strategy. 2009. *Development of Australian Standards and Guidelines for the Welfare of Livestock Business Plan.*

Australian Associated Press. 2019. "Man Who Tore Head Off Kookaburra in Perth Pub Fined $2,500." *Guardian*, 15 November 2019. https://www.theguardian.com/australia-news/2019/nov/15/man-who-tore-head-off-kookaburra-in-perth-pub-fined-2500.

Australian Associated Press. 2018. "Former Live Exports Boss Who Falsified Documents Before Sheep's Deaths Won't be Jailed." *Guardian*, 22 May 2018. https://www.theguardian.com/australia-news/2018/may/22/former-live-exports-boss-who-falsified-documents-before-sheeps-deaths-wont-be-jailed.

Australian Broadcasting Corporation. 2019. "Mass Slaughter and Abuse of Racehorses Undermines Industry's Commitment to AW." *ABC News*, 18 October 2019. https://www.abc.net.au/news/2019-10-18/slaughter-abuse-of-racehorses-undermines-industry-animal-welfare/11603834.

Australian Broadcasting Corporation. 2016. "Mike Baird's Greyhound Racing Industry Ban Backflip: Everything You Need to Know." *ABC News*, 11 October 2016, updated 12 July 2018. https://www.abc.net.au/news/2016-10-11/everything-you-need-to-know-about-mike-baird-greyhounds/7921306.

Australian Chicken Meat Federation. n.d. "Facts & Figures." https://www.chicken.org.au/facts-and-figures/. Accessed 3 November 2021.

Australian Chicken Meat Federation. n.d. "Infographics." https://www.chicken.org.au/infographics/. Accessed 3 November 2021.

Australian Conservation Foundation. 2020. *The Extinction Crisis in Australia's Cities and Towns: How Weak Environmental Laws Have Let Urban Sprawl Destroy the Habitat of Australia's Threatened Species*. https://www.acf.org.au/extinction_crisis_in_australias_cities_and_towns.

Australian Dairy Farmers and Dairy Australia. 2011. Submission No 7. Bobby Calf TOF RIS, January 2011. http://www.animalwelfarestandards.net.au/land-transport/bobby-calf-time-off-feed-submissions/.

Australian Egg Corporation Limited. 2009. *Annual Report 2009: From the Farm to the Table*. https://www.australianeggs.org.au/who-we-are/annual-reports.

Australian Eggs Limited. 2020. *Annual Report 2019/20*. https://www.australianeggs.org.au/who-we-are/annual-reports.

Australian Government. 2015. *Threatened Species Strategy 2015–20*. https://www.awe.gov.au/environment/biodiversity/threatened/publications/threatened-species-strategy-2015-2020.

Australian Harness Racing. 2017. "Industry Notice – Whips." 30 August 2017. http://www.harness.org.au/media-room/news-article/?news_id=34657.

Australian Veterinary Association. 2020. Submission No 180 to the House of Representatives Standing Committee on the Environment and Energy. Parliament of Australia. Inquiry into the Problem of Feral and Domestic Cats in Australia, September 2020. https://www.aph.gov.au/Parliamentary_Business/Committees/House/Environment_and_Energy/Feralanddomesticcats/Submissions.

Australian Veterinary Association. 2019. Submission. *Response to Proposed Conditions for Live Sheep Exports to the Middle East during September and October 2019*.

Australian Veterinary Association. 2012. Dangerous Dogs – A Sensible Solution.

Bain, Simon and Kelly Debono. 2014. "Australian Scientific Animal Use Statistics: A History of Fragmentation, a Future of Hope." *Proceedings of the 2013 ANZCCART Conference*: "*Can We Do Better?*" 23–25 July 2013, 22–6. Sydney, NSW: ANZCCART.

Bainbridge, Amy and Alison Branley. 2021a. "Australia Was Planning to Phase Out Caged Eggs by 2036, But One State is Threatening to Derail That." *ABC News*, 4 November 2021. https://www.abc.net.au/news/2021-11-04/australia-plans-to-phase-out-battery-hens-cage-eggs-at-risk/100566732.

Bainbridge, Amy and Alison Branley. 2021b. "Battery Hens to be Outlawed by 2036 Under New National Proposal." *ABC News*, 23 June 2021. https://www.abc.net.au/news/2021-06-23/caged-eggs-phased-out-by-2036-under-national-proposal/100236246.

Baker, Richard. 2022. "Dying Sheep, Cattle Unable to Stand: Vets Identify Cruelty in Meat Industry." *Sydney Morning Herald*, 30 January 2022. https://www.smh.com.au/national/dying-sheep-cattle-unable-to-stand-vets-identify-cruelty-in-meat-industry-20220126-p59reo.html.

Balcombe, Jonathan. 2016. *What a Fish Knows: The Inner Lives of our Underwater Cousins*. London: Oneworld Publications.

Barilaro, John. 2019. "Farm Invaders and Vegan Vigilantes to Face Toughest Penalties in the Nation." Media Release, 22 July 2019. https://www.nsw.gov.au/media-releases/farm-invaders-and-vegan-vigilantes-to-face-toughest-penalties-nation.

Barnett, Guy. "Strengthening Animal Welfare Laws." Media Release, 9 September 2021. http://www.premier.tas.gov.au/site_resources_2015/additional_releases/strengthening_animal_welfare_laws.

Barrett, Chris. 2021. "On the Kill Floor: Shocking Indonesian Footage Sparks New Live Exports Probe." *Sydney Morning Herald*, 7 November 2021. https://www.smh.com.au/world/asia/on-the-kill-floor-shocking-indonesian-footage-sparks-new-live-exports-probe-20211031-p594qk.html#comments.

Bartlett, Liam. 2018. "Sheep, Ships and Videotape." *60 Minutes*. Aired on Nine Network, 8 April 2018. https://9now.nine.com.au/60-minutes/sheep-ships-and-videotapes/5c6e8bce-b910-4287-87f7-2ac7fa5a80eb.

Beauchamp, Tom L. and R.G. Frey, eds. 2011. *The Oxford Handbook of Animal Ethics*. Oxford: Oxford University Press. https://doi.org/10.1093/oxfordhb/9780195371963.001.0001.

Bengsen, A.J. 2016. *A Systematic Review of Ground-based Shooting for Pest Animal Control*. Pestsmart Toolkit publication. Canberra: Invasive Animals Cooperative Research Centre. https://pestsmart.org.au/resources/page/2/.

Bengsen, A.J. and Jessica Sparkes. 2016. "Can Recreational Hunting Contribute to Pest Mammal Control on Public Land in Australia?" *Mammal Review*. 46: 297–310. https://doi.org/10.1111/mam.12070.

Bentham, Jeremy. 1823. *An Introduction to the Principles of Morals and Legislation*. In Two Volumes. Vol II. London: Printed for W. Pickering, Lincoln's-Inn Fields; and E. Wilson, Royal Exchange. https://hdl.handle.net/2027/uc2.ark:/13960/t6tx3n73s.

Beri, V., A. Tranent and P. Abelson. 2010. "The Economic and Social Contribution of the Zoological Industry in Australia." *International Zoo Yearbook* 44: 192–200. https://doi.org/10.1111/j.1748-1090.2009.00104.x.

Bettles, Colin. 2016. "Nationals Slam NSW Greyhound Racing Ban." *The Land*, 13 July 2016. https://www.theland.com.au/story/4029491/nationals-slam-nsw-greyhound-ban/.

Birch, Jonathan, Charlotte Burn, Alexandra Schnell, Heather Browning and Andrew Crump. 2021. *Review of the Evidence of Sentience in Cephalopod Molluscs and Decapod Crustaceans*. London: LSE Consulting. https://www.lse.ac.uk/business/consulting/reports/review-of-the-evidence-of-sentiences-in-cephalopod-molluscs-and-decapod-crustaceans.

Black, Celeste. 2013. "The Conundrum of Fish Welfare." In *Animal Law in Australasia: Continuing the Dialogue*, edited by Peter Sankoff, Steven White and Celeste Black, 245–63. Leichhardt, NSW: Federation Press.

Blair, Niall. 2015. "Puppy Breeding Practices to be Investigated." Media Release, NSW Department of Primary Industries, 12 May 2015. https://bit.ly/38l8jnl.

Bogdanoski, Tony. 2013. "A Companion Animal's Worth: The Only 'Family Member' Still Regarded as Legal Property." In *Animal Law in Australasia: Continuing the Dialogue*, edited by Peter Sankoff, Steven White and Celeste Black, 84–103. Leichhardt, NSW: Federation Press.

Boom, Keely and Dror Ben-Ami. 2013. "Kangaroos at a Crossroads: Environmental Law and the Kangaroo Industry." *Environment Planning and Law Journal* 30 (2): 162–81. https://www.researchgate.net/publication/256325978_Kangaroos_at_a_Crossroads_Environmental_Law_and_the_Kangaroo_Industry.

Boom, Keely and Elizabeth Ellis. 2009. "Enforcing Animal Welfare Law: The NSW Experience." *Australian Animal Protection Law Journal* 3: 6–32.

Boom, Keely, Dror Ben-Ami and Louise Boronyak. 2012. *Kangaroo Court: Enforcement of the Law Governing Commercial Kangaroo Killing*. Sydney: THINKK, the Kangaroo Think Tank, University of Technology Sydney. http://thinkkangaroos.uts.edu.au/news/kangaroo-court-new-report-on-enforcement.html.

Boom, Keely, Dror Ben-Ami, Louise Boronyak and Sophie Riley. 2013. "The Role of Inspections in the Commercial Kangaroo Industry." *International Journal of Rural Law and Policy*, Occasional Papers: 1–19. http://doi.org/10.5130/ijrlp.i2.2013.2725.

Booth, Carol. 2020. *1080: A Weighty Ethical Issue*. Fairfield, Victoria: Invasive Species Council. https://invasives.org.au/resources/reports/.

Booth, Carol. 2009. "Is Recreational Hunting Effective for Feral Animal Control?" Essay Project, Invasive Species Council Australia. 13 January 2009. https://invasives.org.au/resources/reports/?fwp_paged=3.

Borschmann, Gregg. 2017. "'Leasing' Rare Animals Flagged as a Way to Fund Wildlife Conservation Programs." *ABC News*, 6 October 2017. https://www.abc.net.au/news/2017-10-06/leasing-endangered-animals-could-help-biodiversity-crisis/9022554.

Bourke, Latika. 2019. "Dept of Ag Refuses to Release Live Export Footage." *Sydney Morning Herald*, 31 August 2019. https://www.smh.com.au/politics/federal/department-of-agriculture-refuses-to-release-live-export-footage-20190829-p52lt4.html.

Braid, Andrew and Chris Buller. 2007. *Codes of Practice for Humane Vertebrate Pest Control. Finalisation for National Adoption by Australian States and Territories.* Final Report to the Vertebrate Pest Committee.

Brambell, F.W. Rogers. 1965. *Report of the Technical Committee to Enquire into the Welfare of Animals kept under Intensive Livestock Husbandry Systems.* London: Her Majesty's Stationery Office.

Brammer, Jenne. 2017. "Alannah MacTiernan Calls Foul over Battery Fowl Welfare Standards 'Fail.'" *West Australian*, 29 November 2017. http://www.thewest.com.au/business/agriculture/alannah-mactiernan-calls-foul-over-battery-fowl-welfare-standards-fail-ng-b88673833z.

Branco, Jorge. 2016. "Greyhound Live Baiting: Nine of 22 Trainers had Life Bans Cut." *Brisbane Times*, 15 February 2016. https://www.brisbanetimes.com.au/national/queensland/greyhound-live-baiting-nine-of-22-trainers-had-life-bans-cut-20160215-gmutsc.html.

Bray, Heather. 2018. *Australian Animal Welfare Standards and Guidelines – Poultry, Independent Public Consultation Report.* 9 July 2018. http://www.animalwelfarestandards.net.au/poultry/poultry-submissions/.

Broom, Donald M. 2017. *Animal Welfare in the European Union.* Brussels: Policy Department for Citizens' Rights and Constitutional Affairs. https://www.researchgate.net/publication/315721435_Animal_Welfare_in_the_European_Union.

Broom, Donald M. 2016. "International Animal Welfare Perspectives, Including Whaling and Inhumane Seal Killing as a W.T.O. Public Morality Issue." In *Animal Law and Welfare – International Perspectives*, edited by Deborah Cao and Steven White, 45–61. Switzerland: Springer International. https://doi.org/10.1007/978-3-319-26818-7_3.

Broom, Donald. 2011. "A History of Animal Welfare Science." *Acta Biotheoretica* 59 (2): 121–37. http://doi.org/10.1007/s10441-011-9123-3.

Broom, D.M. 1986. "Indicators of Poor Welfare." *British Veterinary Journal* 142 (6): 524–6. https://doi.org/10.1016/0007-1935(86)90109-0.

Browman, Howard I., Steven J. Cooke, Ian G. Cowx, Stuart W.G. Derbyshire, Alexander Kasumyan and Brian Key et al. 2019. "Welfare of Aquatic Animals: Where Things are, Where They are Going, and What it Means for Research, Aquaculture, Recreational Angling, and Commercial Fishing." *ICES Journal of Marine Science* 76 (1): 82–92. https://doi.org/10.1093/icesjms/fsy067.

Brown, Culum. 2015. "Fish Intelligence, Sentience and Ethics." *Animal Cognition* 18 (1): 1–17. https://doi.org/10.1007/s10071-014-0761-0.

Bruce, Alex. 2018. *Animal Law in Australia: An Integrated Approach*. 2nd edn. Sydney: LexisNexis.

Burgess, Elise. 2017. *Unscrambled: The Hidden Truth of Hen Welfare in the Australian Egg Industry*. A Report on the Australian Egg Industry. Paddington, NSW: Voiceless. https://voiceless.org.au/unscrambled-the-hidden-truth-of-hen-welfare/.

Cao, Deborah and Steven White, eds. 2016. *Animal Law and Welfare – International Perspectives*. Switzerland: Springer International. https://doi.org/10.1007/978-3-319-26818-7.

Cao, Deborah, with Katrina Sharman and Steven White. 2015. *Animal Law in Australia*. 2nd edn. Pyrmont, NSW: Thomson Reuters.

Carleton, Richard. 2006. "A Cruel Trade." *60 Minutes*. Aired on Nine Network, 26 February 2006.

Cattle Standards and Guidelines Writing Group. 2013. *Cattle Standards and Guidelines – Disbudding and Dehorning Discussion Paper*.

Caulfield, Malcolm. 2018. *Animals in Australia: Use and Abuse*. Fremantle WA: Vivid Publishing.

Caulfield, Malcolm. 2017. "The Australian Animal Use Industry Rejects Anthropomorphism, but Relies on Questionable Science to Block Animal Welfare Improvements." *Animal Studies Journal* 6 (1): 155–74. https://ro.uow.edu.au/asj/vol6/iss1/9/

Caulfield, Malcolm. 2008. *Handbook of Australian Animal Cruelty Law*. North Melbourne: Animals Australia.

Chalmers. 2021. "Spanish Court Rules on Dog Custody – The Backstory with Max Chalmers." *ABC RN Breakfast*, 29 October 2021. https://www.abc.net.au/radionational/programs/breakfast/the-backstory-with-max-chalmers-spain-dogs-custody/13608878.

Chen, Peter. 2016. *Animal Welfare in Australia: Politics and Policy*. Sydney: Sydney University Press. https://doi.org/10.30722/sup.9781743324738.

Claughton, David. 2022. "Rodeo Sport of Calf Roping Causes Stress, Fear and Should Be Banned: RSPCA." *ABC Rural*, 14 January 2022. https://www.abc.net.au/news/rural/2022-01-14/rspca-call-for-calf-roping-ban-a-rodeos/100753936.

Coalition for the Protection of Greyhounds. 2020. *Track Deaths and Injuries*. http://greyhoundcoalition.com/2020-track-deaths-and-injuries/.

Coalition for the Protection of Racehorses. 2021. *Deathwatch Report 2021*. https://horseracingkills.com/issues/deathwatch/.

Cochrane, Alasdair. 2009. "Ownership and Justice for Animals." *Utilitas* 21 (4): 424–42. https://doi:org/10.1017/S0953820809990203.

Cockburn, Paige. 2020. "Greyhounds Still Disappearing in NSW as Integrity Commission Tries to Seal Cracks." *ABC News*, 22 February 2020. https://www.abc.net.au/news/2020-02-22/greyhounds-still-disappearing-in-nsw-tracking-failing/11965030.

Commonwealth of Australia. 2015. *Export Supply Chain Assurance System Report*, January 2015.

Comrie, Neil. 2016. *Transformation of the RSPCA Victoria Inspectorate. Independent Review of the RSPCA Victoria Inspectorate*. Final Report, 1 September 2016.

Cox, Lisa. 2020a. "Australia's Environment Minister Orders Investigation into Exports of Hundreds of Endangered Parrots." *Guardian*, 3 September 2020. https://www.theguardian.com/environment/2020/sep/04/australias-environment-minister-orders-investigation-into-export-of-hundreds-of-endangered-parrots.

Cox, Lisa. 2020b. "No Penalty for Victoria Despite 'Wanton Destruction' of Trees Vital to Red-tailed Black Cockatoo." *Guardian*, 27 September 2020. https://www.theguardian.com/environment/2020/sep/28/no-penalty-for-victoria-despite-wanton-destruction-of-trees-vital-to-red-tailed-black-cockatoo.

Craig, Haley. 2020. "Government Launches Statewide RSPCA Taskforce to Target Puppy Farmers Profiting Off Social Media." *ABC New England*, 22 October 2020. https://www.abc.net.au/news/2020-10-22/rscpa-taskforce-to-target-puppy-farms-statewide-nsw/12801116.

Crockford, Toby and Stuart Layt. 2020. "Animal Cruelty Charges Laid Over Queensland Retired Racehorse Slaughter Scandal." *Brisbane Times*, 10 July 2020. https://www.brisbanetimes.com.au/national/queensland/animal-cruelty-charges-laid-over-queensland-retired-racehorse-slaughter-scandal-20200710-p55auu.html.

Dal Pont, Gino. 2015. *Equity and Trusts in Australia*. 6th edn. Pyrmont, NSW: Thomson Reuters.

Daly, Brian. 2020. "Live Export: Why is it Still Happening?" *Humane Food Podcast*, Season 2, RSPCA Australia. https://www.rspca.org.au/media-centre/humane-food-podcast.

Daly, Jon. 2020. "Inhumane Slaughter of Cattle in Indonesian Abattoirs Footage Prompts New Live Export Probe." *ABC Rural, NT Country Hour*, 11 August 2020. https://www.abc.net.au/news/rural/2020-08-11/live-export-investigation-into-inhumane-indonesian-slaughter/12545460.

Dam, Monique and Christine McCaskill. 2020. *Animals and People Experiencing Domestic Violence: How Their Safety and Wellbeing are Interconnected.* Domestic Violence NSW Inc. https://www.dvnsw.org.au/releases/.

Dandie, Geoff. 2013. "The New Code Has a New Name." *ANZCCART News* 26 (2): 1–3. https://anzccart.adelaide.edu.au/latest-news-and-events/anzccart-newsletters#2013-volume-26-issues-1-3-anzccart-news-survey-results-2013.

Dandie, Geoff. 2005. "The Australian Animal Welfare Strategy." *ANZCCART News*, 18 (2): 1–3. https://anzccart.adelaide.edu.au/latest-news-and-events/anzccart-newsletters#2005-volume-18-issues-1-2.

Darwin, Charles. 1871. *The Descent of Man and Selection in Relation to Sex.* Princeton, NJ: Princeton University Press (Reprinted 1981). https://doi.org/10.5962/bhl.title.2092.

Dawkins, Marian Stamp. 2006. "Through Animal Eyes: What Behaviour Tells Us." *Applied Animal Behaviour Science* 100 (1): 4–10. http://doi.org/10.1016/j.applanim.2006.04.010.

Day, Lauren. 2017. "Dumped dead ducks reignite debate over hunting." *7.30*, ABC TV, 29 March 2017. https://www.abc.net.au/7.30/dumped-dead-ducks-reignite-debate-over-hunting/8398902.

Deckha, Maneesha. 2021. *Animals as Legal Beings: Contesting Anthropocentric Legal Orders*. Toronto: University of Toronto Press. https://doi.org/10.3138/9781487538248.

Derkson, Bruce. 2019. "Australia Makes Positive Moves Forward for Loose Housed Sows and New Farrowing Technology." *The Pig Site*, 14 October 2019. https://www.thepigsite.com/articles/australia-makes-positive-moves-forward-for-loose-housed-sows-and-farrowing-technology.

Diamond, Cora. 2004. "Eating Meat and Eating People." In *Animal Rights: Current Debates and New Directions*, edited by Cass R. Sunstein and Martha C. Nussbaum, 93–107. Oxford: Oxford University Press. https://doi.org/10.1093/acprof:oso/9780195305104.003.0005.

Dingle, Sarah and Lesley Robinson. 2012. "Dugongs Cruelly Slaughtered in Illegal Meat Trade." *ABC News*, 8 March 2012. https://www.abc.net.au/news/2012-03-08/dugongs-cruelly-slaughtered-in-illegal-meat-trade/3877908.

Doherty Tim S., Don A. Driscoll, Dale G. Nimmo, Euan G. Ritchie and Ricky-John Spencer. 2019. "Conservation or Politics? Australia's Target to Kill 2 Million Cats." *Conservation Letters* 12 (4): 1–6. https://doi.org/10.1111/conl.12633.

Donovan, Josephine. 2007. "Animal Rights and Feminist Theory." In *The Feminist Care Tradition in Animal Ethics*, edited by Josephine Donovan and Carol J. Adams, 58–86. New York: Columbia University Press.

Donovan, Josephine and Carol J. Adams, eds. 2007. *The Feminist Care Tradition in Animal Ethics.* New York: Columbia University Press.

Dorning, Jo, Stephen Harris and Heather Pickett. 2016. *The Welfare of Wild Animals in Travelling Circuses.* A review commissioned by the Welsh Government. April 2016. https://gov.wales/welfare-wild-animals-travelling-circuses#description-block.

Duff, Eamonn. 2015. "Parliamentary Inquiry Called into Puppy Factories." *Sydney Morning Herald,* 12 May 2015. https://www.smh.com.au/national/nsw/parliamentary-inquiry-called-into-puppy-factories-20150512-ggzuqp.html.

Dunn, Steve, Steve Corrigan and Russell Watkinson. 2012. *Governance Review of the Game Council of NSW* for NSW Department of Primary Industries, Independent Consulting.

Easton Brian, Lynsey Warbey, Bruno Mezzatesta and Ashley Mercy. 2015. *Animal Welfare Review.* Report of an Independent Review of the Investment in and Administration of the *Animal Welfare Act 2002* in Western Australia.

Ellis, Elizabeth. 2018. "Governments Can't Be Trusted to Deliver Welfare Standards for Chickens". *Conversation,* 12 February 2018. https://theconversation.com/governments-cant-be-trusted-to-deliver-welfare-standards-for-chickens-90091.

Ellis, Elizabeth. 2016. "The Will of the People, or the Party?" *Policy Forum.* Asia & the Pacific Policy Society. https://www.policyforum.net/will-people-party/.

Ellis, Elizabeth. 2013a. "Bearing the Burden: Shifting Responsibility for the Welfare of the Beast." *Macquarie Law Journal* 11 (4): 39–49. https://ro.uow.edu.au/lhapapers/1207/.

Ellis, Elizabeth. 2013b. "The Animal Welfare Trade-off or Trading Off Animal Welfare?" In *Animal Law in Australasia: Continuing the Dialogue,* edited by Peter Sankoff, Steven White and Celeste Black, 344–66. Leichhardt, NSW: Federation Press.

Ellis, Elizabeth. 2009. "Collaborative Advocacy: Framing the Interests of Animals as a Social Justice Concern." In *Animal Law in Australasia: A New Dialogue,* edited by Peter Sankoff and Steven White, 354–75. Leichhardt, NSW: Federation Press.

Environment, Natural Resources and Regional Development Committee. Parliament of Victoria. 2017. *Inquiry into the Control of Invasive Animals on Crown Land.* https://www.parliament.vic.gov.au/435-enrrdc/inquiry-into-the-control-of-invasive-animals-on-crown-land.

Environmental Justice Australia. 2020. *Failing our Wildlife: Why Victoria's Wildlife Protection Laws Need to be Modernised.* Environmental Justice Australia and Humane Society International, 11 December 2020. https://www.envirojustice.org.au/failing-our-wildlife-why-victorias-wildlife-protection-laws-need-to-be-modernised/.

Ernst & Young. 2019. *Prevention of Cruelty to Animals Regulatory Impact Statement*, 15 August 2019. Victoria, Department of Jobs, Precincts and Regions.

European Commission. 2021. Brussels, 30 June 2021, C(2021) 4747 final, Communication from the Commission on the European Citizens' Initiative (ECI) "End the Cage Age".

European Court of Auditors. 2018. *Animal Welfare in the EU: Closing the Gap Between Ambitious Goals and Practical Implementation*. Special Report No 31. https://www.eca.europa.eu/en/Pages/DocItem.aspx?did=47557.

Farm Animal Welfare Council. October 2009. *Farm Animal Welfare in Great Britain: Past, Present and Future*. October 2009. London, UK: FAWC. https://www.gov.uk/government/publications/fawc-report-on-farm-animal-welfare-in-great-britain-past-present-and-future.

Farm Animal Welfare Council. 1993. *Report on Priorities for Animal Welfare Research and Development*. May 1993. Surrey, England: FAWC.

Farm Transparency Project. 2021. "Animal Advocates Mount Landmark High Court Challenge to Australia's Ag-gag Laws." Media Release, 29 June 2021. https://www.farmtransparency.org/media.

Farmer, Richard. 2011. *Independent Review of Australia's Livestock Export Trade.* Commonwealth of Australia. https://www.awe.gov.au/biosecurity-trade/export/controlled-goods/live-animals/livestock/regulatory-framework/acts-regulations-orders-standards/review-live-export-trade.

Favre, David. 2016. "An International Treaty for Animal Welfare." In *Animal Law and Welfare – International Perspectives*, edited by Deborah Cao and Steven White, 87–106. Switzerland: Springer International. https://doi.org/10.1007/978-3-319-26818-7_5.

Favre, David. 2010. "Living Property: A New Status for Animals Within the Legal System." *Marquette Law Review* 93 (3): 1021–72. https://scholarship.law.marquette.edu/mulr/vol93/iss3/3/.

Favre, David. 2004. "A New Property Status for Animals: Equitable Self-Ownership." In *Animal Rights: Current Debates and New Directions*, edited by Cass R. Sunstein and Martha C. Nussbaum, 234–50. Oxford: Oxford University Press. https://doi.org/10.1093/acprof:oso/9780195305104.003.0011.

Ferguson, Sarah. 2011. "A Bloody Business." *Four Corners*. ABC TV, 30 May 2011. https://www.abc.net.au/4corners/4c-full-program-bloody-business/8961434.

Field & Game Australia Inc. n.d. https://www.fieldandgame.com.au/home. Accessed 5 May 2022.

Figgis, Honor and Gareth Griffith. 1998. *Animal Experimentation*, Background Paper No 3/98. NSW Parliamentary Library Research Service. https://parlinfo.aph.gov.au/parlInfo/search/display/display.w3p;query=Id:%22library/lcatalog/00079942%22.

Fisher, Roger and Alistair Davey. 2017. *Assessment of the GMA's Compliance and Enforcement Function*. Macquarie, ACT: Pegasus Economics.

Fitzgibbon, Joel. 2013. "New Independent Inspector-General of Animal Welfare and Live Animal Exports." Media Release, 31 July 2013. https://parlinfo.aph.gov.au/parlInfo/search/display/display.w3p;query=Id:%22media/pressrel/2630420%22.

Food and Agriculture Organization of the United Nations. 2018. FAOSTAT, Livestock Primary. http://www.fao.org/faostat/en/?#data/QL.

Fox Koob, Simone. 2019. "How Might Horse Racing Be Cruel?" *Sydney Morning Herald*, 18 October 2019. https://www.smh.com.au/national/how-is-horse-racing-cruel-20191018-p5325q.html.

Francione, Gary L. 2008. *Animals as Persons: Essays on the Abolition of Animal Exploitation*. New York: Columbia University Press.

Francione, Gary L. 2004. "Animals – Property or Persons?" In *Animal Rights: Current Debates and New Directions*, edited by Cass R. Sunstein and Martha C. Nussbaum, 108–42. Oxford: Oxford University Press. https://doi.org/10.1093/acprof:oso/9780195305104.003.0006.

Francione, Gary L. 1995. *Animals, Property and the Law*. Philadelphia: Temple University Press.

Francione, Gary L. and Robert Garner. 2010. *The Animal Rights Debate: Abolition or Regulation?* New York: Columbia University Press.

Franklin, Adrian. 2006. *Animal Nation: The True Story of Animals and Australia*. Sydney: UNSW Press.

Friends of Leadbeater's Possum Inc. 2021. "We Are Off to the High Court, Hopefully – June 2021." https://www.leadbeaters.org.au/we-are-off-to-the-high-court-7-june-2021/.

Furner, Mark. 2020. "Queensland Launches First Review of Animal Welfare Laws in Almost Two Decades." Ministerial media statement, 8 December 2020. https://statements.qld.gov.au/statements/91120.

Futureye Pty. Ltd. 2018. *Australia's Shifting Mindset on Farm Animal Welfare*. Windsor, Victoria: Futureye Pty Ltd. https://futureye.com/resources/.

Garner, Robert. 2006. "Animal Welfare: A Political Defense." *Journal of Animal Law and Ethics* 1: 161–74.

Garner, Robert. 2002. "Political Ideology and the Legal Status of Animals." *Animal Law* 8: 77–91.

Garrett, Aaron. 2011. "Animals and Ethics in the History of Modern Philosophy." In *The Oxford Handbook of Animal Ethics*, edited by Tom L. Beauchamp and R. G. Frey, 61–87. Oxford: Oxford University Press. https://doi.org/10.1093/oxfordhb/9780195371963.013.0003.

Gelber, Katherine and Siobhan O'Sullivan. 2020. "Cat Got Your Tongue? Free Speech, Democracy and Australia's 'Ag-Gag' Laws." *Australian Journal of Political Science* 56 (1): 19–34. https://doi.org/10.1080/10361146.2020.1799938.

Gemmell, Bruce. 2009. *Review of the Australian Animal Welfare Strategy (AAWS)*. Canberra: Australian Department of Agriculture, Fisheries and Forestry.

Geoff Neumann & Associates Pty Ltd. 2005. *Review of the Australian Model Codes of Practice for the Welfare of Animals*, Final Report. Brighton, SA: Geoff Neumann & Associates Pty Ltd.

Gerber, Paula. 2009. "Scientific Experimentation on Animals: Are Australia and New Zealand Implementing the 3Rs?" In *Animal Law in Australasia: A New Dialogue*, edited by Peter Sankoff and Steven White, 212–29. Leichhardt, NSW: Federation Press.

Geysen, Tracy-Lynne, Jenni Weick and Steven White. 2010. "Companion Animal Cruelty and Neglect in Queensland: Penalties, Sentencing and 'Community Expectations'." *Australian Animal Protection Law Journal* 4: 46–63.

Global Animal Law. n.d. "UN Convention on Animal Health and Protection." https://www.globalanimallaw.org/gal/projects/uncahp.html. Accessed 3 November 2021.

Goodfellow, Jed. 2016. "Regulatory Capture and the Welfare of Farm Animals." In *Animal Law and Welfare – International Perspectives*, edited by Deborah Cao and Steven White, 195–235. Switzerland: Springer International. https://doi.org/10.1007/978-3-319-26818-7_10.

Goodfellow, Jed. 2015. "Animal Welfare Regulation in the Australian Agricultural Sector: A Legitimacy Maximising Analysis." PhD thesis, Macquarie University. https://www.researchonline.mq.edu.au/vital/access/manager/Repository/mq:45113.

Goodfellow, Jed. 2013. "Animal Welfare Law Enforcement: to Punish or Persuade?" In *Animal Law in Australasia: Continuing the Dialogue*, edited by Peter Sankoff, Steven White and Celeste Black, 183–207. Leichhardt, NSW: Federation Press.

Gotsis, Tom. 2018. *Exotic Animals in Circuses*, e-brief Issue 2: 1–13. Sydney: NSW Parliamentary Research Service. https://www.parliament.nsw.gov.au/researchpapers/Pages/Exoticanimalsincircuses.aspx.

Gray, Jenny. 2017. *Zoo Ethics: The Challenges of Compassionate Conservation*. Clayton South, VIC: CSIRO Publishing. https://doi.org/10.1071/9781486306992.

Green, T.C. and D.J. Mellor. 2011. "Extending Ideas About Animal Welfare Assessment to Include 'Quality of Life' and Related Concepts." *NZ Veterinary Journal* 59 (6): 263–71. https://doi.org/10.1080/00480169.2011.610283.

Greyhound Welfare and Integrity Commission. 2021. *Annual Report 2020/21*. https://www.gwic.nsw.gov.au/about/annual-report.

Greyhound Welfare and Integrity Commission. 2020. *Annual Report 2019/20*. https://www.gwic.nsw.gov.au/about/annual-report.

Greyhound Welfare and Integrity Commission. 2019. *Annual Report 2018/19*. https://www.gwic.nsw.gov.au/about/annual-report.

Gruen, Lori. 2014. *Entangled Empathy: An Alternative Ethic for our Relationship with Animals*. New York: Lantern Books.

Gullone, Eleonora. 2017. "Why Eating Animals is Not Good for Us." *Journal of Animal Ethics* 7 (1): 31–62. https://doi.org/10.5406/janimalethics.7.1.0031.

Hagen, Kristin, Ruud Van den Bos and Tjard de Cock Buning. 2011. "Editorial: Concepts of Animal Welfare." *Acta Biotheoretica* 59: 93–103. https://doi.org/10.1007/s10441-011-9134-0.

Hambrett, Micaela, Andy Burns and Charlotte King. 2021. "NSW Government Under Pressure Over Kangaroo Culling as Leaked Documents Reveal Questions Over the Program's Sustainability." *7.30/ABC Regional Investigations*, 4 November 2021. https://www.abc.net.au/news/2021-11-04/nsw-government-pressure-kangaroo-culling-leaked-documents-progr/100590328.

Hannah, Frances. 2009. "Pets in Wills: Leaving a Legacy to an Animal Friend." *Law Society Journal* March 2009: 66–9. https://search.informit.org/doi/10.3316/IELAPA.200903867.

Harding, Tim and George Rivers. 2019. *Australian Animal Welfare Standards and Guidelines. Exhibited Animals – Decision Regulation Impact Statement*. NSW Department of Primary Industries. Edition 1. June 2019.

Harrison, Ruth. 1964. *Animal Machines: The New Factory Farming Industry*. London: Vincent Stewart.

Hartcher, K.M. and Bidda Jones. 2017. "The Welfare of Layer Hens in Cage and Cage-free Housing Systems." *World's Poultry Science Journal* 73 (4): 767–82. https://doi.org/10.1017/S0043933917000812.

Hatten, Ruth. 2013. "International Dimensions of Animal Cruelty Law." In *Animal Law in Australasia: Continuing the Dialogue*, edited by Peter Sankoff, Steven White and Celeste Black, 289–307. Leichhardt, NSW: Federation Press.

Heikkila, Karina Elizabeth. 2018. "Could s 17 of the *Animal Care and Protection Act 2001* (Qld) Represent a Derridean Justice-based Approach to Animal Protection?" PhD thesis, Victoria University, Melbourne. https://vuir.vu.edu.au/36758/.

Hemsworth, Lauren, Paul Hemsworth, Rutu Acharya and Jeremy Skuse. 2018. *Review of the Scientific Literature and the International Pig Welfare Codes and Standards to Underpin the Future Standards and Guidelines for Pigs*. Final Report, APL Project 2017/2217, August 2018, APL.

Herrmann, Kathrin. 2019. "Refinement on the Way towards Replacement: Are We Doing What We Can?" In *Animal Experimentation: Working Towards a Paradigm Change*, edited by Kathrin Herrmann and Kimberley Jayne, 3–64. Leiden, Boston: Brill Human-Animal Studies Series. https://doi.org/10.1163/9789004391192_002.

Herrmann, Kathrin and Kimberley Jayne. 2019. *Animal Experimentation: Working Towards a Paradigm Change*. Leiden, Boston: Brill Human-Animal Studies Series. https://doi.org/10.1163/9789004391192.

Hing, Stephanie, Sue Foster and Di Evans. 2021. "Animal Welfare Risks in Live Cattle Export from Australia to China by Sea." *Animals* 11: 2862. https://doi.org/10.3390/ani11102862.

House of Representatives Standing Committee on the Environment and Energy. Parliament of Australia. 2020. *Inquiry into Feral and Domestic Cats in Australia*. https://www.aph.gov.au/feralanddomesticcats.

Humane Research Australia. 2021. "Proposed EU Phase Out of Animal Experimentation Is a Wake up Call for Australia." Media Release, 28 September 2021. https://www.humaneresearch.org.au/proposed-eu-phase-out-of-animal-experimentation-is-a-wake-up-call-for-australia/.

Humane Research Australia. 2020. "New Legislation Restricts the Use of Animal Testing." 30 June 2020. https://www.humaneresearch.org.au/new-legislation-restricts-the-use-of-animal-testing/.

Humane Research Australia. 2019. "Ban Primate Experiments." 1 October 2019. https://www.humaneresearch.org.au/great-apes/.

Humane Research Australia. 2017. "Statistics 2017." 29 December 2017. https://www.humaneresearch.org.au/2017-australian-statistics-of-animal-use-in-research-teaching/.

Humane Research Australia. 2016. "Statistics 2016." 31 December 2016. https://www.humaneresearch.org.au/statistics_2016/.

Humphries, Gary and Jed Goodfellow. 2016. "Failure to Protect." *Policy Forum*. 24 August 2016. Asia & the Pacific Policy Society. https://www.policyforum.net/failure-to-protect/.

Huntingford, Felicity, Colin Adams, Victoria A. Braithwaite, Sunil Kadri, Tom G. Pottinger, Peter Sandoe and James F. Turnbull. 2007. "The Implications of a Feelings-based Approach to Fish Welfare: A Reply to Arlinghaus et al." *Fish and Fisheries* 8 (3): 277–80. https://doi.org/10.1111/j.1467-2679.2007.00254.x.

Hursthouse, Rosalind. 2011. "Virtue Ethics and the Treatment of Animals." In *The Oxford Handbook of Animal Ethics*, edited by Beauchamp, Tom L. and R.G. Frey, 119–43. Oxford: Oxford University Press. https://doi.org/10.1093/oxfordhb/9780195371963.013.0005.

Iemma, Morris, Simon Draper, Brenton Scott, Steve Coleman, Christine Middlemiss. 2017. *Recommendations of the Greyhound Industry Reform Panel*, February 2017. https://www.industry.nsw.gov.au/__data/assets/pdf_file/0020/101738/final-panel-report-february-2017.pdf.

Independent Heat Stress Risk Assessment Technical Reference Panel. 2019. *Final Report*, May 2019. Canberra: Australia, Department of Agriculture.

Inspector-General of Live Animal Exports. 2021. *Review of the Exporter Supply Chain Assurance System*, Review Report No. 2021/01. Canberra: Commonwealth of Australia. https://www.iglae.gov.au/current-reviews.

Inspector-General of Live Animal Exports. 2020. *Implementation of Moss Review Recommendations*, Review Report No. 2020/02. Canberra: Commonwealth of Australia. https://www.iglae.gov.au/current-reviews.

International Whaling Commission. n.d. "Commercial Whaling." https://iwc.int/commercial. Accessed 3 November 2021.

Invasive Plants and Animals Committee. 2016. *Australian Pest Animal Strategy 2017–2027*. Canberra: Australian Government Department of Agriculture and Water Resources. https://www.awe.gov.au/biosecurity-trade/pests-diseases-weeds/pest-animals-and-weeds.

Jamieson, Philip. 1991. "Duty and the Beast: The Movement of Reform in Animal Welfare Law." *University of Queensland Law Journal* 16: 238–55.

Jamieson, Philip. 1989. "Animal Welfare: A Movement in Transition." In *Law and History in Australia: A Collection of Papers Presented at the 1989 Law and History Conference*, edited by Suzanne Corcoran.

Japan. Ministry of Foreign Affairs, Agriculture, Fisheries and Forest. 2018. "Statement by Chief Cabinet Secretary." 26 December 2018. https://www.mofa.go.jp/ecm/fsh/page4e_000969.html#header.

Johnson, Jane. 2014. "Some Challenges with Animal Ethics Committees – Can Greater Transparency Help?" *Proceedings of the 2013 ANZCCART Conference: "Can We Do Better?"* 23–25 July 2013, 18–21. Sydney: ANZCCART. https://anzccart.adelaide.edu.au/publications/conference-proceedings-and-notes.

Joint Select Committee on Companion Animal Breeding Practices in NSW. Parliament of NSW. 2015. *Report 1/56, Inquiry into Companion Animal Breeding Practices in NSW*, August 2015. https://www.parliament.nsw.gov.au/la/papers/Pages/tabled-paper-details.aspx?pk=30564.

Jones, Bidda and Julian Davies. 2016. *Backlash: Australia's Conflict of Values Over Live Exports*. Braidwood, NSW: Finlay Lloyd. https://finlaylloyd.com/books/.

Kawharu, Amokura. 2013. "Animal Welfare Regulation and International Trade Law: Developments at the World Trade Organization." In *Animal Law in Australasia: Continuing the Dialogue*, edited by Peter Sankoff, Steven White and Celeste Black, 308–29. Leichhardt, NSW: Federation Press.

Kelly, Fran. 2020. "Federal Court to Decide if Live Sheep Can Be Shipped to the Middle East." Guest speaker Mark Harvey-Sutton. ABC Radio National, 16 June 2020. https://www.abc.net.au/radionational/programs/breakfast/federal-court-to-decide-if-live-sheep/12358956.

Keniry, John. 2003. *Livestock Export Review: Final Report*. A Report to the Minister for Agriculture, Fisheries and Forestry. Canberra: Department of Agriculture, Fisheries and Forestry. 23 December 2003.

Kotzmann, Jane. 2020a. "Recognising the Sentience of Animals in Law: A Justification and Framework for Australian States and Territories." *Sydney Law Review* 42 (3): 281–310. https://papers.ssrn.com/sol3/papers.cfm?abstract_id=3741746.

Kotzmann, Jane. 2020b. "Animal Welfare: The Hunt for Clarity." *Law Institute Journal* 1 September 2020. Law Institute of Victoria. https://www.liv.asn.au/Web/Law_Institute_Journal_and_News/Web/LIJ/Year/2020/09September/Animal_welfare__The_hunt_for_clarity.aspx.

Kotzmann, Jane and Nick Prendergast. 2019. "Animal Rights: Time to Start Unpacking What Rights and for Whom." *Mitchell Hamline Law Review* 46 (1): 158–200. https://open.mitchellhamline.edu/mhlr/vol46/iss1/.

KPMG. 2020. *Regulation of the Export of Native and Exotic Birds*. Independent Review. Department of Agriculture, Water and the Environment.

Lascelles, Reem and Alexandra McEwan. 2019. "A Spira Inspired Approach to Animal Protection Advocacy for Rabbits in the Australian Meat Industry." *Animal Studies Journal* 8 (2): 81–112. https://doi.org/10.14453/asj.v8i2.8.

Law Institute of Victoria. 2019. Submission No 424 to Legislative Council Economic and Infrastructure Committee, *Inquiry into the Impact of Animal Rights Activism on Victorian Agriculture*, 8 August 2019. https://www.parliament.vic.gov.au/eic-lc/inquiries/article/4202.

Law Society of NSW. Young Lawyers' Animal Law Committee. 2014. *Companion Animal Law Guide NSW*. 2nd edn. The Law Society of NSW Young Lawyers. LexisNexis Butterworths.

Legge, S., B.P. Murphy, H. McGregor, J.C.Z. Woinarski, J. Augusteyn, G. Ballard, M. Baseler et al. 2017. "Enumerating a Continental-scale Threat: How Many Feral Cats Are in Australia?" *Biological Conservation* 206: 293–303. https://doi.org/10.1016/j.biocon.2016.11.032.

Legislative Assembly Social Policy Scrutiny Committee. Parliament of the Northern Territory. 2018. *Inquiry into the Animal Protection Bill 2018*, May 2018. https://parliament.nt.gov.au/committees/previous/spsc/44-2018.

Legislative Council Economic and Infrastructure Committee. Parliament of Victoria. 2020. *Inquiry into the Impact of Animal Rights Activism on Victorian Agriculture*, February 2020. https://www.parliament.vic.gov.au/eic-lc/inquiries/inquiry/965.

Legislative Council Portfolio Committee No 4. Parliament of NSW. 2020. *The Use of Exotic Animals in Circuses and Exhibition of Cetaceans in New South Wales*. Report 46, December 2020. https://www.parliament.nsw.gov.au/committees/inquiries/Pages/inquiry-details.aspx?pk=2555#tab-reportsandgovernmentresponses.

Legislative Council Portfolio Committee No. 7 – Planning and Environment. Parliament of NSW. 2021. *Health and Wellbeing of Kangaroos and Other Macropods in New South Wales*, Report 3, June 2021. https://www.parliament.nsw.gov.au/committees/inquiries/Pages/inquiry-details.aspx?pk=2707#tab-reportsandgovernmentresponses.

Legislative Council Portfolio Committee No. 7 – Planning and Environment. Parliament of NSW. 2020. *Koala Populations and Habitat in New South Wales*, Report 11, October 2020. https://www.parliament.nsw.gov.au/committees/inquiries/Pages/inquiry-details.aspx?pk=2536#tab-reportsandgovernmentresponses.

Legislative Council Select Committee on Animal Cruelty Laws in New South Wales. Parliament of NSW. 2020. *Inquiry into Animal Cruelty Laws in New South Wales*. Report 1, June 2020. https://www.parliament.nsw.gov.au/committees/listofcommittees/Pages/committee-details.aspx?pk=263#tab-reportsandgovernmentresponses.

Legislative Council Select Committee on Greyhound Racing in NSW. Parliament of NSW. 2014. *Greyhound Racing in NSW First Report*, March 2014. https://www.parliament.nsw.gov.au/committees/listofcommittees/Pages/committee-details.aspx?pk=193#tab-reportsandgovernmentresponses.

LexisNexis. 2018. "Persons and Objects in Whose Favour Trusts May Be Created." *Halsbury's Laws of Australia* [430-275]. Accessed 2 July 2020.

Lind, Judy. 2020. "Greyhound Industry Bites Back." A Letter From the Chief Executive Officer of the NSW Greyhound Welfare & Integrity Commission. *Crikey*, 20 January 2020. https://www.crikey.com.au/2020/01/20/greyhound-industry-bites-back/.

Linzey, Andrew and Clair Linzey. 2019. "An Egregious Slander." *Journal of Animal Ethics* 9 (2) v–vi. https://doi.org/10.5406/janimalethics.9.2.000v.

MacTiernan, Alannah. 2021. "Court Decision in Animal Welfare Case Welcomed." Media Statement, 4 June 2021. https://www.mediastatements.wa.gov.au/Pages/McGowan/2021/06/Court-decision-in-animal-welfare-case-welcomed.aspx.

Marino, Lori. 2017. "Thinking Chickens: A Review of Cognition, Emotion and Behaviour in the Domestic Chicken." *Animal Cognition* 20 (2): 127–47. https://doi.org/10.1007/s10071-016-1064-4.

Marino, Lori and Christina M. Colvin. 2015. "Thinking Pigs: A Comparative Review of Cognition, Emotion, and Personality in Sus Domesticus." *International Journal of Comparative Psychology* 28. https://doi.org/10.46867/ijcp.2015.28.00.04.

Markham, Annabel. 2013. In *Animal Law in Australasia: Continuing the Dialogue*, edited by Peter Sankoff, Steven White and Celeste Black, 208–25. Leichhardt, NSW: Federation Press.

Marks, Clive A. 2013. "Killing Schrödinger's Feral Cat." *Animal Studies Journal* 2 (2): 51–66. https://ro.uow.edu.au/asj/vol2/iss2/4/.

Marshall, Adam. 2020a. *Government Response to the Report of the Select Committee on Animal Cruelty Laws in NSW*, 30 November 2020. https://www.parliament.nsw.gov.au/committees/listofcommittees/Pages/committee-details.aspx?pk=263#tab-reportsandgovernmentresponses.

Marshall, Adam, 2020b. "NSW Set to Unleash Toughest Penalties for Animal Cruelty in Australia." Media Release, 8 November 2020. https://www.dpi.nsw.gov.au/about-us/media-centre/releases/2020/ministerial/nsw-set-to-unleash-toughest-penalties-for-animal-cruelty-in-australia.

Marston, Helen. 2015. "Is Wildlife Research Justified if it's to Benefit the Species? Let's End Animal Experiments." 13 July 2015. http://humaneresearch.blogspot.com/2015/07/is-wildlife-research-justified-if-its.html.

Martin, Terry and Peter Reid. 2020. *Inquiry into Animal Cruelty in the Management of Retired Racehorses in Queensland*. Final Report. State of Queensland. Queensland Racing Integrity Commission, 14 January 2020. https://www.daf.qld.gov.au/business-priorities/biosecurity/animal-biosecurity-welfare/welfare-ethics/management-of-retired-racehorses.

Matthews, Ken, Anne Astin, Mary Corbett and Craig Suann. 2021. *Final Report of the Independent Review of the Pesticides and Veterinary Medicines Regulatory System in Australia*. Canberra: Department of Agriculture, Water and the Environment. Canberra: DAWE. https://www.awe.gov.au/agriculture-land/farm-food-drought/ag-vet-chemicals/better-regulation-of-ag-vet-chemicals/independent-review-agvet-chemical-regulatory-framework.

McCarthy, Michael. 2018. *Independent Review of Conditions for the Export of Sheep to the Middle East During the Northern Hemisphere Summer*. https://www.awe.gov.au/biosecurity-trade/export/controlled-goods/live-animals/livestock/history/review-northern-summer#review.

McEwan, Alexandra and Emma L. Turley. 2021. "Green Criminology – Law Interdisciplinarity Towards Multispecies Justice: The Case of Wildlife Trafficking in Vietnam." *International Journal for Crime Justice and Social Democracy* 10 (3): 1804. https://doi.org/10.5204/ijcjsd.1804.

McEwen, Graeme. 2008. "Do the New Commonwealth Live Export Laws Exclude the State Animal Protection Laws." Memorandum of Advice, Barristers Animal Welfare Panel, 21 April 2008. http://bawp.org.au/live-exports/.

McEwen, Graeme, with Adam Ray and Gian-Maria Antonio Fini. 2011. *Animal Law: Principles and Frontiers*. Barristers Animal Welfare Panel. http://bawp.org.au/animal-law-e-book/.

McGrath, Pat. 2017. "Chickens Boiled Alive at Star Poultry Supply Abattoir in Melbourne, Secret Footage Reveals." *ABC News*, 16 November 2017. https://www.abc.net.au/news/2017-11-16/chickens-boiled-alive-inside-melbourne-abattoir/9157186/.

McGreevy, Paul and Bidda Jones. 2020. "10 Reasons to Stop Whipping Racehorses, Including New Research Revealing the Likely Pain it Causes." *Conversation*, 12 November 2020. https://theconversation.com/10-reasons-to-stop-whipping-racehorses-including-new-research-revealing-the-likely-pain-it-causes-149271.

McGreevy, Paul D., Robert A. Corken, Hannah Salvin, Celeste M. Black. 2012. "Whip Use by Jockeys in a Sample of Australian Thoroughbred Races – An Observational Study". PLoS ONE 7 (3): e33398. https://doi.org/10.1371/journal.pone.0033398.

McHugh, Michael. 2016, 107–8. *Special Commission of Inquiry into the Greyhound Racing Industry in New South Wales*. Report. Vol 1, 16 June 2016.

McKinnon, Catherine A. 2004. "Of Mice and Men: A Feminist Fragment on Animal Rights." In *Animal Rights: Current Debates and New Directions*, edited by Cass R. Sunstein and Martha C. Nussbaum, 263–76. Oxford: Oxford University Press. https://doi.org/10.1093/acprof:oso/9780195305104.003.0013.

McLeod S.R. and R.B. Hacker. 2019. "Balancing Stakeholder Interests in Kangaroo Management – Historical Perspectives and Future Prospects." *The Rangeland Journal* 41 (6): 567–79. https://doi.org/10.1071/RJ19055.

McLeod, Steven R. and Trudy M. Sharp. 2014. *Improving the Humaneness of Commercial Kangaroo Harvesting*. Canberra: Rural Industries Research and Development Corporation.

Meldrum-Hanna, Caro. 2015. "Making a Killing." *Four Corners*. ABC TV, 16 February 2015. https://www.abc.net.au/4corners/making-a-killing/6127124.

Meldrum-Hanna, Caro and Amy Donaldson. 2019. "The Final Race." *7.30*. ABC TV, 17 October 2019. https://www.abc.net.au/7.30/the-dark-side-of-the-horse-racing-industry/11614022.

Mellor, David J. 2019. "Welfare-aligned Sentience: Enhanced Capacities to Experience, Interact, Anticipate, Choose and Survive." *Animals* 9 (7): 440–455. https://doi.org/10.3390/ani9070440.

Mellor, David J. 2016. "Updating Animal Welfare Thinking: Moving Beyond the 'Five Freedoms' Towards 'A Life Worth Living'." *Animals* 6 (3): 21–41. https://doi.org/10.3390/ani6030021.

Mellor, David J. 2015. "Positive Animal Welfare States and Reference Standards for Welfare Assessment." *New Zealand Veterinary Journal* 63 (1): 17–23. https://doi.org/10.1080/00480169.2014.926802.

Mercer, Daniel and Tom Edwards. 2020. "WA's Shrinking Sheep Flock Tipped to Increase Lamb Prices and Cause Abattoir Closures." *ABC Great Southern*, 16 June 2020. https://www.abc.net.au/news/2020-06-16/wa-shrinking-sheep-flock-expected-to-cause-abattoir-closures/12359790.

Merkes, Monika and Rob Buttrose. 2019. "Increasing the Transparency of Animal Experimentation: An Australian Perspective." In *Animal Experimentation: Working Towards a Paradigm Change*, edited by Kathrin Herrmann and Kimberley Jayne, 224–43. Leiden, Boston: Brill Human-Animal Studies Series. https://doi.org/10.1163/9789004391192_010.

Merkes, Monika and Rob Buttrose. 2013. "New Code, Same Suffering: Animals in the Lab." *Drum*, *ABC News*, 1 August 2013. https://www.abc.net.au/news/2013-08-01/merkes-and-buttrose-animal-testing/4857604.

Mochan, Kit. 2019. "Farm Trespass Laws Paused by WA Attorney-General After ABC 7.30 Expose into Horse Racing Industry." *ABC Great Southern*, 12 November 2019. https://www.abc.net.au/news/2019-11-12/wa-animal-trespass-legislation-paused-after-racing-investigation/11687824.

Morfuni, Laura. 2011. "Pain for Profit: An Analysis of the Live Export Trade." *Deakin Law Review* 16 (2): 497–538. https://doi.org/10.21153/dlr2011vol16no2art111.

Morton, Rochelle, Michelle L. Hebart and Alexandra L. Whittaker. 2020. "Explaining the Gap Between the Ambitious Goals and Practical Reality of Animal Welfare Law Enforcement: A Review of the Enforcement Gap in Australia." *Animals* 10: 482–502. https://doi.org/10.3390/ani10030482.

Moss, Philip. 2018. *Review of the Regulatory Capability and Culture of the Department of Agriculture and Water Resources in the Regulation of Live Animal Exports.* 27 September 2018. https://www.awe.gov.au/agriculture-land/animal/welfare/export-trade/independent-review-of-regulation.

National Code of Practice for the Humane Shooting of Kangaroos and Wallabies for Commercial Purposes. 2020. AgriFutures Australia Publication No. 20–126. https://www.agrifutures.com.au/product/national-code-of-practice-for-the-humane-shooting-of-kangaroos-and-wallabies-for-commercial-purposes/.

National Council to Reduce Violence against Women and their Children. 2009. *Domestic Violence Laws in Australia*, June 2009. Canberra: Commonwealth of Australia.

National Health and Medical Research Council. 2019. *Information Paper: The Implementation of the 3Rs in Australia.* September 2019. Canberra: National Health and Medical Research Council. https://www.nhmrc.gov.au/about-us/publications/information-paper-implementation-3rs-australia.

National Health and Medical Research Council. 2016. *Principles and Guidelines for the Care and Use of Non-human Primates for Scientific Purposes.* September 2016. Canberra: National Health and Medical Research Council. https://www.nhmrc.gov.au/about-us/publications/principles-and-guidelines-care-and-use-non-human-primates-scientific-purposes.

Newby, Jonica. 2015. "Horse Whip." *Catalyst.* ABC TV, 24 March 2015. https://www.abc.net.au/catalyst/horse-whip/11015810.

Nguyen, Kevin. 2020. "The Baboons That Escaped at Sydney Hospital Were From a Medical Research Facility – This is What Happens There." *ABC News*, 26 February 2020. https://www.abc.net.au/news/2020-02-26/baboons-that-escaped-at-sydney-hospital-were-from-research-lab/12001260.

Nicol, C.J., J. Bouwsema, G. Caplen, A.C. Davies, J. Hockenhull and S.L. Lambton et al. 2017. *Farmed Bird Welfare Science Review.* Melbourne: Department of Economic Development, Jobs, Transport and Resources. https://www.vgls.vic.gov.au/client/en_AU/VGLS-public/search/detailnonmodal?qu=Nicol%2C+S.&d=ent%3A%2F%2FSD_ILS%2F0%2FSD_ILS%3A556652%7E%7E0&ic=true&ps=300&h=8.

Nonhuman Rights Project. n.d. "Challenging the Legal Thinghood of Autonomous Nonhuman Animals 2021." https://www.nonhumanrights.org/litigation/. Accessed 3 November 2021.

NSW Companion Animals Taskforce. 2013. *Report to the Minister for Local Government on the Management of Dangerous Dogs*, February 2013. https://www.olg.nsw.gov.au/public/dogs-cats/companion-animals-taskforce/information-about-the-companion-animals-taskforce/.

NSW Companion Animals Taskforce. 2012a. *Report to the Minister for Local Government and the Minister for Primary Industries*, October 2012. https://www.olg.nsw.gov.au/public/dogs-cats/companion-animals-taskforce/information-about-the-companion-animals-taskforce/.

NSW Companion Animals Taskforce. 2012b. *Discussion Paper*. May 2012.

NSW. Department of Planning and Environment. 2021a. *NSW Commercial Kangaroo Harvest Management Plan: 2020 Annual Report*. NSW Commercial Kangaroo Harvest Management Plan 2017–21. https://www.environment.nsw.gov.au/research-and-publications/publications-search/2020-annual-report-nsw-commercial-kangaroo-harvest-management-plan-2017-21.

NSW. Department of Planning and Environment. 2021b. "Animal Dealer (Live Reptile) Licence." Last updated 12 May 2021. https://www.environment.nsw.gov.au/licences-and-permits/wildlife-licences/trading-in-native-animals/licences-to-commercially-trade-in-native-animals/animal-dealer-live-reptile-licence.

NSW. Department of Planning and Environment. 2021c. "Public Register of Licences to Harm." Last updated 2 March 2021. https://www.environment.nsw.gov.au/licences-and-permits/wildlife-licences/licences-to-control-or-harm/public-register-of-licences-to-harm.

NSW. Department of Planning and Environment. 2020a. *NSW Commercial Kangaroo Harvest Management Plan: 2019 Annual Report*. NSW Commercial Kangaroo Harvest Management Plan 2017–21. https://www.environment.nsw.gov.au/research-and-publications/publications-search/2019-annual-report-nsw-commercial-kangaroo-harvest-management-plan-2017-21.

NSW. Department of Planning and Environment 2020b. "Professional Kangaroo Harvester Licence." 4 December 2020. https://www.environment.nsw.gov.au/research-and-publications/publications-search/licence-conditions-commercial-harvester-kangaroo-professional.

NSW. Department of Planning and Environment. 2019. "Animal Dealer (Live Bird) Licence." Last updated 27 August 2019. https://www.environment.nsw.gov.au/licences-and-permits/wildlife-licences/trading-in-native-animals/licences-to-commercially-trade-in-native-animals/animal-dealer-live-bird-licence.

NSW Department of Primary Industries. 2021. *NSW Animal Welfare Reform – Discussion Paper*. July 2021. https://www.dpi.nsw.gov.au/animals-and-livestock/animal-welfare/animal-welfare-reform/discussion-paper.

NSW Department of Primary Industries. 2020a. *NSW 2019 Animal Use in Research Statistics*. https://www.animalethics.org.au/animal-use-statistics.

NSW Department of Primary Industries. 2020b. *NSW 2018 Animal Use in Research Statistics.* https://www.animalethics.org.au/animal-use-statistics.

NSW Department of Primary Industries. 2020c. *NSW Animal Welfare Reform – Issues Paper*, February 2020.

NSW Department of Primary Industries. 2019. Submission No. 173 to Legislative Council Portfolio Committee No 4. Parliament of NSW, *Inquiry into Exhibition of Exotic Animals in Circuses and Exhibition of Cetaceans in NSW*, 22 November 2019. https://www.parliament.nsw.gov.au/committees/inquiries/Pages/inquiry-details.aspx?pk=2555#tab-submissions.

NSW Department of Primary Industries. 2018. *Animal Welfare Discussion Paper: Improving the Current Legislation – Penalties and Critical Situations.* June 2018.

NSW Department of Primary Industries. 2017. *Performance, Data & Insights 2017.* https://www.dpi.nsw.gov.au/about-us/publications/pdi/2017.

NSW Department of Primary Industries. 2016a. *Game Licensing Unit Enforcement Policy.* Policy number GLUCO1218. Review Date May 2017. https://www.dpi.nsw.gov.au/hunting/compliance/glu-enforcement-policy.

NSW Department of Primary Industries. 2016b. *Game Licensing Unit Regulatory Policy.* Policy number GLUCO1214. Review Date May 2017. https://www.dpi.nsw.gov.au/hunting/compliance/glu-regulatory-policy.

NSW Department of Primary Industries. 2016c. *Hunt Safe, Hunt Legal.* https://www.dpi.nsw.gov.au/hunting/game-and-pests/be-a-responsible-pig-dogger/hunt-safe,-hunt-legal-be-a-responsible-pig-dogger-guide.

NSW Department of Primary Industries. n.d. "Dehorning Cattle." https://www.dpi.nsw.gov.au/animals-and-livestock/beef-cattle/husbandry/general-management/dehorning-cattle. Accessed 3 November 2021.

NSW Department of Primary Industries. n.d. "Game Licensing Unit Outcomes." https://www.dpi.nsw.gov.au/hunting/compliance. https://www.dpi.nsw.gov.au/hunting/compliance. Accessed 3 November 2021.

NSW Department of Primary Industries. n.d. Hunting. "R-Licence Accreditation Course." https://www.dpi.nsw.gov.au/hunting/education-and-training-for-hunters/restricted-licence-accreditation. Accessed 3 November 2021.

NSW Department of Primary Industries. n.d. Recreational fishing. "Free Kids Resources." https://www.dpi.nsw.gov.au/fishing/recreational/kids-resources. Accessed 3 November 2021.

NSW Department of Primary Industries. n.d. Recreational Fishing. "Get Hooked ... it's Fun to Fish." https://www.dpi.nsw.gov.au/fishing/recreational/resources/fishing-workshops/get-hooked. Accessed 3 November 2021.

NSW Department of Primary Industries. n.d. Zoo, Circus and Other Exhibited Animals. "Preparing for an Audit." https://www.dpi.nsw.gov.au/animals-and-livestock/animal-welfare/exhibit/compliance. Accessed 3 November 2021.

NSW Government. 2021. *Greyhound Racing Act 2017*. Statutory Review Report, April 2021. https://www.parliament.nsw.gov.au/la/papers/Pages/tabled-paper-details.aspx?pk=79470.

NSW Government. 2020. *Greyhound Welfare – Code of Practice*. May 2020. https://www.gwic.nsw.gov.au/welfare/code-of-practice-for-the-welfare-of-greyhounds.

NSW Government. 2016. *Response to Report 1/56 of the Joint Select Committee on Companion Animals Breeding Practices in NSW*, February 2016. https://www.parliament.nsw.gov.au/la/papers/Pages/tabled-paper-details.aspx?pk=67636.

NSW Natural Resources Commission 2017, 1. *Supplementary Pest Control Trial. Final Evaluation*. February 2017.

NSW Office of Environment and Heritage. 2018a. *2018 Annual Report*. NSW Commercial Kangaroo Harvest Management Plan 2017–21. https://www.environment.nsw.gov.au/research-and-publications/publications-search/nsw-commercial-kangaroo-harvest-management-plan-2018-annual-report.

NSW Office of Environment and Heritage. 2018b. *Commercial Trade of Native Animals Policy*. https://www.environment.nsw.gov.au/research-and-publications/publications-search/commercial-trade-of-native-animals-policy.

NSW Office of Environment and Heritage. 2018c. *Discussion Paper: Towards a Risk-based Approach to Wildlife Licences*.

NSW. Office of Local Government. n.d. Annual Permits. https://www.olg.nsw.gov.au/councils/responsible-pet-ownership/nsw-pet-registry/annual-permits/. Accessed 3 November 2021.

NSW. Office of Local Government. n.d. Pound and Dog Attack Statistics. https://www.olg.nsw.gov.au/public/dogs-cats/responsible-pet-ownership/pound-and-dog-attack-statistics/. Accessed 3 November 2021.

NSW. Office of Local Government. n.d. Response to Companion Animals Taskforce Recommendations. https://www.olg.nsw.gov.au/public/dogs-cats/companion-animals-taskforce/information-about-the-companion-animals-taskforce/. Accessed 3 November 2021.

Nussbaum, Martha C. 2004. "Beyond 'Compassion and Humanity': Justice for Nonhuman Animals." In *Animal Rights: Current Debates and New Directions*, edited by Cass R. Sunstein and Martha C. Nussbaum, 299–320. Oxford: Oxford University Press. https://doi.org/10.1093/acprof:oso/9780195305104.003.0015.

O'Donnell, Erin L. and Julia Talbot-Jones. 2018. "Creating Legal Rights for Rivers: Lessons From Australia, New Zealand, and India." *Ecology and Society* 23 (1): 7. https://doi.org/10.5751/ES-09854-230107.

OIE. World Organisation for Animal Health. 2019. *Terrestrial Animal Health Code*. https://www.oie.int/en/what-we-do/standards/codes-and-manuals/terrestrial-code-online-access/.

OIE. World Organisation for Animal Health. 2017. 24 May 2017. "Adoption of the First OIE Global Strategy on Animal Welfare." https://www.oie.int/en/adoption-of-the-first-oie-global-strategy-on-animal-welfare/.

Oogjes, Glenys. 2011. "Australian Live Transport Standards and Guidelines: Is the New Review Process Providing Protection for Transported Farm Animals?" *Australian Animal Protection Law Journal* 6: 8.

Orr, Bronwyn and Bidda Jones. 2019. "A Survey of Veterinarian Attitudes Toward Prepubertal Desexing of Dogs and Cats in the Australian Capital Territory." *Frontiers in Veterinary Science* 6: 1–7. https://doi.org/10.3389/fvets.2019.00272.

O'Sullivan, Siobhan. 2011. *Animals, Equality and Democracy*. Palgrave Macmillan Animal Ethics Series. Houndmills: Palgrave Macmillan.

Pallotta, Nicole. 2019. "Chattel or Child: The Liminal Status of Companion Animals in Society and Law." *Social Sciences* 8:158–201. https://doi.org/10.3390/socsci8050158.

Pallotta, Nicole. 2018. "Brussels Recognises Animals as Sentient Beings Distinct from Objects." *Animal Law Update*. Animal Legal Defense Fund, 8 December 2018. https://aldf.org/article/brussels-recognizes-animals-as-sentient-beings-distinct-from-objects/.

Pallotta, Nicole. 2017. "Alaska Legislature Becomes First to Require Consideration of Animals' Interests in Custody Cases." *Animal Law Update*. 20 January 2017. Animal Legal Defense Fund. https://aldf.org/article/alaska-legislature-becomes-first-to-require-consideration-of-animals-interests-in-custody-cases/.

Parker, Christine, Gyorgy Scrinis and Rachel Carey. 2018. "A Public Appetite for Poultry Welfare Regulation Reform: Why Higher Welfare Labelling Is Not Enough." *Alternative Law Journal* 43 (4): 238–43. https://doi.org/10.1177/1037969X18800398.

Parker, Christine and Josephine De Costa. 2016. "Misleading the Ethical Consumer: The Regulation of Free-range Egg Labelling." *Melbourne University Law Review* 39 (3): 895–949.

Peck, Jackson. 2021. "Call for National Puppy Farm, Animal Cruelty Laws as Breeders Eye NSW's More Lenient Rules." *ABC Goulburn Murray*, 2 March 2021. https://www.abc.net.au/news/2021-03-02/call-for-national-puppy-farm-and-animal-cruelty-laws/13191968.

Peters, Anne. 2016. "Global Animal Law: What it is and Why We Need it." *Transnational Environmental Law* 5 (1): 9–23. http://doi.org/10.1017/S2047102516000066.

Petrie, Claire. 2019. *Live Export – a Chronology*. Research Paper Series, 2019–20, Parliament of Australia, Department of Parliamentary Services. iommonwealth of Australia. https://www.aph.gov.au/About_Parliament/Parliamentary_Departments/Parliamentary_Library/pubs/rp/rp1920/Chronologies/LiveExport.

Phillips, C.J.C. and J.C. Petherick. 2015. "The Ethics of a Co-regulatory Model for Farm Animal Welfare Research." *Journal of Agricultural and Environmental Ethics* 28: 127–42. https://doi.org/10.1007/s10806-014-9524-9.

Press, Tony and Indi Hodgson-Johnston. 2015. "Japan's Whaling Fleet Sets Sail Again, and There's Not Much That Can Stop it." *Conversation*, 1 December 2015. https://theconversation.com/japans-whaling-fleet-sets-sail-again-and-theres-not-much-that-can-stop-it-51556.

Productivity Commission. 2016. *Regulation of Australian Agriculture*, 15 November 2016. https://www.pc.gov.au/inquiries/completed/agriculture#report.

Queensland. Department of Agriculture and Fisheries. 2021. *Annual Report 2020–21*. https://www.daf.qld.gov.au/strategic-direction/annual-report.

Queensland. Department of Agriculture and Fisheries. 2020. *Annual Report 2019–20*. https://www.daf.qld.gov.au/strategic-direction/annual-report.

Queensland Government. 2021. *Review of the Animal Care and Protection Act 2001*. Discussion Paper. https://www.daf.qld.gov.au/business-priorities/biosecurity/animal-biosecurity-welfare/welfare-ethics/review-of-the-animal-care-and-protection-act-2001.

Queensland Sentencing Advisory Council. 2019. *Sentencing Spotlight on Animal Welfare Offences*. https://www.sentencingcouncil.qld.gov.au/research/reports/sentencing-spotlight/animal-welfare-offences.

Racing SA. 2021. "Jumps Racing Removed From SA Racing's Calendar." 1 October 2021. https://racingsa.com.au/blog/2021/10/01/3491/jumps-racing-removed-from-sa-racings-calendar.

Radan, Peter and Cameron Stewart. 2018. *Principles of Australian Equity and Trusts*. 4th edn. Sydney: LexisNexis Butterworths.

Radan, Peter. 2013. "Antivivisection and Charity." *Sydney Law Review* 35 (3): 519–39.

Radford, Mike. 2001. *Animal Welfare Law in Britain: Regulation and Responsibility*. Oxford: Oxford University Press.

Ramp, Daniel, Dror Ben-Ami, Keely Boom and David Benjamin Croft. 2013. "Compassionate Conservation: A Paradigm Shift for Wildlife Management in Australasia." In *Ignoring Nature No More: The Case for Compassionate Conservation*, edited by Marc Bekoff, 295–315. London: University of Chicago Press. https://doi.org/10.7208/chicago/9780226925363.003.0021.

Ray, Adam. 2011. "The Conception of Animals as Property." In *Animal Law: Principles and Frontiers*, Graeme McEwen with Adam Ray and Gian-Maria Antonio Fini. Barristers Animal Welfare Panel. http://bawp.org.au/animal-law-e-book/.

Regan, Tom. 1983. *The Case for Animal Rights*. Berkeley and Los Angeles, California: University of California Press.

Reynolds, Annika, Lilly Deluca, Adam Gottschalk, Kelsey Gray, Stella Leonardi and Imogen Picker. 2021. *The Climate Gap: Report on Climate Threat Management for Critically Endangered Species and Ecological Communities under the EPBC Act*. GreenLaw, Australian Conservation Foundation.

Riga, Rachel. 2018. "Greyhounds Still Killed in the Hundreds as Government and Industry Accused of Dragging Feet on Reforms." *ABC News*, 24 November 2018. https://www.abc.net.au/news/2018-11-24/hundreds-of-greyhounds-killed-as-reforms-not-implemented/10547874.

Riley, Sophie. 2020a. "Brighton v Will: The Legal Chasm Between Animal Welfare and Animal Suffering." *Animals* 10 (9): 1497–1511. https://doi.org/10.3390/ani10091497.

Riley, Sophie, with contributions from Peter Wolf, Joan Schaffner and Geoffrey Wandesforde-Smith. 2020b. Submission No 151 to House of Representatives Standing Committee on the Environment and Energy, *Inquiry into the Problem of Feral and Domestic Cats in Australia*, July 2020. https://www.aph.gov.au/Parliamentary_Business/Committees/House/Environment_and_Energy/Feralanddomesticcats/Submissions.

Riley, Sophie, Julie Levy, Joan Schaffner, Geoffrey Wandesforde-Smith and Peter J. Wolf. 2021. "Protection of Biodiversity in Australia: Is Killing Cats an Effective and Ethical Approach?" *Juriste International* 1: 49–52.

Rizzuto, Sally, Di Evans, Bethany Wilson and Paul McGreevy. 2020. "Exploring the Use of a Qualitative Behavioural Assessment Approach to Assess Emotional State of Calves in Rodeos." *Animals* 10 (1): 113–128. https://doi.org/10.3390/ani10010113.

Rollin, Bernard. 2019. "Animal Welfare Across the World." *Journal of Applied Animal Ethics Research* 1 (1): 146–70. https://doi.org/10.1163/25889567-12340008.

Rollin, Bernard E. 2009. "Ethics and Euthanasia." *Canadian Veterinary Journal* 50 (10): 1081–86.

Rollin, Bernard E. 2006. *Animal Rights and Human Morality*. New York, NY: Prometheus Books.

Rosalky, Mike. 2019. "Deserving of Rights: Legal Personhood and Animal Law." *Ethos*, Law Society of the ACT Journal, Spring 2019: 30–5.

Rose, Margaret. 2013. "Ethical Decision-making: Do We Need to Re-set the GPS?" *Proceedings of the 2013 ANZCCART Conference 'Can We Do Better?'* Sydney: ANZCCART. https://anzccart.adelaide.edu.au/publications/conference-proceedings-and-notes.

Roth, Ian. 2018. *Australian Animal Welfare Standards and Guidelines – Poultry, Report for NSW Government Following the Independent Consultation Process.*

Roy, Tahlia. 2020. "Coronavirus Restrictions See Demand for Pets Surge as Shelters Issue Warning to Prospective Owners." *ABC News*, 5 April 2020. https://www.abc.net.au/news/2020-04-05/demand-for-pets-surge-as-australians-stay-at-home/12118888.

Royal Commission into National Natural Disaster Arrangements. 2020. *Report*, 28 October 2020. Commonwealth of Australia. https://naturaldisaster.royalcommission.gov.au/publications/royal-commission-national-natural-disaster-arrangements-report.

RSPCA Australia. 2021a. *Animal Welfare in Abattoirs, Poultry Processors and Knackeries – Regulatory Scorecard*. Deakin West, ACT: RSPCA Australia. Revised May 2021. https://scorecard.rspca.org.au/reports/animal-welfare-in-slaughtering-establishments-regulatory-scorecard/.

RSPCA Australia. 2021b. "44 Strikes and You're … Not Out? RSPCA Calls For Export Licence to be Stripped After Further Animal Welfare Breaches." Media Release, 30 July 2021. https://www.rspca.org.au/media-centre/news/2021/44-strikes-and-you%E2%80%99re-%E2%80%A6-not-out-rspca-calls-export-licence-be-stripped-after.

RSPCA Australia. 2020a. Knowledgebase. "Policy Co8 Rodeos." Updated 9 December 2020. https://kb.rspca.org.au/knowledge-base/rspca-policy-c08-rodeos/.

RSPCA Australia. 2020b. Knowledgebase. "What Laws Protect Animals in Rodeos?" Updated 14 October 2020. https://kb.rspca.org.au/knowledge-base/what-laws-protect-animals-in-rodeos/.

RSPCA Australia. 2020c. Knowledgebase. "What is the Difference Between Non-Commercial and Commercial Kangaroo Shooting?" 26 November 2020. https://kb.rspca.org.au/knowledge-base/what-is-the-difference-between-non-commercial-and-commercial-kangaroo-shooting/.

RSPCA Australia. 2020d. *National Statistics 2019–2020*. https://www.rspca.org.au/what-we-do/our-role-caring-animals/annual-statistics.

RSPCA Australia. 2020e. *Recreational Hunting and Animal Welfare*. An RSPCA Australia information paper. July 2020. https://kb.rspca.org.au/downloads/information-papers/.

RSPCA Australia. 2020f. Submission No 124 to House of Representatives Standing Committee on the Environment and Energy, *Inquiry into Feral and Domestic Cats in Australia*, 30 July 2020. https://www.aph.gov.au/Parliamentary_Business/Committees/House/Environment_and_Energy/Feralanddomesticcats/Submissions.

RSPCA Australia. 2019a. Submission 175 to Legislative Council Portfolio Committee No 4, Parliament of NSW, *Inquiry into Exhibition of Exotic Animals in Circuses and Exhibition of Cetaceans in NSW*, 22 November 2019. https://www.parliament.nsw.gov.au/committees/inquiries/Pages/inquiry-details.aspx?pk=2555#tab-submissions.

RSPCA Australia. 2019b. "Final ASEL Report Falls Short on Animal Welfare." Media Release, 21 March 2019. https://www.rspca.org.au/media-centre/news/2019/final-asel-report-falls-short-animal-welfare.

RSPCA Australia. 2019c. "FOI Reports Reveal Death, Disease and Heat Stress on Board Live Sheep Export Ships." Media Release, 31 January 2019. https://www.rspca.org.au/media-centre/news/2019/foi-reports-reveal-death-disease-and-heat-stress-board-live-sheep-export.

RSPCA Australia. 2019d. Knowledgebase. "What is the RSPCA's Position on Breed-Specific Legislation?" Updated 30 April 2019. https://kb.rspca.org.au/knowledge-base/what-is-the-rspcas-view-on-breed-specific-legislation/.

RSPCA Australia. 2019e. *National Statistics 2018–2019*. https://www.rspca.org.au/what-we-do/our-role-caring-animals/annual-statistics.

RSPCA Australia. 2018a. Submission No 29b. Proposed Draft Australian Animal Welfare Standards and Guidelines for Poultry. Version Public Consultation, February 2018. http://www.animalwelfarestandards.net.au/poultry/poultry-submissions/.

RSPCA Australia. 2018b. *Identifying Best Practice Domestic Cat Management in Australia*. May 2018. Deakin West, ACT: RSPCA Australia. https://www.rspca.org.au/facts/science/cat-management-paper.

RSPCA Australia. 2018c. "Weak McCarthy Review Decisions Guarantee More Suffering, Deaths." Media Release, 17 May 2018. https://www.rspca.org.au/media-centre/news/2018/weak-mccarthy-review-decisions-guarantee-more-suffering-deaths-rspca.

RSPCA Australia. 2018d. "New Poll Finds 3 in 4 Australians Want Live Export to End, Greatest Concern Over Standards in Rural and Country Areas." Media Release, 27 April 2018. https://www.rspca.org.au/media-centre/news/2018/new-poll-finds-3-4-australians-want-live-export-end-greatest-concern-over.

RSPCA Australia. 2018e. "The Prevalence of Microfractures Due to Bone Fatigue in Thoroughbred Racing Horses." *Science Update* 59: 2. https://www.rspca.org.au/what-we-do/our-role-in-animal-welfare-science/science-update-newsletter.

RSPCA Australia. 2018f. *National Statistics 2017–2018*. https://www.rspca.org.au/what-we-do/our-role-caring-animals/annual-statistics.

RSPCA Australia. 2017. "Welfare Issues Associated with the Illegal Wildlife Trade." https://kb.rspca.org.au/downloads/information-papers/.

RSPCA Australia. 2010. *Puppy Farms*. RSPCA Australia Discussion Paper. https://kb.rspca.org.au/downloads/discussion-papers/.

RSPCA Australia. 2002. *Kangaroo Shooting Code Compliance – A Survey of the Extent of Compliance with the Requirements of the Code of Practice for the Humane Shooting of Kangaroos*. Prepared for Environment Australia by RSPCA Australia, July 2002.

RSPCA Australia. n.d. "About Us." https://www.rspca.org.au/about-us. Accessed 3 November 2021.

RSPCA Australia. n.d. "Our History." https://www.rspca.org.au/about-us/our-history. Accessed 3 November 2021.

RSPCA NSW. 2020a Response to Supplementary Questions and Questions on Notice, Legislative Council Select Committee on Animal Cruelty Laws in NSW, 12 March 2020. https://www.parliament.nsw.gov.au/committees/listofcommittees/Pages/committee-details.aspx?pk=263#tab-otherdocuments.

RSPCA NSW. 2020b. Submission No 62, Draft NSW Greyhound Welfare Code of Practice, 31 March 2020.

RSPCA NSW. 2019. Submission No 136 to Legislative Council Select Committee. Parliament of NSW, Inquiry into Animal Cruelty Laws in NSW, 6 December 2019. https://www.parliament.nsw.gov.au/committees/listofcommittees/Pages/committee-details.aspx?pk=263#tab-submissions.

RSPCA NSW. 2018a. Comments on OEH Discussion Paper – Towards a risk-based approach. 23 July 2018.

RSPCA NSW. 2018b. *Annual Report of the Board*. 30 June 2018. https://www.rspcansw.org.au/annual-report/#1564124892064-85c4b091-e3dd.

RSPCA Queensland. 2019. *Annual Report 2018–19*. https://www.rspcaqld.org.au/who-we-are/annual-report.

RSPCA South Australia and AWL. 2019. Cat Management Plan for South Australia, November 2019. https://www.rspcasa.org.au/wp-content/uploads/2019/11/RSPCA-AWL-Cat-Management-Plan-for-South-Australia.pdf.

RSPCA UK. 2020. "We're Delighted as Welsh Parliament Votes to Ban Use of Wild Animals in Circuses", 15 July 2020. https://www.rspca.org.uk/-/welsh-parliament-votes-for-ban-on-wild-animals-in-circuses.

Russell, Denise. 2012. "Why Animal Ethics Committees Don't Work." *Between the Species: An Online Journal for the Study of Philosophy and Animals* 15 (1): 127–42. https://doi.org/10.15368/bts.2012v15n1.1.

Russell, William M.S. 2009. "The Progress of Humane Experimental Technique: The First Annual FRAME Lecture" presented at the Royal Society of Medicine, London on 24 September 1999. *Alternatives to Laboratory Animals* 37: 3, 277–83. https://doi.org/10.1177/026119290903700309.

Russell, William and Rex Burch. 1959. *The Principles of Humane Experimental Technique*. London: Methuen & Co.

Rutledge-Prior, Serrin and Tara Ward. 2021. "Pricking the Public's Conscience: Implications of *R v Radunz* for the Future of Political Protest in Australia." *Ethos*, Law Society of the ACT Journal, 259: 44–51.

Samuel, Graeme. 2020. *Independent Review of the EPBC Act – Final Report*. Canberra: Department of Agriculture, Water and the Environment. October 2020. https://epbcactreview.environment.gov.au/resources/final-report.

Sankoff, Peter. 2013. "The Protection Paradigm: Making the World a Better Place for Animals?" In *Animal Law in Australasia: Continuing the Dialogue*, edited by Peter Sankoff, Steven White and Celeste Black, 1–30. Leichhardt, NSW: Federation Press.

Sankoff, Peter, Steven White and Celeste Black, eds. 2013. *Animal Law in Australasia: Continuing the Dialogue*. Leichhardt, NSW: Federation Press.

Sankoff, Peter and Steven White, eds. 2009. *Animal Law in Australasia: A New Dialogue*. Leichhardt, NSW: Federation Press.

Saunders, Glen and Trudy Sharp. 2008. "The Welfare of Introduced Wild Animals in Australia: A Balanced Response." Letter to the Editor. *Environment and Planning Law Journal* 25 (3): 157–60.

Schipp M.A. and A.D. Sheridan. 2013. "Applying the OIE *Terrestrial Animal Health Code* to the Welfare of Animals Exported from Australia." *Rev. Sci. Tech. 32* (3): 669–83. https://doi.org/10.20506/rst.32.2.2224.

Schmidt, Kirsten. 2011. "Concepts of Animal Welfare in Relation to Positions in Animal Ethics." *Acta Biotheoretica* 59 (2): 153–71. https://doi.org/10.1007/s10441-011-9128-y.

Select Committee on Jumps Racing, Parliament of South Australia. 2016. *Final Report*.

Senate Rural and Regional Affairs and Transport Legislation Committee. Parliament of Australia. 2015. *Inquiry into the Voice for Animals (Independent Office of Animal Welfare) Bill 2015*. https://www.aph.gov.au/Parliamentary_Business/Committees/Senate/Rural_and_Regional_Affairs_and_Transport/Voice_for_Animals_Bill_15.

Senate Rural and Regional Affairs and Transport Legislation Committee. Parliament of Australia. 2006. *National Animal Welfare Bill 2005*. https://www.aph.gov.au/Parliamentary_Business/Committees/Senate/Rural_and_Regional_Affairs_and_Transport/Completed_inquiries/2004-07/animal_welfare05/index.

Senate Select Committee on Animal Welfare. Commonwealth Parliament. 1985. *Export of Live Sheep from Australia*. Canberra: AGPS. https://www.aph.gov.au/Parliamentary_Business/Committees/Senate/Significant_Reports/animalwelfarectte/exportlivesheep/index.

Senate Select Committee on Animal Welfare. Parliament of Australia. 1991. *Aspects of Animal Welfare in the Racing Industry*. Canberra: AGPS. https://www.aph.gov.au/Parliamentary_Business/Committees/Senate/Significant_Reports/animalwelfarectte/welfareracingindustry/index.

Senate Select Committee on Animal Welfare. Parliament of Australia. 1990. *Intensive Livestock Production*. Canberra: AGPS. https://www.aph.gov.au/Parliamentary_Business/Committees/Senate/Significant_Reports/animalwelfarectte/intensivelivestockproduction/index.

Senate Select Committee on Animal Welfare. Parliament of Australia. 1989. *Animal Experimentation*. Canberra: AGPS. https://www.aph.gov.au/Parliamentary_Business/Committees/Senate/Significant_Reports/animalwelfarectte/animalexperimentation/index.

Senate Standing Committee on Rural and Regional Affairs and Transport. Parliament of Australia. 2019. *Feasibility of a National Horse Traceability Register for All Horses*. Canberra: Commonwealth of Australia. https://www.aph.gov.au/Parliamentary_Business/Committees/Senate/Rural_and_Regional_Affairs_and_Transport/NationalHorseRegister46/Report.

Sentencing Advisory Council. Victoria. 2019. *Animal Cruelty Offences in Victoria*. Melbourne: Sentencing Advisory Council. https://www.sentencingcouncil.vic.gov.au/publications/animal-cruelty-offences-victoria.

Shanks, Niall, Ray Greek and Jean Greek. 2009. "Are Animal Models Predictive for Humans?" *Philosophy, Ethics, and Humanities in Medicine* 4 (2): 1–20. https://doi.org/10.1186/1747-5341-4-2.

Sharp, Trudy. 2012. *Model Code of Practice for the Humane Control of Feral Pigs. Code of Practice*. PestSmart. https://pestsmart.org.au/toolkit-resource/code-of-practice-feral-pigs/.

Sharp, Trudy and Steven McLeod. 2020. *The Development of a New Code of Practice for the Commercial Harvesting of Kangaroos*. AgriFutures Australia Publication No. 20-081. https://www.agrifutures.com.au/publications-resources/publications/?fwp_rural_industry_search=kangaroos.

Sharp, Trudy and Glen Saunders. 2011. *A Model for Assessing the Relative Humaneness of Animal Pest Control Methods*. 2nd edn. Canberra, ACT: Australian Government Department of Agriculture, Fisheries and Forestry. https://www.awe.gov.au/agriculture-land/animal/welfare/aaws/humaneness-of-pest-animal-control-methods.

Sheep Standards and Guidelines Writing Group. 2013. *Sheep Standards and Guidelines – Mulesing*. Discussion Paper. https://www.animalwelfarestandards.net.au/files/2011/05/Sheep-Mulesing-discussion-paper-5.3.13.pdf

Siganto, Talissa. 2020. "Men Fined After Pleading Guilty to Animal Cruelty Over Caboolture Abattoir Horse Slaughter." *ABC News*, 22 July 2020. https://www.abc.net.au/news/2020-07-22/men-fined-over-meramist-abattoir-animal-cruelty-offences/12481800.

Sinclair, Michelle, Tessa Derkley, Claire Fryer and Clive J.C. Phillips. 2018. "Australian Public Opinions Regarding the Live Export Trade Before and After an Animal Welfare Media Expose." *Animals* 8 (7): 106–17. https://doi.org/10.3390/ani8070106.

Sinclair, Michelle, Tamara Keeley, Anne-Cecile Lefebvre and Clive J.C. Phillips. 2016. "Behavioural and Physiological Responses of Calves to Marshalling and Roping in a Simulated Rodeo Event." *Animals* 6 (5): 30–41. https://doi.org/10.3390/ani6050030.

Singer, Peter. 2011. *Practical Ethics*. 3rd edn. Cambridge University Press. https://doi.org/10.1017/CBO9780511975950.

Singer, Peter. 1995. *Animal Liberation*. 2nd edn. London: Pimlico.

Smith, Douglas. 2019. "Aboriginal Elders Defend Traditional Hunting After Wombat Stoning Outrage." 9 October 2019. *NITV*. https://www.sbs.com.au/nitv/article/2019/10/09/aboriginal-elders-defend-traditional-hunting-after-wombat-stoning-outrage.

Sneddon, Joanne. 2011. "How the Wool Industry has Undercut Itself on Mulesing." *Conversation*, 3 May 2011. https://theconversation.com/how-the-wool-industry-has-undercut-itself-on-mulesing-956.

Sneddon, Lynne U. 2019. "Evolution of Nociception and Pain: Evidence From Fish Models." *Philosophical Transactions of the Royal Society B* 374–381 (1785). https://doi.org/10.1098/rstb.2019.0290.

Sowry, Alice. 2015. "Reconciling the Clash: A Comparison of the Australian and Canadian Legal Approaches to Burdening Indigenous Hunting Rights." *Public Interest Law Journal of New Zealand* 4: 155–65.

Stevens, Grant. 2019. "Outcome of SAPOL Internal Investigation." Media statement, South Australia Police, 6 December 2019.

Stevenson, Peter. 2009. "European and International Legislation: A Way Forward for the Protection of Farm Animals?' In *Animal Law in Australasia: A New Dialogue*, edited by Peter Sankoff and Steven White, 307–32. Leichhardt, NSW: Federation Press.

Sunstein, Cass R. and Martha C. Nussbaum, eds. 2004. *Animal Rights: Current Debates and New Directions*. Oxford: Oxford University Press. https://doi.org/10.1093/acprof:oso/9780195305104.001.0001.

Tasmania. Department of Primary Industries, Parks, Water and Environment. Biosecurity Tasmania. 2021. "Animal Welfare Standards – Poultry." Last published 23 July 2021. https://dpipwe.tas.gov.au/biosecurity-tasmania/animal-biosecurity/animal-welfare/legislation-standards-guidelines/animal-welfare-standards-guidelines/animal-welfare-standards/poultry-welfare.

Tasmania. Department of Primary Industries, Parks, Water and Environment. Wildlife Management. 2021. "Waterfowl Identification Testing." Last published 5 February 2021. https://dpipwe.tas.gov.au/wildlife-management/management-of-wildlife/game-management/species-of-game/waterfowl-identification-testing.

Tatnell, Paul. 2020. "RA Fails to Adopt RV Whip Reforms." RACING.COM, 12 November 2020. https://www.racing.com/news/2020-11-12/news-ra-fails-to-adopt-rv-whip-reforms.

Taylor, Katy and Laura Rego Alvarez. 2019. "An Estimate of the Number of Animals Used for Scientific Purposes Worldwide in 2015." *Alternatives to Laboratory Animals* 47 (5-6): 196–213. http://doi.org:/10.1177/0261192919899853.

Taylor, Maria. 2017. "CSIRO Independent Analysis: No Support for Kangaroo Research Assumptions." *The District Bulletin*, 18 October 2017. https://districtbulletin.com.au/csiro-independent-analysis-no-support-kangaroo-research-assumptions-2/.

Taylor, Martin, Carol Booth and Mandy Paterson. 2017. *Tree-clearing: The Hidden Crisis of Animal Welfare in Queensland*, Report. WWF Australia in collaboration with RSPCA Queensland.

Taylor, Nik and Tania Signal. 2009a. "Lock 'Em Up and Throw Away the Key? Community Opinions Regarding Current Animal Abuse Penalties." *Australian Animal Protection Law Journal* 3: 33–52.

Taylor, Nicola and Tania D. Signal. 2009b. "Pet, Pest, Profit: Isolating Differences in Attitudes Towards the Treatment of Animals." *Anthrozoös. A Multidisciplinary Journal of the Interactions of People and Animals* 22 (2): 129–35. https://doi.org/10.2752/175303709X434158.

Taylor, Nik, Damien W. Riggs, Catherine Donovan, Tania Signal and Heather Fraser. 2019. "People of Diverse Genders and/or Sexualities Caring for and Protecting Animal Companions in the Context of Domestic Violence." *Violence Against Women* 25 (9): 1096–1115. http://doi.org/10.1177/10778012188099.

The Panpsycast Philosophy Podcast. 2018. *The Peter Singer Interview* (Part I) 4 March 2018. Episode 34. https://thepanpsycast.com/panpsycast2/singer1.

Thiriet, Dominique. 2013. "Out of Eden: Wild Animals and the Law." In *Animal Law in Australasia: Continuing the Dialogue* edited by Peter Sankoff, Steven White and Celeste Black, 226–44. Leichhardt, NSW: Federation Press.

Thiriet, Dominique. 2009. "Recreational Hunting – Regulation and Animal Welfare Concerns." In *Animal Law in Australasia: A New Dialogue* edited by Peter Sankoff and Steven White, 259–88. Leichhardt, NSW: Federation Press.

Thiriet, Dominique. 2007a. "In the Spotlight – The Welfare of Introduced Wild Animals in Australia." *Environment and Planning Law Journal* 24 (6): 417–26.

Thiriet, Dominique. 2007b. "Out of the 'Too Hard Basket' – Traditional Hunting and Animal Welfare." *Environment and Planning Law Journal* 24 (1): 59–73.

Thiriet, Dominique. 2004. "Tradition and Change – Avenues for Improving Animal Welfare in Indigenous Hunting." *James Cook University Law Review* 11: 195–214.

Thomas, James. 2018. "Executive Email Reveals Stoush over 'Stage-managed' Process to Benefit Egg Industry." *ABC News*, 8 January 2018. https://www.abc.net.au/news/2018-01-08/concerns-poultry-welfare-standards-stage-managed-by-industry/9299256.

Thomas, James and Alison Branley. 2017. "Western Australian Government Threatens to Pull Out of Review of Chicken Welfare Standards." *ABC News*, 22 December 2017. https://www.abc.net.au/news/2017-12-22/western-australia-may-leave-chicken-welfare-review/9283274.

Thompson, Kirrilly, Phil McManus, Dene Stansall, Bethany J. Wilson and Paul McGreevy. 2020. "Is Whip Use Important to Thoroughbred Racing Integrity? What Stewards' Reports Reveal about Fairness to Punters, Jockeys and Horses." *Animals* 10 (11): 1985. https://doi.org/10.3390/ani10111985.

Thoroughbred Welfare Initiative. 2021. *The Most Important Participant: A Framework for Thoroughbred Welfare*. Report of the Thoroughbred Aftercare Welfare Working Group. https://www.tbaus.com/welfare/thoroughbred-welfare-initiative-2/.

Tim Harding & Associates. 2017. *Proposed Australian Animal Welfare Standards and Guidelines, Poultry, Consultation Regulatory Impact Statement*. Canberra: Animal Health Australia. http://www.animalwelfarestandards.net.au/poultry/poultry-public-consultation/.

Tim Harding & Associates in Association with Rivers Economic Consulting. 2014. *Proposed Australian Animal Welfare Standards and Guidelines – Sheep. Decision Regulation Impact Statement*, Version 1, 30 July 2014. Canberra: Animal Health Australia.

Tim Harding & Associates in Association with Rivers Economic Consulting. 2013. *Proposed Australian Animal Welfare Standards and Guidelines, Cattle, Consultation Regulation Impact Statement,* Version 1, 1 March 2013. Canberra: Animal Health Australia. http://www.animalwelfarestandards.net.au/cattle/consultative-process/.

Timoshanko, A., Helen Marston and Brett A. Lidbury. 2016. "Australian Regulation of Animal Use in Science and Education: A Critical Appraisal." *ILAR Journal* 57 (3): 324–32. https://doi.org/10.1093/ilar/ilw015.

Tong, Lydia, Melinda Stewart, Ian Johnson, Richard Appleyard, Bethany Wilson and Olivia James et al. 2020. "A Comparative Neuro-Histological Assessment of Gluteal Skin Thickness and Cutaneous Nociceptor Distribution in Horses and Humans." *Animals* 10 (11): 2094–2108. https://doi.org/10.3390/ani10112094.

Veit, Walter and Heather Browning. 2021. "Perspectival Pluralism for Animal Welfare." *European Journal for Philosophy of Science* 11: 9–22. https://doi.org/10.1007/s13194-020-00322-9.

Vets Against Live Exports. n.d. http://www.vale.org.au/. Accessed 3 November 2021.

Victoria. Conservation Regulator. 2022. Operational Information – Licences and Permits Issued by the Conservation Regulator. Last reviewed 16 May 2022. https://www.vic.gov.au/operational-licences-permits-issued-conservation-regulator.

Victoria. Conservation Regulator. 2020. *Year in Review 2019–20*. Victoria. Department of Environment, Land, Water and Planning. https://www.vic.gov.au/publications-conservation-regulator.

Victoria. Conservation Regulator. 2018. Operational Information – Licences and Permits Issued by the Conservation Regulator. *2009–2019 ATCW Annual Data*. https://www.vic.gov.au/operational-licences-permits-issued-conservation-regulator.

Victoria. Department of Economic Development, Jobs, Transport and Resources. 2017. *Animal Welfare Action Plan*. https://agriculture.vic.gov.au/livestock-and-animals/animal-welfare-victoria/animal-welfare/animal-welfare-action-plan.

Victoria. Department of Environment, Land, Water and Planning. 2018. *The Authority to Control Wildlife (ATCW) System Review*. Discussion Paper.

Victoria. Department of Jobs, Precincts and Regions. 2021. *A New Animal Welfare Act for Victoria – Engagement Summary Report*. https://engage.vic.gov.au/new-animal-welfare-act-victoria.

Victoria. Department of Jobs, Precincts and Regions. 2020. *A New Animal Welfare Act for Victoria – Directions Paper*. https://engage.vic.gov.au/new-animal-welfare-act-victoria.

Victoria. Game Management Authority. 2020a. *Annual Report 2019–20*. Melbourne: Game Management Authority. https://www.gma.vic.gov.au/about-us/annual-reports.

Victoria. Game Management Authority. 2020b. *Summary Report of Hunters' Knowledge Survey Findings*, December 2020. Melbourne: Game Management Authority. https://www.gma.vic.gov.au/research/hunting-research.

Victoria. Game Management Authority. 2020c. "Education. Duck Hunting Education. Duck WISE Education Video." Last updated 30 January 2020. https://www.gma.vic.gov.au/education/duck-hunting-education/duck-wise-education-video.

Victoria. Game Management Authority. 2014. "Duck WISE by Chapters. Introduction." 20 October 2014. https://www.youtube.com/watch?v=K7Edb4PVtoc&list=PLrm3E-zEKA43BmYGuj0ek1XOZlq25vMb6. Accessed 3 November 2021.

Vidot, Anna. 2013. "Federal Government Scraps Animal Welfare Advisory Group." *ABC Rural*, 8 November 2013. https://www.abc.net.au/news/rural/2013-11-08/animal-welfare-committee-scrapped/5079284.

Wahlquist, Calla. 2020. "South Australia Blasted for Issuing Permit to Cull Hairy-nosed Wombats." *Guardian*, 2 March 2020. https://www.theguardian.com/environment/2020/mar/03/south-australia-blasted-for-issuing-permit-to-cull-southern-hairy-nosed-wombat.

Wahlquist, Calla. 2019. "'Horrific' Footage of Live Cattle Having Horns Removed in Australia Sparks Outrage." *Guardian*, 5 December 2019. www.theguardian.com/world/2019/dec/05/despicable-and-horrific-footage-of-cattle-in-distress-prompts-calls-for-mandatory-pain-relief-in-australia.

Wallach, Arian D., Marc Bekoff, Chelsea Batavia, Michael Paul Nelson and Daniel Ramp. 2018. "Summoning Compassion to Address the Challenges of Conservation." *Conservation Biology* 32 (6): 1255–65. https://doi.org/10.1111/cobi.13126.

Ward, Michelle S., Jeremy S. Simmonds, April E. Reside, James E.M. Watson, Jonathan R. Rhodes, Hugh P. Possingham, James Trezise, Rachel Fletcher, Lindsey File and Martin Taylor. 2019. "Lots of Loss with Little Scrutiny: The Attrition of Habitat Critical for Threatened Species in Australia." *Conservation Science and Practice* 1 (11) e117. https://doi.org/10.1111/csp2.117.

Webster, John. 2016. "Animal Welfare: Freedoms, Dominions and 'A Life Worth Living.'" *Animals* 6 (6): 35–40. https://doi.org/10.3390/ani6060035.

Webster, John. 2006. "Animal Sentience and Animal Welfare: What is it to Them and What is it to Us?" *Applied Animal Behaviour Science* 100: 1–3. https://doi.org/10.1016/j.applanim.2006.05.012.

Webster, John. 2005. *Animal Welfare: Limping Towards Eden*. Oxford: Blackwell Publishing. https://doi.org/10.1002/9780470751107.

Western Australia Agriculture Authority. 2020. *Review of the Animal Welfare Act 2002 – Summary Report on the Public Consultation*, June 2020. https://www.agric.wa.gov.au/animalwelfare/review-animal-welfare-act-2002-government-response?page=0%2C0#smartpaging_toc_p0_s1_h3.

Western Australia. Department of Mines, Industry Regulation and Safety. n.d. "A Guide to Consumer Rights When Buying a Pet." Last updated 25 September 2019. https://www.commerce.wa.gov.au/publications/guide-consumer-rights-when-buying-pet.

Western Australia. Department of Primary Industries and Regional Development. 2020. *Animal Welfare Act Review 2020 – Report of the Independent Review of the Animal Welfare Act 2002 of Western Australia*, December 2020. https://www.agric.wa.gov.au/animalwelfare/review-animal-welfare-act-2002-government-response.

White, Steven. 2016a. "Standards and Standard-Setting for Companion and Farm Animal Protection in Queensland, Australia." PhD thesis, Griffith University.

White, Steven. 2016b. "Animal Protection Law in Australia: Bound by History." In *Animal Law and Welfare – International Perspectives*, edited by Deborah Cao and Steven White, 109–29. Switzerland: Springer International. https://doi.org/10.1007/978-3-319-26818-7_6.

White, Steven. 2013a. "Exploring Different Philosophical Approaches to Animal Protection in Law." In *Animal Law in Australasia: Continuing the Dialogue* edited by Peter Sankoff, Steven White and Celeste Black, 31–60. Leichhardt, NSW: Federation Press.

White, Steven. 2013b. "British Colonialism, Australian Nationalism and the Law: Hierarchies of Wild Animal Protection." *Monash University Law Review* 39 (2): 452–72.

White, Steven. 2013c. "Into the Void: International Law and the Protection of Animal Welfare." *Global Policy* 4 (4): 391–8. https://doi.org/10.1111/1758-5899.12076.

White, Steven. 2012. "Animal Law in Australian Universities: Towards 2015." *Australian Animal Protection Law Journal* 7: 70–81.

White, Steven. 2009a. "Companion Animals: Members of the Family or Legally Discarded Objects?" *UNSW Law Journal* 32 (3): 852–78.

White, Steven. 2009b. "Animals in the Wild, Animal Welfare and the Law." In *Animal Law in Australasia: A New Dialogue*, edited by Peter Sankoff and Steven White, 230–58. Leichhardt, NSW: Federation Press.

White, Steven. 2007. "Regulation of Animal Welfare in Australia and the Emergent Commonwealth: Entrenching the Traditional Approach of the States and Territories or Laying the Ground for Reform." *Federal Law Review* 35 (3): 347–74. https://doi.org/10.22145/flr.35.3.1.

Wickins-Drazilova, Dita. 2006. "Zoo Animal Welfare." *Journal of Agricultural and Environmental Ethics* 19: 27–36. https://doi.org/10.1007/s10806-005-4380-2.

Wicks, Deidre. 2018. "Demystifying Dairy." *Animal Studies Journal* 7 (2): 45–75. https://ro.uow.edu.au/asj/vol7/iss2/5.

Wilderness Society of Australia. 2020. Submission to the Environment Protection and Biodiversity Conservation Act Review, April 2020. NSW: The Wilderness Society of Australia Ltd.

Wilkins, Roger, Ferdi Botha, Esperanza Vera-Toscana and Mark Wooden. 2020. *The Household, Income and Labour Dynamics in Australia Survey: Selected Findings from Waves 1 to 18*. Melbourne Institute: Applied Economic & Social Research, University of Melbourne.

Willett, Walter, Johan Rockström, Brent Loken, Marco Springmann, Tim Lang, Sonja Vermeulen et al. 2019. "Food in the Anthropocene: The EAT-*Lancet* Commission on Healthy Diets from Sustainable Food Systems." *Lancet* 393: 447–92. https://doi.org/10.1016/S0140-6736(18)31788-4.

Wintle, Brendan and Sarah Bekessy. 2017. "Let's Get This Straight, Habitat Loss is the Number One Threat to Australia's Species." *Conversation*, 17 October 2017. https://theconversation.com/lets-get-this-straight-habitat-loss-is-the-number-one-threat-to-australias-species-85674.

Wisch, Rebecca F. 2021. *Domestic Violence and Pets: List of States that Include Pets in Protection Orders*. Michigan State University, Animal Legal & Historical Center. https://www.animallaw.info/article/domestic-violence-and-pets-list-states-include-pets-protection-orders.

Wise, Steven M. 2002. *Drawing the Line: Science and the Case for Animal Rights*. Cambridge, Massachusetts: Perseus Books.

Woods, Abigail. 2012. "From Cruelty to Welfare: The Emergence of Farm Animal Welfare in Britain, 1964–71." *Endeavour* 36 (1): 14–22. https://doi.org/10.1016/j.endeavour.2011.10.003.

World Animal Protection. 2020a. *Animal Protection Index*. Commonwealth of Australia. https://api.worldanimalprotection.org/country/australia.

World Animal Protection. 2020b. *Animal Protection Index*. Republic of France https://api.worldanimalprotection.org/country/france.

World Animal Protection. n.d. *Animal Protection Index*. https://api.worldanimalprotection.org/methodology. Accessed 3 November 2021.

World Trade Organization. 2015. *European Communities – Measures Prohibiting the Importation and Marketing of Seal Products*, Status Report by European Union, 16 October 2015. https://trade.ec.europa.eu/wtodispute/show.cfm?id=475&code=2.

World Wide Fund for Nature Australia. 2020. *Australia's 2019–2020 Bushfires: The Wildlife Toll*. Interim Report. https://www.wwf.org.au/what-we-do/bushfire-recovery/in-depth/resources/australia-s-2019-2020-bushfires-the-wildlife-toll#gs.fhuuz6.

WWF-Australia and Nature Conservation Council of NSW. 2018. *Bulldozing of Bushland Nearly Triples Around Moree and Collarenebri After Safeguards Repealed in NSW*.

Zacharin, Will. 2017. Animal Welfare Task Group. *ABC 7.30 – Statement Regarding Development of Poultry Guidelines*, December 2017. https://www.animalwelfarestandards.net.au/files/2017/12/ABC-730-poultry-guidelines-AWTG-statement.pdf.

Table of Cases

Table of Legislation

AUSTRALIA

Australian Constitution

COMMONWEALTH

AUSTRALIAN CAPITAL TERRITORY

NEW SOUTH WALES

NORTHERN TERRITORY

QUEENSLAND

SOUTH AUSTRALIA

TASMANIA

VICTORIA

WESTERN AUSTRALIA

CANADA

ENGLAND

NEW ZEALAND

UNITED KINGDOM

Index

www.ingramcontent.com/pod-product-compliance
Lightning Source LLC
Chambersburg PA
CBHW070710280326
41926CB00089B/3383